Scoring Off the Field

South Asian History and Culture

Series Editors:
David Washbrook, University of Cambridge, UK
Boria Majumdar, University of Central Lancashire, UK
Sharmistha Gooptu, South Asia Research Foundation, India
Nalin Mehta, Institute of South Asian Studies, National University of Singapore

This series brings together research on South Asia in the humanities and social sciences, and provides scholars with a platform covering, but not restricted to, their particular fields of interest and specialization.

A significant concern for the series is to focus across the whole of the region known as South Asia, and not simply on India, as is often the case. We are most conscious of this gap in South Asian studies and work to bring into focus more scholarship on and from Pakistan, Bangladesh, Sri Lanka, Nepal and other parts of South Asia. At the same time, there will be a conscious attempt to publish regional studies, which will open up new aspects of scholarly inquiry going into the future.

This series will consciously initiate synergy between research from within academia and that from outside the formal academy. A focus will be to bring into the mainstream more recently developed disciplines in South Asian studies which have till date remained in the nature of specialized fields: for instance, research on film, media, photography, sport, medicine, environment, to mention a few. The series will address this gap and generate more comprehensive knowledge fields.

Also in this Series

'How Best Do We Survive?' A Modern Political History of the Tamil Muslims
Kenneth McPherson
978-0-415-58913-0

Health, Culture and Religion in South Asia: Critical Perspectives
Editors: **Assa Doron and Alex Broom**
978-81-89643-16-4

Gujarat beyond Gandhi: Identity, Conflict and Society
Editors: **Nalin Mehta and Mona Mehta**
978-81-89643-17-1

India's Foreign Relations, 1947–2007
Jayanta Kumar Ray
978-0-415-59742-5

Land, Water, Language and Politics in Andhra: Regional Evolution in India since 1850
Brian Stoddart
978-0-415-67795-0

Scoring Off the Field
Football Culture in Bengal, 1911–80

Kausik Bandyopadhyay

LONDON NEW YORK NEW DELHI

First published 2011 in India
by Routledge
912–915 Tolstoy House, 15–17 Tolstoy Marg, Connaught Place, New Delhi 110 001

Simultaneously published in the UK
by Routledge
2 Park Square, Milton Park, Abingdon, Oxfordshire OX14 4RN

First issued in paperback 2015

Routledge is an imprint of the Taylor & Francis Group, an informa business

© 2011 Kausik Bandyopadhyay

Typeset by
Star Compugraphics Private Limited
5, CSC, Near City Apartments
Vasundhara Enclave
Delhi 110 096

All rights reserved. No part of this book may be reproduced or utilised in any form or by any electronic, mechanical or other means, now known or hereafter invented, including photocopying and recording, or in any information storage and retrieval system without permission in writing from the publishers.

British Library Cataloguing-in-Publication Data
A catalogue record of this book is available from the British Library

ISBN-13: 978-1-138-65996-4 (pbk)
ISBN-13: 978-0-415-67800-1 (hbk)

For

Baba, who gave me football

and

Mono, who keeps me playing

Contents

List of Plates	ix
Acknowledgements	xi
Introduction	1
1. The Culture of a 'Masculine' English Game in an 'Effeminate' Native Colony: Football in Bengal	19
2. From Imperialism to Nationalism: The Changing Culture of Soccer in Late Colonial Bengal	57
3. Communalism on the *Maidan*: Community and Identity in Bengali Football	108
4. Tussle in Football Administration: Bengal and the Regional Politics of Soccer in Colonial India	143
5. Mohun Bagan vs East Bengal: Social Conflict, Club Rivalry and Supporters' Culture in Bengali Football	167
6. Open Space, Stadium Imbroglio and Spectator Culture: Ground Realities of Bengali Soccer	199
7. Football, Literature and Performing Arts: Perceptions and Sensibilities Towards the Game	236
Epilogue	261
Appendices	264
Bibliography	292
About the Author	307
Index	308

List of Plates

◘

Between pages 142 and 143

1. Dukhiram Majumdar
2. Birth of Indian Football or that Historic 1911 IFA Shield Final
3. Mohun Bagan Match: A Study in Expression
4. The Victorious Mohun Bagan Team with the IFA Shield in 1911
5. Mohun Bagan Captain Shibdas Bhaduri and Honorary Secretary S. N. Bose with the IFA Shield in 1911
6. IFA Shield Winning Aryan Team in 1940
7. Queue for Tickets at a Match in Calcutta First Division League in the 1960s
8. Mounted Police Trying to Discipline the Spectators in Queue for Tickets Outside the Ground
9. Football Fans Sitting atop a Monument to View a Match
10. Effusion of the Fans Behind the Goalpost after Their Favourite Club Scored a Goal
11. Referee and Linesmen being Cordoned by Police after the League Match between Mohun Bagan and East Bengal in 1975
12. One Mohammedan Sporting Player Hitting the Referee during a League Match
13. Mohun Bagan Footballer Prasun Banerjee being Garlanded by a Woman Fan during the Course of a Match

14　Dead Body being Taken from Upper to Lower Tier of the Eden Gardens during the Tragedy on 16 August 1980

15　Dead Bodies of the Victims of 16 August 1980 Tragedy Kept at the Club House of the Eden Gardens

16　Statue of Gostho Paul, the Legendary Mohun Bagan Footballer, at Kolkata Maidan

Acknowledgements

I was only 4 when my father first took me to Kolkata *maidan* to watch a football match. He introduced me to the world of football with a number of stories on Bengali football including the Mohun Bagan Club's epochal Indian Football Association (IFA) Shield victory of 1911. This was something that became an inspiration for me to look upon sport as an integral part of my life. Although I never played the game beyond the standard of school, I have never lost an occasion to watch the Kolkata League or Shield matches since the early 1980s. The passion for the game drove me to take up the social history of Bengali football as the subject of my doctoral research. Thanks to all who have either inspired or discouraged me in my short journey to study sport in a historical perspective.

I am grateful to Professor Arun Bandopadhyay, who has read many earlier drafts of this work and provided invaluable suggestions. Professor J. A. Mangan, Professor Jayanta Kumar Ray, Professor Brian Stoddart, and Dr Boria Majumdar provided valuable comments at different stages of this research. My professors at the Scottish Church College and the Department of History, Calcutta University, have always been a source of inspiration. I am especially grateful to Sri Sibaji Koyal, Professor Bhaskar Chakraborty, Professor Suranjan Das, and the late Basudeb Chattopadhyay.

I am immensely thankful to the authorities and staff of all the libraries and institutions wherever I have worked to collect research materials: British Library and School of Oriental and African Studies Library (London); Central Library, Dhaka University and Central Public Library (Dhaka); Nehru Memorial Museum and Library (New Delhi); West Bengal State Archives National Library, Ramkrishna Mission Institute of Culture Library, the Scottish Church College Library, Department of History Seminar Library of the Calcutta University, Maulana Abul Kalam Azad Institute of Asian Studies Library, the Indian Football Association Archives, and the Cricket Association of Bengal Library (all in Kolkata); North Bengal University Central and Departmental Libraries, and Udayan Memorial Sports Library (Siliguri); and Basirhat Public Library (Basirhat).

The feedback I received at various seminars in Kolkata and elsewhere has enriched the manuscript immensely.

Over the years, many friends have contributed to my pursuit of sport as a serious subject of historical research. In particular, I must thank the late Ranjit Roy, Dhruba Gupta and Moti Nandy, Anita Bagchi, Anirban Mukherjee, Rakhee Bhattacharya, Sabyasachi Chatterjee, Suchanadana Chatterjee, Anand Gopal Ghosh, Sabyasachi Mallick, Subhrangshu Roy, and Shamee Bhattacharya. I also recount with deep gratitude the support and inspiration provided by Professor Ashoke Ranjan Thakur, Professor Kamales Bhaumik, Sri Paritosh Kanjilal, Sri Narayan Mukhopadhyay and Sri Dipak Chatterjee during one of the most critical stages of my life preceding the writing of this book.

I am also grateful to Professor Hari S. Vasudevan for having encouraged me to undertake a field trip to England, which made possible my access to an interesting gamut of research materials unavailable in India. I express my sincere debt to Subrata Dutta, former honorary secretary of the Indian Football Association, who supported my research by all possible means. Ajay Chakraborty deserves special thanks for his unfailing support while I worked at the Nehru Memorial Museum and Library, New Delhi. My thanks to all my colleagues and friends at different institutions wherever I have taught and worked, for their constant encouragement. My special thanks to Mona Chowdhury, Sabyasachi Mallick and Mohun Bagan Club for providing the excellent photographs and illustrations for this work.

Finally, my heartfelt thanks o Boria and Sharmishtha for taking keen interest in my research and giving me the opportunity to publish in the series *South Asian History and Culture* of Routledge. It has been a pleasure to work with the Routledge team.

My family and relations have been a constant source of sustenance all through. I owe a lot to my parents who nurtured my passion for sports since my childhood. And Tania and Aman, with their love and care, have made this venture a reality.

Introduction

> And across the globe, sport is now too important to be left in the hands of sportsmen and women. More and more, it is the property of the 'People' in their various manifestations as politicians, entrepreneurs, educationists, commercialists, publicists, and, not least, academics.[1]

> As such the history of sport gives a unique insight into the way a society changes and impacts on other societies it comes into contact with and, conversely, the way those societies react back upon it.[2]

As a distinctive part of human civilisation, sport has always been an interesting and complex aspect of social life. Eric Hobsbawm described it as 'one of the most important new social practices' of Europe of the late 19th and early 20th centuries,[3] which, as such, 'played a central role in the creation of politically and socially cohesive "invented traditions"'.[4] However, it became a major social phenomenon in the modern world, particularly in the 20th century with political, cultural, economic, spiritual, and aesthetic dimensions. When James Walvin wrote his influential essay, 'Sport, Social History and the Historian', for the first volume of the *British Journal of Sports History* in 1984, he was fully convinced that 'the history of a

---

[1] J. A. Mangan, 'Series Editor's Foreword', in Mike Cronin and David Myall (eds), *Sporting Nationalisms: Identity, Ethnicity, Immigration and Assimilation*, London: Frank Cass, 1998, pp. xi–xii.

[2] Harold Perkin, 'Teaching the Nations How to Play: Sport and Society in the British Empire and Commonwealth', in J. A. Mangan (ed.), *The Cultural Bond: Sport, Empire, Society*, London: Frank Cass, 1992, p. 212.

[3] Eric Hobsbawm, 'Mass-Producing Traditions: Europe, 1870–1914', in Eric Hobsbawm and Terence Ranger (eds), *The Invention of Tradition*, Cambridge: Cambridge University Press, 1983, p. 298.

[4] J. A. Mangan, 'Introduction', in J. A. Mangan (ed.), *Pleasure, Profit, Proselytism: British Culture and Sport at Home and Abroad: 1700–1914*, London: Frank Cass, 1988, p. 1. For a study of how mass and middle-class sport combined the invention of political and social traditions in Europe between 1870 and 1914, see Hobsbawm, 'Mass-Producing Traditions', pp. 300–2.

particular game had an importance which far transcended the game itself' and that 'ultimately, sport could (and perhaps ought to) provide a reflection of wider issues and relationships in society at large'.[5] Yet what seemed difficult for him to reconcile at that time was 'the manifest discrepancy between the undeniable significance of sport in the contemporary world and the refusal of many to accept the importance of sport in its historical setting'.[6]

While sport in the modern world is a proper subject of study for historians, it has taken an inordinately long time for them to appreciate its relevance for the lives of both the influential and the insignificant of past communities.[7] Failure to get sport into sharp academic focus may be 'a form of intellectual myopia born of long-established prejudice'.[8] Sport now has a significant place in Indian life. The study of sport as a serious intellectual discipline, however, remains underdeveloped in India.[9] While the Western academic world in the past three decades has appreciated the relevance of sport in the history of past and present communities, India remained for long far backward in its appreciation of the role of sport in Indian society.[10] In the same way, football, one of the central components of the popular culture of 20th-century India, was mostly neglected by

---

[5] James Walvin, 'Sport, Social History and the Historian', *British Journal of Sports History*, vol. 1, no. 1, 1984, pp. 5–13, especially p. 6.

[6] *Ibid.*, p. 13.

[7] Mangan, 'Introduction', p. 1.

[8] *Ibid.*

[9] Boria Majumdar, 'The Vernacular in Sports History', *Economic and Political Weekly*, vol. 37, no. 29, 2002, p. 3069.

[10] Academic pursuit of sports history in the West began in the 1970s and was concretised in the next decade with the publication of a series of works by a galaxy of social scientists that included such names as J. A. Mangan, Wray Vamplew, Tony Mason, Allen Guttman, Richard Holt, and Peter McIntosh. Institutional organisation to support their efforts began in 1982 when the British Society of Sports History was founded. Distinguished publishers such as Frank Cass offered instant active support and launched the *British Journal of Sports History* that was later transformed into *The International Journal of the History of Sport*. These institutional efforts met with welcome parallels in other Western countries like Scotland, Finland, Sweden, Denmark, Brazil, and the USA. Scholars from Asian countries like China, Japan and South Korea as well as Australia too were quick to recognise the importance of sports history and joined the venture in right earnest since the early 1990s. Finally, Cass launched three more journals, viz., *Culture, Sport, Society*; *Soccer and Society* and *European Sports History Review* and most importantly the *Sport in*

historians as unworthy of serious research until recently.[11] The present work is set in this context, and makes an attempt to understand the growth of football culture in Bengal from 1911 to 1980 in a historical perspective and to demonstrate its social and political implications.

Sport in Social History: The Indian Context

Like many other forms of social behaviour, as Walvin rightly noted, sporting activity is largely socially and historically determined.[12] He further pointed out that 'the sports historian and sociologist need to reach beneath the surface, behind the obvious facts of sporting history, if their studies are to be any more than yet another quasi-antiquarianism masquerading as serious social history'.[13] Following Walvin, Boria Majumdar argues that 'a study of sport history is crucial not only for an understanding of the evolution of the sporting heritage of the Indian nation, but for a deeper appreciation of the seemingly unrelated political processes such as nationalism, [and] colonial culture . . .'.[14] The prime purpose in this academic exercise is not the descriptive study of a particular sport, but what it says about the society of a particular period. There have been, as Ramachandra Guha has suggested, two approaches to the Indian history

---

the Global Society Series in the late 1990s under the auspices of the International Research Centre for Sport, Socialisation and Society instituted at the Strathclyde University, Scotland with J. A. Mangan as the executive academic editor. The huge success of all these ventures further point to the current healthy state of sports history in the West.

According to Gautam Bhadra, professor of History, Centre for Studies in Social Sciences, Kolkata, the aversion of Indian historians to study sport as part of history probably emanates from their uneasiness about the *unconventionality* of the subject as well as the sources of research, which mostly lay beyond the archives and libraries. Discussion with Gautam Bhadra, February 2000. Binay Bhushan Chaudhuri, former professor of History, Calcutta University, also considered this very *unconventionality* of research to be a hindrance in accepting sport as a viable theme of historical research for long in Indian academia. Discussion with Binay Bhushan Chaudhuri, 28 May 2001.

[11] Surendra Gopal, former professor of History, University of Patna, argued that neglect of football as a subject of historical study has much to do with the over-emphasis on cricket even in Indian academia in the last two decades of the 20th century, a period which witnessed huge strides being made in the history of sport in the West. Interview with Surendra Gopal, February 2001.

[12] Walvin, 'Sport, Social History and the Historian', p. 8.
[13] *Ibid*.
[14] Majumdar, 'The Vernacular', p. 3069.

of sport.[15] The first has focused narrowly on its practice, the background of its patrons and players, the evolution of its associations and tournaments, and on how it pays or does not pay for itself. The second approach, which Guha himself prefers, uses sport to illuminate themes of wider interest and relevance. 'It views sport as a *relational idiom*, a sphere of activity which expresses, in concentrated form, the values, prejudices, divisions and unifying symbols of a society.'[16] He goes on to suggest proficiently that the game of cricket can provide valuable insights into the history of modern India, in particular to the three overarching themes of Indian history: those of race, caste and religion.[17] Guha further asserts that the sociology and politics of cricket 'presumes no technical knowledge of the game itself'.[18] This view, however, is not tenable because, as the history of the game over the last century ranging from the infamous 'Bodyline' series of the 1930s to the launch of the T-20 Indian Premier League shows, changes in its rules, rituals and vocabulary are intimately related to, and highly influenced by the politics, culture and economy of the game.[19]

To study sport in the wider perspective of history and culture will help us understand the importance of sport as more than entertainment and locate sport within the broader cultural, social, political, and economic

---

[15] Ramachandra Guha, 'Cricket and Politics in Colonial India', *Past and Present*, no. 161, November 1998, p. 157.

[16] *Ibid.*

[17] Guha deals with these themes in his later publication, viz., *A Corner of a Foreign Field: The Indian History of a British Sport*, Delhi: Picador, 2002. For a more elaborate but different analysis of these important aspects of Indian history through cricket, see Boria Majumdar, 'Cricket in Colonial India, 1850–1947', D. Phil. dissertation, University of Oxford, spring 2004. See also his *Twenty-Two Yards to Freedom: A Social History of Indian Cricket*, New Delhi: Penguin/Viking, 2004.

[18] By this, Guha in fact suggests that the 'sociology and politics' of sport can be studied without any 'technical knowledge of the game', which, broadly speaking, includes, apart from playing style and techniques, the rules, rituals and vocabulary of the game. By implication, therefore, it leads to the conclusion that the technicalities of the game have no bearing on the 'sociology and politics of the game'.

[19] In the 1930s, English fast bowler Douglas Jardine used the method of 'bodyline' bowling to stop Don Bradman, the Australian batting wizard, from scoring runs. Hence the series goes down in history as the 'Bodyline Series'.

The Board of Control for Cricket in India in 2008 launched IPL cricket tournament in India, which attracted as much big money as mass support. The teams, named after some of the most important cities of the country and comprising players from India as well as other test-playing nations, bought by the respective teams in a live auction, played 20-over games with each other on a double leg format followed by semi-finals and a final.

contexts of colonial and post-colonial South Asian societies. The study of sport as history offers major correctives to the range of our understanding of the social and economic history of late 19th- and 20th-century India. For instance, the existing historiography of nationalism, communalism, social conflict, colonial culture, or developing economy in India fails to recognise the importance of football as an arena for spontaneous articulation of nationalism, communalism and popular culture or the role cricket has played as a major nationalist, communal and commercial force in the 20th century.[20]

There has also been an irrational yet popular belief that only the 'committed', the insiders or the practitioners are qualified to pursue sports history. This is certainly a flawed assumption. Personal experience or membership of course can be useful at times in understanding 'certain distinct sensibilities which outsiders could never experience'.[21] But that should never be considered a deciding factor in pursuing academic research on sport. Walvin is again pertinent in his comment:

> (S)uch claims to exclusivity are intellectually crippling and depend ultimately for their *rationale* on the belief that there is, or ought to be, only one particular approach or interpretation of historical experience. It is to be hoped that sports history will avoid such factional fights, although this is not to claim that sporting practitioners have *nothing* to tell us. Far from it. What is quite clear however is that one does not need to be player, spectator or *aficionado* — of any sport — to appreciate its broader social, or historical significance.[22]

It is not necessary therefore for social historians to describe events or matches that they never saw or to engage in discussions of the tactics employed in a match. In other words, it is less important for our purposes to understand the genius of Sachin Tendulkar and Diego Maradona than to analyse what sport means and why it matters.[23] Nevertheless, as noted earlier, it can be useful to have a workable knowledge of the evolution of a game's technicalities, which sometimes exert important sway on its social history and vice versa.

---

[20] The case of cricket in this regard is illustrated in the thesis of Boria Majumdar mentioned earlier.

[21] Walvin, 'Sport, Social History and the Historian', p. 7.

[22] *Ibid.*

[23] Sachin Tendulkar, the batting maestro of the present Indian cricket team, is considered to be one of the greatest batsmen world cricket has ever produced.

Diego Maradona was the captain of the 1986 World Cup Football champions Argentina. Maradona, for his sheer footballing talent, can be compared only to the legendary Brazilian footballer Pele.

Socio-historical research on aspects of popular culture in India commonly tends to generalise the regional thrust of particular cultural elements into a national pattern. The history of sport to date in India, too, suffers from such sweeping generalisations. For instance, a history of Indian football is often identified with that of Bengali football and the latter with Calcutta football.[24] Cricket in colonial India, in the same way, until recently, was understood to be primarily a Bombay-based phenomenon.[25] But both these approaches are mistaken. Without prior consideration of a sport's local origins, developments and specificities, construction of its wider national history can be a flawed exercise.

Finally, the study of sport in India from the perspective of social history needs to put a strong emphasis on vernacular sources. This has not been true of the past. Furthermore, I work on the assumption that 'historians are made for history and the reverse can not be true' and that a social historian has certain social responsibilities.[26] As S. N. Mukherjee has aptly remarked: 'We should not only concern ourselves with the problems which the man in the street faced in the past, but make them entertaining and instructive for the man in the street today . . . the questions we ask about our past must be related to our present day problems.'[27] Historians of sport, in short, also have a duty to make people aware of the problems, realities and potentials of sport in the country today, and inform and impress the authorities so as to keep them on the right track towards progress and excellence.[28] E. H. Carr once made a splendid comment:

---

[24] Both Soumen Mitra and Paul Dimeo considered Calcutta football to be synonymous with Bengali football and, hence, missed its local character completely. Soumen Mitra, *In Search of an Identity: History of Football in Colonial Calcutta*, Kolkata: Das Gupta & Co., 2006; Paul Dimeo, 'Football and Politics in Bengal', in Paul Dimeo and James Mills (eds), *Soccer in South Asia: Empire, Nation, Diaspora*, London: Frank Cass, 2001, pp. 57–74.

[25] Even Ramachandra Guha, one of the most celebrated cricket writers of India, suffers from this flawed understanding in his work. For clarification, see Guha, *A Corner of a Foreign Field*. For a different view, see Majumdar, *Twenty-Two Yards to Freedom*.

[26] S. N. Mukherjee, *Citizen Historian: Explorations in Historiography*, Delhi: Manohar, 1996, p. 8.

[27] *Ibid.*

[28] This statement, relating to the moral duty of the historian of sport, however, should not be mistaken as typically reflective of the early stage of the development of the history of sport in India. It is applicable to historians of sport in countries which might already have achieved a developed or developing stage of research.

'Good historians... have future in their bones.'[29] Research on the history of sport in India, especially on Indian sport, should not only concern itself with the analytical understanding of specific historical issues, but should offer valuable insights in the light of past historical experience into a better future for sport in India. To achieve this end, it is important to remember what Walvin stated two decades earlier:

> In the determination to establish legitimacy there is the basic danger of overstatement and exaggeration. This, however, is not the most seductive danger, for in seeking to stake out an autonomous historical empire, it is all too easy to wrench sports history from its determining social and economic context. There is no single model upon which the sports historian ought to proceed but in the last resort the viability and even the respectability of sports history must rest upon the quality of the work produced. Unless the traditional canons of historical research and reconstruction are applied to this relatively new field, it will not — and ought not to — gain acceptance. Like sport itself, sports history will ultimately depend on the skills and imagination of its practitioners.[30]

Academic Writings on Indian Sport: Historiography of Football in India

The first serious academic research by an Indian on the history of sport was pursued as early as 1988 when Soumen Mitra, a graduate of Presidency College, Kolkata, and an M.A. in History from Jawaharlal Nehru University, submitted an M.Phil. dissertation on the role of soccer in colonial Bengal.[31] It was also in the late 1980s that cricket was considered seriously by Indian writers such as Ramachandra Guha, Arjun Appadurai, Mihir Bose, and Ashis Nandy.[32] Very little attention, however, was paid either to historical studies of other sports or to sport in general.

---

[29] E. H. Carr, *What is History?* London: Pelican, 1961, p. 108.

[30] Walvin, 'Sport, Social History and the Historian', p. 13.

[31] The dissertation entitled 'Nationalism, Communalism and Sub-regionalism: A Study of Football in Bengal, 1880–1950' was submitted at the Centre for Historical Studies, Jawaharlal Nehru University. Subsequently, he published an article, 'Babu at Play: Sporting Nationalism in Bengal: A Study of Football in Bengal, 1880–1911', in Nisith Roy and Ranjit Roy (eds), *Bengal: Yesterday and Today*, Calcutta: Papyrus, 1991, pp. 45–61. His M.Phil. dissertation was published in 2006 as *In Search of an Identity*.

[32] Guha, 'Cricket and Politics in Colonial India'; *A Corner of a Foreign Field*.

Non-Indian specialists on sport in India have mostly focused on the games introduced by the British during their period of colonial rule. Much of this work has dealt with cricket since it has become the most popular game in India in recent decades. The works of Edward Docker and Richard Cashman bear testimony to this trend.[33] Some of the studies on colonial Indian sport focus on the colonial introduction of modern sports and explore deeper imperial motives behind it.[34] There have been some essays on football by Tony Mason, and most recently in a collection edited by Paul Dimeo and James Mills.[35] Some European scholars have also studied indigenous sports and games of India. Chief among these are J. Alter's works on wrestling and *kabaddi*.[36] The most recent major Indian contribution to the study of social history of sport has come from a young Bengali sports historian, Boria Majumdar.[37]

A. Appadurai, 'Playing with Modernity: The Decolonization of Indian Cricket', in C. A. Breckenridge (ed.), *Consuming Modernity: Public Culture in a South Asian World*, Minneapolis, MN: University of Minnesota Press, 1995, pp. 23–48.

Mihir Bose, *A History of Indian Cricket*, London: Andre Deutsch, 1990.

Ashis Nandy, *The Tao of Cricket: On Games of Destiny and the Destiny of Games*, New Delhi: Oxford India Paperbacks, 2000.

[33] Edward Docker, *History of Indian Cricket*, Delhi: Macmillan, 1976.

Richard Cashman, *Patrons, Players and the Crowd: The Phenomenon of Indian Cricket*, Calcutta: Orient Longman, 1979.

[34] The most standard text on this interpretation is J. A. Mangan, *The Games Ethic and Imperialism: Aspects of the Diffusion of an Ideal*, London and Portland: Frank Cass, 1998, especially Chapters 5 and 7, pp. 122–41, 168–92. Also see Richard Holt, *Sport and the British: A Modern History*, Oxford: Oxford University Press, 1989, pp. 203–18; Allen Guttman, *Games and Empires: Modern Sports and Cultural Imperialism*, New York: Columbia University Press, 1994.

[35] Tony Mason, 'Football on the Maidan: Cultural Imperialism in Calcutta', in Mangan (ed.), *The Cultural Bond*, pp. 142–53.

Dimeo and Mills (eds), *Soccer in South Asia*. Worthy scholarly interventions made in the collection include J. A. Mangan, 'Soccer as Moral Training: Missionary Intention and Imperial Legacies', pp. 41–56; Dimeo, 'Football and Politics in Bengal', pp. 57–74; and James Mills, 'Football in Goa: Sport, Politics and the Portuguese in India', pp. 75–88.

[36] J. Alter, *The Wrestler's Body: Identity and Ideology in North India*, Berkerley, CA: University of California Press, 1992; '*Kabaddi*, a National Sport of India: The Internationalism of Nationalism and the Foreignness of Indianness', in N. Dyck (ed.), *Games, Sports and Cultures*, Oxford: Berg, 2000.

[37] Boria Majumdar, who has done his Ph.D. on the social history of Indian cricket at St. John's College, University of Oxford as a Rhodes scholar, is presently

It is surprising to note that the modern Indian historian has more or less neglected football as worthy of serious historical scholarship. Perhaps the academic historian regards sport as falling in the area of popular history to be left in the hands of literateurs, journalists, sports-specialists, and sportsmen themselves. Hence, the production of scholarly studies on the social and cultural history of football in Bengal/India has been few and far between. While only a few books and articles deal with this topic in historical perspective,[38] a vast terrain of vernacular sporting literature written mostly by journalists, sports-writers and players themselves, too numerous to mention here, throws great light on different aspects of football's socio-historical face and helps us construct the history of the evolution of football culture in Bengal.

It is important here to assess the merit of those few academic works and articles which deal with this topic in historical perspective. Soumen Mitra, in his first work, analyses the nationalist implications of football

---

the Executive Academic Editor, *The International Journal of the History of Sport*. His most influential writings include *Once Upon a Furore: Lost Pages of Indian Cricket*, New Delhi: Yoda Press, 2004; *Twenty Two Yards to Freedom*; *Goalless: The Story of a Unique Footballing Nation* (with Kausik Bandyopadhyay), New Delhi: Penguin/Viking, 2006; and *Olympics: The India Story* (with Nalin Mehta), New Delhi: HarperCollins, 2008. He has also edited with J. A. Mangan *The Cricket World Cup: Cultures in Conflict*, London: Routledge, 2004 and *Sport in South Asian Society: Past and Present*, London: Routledge, 2004.

[38] These works include: Dimeo and Mills, *Soccer in South Asia*; Majumdar and Bandyopadhyay, *Goalless*; Mitra, *In Search of an Identity*; and 'Babu at Play'; Moti Nandy, 'Calcutta Soccer', in Sukanta Chaudhuri (ed.), *Calcutta: The Living City*, vol. 1, Oxford: Oxford University Press, 1990, pp. 316–20, and 'Football and Nationalism', transl. Shampa Banerjee, in Geeti Sen (ed.), *The Calcutta Psyche*, New Delhi: India International Centre, 1991–92, pp. 241–54; Mason, 'Football on the Maidan'; Dimeo, 'Football and Politics in Bengal'; Dimeo, '"Team Loyalty Splits the City into Two": Football, Ethnicity and Rivalry in Calcutta', in G. Armstrong and R. Giulianotti (eds), *Fear and Loathing in World Football*, Oxford: Berg, 2001, pp. 96–107; Paul Dimeo, 'Colonial Bodies, Colonial Sport: "Martial" Punjabis, "Effeminate" Bengalis and the Development of Indian Football', *The International Journal of the History of Sport*, vol. 19, no. 1, March 2002, pp. 72–90; Dimeo, '"With Political Pakistan in the Offing …": Football and Communal Politics in South Asia, 1887–1947', *Journal of Contemporary History*, vol. 38, no. 3, July 2003, pp. 377–94; Dwaipayan Sen, 'Wiping the Stain Off the Field of Plassey: Mohun Bagan in 1911', *Soccer and Society*, vol. 7, nos 2–3, 2006; Sharmishtha Gooptu, 'Celluloid Soccer: The Peculiarities of Soccer in Bengali Cinema', *The International Journal of the History of Sport*, vol. 22, no. 4, July 2005, pp. 689–98.

in early 20th-century Calcutta and explains the significance of Mohun Bagan's IFA Shield victory of 1911 in that context.[39] Mitra's unpublished M.Phil. dissertation 'Nationalism, Communalism and Sub-regionalism: A Study of Football in Bengal; 1880–1950' (Centre for Historical Studies, Jawaharlal Nehru University, 1988), later published as a book, interprets the articulation of nationalism, communalism and sub-regionalism through football in Bengal.[40] The work, despite being an excellent treatment of football's social history in a nationalist paradigm, betrays a purely Calcutta-centric approach and does not take into consideration significant issues like football's distinct cultural dimensions, articulation of social power relations through football and football's emotional overtones.

Moti Nandy, the renowned Bengali sport-literateur, contributed two important articles on the history of football in Bengal. In the first one, 'Calcutta Soccer', which is preciously informative, he neatly delineates the origin, growth and development of Calcutta soccer in its entire vicissitudes. In the second, 'Football and Nationalism', Nandy takes up the more complex aspects of football's socio-historical development in Bengal — nationalism, communalism, Ghoti–Bangal conflict, *maidan* culture, football finance, and other social aspects of the game. Both the works, however, remain in the nature of narratives, being unable to become interpretative in a way that may lead to the formulation of any hypothesis at a more conceptual level.

Tony Mason's article, 'Football on the Maidan: Cultural Imperialism in Calcutta', deals with the implications of the concept of 'cultural imperialism' in a colonised society like India and takes up football on the Calcutta maidan as the mirror through which specific forms of this cultural imperialism were reflected.[41] He also discusses how the native Indian responded to this new imperial 'offence' with a case study of Mohun Bagan's 1911 victory. Mason, however, ignores the broader political, cultural and social implications of the victory in contemporary Bengal.

The publication of *Soccer in South Asia: Empire, Nation, Diaspora* in 2001 was an important step in the direction of historical studies on Indian football. This book could be viewed as a part of the growing concern on the part of the sports historians in the West to give soccer its deserved status as a

---

[39] Mitra, 'Babu at Play'.

[40] Mitra, *In Search of an Identity*.

[41] 'Maidan' refers to the vast open playing fields of Calcutta opposite to the Eden Gardens at the eastern banks of the river Hoogly. The term will be generically used throughout the book denoting the same meaning.

subject of historical scholarship so long overdue in South Asia. In fact, it pointed the way in this regard for Indians. It contains some excellent essays, especially those by J. A. Mangan and James Mills. But the work which did have the potential of becoming a path breaking contribution towards the study of sport in South Asia, sadly belies much of it owing to gross factual errors, omission of the most important primary sources, utter neglect of the vernacular sources, and miserable editorial lapses.[42] Moreover, the

---

[42] Such errors are abundant throughout the volume (*Soccer in South Asia*). To give a few examples, Mohun Bagan Club, the National Club of India, is said to mean 'sweet' (Mohun) 'group' (Bagan). In reality, it actually means 'beautiful' (Mohun) 'garden' (Bagan). It derives its name from the Mohun Bagan Villa of north Calcutta where the club was actually founded in 1889. Again, East Bengal Club which is supposed to be founded in 1924 by poor East Bengali refugees was actually formed in 1920 by respectable East Bengali intelligentsia as a part of their reaction against the ill treatment and discrimination meted out to them by their West Bengali counterparts in wider social life including sports. Furthermore, it is wrongly mentioned that the Sovabazar club was formed in 1885 and the soccer team of the Presidency College in 1884. The first, in fact, was formed in 1887 while the earliest mention of soccer at the college goes back to 1879. Then, sweeping generalisations such as 'domestic matches in India in those days (1950s and 60s) were still limited to seventy minutes and the players were not used to playing full ninety minutes' (p. 24) or 'the professionalization of football had begun in the early 1980s' (p. 109) make matters worse. While Calcutta League matches were limited to 70 minutes at that time, most of the other tournaments across the country were in tune with the international stipulation of 90 minutes. The professionalisation of Indian football, on the other hand, has been a feature from only the 1990s, still awaiting its much-desired maturity.

The book suffers from a miserable omission of important primary sources. Except J. A. Mangan's brilliant piece, in most cases, the contributors depend heavily on secondary works and sometimes on not-too-reliable popular writings available in the newspapers and internet websites.

Unfortunately, most of the writers either ignore or fail to consult a large number of vernacular primary sources as well as numerous important popular sporting histories written in the vernacular. Even when vernacular sources are consulted, the exercise is a flawed one. For the much-reported event in the history of Indian soccer, Mohun Bagan's victory of 1911, mention is made of R. Saha's *Ekadashe Surya*. The title of the book is *Ekadashe Suryodaya* meaning 'Sun-Rise in 1911', hardly conveyed by the error in the book. The book fails to take into account some invaluable sources like the *Mohun Bagan Platinum Jubilee Souvenir, IFA Golden Jubilee Souvenir, Mohammedan Sporting Club League Champions Souvenir, East Bengal Club Golden Jubilee Souvenir,* Nagendra Prasad Sarvadhikari's two biographies by P. L. Dutt and Sourindra Kumar Ghosh, Paresh Nandy's *Mohun Bagan 1911*

editors fail to understand that sports journalists, TV commentators and experienced coaches, save very few exceptions, can hardly make up for academic writers.[43]

Paul Dimeo, who deals with football in colonial Bengal in this book, focuses on the inception, development and politics of football in Calcutta.[44] Although he reiterates J. A. Mangan's broader thematic observations about the importance of public school spirit to explain football's introduction and organisation in Calcutta, he recognises the inherent contradiction with the colonial designs in that purpose. Dimeo relates the Bengali desire to adopt and excel in the game to the latter's attempt to dispel the charge of so-called effeminacy labelled upon them by the Europeans. He rightly points out that at the heart of the appropriation of the game on nationalist lines lay a paradox since it was couched in the very British idiom of masculinity and competition. Dimeo, however, fails to highlight the actual roles played by persons like Nagendra Prasad Sarvadhikari and clubs like National Association in that process. He is also utterly silent on the nature, pattern and specific forms of footballing nationalism in late colonial Calcutta. He, not unlike his predecessors, put all the emphasis on Mohun Bagan's IFA Shield victory of 1911. Moreover, his one short paragraph on the relation between communalism and football suffers from

---

(Calcutta: Karuna Prakashani, 1976) and *East Bengal Club: 1920–1970* (Calcutta: Bichitra, 1973), RB's (Rakhal Bhattacharyya) *Kolkatar Football* (Calcutta: East Light Book House, 1955), Rupak Saha's *Itihase East Bengal* (Calcutta: Deep, 2000) and so on, not to speak of the massive collections of vernacular newspaper reports and sports magazines.

Editorial lapses, unfortunately, are more serious. The Durand Cup, the oldest tournament in the country, gets two foundation dates thanks to Kapadia (1888) and Dimeo (1886), of whom the former is correct. In his notes, Bill Adams refers to one crore as equal to 10,000. Numerous such lapses only mar the academic value of the publication.

[43] For instance, the articles by Mario Rodrigues, Bill Adams or John Hammond dealing respectively with issues of the game's commercialisation and professionalisation in the 1990s, the problems and possibilities of the future and talent identification and development have hardly any constructive analysis or original insight to offer. To furnish one specific example, Mario Rodrigues's statement that the policies of liberalisation in the Indian economy were initiated by Rajiv Gandhi (p. 110) is grossly mistaken since such policies were introduced by Manmohun Singh, the finance minister under the P. V. Narsimha Rao government after Rajiv's death in 1991.

[44] Dimeo, 'Football and Politics in Bengal'.

gross oversimplification because, in identifying the Mohammedan Sporting Club with footballing communalism, he totally ignores the other side of the coin, that is, the Hindu involvement in, and response to this. Dimeo tries to amend the deficiencies of his interpretation of the communalisation of Bengal football in another essay, where he claims to introduce 'a history of sport and politics' and discusses 'how a sports club took on political meaning in a charged climate of antagonism and emerging identities, when anti-colonial nationalism gave way to religious communalism between Hindus and Muslims as Indians fought over spoils of decolonization'.[45] However, he does not delve into the long-term conflict between the Mohammedan Sporting Club and the Indian Football Association, which had a visible impact on Hindu–Muslim relations of the time. Dimeo's other article entitled 'Colonial Bodies, Colonial Sport' compares and contrasts the efforts of the 'effeminate Bengalis' with that of the 'martial Punjabis' in the development of Indian football, albeit superficially, given the dearth of primary sources to substantiate his interesting inferences.

In another article on the history of club conflict in Calcutta football, Dimeo has argued that the most fascinating rivalry in India's club football between Mohun Bagan and East Bengal can be interpreted in terms of an ethnic conflict between the Hindu settlers of West Bengal and the Hindu immigrants from East Bengal in the aftermath of the Partition of 1947.[46] But this rigid ethnic polarisation, probably emanating from the writer's lack of awareness about the fluidity of cultural identities of the two groups of people sharing more or less a broadly common language, religion and cultural past, seems not only oversimplistic but also flawed. More importantly, Dimeo's further argument that Mohun Bagan and East Bengal — two Hindu clubs — were on friendly terms and his conception of Mohun Bagan–East Bengal cooperation in opposition to a Muslim club, that is, Mohammedan Sporting, require critical observation.

A most recent work on the history of Indian football, *Goalless: The Story of a Unique Footballing Nation*, concentrates on exploring the relationships between the national, the regional and the local in the history of Indian soccer.[47] It seeks to explore the relationship between soccer on the one hand and forces like imperialism, nationalism, communalism, regionalism, commercialism, and professionalism on the other. It has rather tried to pave the way for further and fuller coverage of the significant issues

---

[45] Dimeo, 'With Political Pakistan in the Offing …', p. 378.
[46] Dimeo, '"Team Loyalty Splits the City into Two"'.
[47] *Goalless*, by Boria Majumdar and Kausik Bandyopadhyay.

revealed through attitudes to soccer in Indian society. Among these are: gender relations (the presence and absence of women within the ambit of the sport); the limits of access to the game (for the lower classes and castes); the role of the sport within the imperial educational establishments and their 'Anglo-Saxon' educators in the implication of the 'values' deemed important in metropolitan middle-class public schools; the increasing importance of commerce and its interaction with nationalism; and, internecine political and personal conflicts between Indians themselves. The work, however, attends to a much broader spatial dimension covering the most important centres of soccer throughout India, in which Bengal only gets its due attention. Naturally therefore, some of the crucial inner dynamics of the game's evolution such as football ground/stadium development and spectator violence, typical of Bengal, are largely ignored. It also does not deal with the patterns of football culture or cultural representations of the game at either national or regional level.

Dwaipayan Sen, in his recent article on the significance of Mohun Bagan's IFA Shield victory of 1911, examines the varied response to, and the larger meaning of, the historic event in trying to destabilise rigidly imperialist or nationalist historical interpretations of this occasion.[48] He focuses his analysis on the varied responses to the phenomenon of Indians having defeated the British, and argues that in each case the writer of the report brought his ideological commitments to bear on his interpretation of the victory. Analysing an entire range of newspaper reports, Sen documents how the larger meaning of Mohun Bagan's victory came into being only through very particular connotations football had acquired in the cultural and political schema of early 20th-century Bengali society. The study also tries to reveal how received notions of modernity, tradition, race, governance, and masculinity acquired significantly different, and at times, conflicting meanings in the minds of the football- and Mohun Bagan-crazy newspaper correspondents, and presumably, the newspaper reading public. It accounts for the larger significance of this event in terms of the differences and similarities both between and within nationalist (Indian) and imperialist (British) interpretations. While Sen's study admittedly offers a valid area for future research, it seems to suffer from over-assessment of the consequential circumstances such as media representations of a particular event.

My earlier work *Playing for Freedom: A Historic Sports Victory* concentrates only on the IFA Shield victory of Mohun Bagan as the first Indian team in

---

[48] Sen, 'Wiping the Stain Off the Field of Plassey'.

1911 and tries to bring to light the political, social and cultural importance of that event in a historical perspective.[49]

Finally, Sharmishtha Gooptu's article on 'Celluloid Soccer: the Peculiarities of Soccer in Bengali Cinema' deals with popular representations of football in Bengali cinema in the last three decades of the 20th century. While films with football as central or peripheral themes were popular in Bengal, she argues that the marginality of sport sans cricket in popular cinema is most striking in the case of Bengali soccer. She also identifies some of the problematic elements of the Bengali identification with soccer pointing to what she calls 'the uneasy relationship between soccer and Bengali cinema'.[50] She emphasises that there are only a handful of films that have plots centring on the game, or that at least feature the game as a key element. However, her case studies of three films, which include *Dhanyi Meye*, *Saheb* and *Ashray*, do not consider the most important movie on Bengali football, namely *Mohun Baganer Meye*, leaving, in effect, the most probable illumination of Bengali football culture of post-colonial Bengal.

Thus the fact that the culture of football in 20th-century Bengal has not been thoroughly explored in socio-historical perspective suggests the pre-eminent significance of an interdisciplinary research on the football culture in 20th-century Bengal, which this work has attempted to offer.

Scoring Off the Field: Football Culture in Bengal

The purpose of this book is to examine how football, as a mass spectator sport, came to represent a novel, unique cultural identity of Bengali people in terms of nation, community, region/locality, and club, contributing to the continuity of everyday socio-cultural life. It also intends to explain how football became a viable popular social force with rare emotional spontaneity and peculiar self-expressive fan culture against the background of the anti-imperial nationalist movement and post-colonial political tension and social transformation. In the process, it investigates certain key questions and problems in the social history of football in Bengal: How did the socio-cultural scenario into which football was introduced in Bengal become conducive to football's widespread popularisation and

---

[49] Kausik Bandyopadhyay, *Playing for Freedom: A Historic Sports Victory*, New Delhi: Standard Publisher, 2008.

[50] Gooptu, 'Celluloid Soccer', pp. 188–89.

social indigenisation? Why did football, instead of cricket, hockey or polo, gain wider popularity in colonial Bengal? How far did British *cultural imperialism* inform and concretise Bengali nationalist identity through a mass spectator sport like football? Was the significance of 1911 limited to this simplistic formulation of the nationalist paradigm or had it wider ramifications for Bengali society and culture? How did Bengali/Indian *footballing identity* under colonial rule come to be fragmented on communal, regional or sub-regional lines? Would it be right to talk about a Bengali *cultural identity* of purely sporting origin? Was spectator violence a direct outcome of the assertion of such identity or were there other geographical factors shaping its forms? How did this identity get reflected through specific forms of culture — literature, media and performing arts such as cinema, theatre or music?

The present work addresses these questions studying the game from 1911 to 1980, those specific years having great significance in the history of football in Bengal. The year 1911 marked India's first greatest nationalist sporting victory over the mighty British on the football field when the barefoot Bengali team Mohun Bagan defeated the booted European East York Regiments to win the Indian Football Association Shield. While the pre-1911 period is important for understanding the socio-historical background of football's introduction in Bengal, the post-1911 period till the mid-1930s is crucial in appreciating the significance of the game as a nationalist force. The political and social volatility of the 1930s and 1940s received ample reflection in the communal and regional politics of soccer that signified the period. The period from the late 1940s to the end of the 1970s witnessed intense club rivalry in Bengali football, leading ultimately to the tragic death of 16 football fans who died in a stampede at the Eden Gardens, Calcutta, during a Mohun Bagan–East Bengal League encounter on 16 August 1980.

The work conforms to the requirements of interdisciplinary Social Science research, depending upon empirically testable information and viability prospective verification. The research is based on primary sources collected from comprehensive fieldwork, especially visits of football clubs and associations; publications and souvenirs; interviews and discussions; detailed study of archival sources including government publications and printed reports; study of contemporary newspapers and periodicals; study of contemporary literature and memoirs and reminiscences, and other published sources; study of sports magazines; critical overview of *sporting* literature and a variety of secondary works; plausible utilisation of photographs, cartoons and audio-visual aids (audio cassettes, films); and use of internet appliances. In short, the specific methodology followed in this work includes the historical methodology of relating archival and literary sources, complemented from time to time by Social Science methodology of fieldwork and interviews in connection with this research. The book comprises seven chapters apart from an introduction and an epilogue, appendices, a bibliography, and photographs.

The first chapter analyses the wider socio-political and cultural context in which football was adopted and adapted as a popular pursuit in late 19th-century Bengali society. It also assesses the validity of the widely popular theory of 'games ethic' in analysing the popular adoption and cultural indigenisation of soccer in Bengal, tracing the local roots and growth of the game to peculiarly regional/local situations. It also examines and refutes the notion that the wider popularity of football throughout Bengal was a post-1911 phenomenon, which most of the existing histories of the game tell us.

Chapter 2 deals with the nature of nationalist response towards European cultural imperialism as manifested on the football field of colonial Bengal. It assesses the notional strengths and weaknesses of the binary of cultural imperialism and cultural nationalism as applied to sport in colonial societies like India. In the process, the chapter reconstructs the nationalist-racist-social-cultural-economic significance of Mohun Bagan's epochal Indian Football Association Shield victory as it also analyses the origin, growth, character, and impact of footballing nationalism in colonial Bengal. It also looks into the question of nationalist appropriation of football and its role as an instrument of reaction, resistance and subversion.

Chapter 3 deals with soccer's burgeoning communal encounter in Bengali football from the 1930s against the backdrop of the socio-political and economic life of the region. While trying to explore and analyse the key factors precipitating such communal conflict in Bengali football, it also explains why Mohun Bagan's victory against East Yorkshire Regiment in the IFA Shield final in 1911 is still perceived as a greater nationalistic triumph than Mohammedan Sporting's five straight Calcutta Football League titles between 1934 and 1938. The chapter, dwelling on the impact of Mohammedan's success on Bengal's footballing society and Indian Football Association's critical relations with the club, pays attention to the transition of Bengali football from nationalist force to communal identity during a tense socio-political context of Bengal in the 1940s.

The next chapter discusses the character and impact of the regional politics of Indian soccer in the 1930s and the part Bengal played in the process. It brings into the fore the important role of the British, especially the Football Association of England and the Army Sports Control Board of India in this regional power conflict between Bengal on the one hand and Delhi and Bombay on the other. The chapter tries to analyse this unhealthy power rivalry and the ultimate formation of the All India Football Association in the wider political canvas of the evolving relationship between the provinces against the backdrop of the towering presence of the colonial state.

Chapter 5 turns its attention to the fascinating social conflict configured in terms of a club rivalry between Mohun Bagan and East Bengal and its associated fan culture in colonial and post-colonial Bengal. Emphasising the notion of 'social differentiation' in the context of Bengali football, it seeks to explore the roots of the origin and concretisation of this football rivalry against the backdrop of social, cultural and sub-regional differences of colonial and post-colonial Bengali society. The chapter examines the evolution of this soccer rivalry in the third quarter of the 20th century in terms of club loyalty and supporters' culture.

The last two chapters attempt to understand the various changing aspects of football culture in Bengal during the period under review, looking into the perceptions and sensibilities towards the game, manifested in behaviour, literature and performing arts. While Chapter 6 throws light on some of the hitherto neglected facets of Bengali football culture such as the relation between the problems of open space and the development of football grounds, Bengal's long-term quest for a football stadium, and the peculiarities of Bengali fan culture, hooliganism and violence, the last chapter reflects upon the representations of the game in the media, literature, film, theatre, and music.

Thus *Scoring Off the Field* is an attempt to understand football's growth, popularity and significance in Bengali social and cultural life from 1911 to 1980. The prime interest of this work is not to study football as a game in its own right, but in what it tells us about the society of this period. Hence, the study wishes to treat football as a cultural phenomenon setting it squarely in the context of politics and society. The point here is not to describe football matches but to study what football meant and why it mattered. In brief, the book intends to understand the relevance of football as a popular cultural force and its centrality in the everyday life of Bengal.

1
The Culture of a 'Masculine' English Game in an 'Effeminate' Native Colony: Football in Bengal

The tide of evolution which rose high and rolled on throughout Bengal with the advent of the English, before it settled down in its calm and fertilizing course, swept away many old landmarks.... Among them were some of our national games of pre-British days. It ushered in football which very soon became a new milestone in the course of our progress and advancement in the field of sports. It captured the imagination of the youths of the land and thrilled our people through and through as no other game had done before.[1]

One of the most striking facts about social life in late colonial Bengal was the adoption, growth and popularisation of association football. A growing number of people played, watched and read about football. The wave of pioneering and creative endeavour that had flowed out of the turbulence generated in literature, art, religion, and society by the Bengal Renaissance, later sent ripples to the football field as well. The Bengalis, however, in the changed socio-political context of the late 19th century, popularised football not as a simple means of entertainment but as a culturally unifying force among themselves. This chapter examines the wider socio-political and cultural context in which football was adopted and adapted as a popular pursuit in late 19th-century Bengali society.

The Socio-political Context: Soccer as 'Games Ethic'

The socio-historical context into which football was introduced and popularised in Bengal was itself situated in a transitory phase of cultural

---
[1] *IFA Shield Souvenir* 1945, Calcutta: Indian Football Association, p. 9.

development in a colonised society. The official policy to anglicise Indian people, established with the famous 'Macaulay Minute' of 1835, was aimed at creating a band of educated anglicised Indians who would imitate the imperialists in their behaviour, values and attitudes and ultimately become the protectors of the Raj. On the one hand, the British, as an integral part of their new modified policy towards Indian aristocracy in the aftermath of the revolt of 1857, began to redefine their relations with the Indian princes.[2] In the 'orientalisation' of British rule after 1857, however, imperial values were to remain distinctly superior, and were diffused with total conviction.[3] The princes were not just to be imbued with Western values but with a distinctly British sense of priorities. British hegemony in India was to be underpinned by the princes themselves, who were not merely to be 'bought off', but rather were to become honorary English gentlemen.[4] Lord Curzon outlined the proper education of an Indian prince as follows: 'Young chiefs . . . to learn the English language, and become sufficiently familiar with English customs, literature, science, modes of thought, standards of truth and honour, and . . . with manly English sports and games . . .'[5] It was this kind of thinking which lay behind the setting up of the 'Chiefs Colleges' on the model of the public school system of Eton and Harrow in the 1870s and 1880s. The curriculum in these colleges was expected to expose the princes to the superiority of British culture and allow them to uphold the status quo out of conviction rather than from greed or from fear. It was in that particular context that sports like cricket and football

---

[2] For an elaborate view of the changing British policy towards Indian princes in the 19th century, see S. R. Ashton, *British Policy towards the Indian States, 1905–39*, London: Curzon Press, 1982; Edward Thompson, *The Making of the Indian Princes*, London: Curzon Press, 1978; Robin Jeffrey (ed.), *People, Princes and Paramount Power: Society and Politics in the Indian Princely States*, Delhi: Oxford University Press, 1978; Thomas R. Metcalf, *The Aftermath of Revolt: India 1857–1870*, Princeton: Princeton University Press, 1964.

[3] The term 'orientalization' is usefully employed by Francis Hutchins in *Illusion of Permanence: British Imperialism in India*, Princeton: Princeton University Press, 1967, p. 154.

See J. A. Mangan, 'Eton in India: The Careful Creation of Oriental Englishmen', in Mangan, *The Games Ethic and Imperialism*, pp. 122–41. See also Mangan (ed.), *The Cultural Bond, passim* but especially the Prologue.

[4] Mangan, 'Eton in India', pp. 125–26.

[5] Quoted from Sir Thomas Raleigh, *Lord Curzon in India: Being a Selection from His Speeches as Viceroy and Governor General. 1898–1905*, London: Macmillan, 1906, p. 245.

came to be utilised by the British as an important means of anglicising the indigenous rulers from the 1880s onwards. Going by the maxim of the diplomat Sir Hercules Robinson, that 'a similarity of taste in amusements is a guarantee for common sympathy in more important matters', the British had little to fear from the 'sporting princes'.[6] The native princes, on their turn, found in Western sports a shortcut to social mobility vis-à-vis the colonial state, or in Ann Morrow's words, an important way of 'sweating the sex' out of the other ranks.[7] Such sports that received royal patronage in the late 19th century included hunting, horse-racing, golf, polo, snooker, or billiards and most importantly, cricket. Especially, for many of the native princes, 'cricket was a tool of social mobility'.[8]

In this politico-cultural setting the British began to employ the concept of 'games ethic' as part of their imperial project. Tony Mason and Paul Dimeo, following the widely discussed theory of 'games ethic' popularised by J. A. Mangan, explain football's introduction and organisation in Calcutta primarily in terms of public school games-playing ethos learnt by the educated Bengali middle classes at the British-run Anglo-Indian colleges.[9] The concept of 'games ethic' had shared with the notion of 'muscular Christianity' propagated by the moral missionary a firm belief in sport as an instrument of imperial moral persuasion.[10] As has been rightly

---

[6] Donald Trelford, *Snookered*, UK: Faber and Faber, 1986, pp. 24–25; Robert Hyam, *Britain's Imperial Century, 1851–1914*, London: Macmillan, 1976, p. 151, cited in Holt, *Sport and the British*, p. 215.

[7] Ann Morrow, *The Maharajas of India*, London: Grafton Books, 1986, quoted in Majumdar, *Twenty-Two Yards to Freedom*, p. 22.

[8] For details on the princely patronage of cricket, see Majumdar, *Twenty-Two Yards to Freedom*, pp. 22–74. Also see W. D. Begg, *Cricket and Cricketers in India*, Ajmer: published by author, 1934.

[9] The accepted definitive study of public school games as moral training is J. A. Mangan's *Athleticism in Victorian and Edwardian Public School: The Emergence and Consolidation of an Educational Ideology*, Cambridge: Cambridge University Press, 1981 and London: Frank Cass, 2000, with a new introduction.

Mason, 'Football on the *Maidan*', p. 144; Dimeo, 'Football and Politics in Bengal', p. 62.

[10] For a reflective discussion on this theme in the Asian context, see J. A. Mangan, 'Imperial Origins, Christian Manliness, Moral Imperatives and Pre-Srilankan Playing Fields' — two chapters dealing respectively with 'Beginnings' and 'Consolidation', in J. A. Mangan and Fan Hong (eds), *Sport in Asian Society: Past and Present*, London: Frank Cass, 2003, pp. 1–49. Mangan's most recent considerations of the role of the imperialist in the spread of modern sport in South Asia are well documented here.

pointed out by J. A. Mangan, the so-called 'games ethic' inculcated in the Victorian public schools was a useful instrument of colonial purpose.[11] In late 19th-century India, too, the public/missionary schools and the headmasters, teachers and missionaries who ran them used sports like football as a moral tool as part of a broader imperial project. As Mangan neatly sums up:

> The game was considered by the colonizers to carry with it a series of moral lessons, regarding hard work and perseverance, about team loyalty and obedience to authority and, indeed, involving concepts of correct physical development and 'manliness'. As such, it was used as key weapon in the battle to win over local populations and to begin transforming them from their 'uncivilized' and 'heathen' state to one where they might be considered 'civilized' and 'Christian'.[12]

The pre-eminent role of the muscular moral missionary in the introduction of football in India was most evident in Kashmir. In the early 1890s, Cecil Earle Tyndale-Biscoe, a missionary of the Church Missionary High School of Srinagar, fought hard against indigenous religious customs and social habits to introduce soccer to his Hindu schoolboys. Despite overall initial resistance from the boys, he emerged successful in popularising the game among the local youth, who, on their part, were introduced to a new code of ethics.[13] Of course, soccer was a mere moral means for Biscoe to serve a wider imperial end:

> It was his profound desire as a Christian to introduce his pupils to HIM who taught all men to love one another and show it by practice . . . talking would not accomplish this . . . bundles could not do this, therefore bundles must be turned into boys by athletic exercises and athletic boys turned into manly citizens by continued acts of kindness.[14]

Later on soccer became popular in different other schools of Kashmir including the famous Srinagar High School. The game's social popularisation is also noted by Eric Dallas Tyndale-Biscoe, Cecil

---

[11] Mangan, *The Games Ethic*, p. 18.

[12] J. A. Mangan, 'Soccer as Moral Training: Missionary Intentions and Imperial Legacies', in Dimeo and Mills, *Soccer in South Asia*, p. 41.

[13] For Tyndale-Biscoe's observations on the matter, see C. E. Tyndale-Biscoe, *Tyndale-Biscoe of Kashmir: An Autobiography*, London: Seeley Service, 1951 and *Character-Building in Kashmir*, London: Church Missionary Society, 1920.

[14] Mangan, *The Games Ethic*, p. 187.

Tyndale-Biscoe's third son, in his biography of his father, 'Now, not only is football played by the schoolboys, but the general public have taken to it with enthusiasm. They have a football league of various teams . . .'[15]

At virtually the same time as Tyndale-Biscoe taught soccer to his Hindu schoolboys in Kashmir, Theodore Leighton Pennell, a medical missionary, posted at Bannu, a small military station on the North-West Frontier, introduced the game to mostly Afghan boys of Bannu High School. For Pennell, like Tyndale-Biscoe, soccer was an effective instrument for character-building among schoolboys. Later Pennell became so much impressed by the locals' enthusiasm towards adoption and adaptation of the game that he entitled one of the chapters in his autobiography as 'An Afghan Football Team'.[16] In fact, he took his school football team for a tour to several mission schools and colleges in north India. Importantly enough, the team represented 'all classes, Moslims, Hindu, Christians and Sikhs'. The Afghan team's display against their more reputed opponents at Bombay, Karachi, Hyderabad, or Calcutta was phenomenal. On the team's return to Bannu after the long tour, a civic reception was arranged to honour them.[17] Thus, as Mangan explains, both Tyndale-Biscoe and Pennell used the game as a 'key weapon in the battle to win over local populations and to begin transforming them from their "uncivilized" and "heathen" state to one where they might be considered "civilized" and "Christian"'.[18]

Apart from the important contributions made by missionaries like Tyndale-Biscoe or Pennell towards the spread of soccer, no less vigorous a proclamation of 'games ethic' was noticed in the city-based public schools and the hill-based boarding schools established during the two decades following the revolt of 1857. Five major public schools, known as the 'Chiefs Colleges' were: Rajkumar College (1870) at Rajkot, Mayo College (1872) at Ajmer, Rajkumar College (1872) at Nowgong, Daly College (1876) at Indore, and Aitchison College (1886) at Lahore. These colleges were modelled in the spirit and ethos of the Victorian English public schools. As a natural corollary to this trend, the games field

---

[15] E. D. Tyndale-Biscoe, *Fifty Years against the Stream*, Mysore: Wesleyan Missionary Press, 1930. He has also mentioned this in his autobiography, *Memoirs of Eric Dallas Tyndale-Biscoe* (in transcript form).

[16] T. L. Pennell, *Among the Wild Tribes of the Afghan Frontier*, London: Seeley, 1909, pp. 153–67.

[17] *Ibid.*, p. 167.

[18] Mangan, 'Soccer as Moral Training', p. 41.

was instrumentalised as a moral tool for character training.[19] The boarding schools of the Raj situated mostly at the British hill stations in India, did not lag much behind in the spread of soccer. The Simla Public School, created at the instance of G. E. L. Cotton in 1863, integrated modern games including football into its curriculum. Other boarding schools set up in Nagpur, Bangalore, Nainital, and Darjeeling were also moulded by the same public school games-playing ethos. In all these schools, 'soccer was a means to moral end'.[20]

In Bengal, especially in Calcutta, the Anglo-Indian schools and colleges certainly integrated sports, including football, as an integral part in their educational curriculum. Soccer, to these early missionaries as well as public school teachers, was a *moral* tool to inculcate 'a series of moral lessons, regarding hard work and perseverance, about team loyalty and obedience to authority and, indeed, involving concepts of correct physical development and "manliness"'.[21] The games ethic of the public school playing field was not confined to the city of Calcutta only. At times, it transgressed the boundaries of city schools to reach out to wider masses through personal efforts of public school teachers.[22] More importantly, British missionaries and public school teachers played a more worthy role in spreading soccer in the hill station of Darjeeling. The St. Paul's School for Boys, established under the guidance of Rev. J. C. Nesfield in 1864, reflected soccer's importance as a moral tool during its first hundred years.[23] Edmund Cox, who joined the school as a classics master in

---

[19] For an in-depth discussion of 'games ethic' in these colleges, see Mangan, *The Games Ethic*, especially Chapter 5, 'Eton in India', pp. 122–41. For Mangan's most pointed reference in this regard, viz., the Mayo College, see Herbert Sherring, *Mayo College, Ajmere, 'The Eton of India': A Record of Twenty Years 1875–1895* (1897), cited in Mangan, *The Games Ethic*, pp. 217–18. For the importance of games in other colleges, two works referred to by Mangan in 'Soccer as Moral Training' deserve mention: *Forty Years of the Rajkumar College 1870–1910*, compiled by H. H. Sir Bhavasinhji, K.C.S.I., Maharaja of Bhavnagar, prepared and abridged from the papers of the late Chester Macnaghten; *Aitchinson Chiefs College: Old Boys Register*, 1928.

[20] Mangan, 'Soccer as Moral Training', p. 52.

[21] *Ibid.*, p. 41.

[22] For example, E. M. Wheeler, a teacher of the Bishops College, who was himself a great footballer of National Association in the 1890s and a noted educationist later on, was primarily responsible for the promotion of the game in Hooghly, an important suburban town of Calcutta.

[23] Two teachers — Edmond Cox in the last quarter of the 19th century and Leslie James Goddard in the middle of the 20th century — played a crucial role in popularising the game among the students of the school.

1877, worked very hard to teach and organise football, cricket, swimming, and riding. The result was, as Cox later noted in his autobiography, 'order emerged out of chaos'.[24] A few decades later Leslie James Goddard, principal of the school from 1934 to 1964, enhanced the popularity of soccer at the school, 'as he created new pitches and played in the school eleven'.[25] The love cultivated for soccer at the school had a much wider impact on the local society as the tea-planters as well as their Indian staff began to take active interest in the game.[26] Especially notable was the close connection between St. Paul's and the local tea-planting fraternity since many of the sons of tea planters had been educated at the school.[27] In fact, sports like football and cricket proved a fruitful means of cultural exchange for the ex-student-turned-tea-planters who used to take part in friendly matches against the boys of the school and other visiting teams.[28] This shows how soccer, in place of its moral flavour intended by its public school promoters, assumed a local dimension fostering a sense of cultural attachment to the game itself.

Notwithstanding the obvious role of the moral educationists and muscular missionaries in the introduction of football in the public schools in north India and parts of Bengal, the formidable growth of the game in Bengal within a short span of time can be least understood in terms of the imperial programme of 'games ethic' only. Ultimately, the impact of public school games-playing ethos seemed to be minimal in the social popularisation of the game among Bengali masses. In fact, how the game was adopted and adapted by various Indian groups at various places is a much more complex story.[29]

---

[24] Sir Edmund L. Cox, *My Thirty Years in India*, London: Mills & Boon, 1909, p. 28.

[25] Mangan, 'Soccer as Moral Training', p. 51.

[26] *Ibid.*

[27] *Ibid.*

[28] *Ibid.* Mangan refers to a privately printed work *Under the Old School Topee* by Hazel Craig Innes (1996), p. 77 for this interesting piece of information. According to Mangan, 'this labour of love, and rightly unashamed exercise in nostalgia, will prove to be record of considerable value to future social historians who reflect on the cultural influences of the English public school system on modern Indian culture and society'. Mangan, 'Soccer as Moral Training', p. 55.

[29] J. A. Mangan, for example, hinted at this reality. As he rightly observes, 'An assessment of the impacts of these (colonizers') intentions and programmes is a different matter altogether. . . . It is no easy matter to begin untangling the responses of Indian communities to the introduction of football.' Mangan, 'Soccer as Moral Training', p. 54.

Effacing the 'Self-Image of Effeteness': From Physical Culture to Football Culture

Importantly enough, the period games ethic meshed with colonial masculinity to produce a fruitful stereotype of Bengali as an effeminate non-military race. In fact, throughout the 19th century, British imperialists, perhaps out of their deep dislike for the climate, topography and inhabitants of Bengal, made the Bengali a butt of satiric criticisms for his supposed physical effeteness — a stereotype that ran all through the period of imperial rule. This colonial construction of the 'effeminate Bengali' could be found in everyday British attitude towards commonplace Bengalis, in their various speeches and most prolifically in their writings, that is, contemporary Anglo-Indian literature. 'A low, lying people in a low-lying land' went the colonial snicker. A Bengali had 'the grit of a rabbit' — an image with which the Bengali elite appeared to concur.[30] The Bengali middle classes, especially the babus, had to bear the brunt of this slur for their supposed physical effeminacy and moral susceptibility. This stereotype of the physical effeminacy of the Bengali as a 'race' found its most blatant expression in Thomas Macaulay's critique:

> The physical organisation of the Bengali is feeble even to effeminacy. He lives in a constant vapour bath. His pursuits are sedentary, his limbs delicate, his movements languid. During many ages he has been trampled upon by men of bolder and more hardy breeds. Courage, independence, veracity are qualities to which his constitution and his situation are equally unfavourable.[31]

G. W. Steevens, a British journalist, wrote in 1899:

> By his legs you shall know the Bengali. The leg of a free man is straight or a little bandy, so that he can stand on it solidly. . . . The Bengali's leg is either skin and bones; the same size all the way down, with knocking knobs for trees, or else it is very fat or globular, also turning in at the knees, with round thighs like a woman's. The Bengali's leg is the leg of a slave.[32]

---

[30] Sir Frank Dunlop Smith, private secretary to the viceroy, 1905–10, in M. Gilbert, *Servant of India*, London: Longman, 1966, p. 56, quoted in John Rosselli, 'The Self-Image of Effeteness', *Past and Present*, no. 86, February 1980, p. 121.

[31] Thomas Macaulay, *Critical and Historical Essays*, London: J. M. Dent & Sons Ltd., 1961, vol. 1, p. 562.

[32] G. W. Steevens, *In India*, London: Thomas Nelson & Sons, 1899, pp. 85–86, cited by I. Chowdhury-Sengupta, 'The Effeminate and the Masculine: Nationalism and the Concept of Race in Colonial Bengal', in Peter Robb (ed.), *The Concept of Race in South Asia*, Oxford: Oxford University Press, 1995, p. 298. Emphasis added.

The colonial charge of 'effeminate' and 'non-martial' against the Bengali continued even in the characterisation of his sporting pursuit in the mid-19th century. As one contemporary commentator observes:

> The most superficial observer of Bengali manners must know that their games and sports are, for the most part, *sedentary*. The amusements of a numerous people, that do not supply the British army with a single sepoy, cannot be expected to bear a military character. The Bengali is certainly the least pugnacious animal in the world. The gods did not make him warlike. His maxim being, that 'walking is better than running, standing than walking, sitting than standing, and lying-down best of all', his amusements have to be for the most part *sedentary*.[33]

He also furnished a list of the most important pre-colonial Bengali sports and games to amplify his observation. The list included *shatranj*, *pasha*, cards, *ashta-kashte*, *das-panchis*, *bhag-bandhi*, the sling, *hadu-gudu*, *danda-guli*, kite-flying, wrestling, ram-fight, *bulbul*-fight, jugglery, cock-fight, gymnastics, yoga, swimming, *chaughan*, *gendua*, and marble throwing or *gulti*.[34]

The Bengali response to this charge of effeminacy was uniquely *cultural*. They reacted to the colonial stereotype by way of the pursuit of a 'neo-traditional physical culture' to efface the 'self-image of effeteness'.[35] In fact, many noted Bengali intellectuals of the age too seemed to have internalised this 'self-image of effeteness', and voiced an urgency to overcome this supposed physical degeneration by way of resurgence of traditional Bengali physical culture and indigenous games. In 1966 Rajnarayan Basu, in his famous prospectus of a 'Nationality Promotion Society', urged the revival of 'national gymnastic exercises'.[36] The motivation spurred up by middle-class cultural nationalists such as Rajnarayan Basu, Bankim Chandra Chatterjee, Krishna Kumar Mitra, Sarala Debi, Nabagopal Mitra, and Swami Vivekananda led to the emergence of a physical culture movement in the second half of the 19th century.[37] This movement led

---

[33] Horatio Smith, 'Bengali Games and Amusements', *Calcutta Review*, 1851.

[34] *Ibid.*

[35] For an in-depth study of this concept, see Rosselli, 'The Self-Image of Effeteness', pp. 121–48. Also see Mrinalini Sinha, *Colonial Masculinity: The 'Manly Englishman' and the 'Effeminate Bengali' in the Late Nineteenth Century*, Manchester: Manchester University Press, 1995.

[36] Jogesh Chandra Bagal, *Hindu Melar Itibritta* (History of the Hindu Mela), Calcutta: Maitrayee, 1945, p. 91.

[37] Rajnarayan Basu, *Se Kaal aar e Kaal* (That Age and This Age), Calcutta: Bangiya Sahitya Parisat, 1951. Basu identified a number of reasons for the physical degeneration of the Bengalis, of which environmental imbalance, untimely hard

and popularised in Bengal by Nabagopal Mitra's Hindu Mela in the 1860–70s began to promote the rejuvenation of the ancient Hindu principle of physical culture.[38] Any involvement in Anglo-Saxon sports like football, cricket or hockey was discouraged and rejected in favour of active participation in physical culture clubs or *akhras*.[39] Thus Hindu Mela represented an indigenous reaction against the British charge of the Bengali's supposed racial effeminacy.

British attitude towards this rejuvenation of Bengali physical culture was rather curious. In fact, British civil servants like Sir George Campbell, who was the lieutenant governor of Bengal from 1871 to 1874, were active promoters of physical education in the civil service and

---

labour, lack of exercises, decrease in nutritious diet and heavy drinking, indulgence in idle pleasure and lack of healthy entertainment remained most important (pp. 38–53).

Bankim Chandra Chatterjee, 'Bangalir Bahubal' (Physical Valour of the Bengalis), in *Bankim Rachanabali* (Collected Works of Bankim Chandra), Calcutta, Sahitya Samsad, 1953–69, vol. II, pp. 209–13. Bankim admitted in this essay that 'Bengalis had never had any physical valour'. But he distinguished physical valour (*bahubal*) from bodily strength (*saririk bal*). For him, physical valour consisted of four qualities: enthusiasm, unity, bravery, and perseverance. And he was hopeful that Bengalis would be able to acquire these qualities soon (pp. 307–14).

Krishna Kumar Mitra, *Atmacharit* (Memoirs), Calcutta, 1937.

Sarala Debi, *Jibaner Jharapata* (Broken Leaves of Life), Calcutta, Rupa, 1964.

In the course of the proliferation of the physical culture movement, circus strong-men and acrobats figured prominently. For contemporary examples on this, see Abanindrakrishna Basu, *Bangalir Sarkus* (Bengali's Circus), Calcutta, 1936; Birendranath Ghosh, *Bangalir Bahubal* (Physical Valour of Bengalis), Calcutta, 1932; Umesh Mallick, *Yader Gaye Jor Achhe* (Those Who Have Bodily Strength), Calcutta, 1946. Later on even Bengali military men came to be looked upon as a symbol of Bengali physical valour. A useful instance is provided by Upendra Krishna Banerjee, *Karnel Suresh Bishvas* (Cornel Suresh Biswas), Calcutta, 1900. For a reflective historical construction on this case, see Chowdhury-Sengupta, 'The Effeminate and the Masculine', pp. 282–303.

[38] For a detailed history of this movement, see Bagal, *Hindu Melar Itibritta*.

[39] The endeavour to restore the ancient physical culture of Bengali people was most distinctly reflected later in the growth and proliferation of physical culture clubs and secret societies throughout Bengal in the 1890s and 1900s. The revolutionary secret societies of the Swadeshi Age including Anushilan Samiti and Yugantar put the greatest emphasis on the physical culture of gymnastic-exercises, *lathi*-sword-dagger play and yoga as the prime requisite for the physical and mental development of the youth.

educational institutions.[40] More importantly, Campbell also became a great patron of the Hindu Mela activities. His physical education measures were motivated by a desire to promote those qualities of 'physical energy, activity and endurance' which were 'the great want among Bengalis'.[41] He was quite certain that 'if the educated Bengalees, instead of giving way to intellectual vanity, set themselves to rival Europeans in qualities depending on physical and moral tone, they are capable of very great things'.[42] But Campbell's hope — a concern shared by many socially upright elite and middle-class Bengalis — could not be fulfilled by a mere recourse to gymnastic exercises or indigenous sports like gymnastics, body-building and wrestling as popularised by the Hindu Mela. Bengalis needed to become more competitive to prove their mettle of masculinity to the Europeans.

Despite the Bengali rejuvenation of physical culture in the 1860–70s, the charge of effeminacy continued to be labelled specifically against the Bengali middle class, or a section of the class, identified as *babus*.[43] Mrinalini Sinha has shown this in her analysis of the political controversies over the Ilbert Bill (1883–84), the Native Volunteer Movement (1884–85), recruitment to the Public Service Commission (1886–87), and the 'age of consent' controversy of 1891.[44] The Ilbert Bill agitation served as an important reminder that the Europeans, so much confident of their 'unchallengeable superiority', would not easily accept the 'equality of Indian ability and character'.[45] The Bengalis probably learnt a lesson from this 'open manifestation of Social Darwinism': 'The remedy for the racist offence was to imitate the successful tactics of the Anglo-Indian middle class.'[46] This might have prompted them to take recourse to Western sports to challenge the Europeans at their own game. The failure of the physical culture movement in establishing the Bengali's physical strength vis-à-vis the British was also in evidence during the 'age of consent' controversy. In fact, it became clear by the 1890s that the physical culture movement

---

[40] The colleges where physical education was started were those of Dacca, Hoogly, Barrackpore, and Howrah.

[41] Rosselli, 'The Self Image of Effeteness', p. 138.

[42] Sir George Campbell, *Memoirs of My Indian Career*, ed. Sir C. E. Bernard, vol. 2, London: Macmillan, 1893.

[43] Sinha, *Colonial Masculinity*, p. 16.

[44] *Ibid.*

[45] Burton Stein, *A History of India*, Oxford: Blackwell, 1998, p. 273.

[46] *Ibid.*

was marked by a conspicuous lack of competitive dimension that distinguished modern Western sports like football, cricket or hockey. Moreover, even if rigorous physical exercise was looked upon as a plausible weapon to counter the British slur of effeminacy, it did not afford the Bengali the opportunity to compete with the British on even terms. Middle-class Bengalis quickly realised the ultimate ineffectuality of the physical culture movement and the urgent need to cultivate new ways to reassert physical prowess and redeem their hurt masculinity. Western sports, especially football, provided the way out. As one anonymous Englishman observed in the 1880s:

> Many educated natives, in Bengal specially, have, for years past, felt the reproach which attaches to their want of courage and corporal activity, and have earnestly set themselves to remedy these defects: hence on all sides we find efforts to follow the Europeans among native students. Football and cricket are becoming popular, and gymnasia introduced.[47]

Dimeo has argued that in taking recourse to modern sports Bengalis followed a 'route of mimicry'.[48] But he fails to admit that they adopted Western sports like football with a conscious design of showing their physical worth by competing with the Europeans on an equal plane. Football's adaptation was therefore more a cultural ploy than a simplistic mimicry. Nagendra Prasad Sarvadhikari, the so-called 'Father of Indian Football', came to introduce and popularise football play with his school and college mates in this particular context. But before appreciating the role of Nagendra Prasad in the growth of football culture in Bengal, it is pertinent to briefly discuss the beginnings of soccer in Bengal, particularly in the third quarter of the 19th century.

The Beginnings: The First Matches and the Earliest Clubs

To ascertain precisely who introduced the game in India and how it was first played in Calcutta is nearly impossible. Records simply do not exist. It is reasonably clear, however, that this game came to India with the East India Company. Football's early pioneers were the officers and men of trading farms and regimental battalions, European professors of

---

[47] *Trust and Fear Not, Ought Natives to be Welcomed as Volunteers?* Calcutta: Thacker, Spink & Co., 1885, p. 18.

[48] Dimeo, 'Colonial Bodies, Colonial Sport', p. 84.

educational institutions, and naval men who used to play at ports of call like Calcutta, Bombay, Madras, and Karachi. According to one source, the record is still extant of a match of only 30 minutes duration. The match 'was played as early as in 1802 between a Military XI and an Island XI at Bombay and it resulted in a 5–0 win for the former'.[49] But it was in Calcutta where soccer got its first toast of popular appeal in India. It has been said that the British regimental footballers and the civilian residents at Calcutta, Barrackpore and Dumdum 'had a big say in establishing the game on a firm footing locally and then spreading it all over the province of Bengal'.[50] The first football match in Calcutta was played in April 1854 between a 'Calcutta Club of Civilians' and the 'Gentlemen of Barrackpore'. As *The Englishman* reported: 'A Calcutta team of civilians had challenged the Gentlemen of Barrackpore to meet for a trial of their skill in the manly game of soccer on Saturday, the 13th April 1854, on the Esplanade Ground, Fort William, Calcutta, at 5.15 p.m.'[51] It was followed by two more notable matches, one in 1868 between the Etonians and the Rest, and the other in 1870 between the public schools of Eton, Harrow and Winchester and the private schools, composed of Miss Tina's pupils.[52]

The oldest football club in India was the Dalhousie Club of Calcutta (1878) although the Calcutta Football Club (1872), devoted to playing rugby football initially, predated it. Other important soccer creations of the Europeans included the Naval Volunteers, the Howrah United Club and the Armenian Club as well as the football teams of colleges like Presidency College, Sibpur Engineering College, Bishop's College, Calcutta Medical College, and La Martiniere. In its early years of growth, football really flowered at the precincts of these colleges in and around Calcutta. The college football clubs had come into the fore immediately after the foundation of the Dalhousie Athletic Club. Most of these clubs came into existence parallel to the emergence of worthy Bengali clubs like Sovabazar, National, Town, or Mohun Bagan in the 1880s. Presidency College, where football was introduced at the turn of 1870s, set the ball rolling and other leading colleges mentioned earlier enthusiastically took up the mantle. In fact, one of the main reasons for football's wider

---

[49] Killum, 'Our Soccer Story', *Sport and Pastime*, vol. 5, no. 25, 23 June 1951.
[50] *Ibid.*
[51] *The Englishman*, 10 June 1854.
[52] *IFA Shield Souvenir*, 1945, Calcutta: IFA, 1945. All the standard sporting chronicles in India, too, testify to these dates.

popularity in Bengal compared to other Western sports like hockey or cricket was the overwhelming patronage it got from the Bengali student community.[53] Most of the students, who had excelled in the game, after leaving their colleges, 'either joined one of the existing clubs or in their zeal became instrumental in forming others'.[54] As Moti Nandy makes the point rightly, 'it was these students, after they left college, who founded the first of today's open clubs in the 1880s and 90s to enable them to go on playing the game'.[55]

However, in the fullness of time, despite the important innovatory role of these middle-class schools and colleges, the role of the public schools for the introduction and promotion of football in Calcutta was minimal. Despite football's inclusion and importance as a form of moral training in the public school curriculum in the leading British educational institutions, football's popularisation in Bengal cannot solely be attributed to this process. The attitude and response of the general Bengali public towards this mass spectator sport was rather different. Football's appropriation by the general public was a complex process with certain elements of spontaneity and calculation.

The Role of Nagendra Prasad Sarvadhikari

Despite considerable debates in Bengali sporting literature, Nagendra Prasad Sarvadhikari is generally acknowledged for his part in popularising the game of football with his fellow-students at Hare School in 1877.[56] Hence, the year goes down in history as the beginning of the Bengali's or rather the Indian's tryst with soccer and Nagendra Prasad is regarded as the 'Father of Indian Football'.[57] With his indomitable

---

[53] This point was specifically noted in 'Sixty Years', *Diamond Jubilee Official Souvenir, Indian Football Association*, Calcutta: IFA, 1956, pp. 42–43.

[54] *Ibid.*

[55] Moti Nandy, 'Calcutta Soccer', in Sukanta Chaudhuri (ed.), *Calcutta: The Living City, 2. Present and Future*, Calcutta: Oxford University Press, 1990, p. 317.

[56] Hare School, a prestigious secondary school of 19th-century Calcutta, was established in 1834 at the initiative of David Hare, a Scotsman, who devoted all his energy and wealth for the betterment of education in contemporary Bengal.

[57] Nagendra Prasad's biographical sketches, one in English and the other in Bengali, are worth reading in this regard. These are: P. L. Dutt, *Memoir of 'Father of Indian Football' Nagendra Prosad Sarvadhikari*, Calcutta: N. P. Sarvadhikari Memorial Committee, 1944 (hereafter *Memoir*); and Sourindra Kumar Ghosh, *Kridasamrat Nagendra Prasad Sarvadhikari* (Nagendra Prasad, the Emperor of Sports), Calcutta: N. P. Sarvadhikari.Memorial Committee, 1963 (hereafter *Kridasamrat*).

sportsman spirit and unparalleled organisational acumen, it is said, Nagendra Prasad almost single-handedly led Bengali society into an engaging popular pursuit of modern sporting culture. His sincere efforts at the development of modern sporting activities among Bengali people contributed to the initiation of a unique sporting identity in Bengali society. Nagendra Prasad's lifelong effort to raise the physical and sporting prowess of the Bengali can be placed in the broader perspective of social reform and regeneration in India, which had started since the days of Raja Rammohun Roy. Nagendra Prasad used sports like football as a viable cultural weapon to reassert hurt Bengali masculinity and to retrieve India's sinking national prestige.[58] While the legend of his kicking off football in India remains a bit of a debatable issue, more mystery surrounds his sudden withdrawal from sporting engagements in only his 30s and consequent self-disappearance into obscurity.[59] However, there is no doubt that he generated an unprecedented sporting spirit in Bengali urban society and organised sport as a bond of social unity. It is therefore important to acknowledge his contributions to the growth and efflorescence of a football culture in contemporary Bengal and accord this legendary figure his much-deserved place in the social history of modern Bengal.[60]

It is said that Nagendra Prasad rose to prominence when he kicked off football for the first time as an Indian on the Calcutta maidan at a very tender age in 1877 and followed it up by introducing and popularising the game among his friends of Hare School. It is of contextual interest here to reproduce this engaging story from his first biography:

> How the ten-year-old boy came to introduce football amongst Bengalees when related will be read like a romance. . . . Nagendra Prasad's mother had the habit of going to the Ganges everyday for her bath. . . . One day Nagendra Prasad was driving with his mother to the Ganges and the

---

[58] Prof. Manmatha Mohan Bose was later said to have remarked: 'Amongst Indians it was Nagendra Prasad who convinced the European that prowess of the Bengalees was in no way inferior to their intellect; and the kick of the naked foot perhaps superior to the kick of the men with boots.' Quoted in *Memoirs*, p. 27.

[59] Nagendra Prasad suddenly withdrew from most of his engagements in sports organisation in 1902 when he joined the Calcutta High Court as an attorney.

[60] Pankaj Kumar Gupta, the famous soccer administrator, noted later: 'Mr. Nagendra Prasad Sarvadhikari took a very leading role amongst the Indians and his enthusiasm, interest, organizational abilities and skill in the game in the nineties, gave great impetus to Indian football.' *IFA Golden Jubilee Souvenir*, Calcutta: IFA, 1943.

carriage approaching the road on the north of the Calcutta F. C. Ground the boy noticed that on the field a number of Europeans were kicking and throwing a pretty roundish thing in air and running and tussling to get it again. The boy was restless and entreating his mother got down there and watched for few minutes the game the Europeans were at. Suddenly the big roundish thing came rolling near the boy. Without hesitation he picked it up and felt it and found to his astonishment that such a large thing was not heavy at all. While holding it a European accosted him and laughingly said, 'kick it to me'. The boy was delighted and after the Europeans kicked it in. This was the first time a Bengali and that a lad of ten kicked a football. The boy was jubilant.[61]

This 'kick off' inspired Nagendra Prasad to mobilise his classmates to play the game. He collected subscriptions from the interested ones and bought a football (in fact a rugby ball as they could not identify it) from Messrs Manton & Co., a renowned sports goods shop at Bowbazar, Calcutta. Next day the schoolboys started playing with the ball under Nagendra's leadership at the Hare School compound. A sizeable crowd enjoyed this unprecedented event from outside the fences. However, a European teacher of the adjacent Presidency College, Prof. G. A. Stack, watched the proceedings from the balcony with great delight.[62] Attracted by the boys' enthusiasm, Stack offered to train them in the rules of the game. Another professor of the college, J. H. Gilligand, also took active interest in the process. Both encouraged Nagendra Prasad and his companions to popularise the game among Bengali students in Calcutta. The Boys' Club, founded by Nagendra Prasad around this time, was the first Bengali, alias Indian, initiative at football organisation.[63] Prof. Stack found in him great aptitude for the game. The boy picked up the rules of the game as well in no time. Indian football thus got a start at the initiative of the young lad,

---

[61] *Memoir*, pp. 6–7; *Kridasamrat*, pp. 87–99. Most standard monographs on Bengal soccer reproduce this story as the beginning of the Bengali's pursuit of the game. For more contemporary layers on the same, see Pabitra Bhushan Gangopadhyay, 'E deshe football er janmo' (Birth of Football in This Country), *Ananda Bazar Patrika*, 25 June 1941; *The Statesman*, 6 August 1944.

[62] According to the Jubilee Number of the Presidency College Magazine, football became popular in the college at the initiative of G. A. Stack, a professor of History in 1883. For further details, see *Presidency College Centenary Volume, 1955*, Calcutta: Presidency College, 1956, pp. 195–97.

[63] Srinibas Chaudhuri, 'Bangali Football Kheloyar' (Bengali Football Player), *Prabartak*, Asadha, June–July 1938, p. 305.

who was destined to hold the helm of the boat and lead it to the shore. Later on he became the greatest centre forward of his time.

It was his honesty and sincerity that enabled Nagendra Prasad to be the leader of the school when he started the game of football for the benefit of the schoolboys. The enterprise caught the imagination of young men in no time and spread all over Calcutta and its suburbs speedily. Proving himself the best in the team, the boy became a true leader of the team in every aspect. Even the students of the Presidency College took the opportunity of playing football with the boys of Hare School. Although very much senior in age, the college boys followed the leadership of Nagendra Prasad without the least demur. It did not give the boy a swelled head. As a born sportsman and leader, Nagendra Prasad, though of tender age, managed to create an atmosphere which bound the school and college boys closely, thereby helping to pave the way for the growth of football among the student communities. Nagendra Mullick, a boy from the famous Mullick family of Chorebagan, happened to be a classmate of Nagendra Prasad. Enamoured by the game of football and eager to start a private club in the spacious confines of Rajendra Mullick's house, Nagendra Mullick sought Nagendra Prasad's help. The latter greeted the offer in right earnest and the Friends Club was founded forthwith with great pomp.[64] As P. L. Dutt comments: 'Belonging to a family of millionaire, it was a sight as to how the young Mullick and his rich relations in honouring the traditional spirit of sports vied with each other.'[65]

Soon, the popularity of football grew by leaps and bounds. Led by Nagendra Prasad, a number of clubs were soon formed in and around Calcutta. Presidency, Wellington and Howrah Sporting were the foremost amongst them. While the first two emerged under Nagendra Prasad's direct leadership, the last one was the creation of Bama Charan Kundu, a son of the famous Iswar Charan Kundu at the instance of Nagendra Prasad, his mentor.[66]

By the time Wellington Club was formed (1884), Nagendra Prasad rose to be an undergraduate of the Calcutta University being a student of the Presidency College. His contemporaries that included illustrious names like Sir Pratul Chatterjee, Bhupendra Nath Mitter, Sir Binod Mitter, Sir Manmatha Nath Mukherjee, Surendra Nath Mullick, K. N. Chaudhuri, and Jatindra Nath Basu, cooperated with Nagendra Prasad in his manly

---

[64] *Kridasamrat*, p. 98.
[65] *Memoir*, p. 11.
[66] *Kridasamrat*, p. 98; *Memoir*, p. 12

effort to improve the physique of the young men of the country and bring them at par with the Europeans in the field of competition.[67] After leaving college, this first generation of footballing Bengalis led by Nagendra Prasad took an active interest in the formation of Bengali football clubs. Nagendra Prasad concentrated on consolidating the Wellington Club. The Club had its ground on the Calcutta maidan. The membership of the club was open to all irrespective of class or creed. Amongst others, influential Mohammedans joined the club in large numbers. Apart from soccer the club played rugby, tennis and cricket.

The foundation of the Sovabazar Club in 1887 was the culmination of Nagendra Prasad's continuous efforts at club formation. Sovabazar was actually the outcome of a severe rift in the organisation of the Wellington Club on the question of entry of a low-caste member into the club's ranks.[68] Nagendra Prasad was the first Indian to voice the critique of caste-based discrimination in the arena of sports. Although he belonged to an orthodox Hindu family, he chose to ignore all caste prejudices while establishing a series of sporting clubs. His position against the discriminatory actions based on caste status is clearest in the incident surrounding the induction of a confectioner's son into the Wellington Club. The club had a membership of nearly 500 from all classes of society. Well-to-do and middle-class young men of Calcutta felt some amount of pride to belong to Wellington at that time. Nagendra Prasad was ever vigilant to keep the team spirit intact. When Nagendra Prasad wanted to induct Moni Das, a confectioner's son, the richer members protested vehemently.[69] But Nagendra Prasad refused to buckle before the pressure, arguing that a sporting association should be free of any prejudice and decided to dismantle the Wellington Club. He made no secret of the exact situation and, in his characteristic gait and demeanour, said: 'I know sooner or later the matter will be asked to be put to vote. It will be a mean move on the part of those who call themselves sportsmen. I cannot allow myself to be party to it.'[70] Greatly irked by the intrigues carried on behind his back, Nagendra Prasad dissolved the Wellington Club and by combining the various sporting clubs he had

---

[67] *The Statesman*, 8 July 1934.

[68] For details on this rift and its consequent outcome, see *Memoir*, pp. 17–18; also see *Kridasamrat*, pp. 118–20.

[69] There is a controversy over Moni Das's actual caste identity. P. L. Dutt mentions Das as a confectioner's son. *Memoir*, p. 17. Saurindra Kumar Ghosh, on the other hand, describes him as a smith's son. *Krida Samrat*, pp. 118–19. Be that as it may, that Moni Das was from a low caste family is beyond doubt.

[70] *Memoir*, pp. 17–18.

earlier established — the Boys Sporting Club, Friends Club, Presidency Club, the erstwhile Wellington Club — founded the famous Sovabazar Club in 1887 at the premises of the Sovabazar Rajbati.[71] Moni Das, whose proposed induction was the cause behind the decimation of the Wellington Club, was one of the first members of the Sovabazar Club. He later distinguished himself as one of the best cricketers of the Mohun Bagan Club. This attempt by Nagendra Prasad to free sport of all caste prejudices in the 1880s was the first of its kind in India.

The Sovabazar Raj family by that time could already boast of a tennis club under the leadership of Kumar Jisnendra Krishna Dev Bahadur. Nagendra Prasad, a son-in-law of the same family, utilised his relations with the Raj family to form the Sovabazar Club. Kumar Jisnendra Krishna along with Nagendra Prasad became the joint honorary secretaries of the club and the then Maharaja of Coochbehar held the office of the president. The club was unique in its policy to throw open its membership to anyone irrespective of his class, caste, community, or religious affiliations.[72] Even the Anglo-Indians and the Europeans were welcome to join the club. It was Nagendra Prasad's practical vision that urged him to create sportsmen as 'a class by themselves'.[73] As a result, the sporting prowess of Sovabazar increased very quickly and it became the only premier Indian club of the time. In fact, Sovabazar under Nagendra Prasad's able leadership played a pioneering role in popularising and spreading football in Bengal.

The first open football tournament in India was the Trades Cup played in Calcutta in 1889.[74] Sovabazar was the first and only Indian team to take

---

[71] For details of how the club was actually formed, see *Memoir*, pp. 17–18; and also *Kridasamrat*, pp. 118–21.

Rajbati means the massive housing premises of the royal family of Sovabazar in north Calcutta.

[72] *Memoir*, p. 19.

[73] *Ibid*.

[74] *The Indian Daily News* published the first advertisement of the tournament on 8 June 1889 thus:

'The "Trades Challenge Cup"'
Presented by the Trading Community of Calcutta to the Committee of the Dalhousie Football Club in trust,

Conditionally
1. That the Cup shall be called "Trades Challenge Cup" and shall be played for in Calcutta during the recognized Football Season (May 15th to August 31st) under the rules of the Football Association by bonafide Football Clubs only …

part in the inaugural edition of the tournament and fight for the native cause at the competitive level. The then lieutenant governor of Bengal was present at Sovabazar's first appearance in the Trades Cup and 'viewed the proceedings from his carriage'.[75] The win of Sovabazar Club over the military team, the East Surrey Regiment, by 2–1 in the 1892 Trades Cup was the first prominent victory of an Indian team at competitive level. Newspapers in England gave prominence to the result, and some concern was expressed at the win of an Indian team against a team representing a British Regiment![76] Thus Sovabazar set the trend for future Indian outfits to fight and defeat the British at their own game.

The Trades Cup soon became very popular and clubs of all communities and categories — Europeans, Indians, Armenians, and students — competed. The steadily growing interest in the game brought to the fore questions of control and coordination. With the need of a well-constituted controlling body clearly obvious, the formation of the Indian Football Association (IFA) in 1892 was a mere formality.[77] But the initiative in this regard was again taken in right earnest by no other person than Nagendra Prasad. He invited the leading members of the two foremost contemporary European clubs — the Calcutta Football Club and the Dalhousie Club — to an informal meeting at the Sovabazar Club tent at the close of the 1892 football season. Mr A. R. Brown, honorary secretary of the Dalhousie Club, Mr B. R. C. Lindsay, a player of distinction of the same club, Mr Watson of the Calcutta F.C. and Nagendra Prasad of Sovabazar

---

2. That the competition shall be controlled by a committee formed of one representative (or his proxy) from each competing club, and in addition two members of the Dalhousie Football Club Committee (to represent the trust), who shall elect a Secretary for the season.

3. Player will be allowed to play for more than one club for the Cup during a season.

4. That the holders of the Cup for the time being be held responsible for the safe custody thereof.

W. Bushby
Hony. Sec. Dalhousie Football Club
6th June, 1889'

[75] *The Englishman*, 12 July 1889.

[76] J. N. Basu, 'My Reminiscences', in Pankaj Kumar Gupta, ed., *IFA Golden Jubilee Souvenir*, Calcutta: IFA, 1943.

[77] All standard chronicles on Indian football attest to this date. It also finds corroboration in the *Golden Jubilee* and *Diamond Jubilee Souvenirs of the Indian Football Association* published in 1943 and 1956 respectively. Also see *The Statesman*, 8 July 1934.

attended the meeting and agreed to launch another tournament that would attract the strongest combinations from all parts of the country. Voluntary financial contributions, chiefly from their Highnesses, the Maharajas of Coochbehar and Patiala, Sir A. A. Apcar and Mr J. Southerland enabled them to place an order for a shield with Messrs Elkington & Co., London through their Calcutta agents, Messrs Walter Locke & Co. The IFA Shield tournament was thus started in 1893.[78] It was again Sovabazar from among the Indian teams to represent the Indian cause and fight against the topmost European teams in the tournament.[79] The First Division Football League also began soon after in 1898, though it was confined to British teams till 1914. The birth of the IFA may truly be regarded as a historic milestone in the development of Indian football. However, the IFA, from the very beginning, became an institution completely dominated by the European members. When the opportunity of nominating the only Indian member in the IFA Council arose in 1900, Nagendra Prasad, who could have easily grabbed the membership coveted by all, surprisingly nominated Kali Mitter, a senior sportsman of the Sovabazar Club to the post.[80] This brings clear testimony to Nagendra Prasad's crass indifference to the lure of either power or position.

It is astonishing to note that such a great and pioneering sporting patron like Nagendra Prasad withdrew from nearly all sporting engagements and organisations all of a sudden in 1902, when he joined the Calcutta High Court as an attorney. There have been very little explanations in the existing literature for this drastic step taken by Nagendra Prasad. Here is one given by one of his biographers:

> When Nagendra Prasad saw Hare Sporting, National Association and Mohun Bagan were dependable to carry on his work and and the work of the Sovabazar Club, when he saw that Sarada Ranjan was moving wholeheartedly in the interest of Indian cricket he felt at ease. So long Nagendra Prasad was their guardian angel. There was no necessity for him to be always hovering over them any longer. So step by step he let them chalk out their own path till he saw the line clear, when he made everything over to them.[81]

---

[78] *IFA Shield Souvenir*, Calcutta: IFA, 1945, pp. 10–11; *The Statesman*, 1 December 1937.

[79] Sovabazar, however, had a very early exit from the tournament as it was defeated by St. Xaviers College 0–3 in their first round match.

[80] *Kridasamrat*, pp. 145–46.

[81] *Memoir*, p. 25.

But this does not seem to be a very convincing explanation for Nagendra Prasad's self-disappearance into obscurity during the last four decades of his life.[82] At the turn of the century, Nagendra Prasad observed a gradual decline in the conviction and performance of Sovabazar. This coincided with the rise of National Association or Mohun Bagan with strong values and sporting acumen. With the declining interest of the Sovabazar Raj family in sports and the death of the Maharaja of Coochbehar, the mantle of sports patronage was taken over by other aristocratic families of Bengal including the Rajas of Bhukoilas and Natore. Other sporting organisers and stalwarts like Sarada Ranjan Roy and Manmatha Ganguly came to the fore to lead the Bengali sportsmen with a different set of values. Moreover, the incoming tide of nationalism was beginning to send its impact on the Bengali sporting psyche, particularly on footballers and spectators in the wake of the anti-Partition movement in Bengal. Nagendra Prasad might be hesitant to adapt to the changing priorities of the time, especially the change in the composition and values of the Bengali aristocratic and bhadralok society at the turn of the century. A man of great foresight, he therefore thought it wise to quit sports organisation with honour.

Nagendra Prasad's organisational effort was followed by enthusiastic Bengalis like Sir Dukhiram Majumdar, Kalicharan Mitter, Manmatha Ganguly, and Haridas Seal.[83] As a result, football clubs emerged in different localities and suburbs of Calcutta in the late 1880s — amongst them National Association, Town Club, Kumartuli, Chandannagar Sporting, Chinsura Sporting, Mohun Bagan, and Aryan being most notable. The early patrons of Bengali football included aristocratic families of Calcutta

---

[82] Nagendra Prasad died in 1941.

[83] Dukhiram Majumdar, the revered 'Sir' of Bengali football, was the greatest football coach and recruiter of footballers from the late 1880s. His original name was Oomesh Chandra Majumdar. He founded the Aryan Club in 1888.

Kalicharan Mitter, son of a respectable aristocratic family of north Calcutta, was a close chum of Nagendra Prasad. An ardent football lover and a fine player himself, Mitter became the first Indian joint secretary of the IFA.

Manmatha Ganguly was a very popular teacher of Kalighat High School in south Calcutta during the 1880s and 1890s. He was a founder member of the National Association. A strict disciplinarian as a teacher, Ganguly trained his students to play football in boots. It was under his able coaching that the National Association won the Trades Cup as the first Indian team in 1900.

Haridas Seal had been a close friend of Nagendra Prasad since his school days. In his youth he always stood by Prasad in the latter's efforts to promote football in and around Calcutta.

like the Sovabazars, Bhukailas and the Lahas, and the Maharajas of Coochbehar, Mahisadal and Burdwan. Muslim representation in Indian football too began in the last decade of the 19th century when Mohammedan Sporting Club gained in prominence in Calcutta thanks to the efforts of some Muslim individuals. In 1887 the Jubilee Club was established, a sporting organisation for the Muslims in Calcutta. The club changed its name twice in the next few years, first to the Crescent Club and then to the Hamidia Club. Finally, in 1891, the latter culminated into the Mohammedan Sporting Club.[84]

The first significant Indian tournament win was achieved in 1893 when the Fort William Arsenal consisting of Indian employees of Fort William won the Coochbehar Cup.[85] Sovabazar's football prowess gradually subsided with the rise of Manmatha Ganguly's National Association that became the first-ever Indian team to lift the Trades Cup in 1900 and repeated the feat again in 1902.[86] Then came the age of Mohun Bagan, which became an emblem of Bengali self-esteem, football prowess and sporting nationalism in the first half of the 20th century. Mohun Bagan created history on the sports field when it defeated crack British military teams one by one in the qualifying rounds and the East Yorkshire Regiment in the final to win the IFA Shield in 1911 as the first native Indian team.

Nagendra Prasad was certainly a pioneer in his efforts to engage Bengali society in a popular pursuit of modern sporting culture. As has been noted in an earlier work, 'Nagendra Prasad's lifelong effort to raise the physical/sporting prowess of the Bengali can be placed in the broader perspective of social reform and regeneration in India, which had started since the days of Raja Rammohun Roy. He looked upon European sports like football as a viable cultural weapon to reassert Bengali masculinity and resurrect India's sinking national prestige.'[87] Nagendra Prasad's ingrained sportsman's spirit led him to a conscious utilisation of sport as a platform of social equality. That he made a very spirited attempt to establish the credibility of the indigenous pursuit of football is quite obvious. But more importantly, he fought against heavy odds to initiate and concretise the formation of a sporting identity among Bengali youths irrespective of

---

[84] For a brief history of the origin and early development of the club, see *Mohammedan Sporting Club — Calcutta League Champions, 1934–1935: A Souvenir*, Calcutta: Mohammedan Sporting Club, 1935, pp. 27, 35–39.

[85] RB, *Kolkatar Football*, p. 100.

[86] *The Indian Daily News*, 11 August 1900.

[87] Majumdar and Bandyopadhyay, *Goalless*, p. 18.

caste, class, community, religion, or such social affiliations at a critical socio-political context.

However, the cultural ethos with which Nagendra Prasad and his followers like Manmatha Ganguly, Kalicharan Mitter, Haridas Seal, or Dukhiram Majumdar equipped the contemporary Bengali football culture had its obvious limitations. At this stage, that is, in the 1880s and 1890s, football was deemed as a cultural weapon to reassert Bengali physical prowess and masculinity and as a medium of social intercourse between the ruler and the ruled. It was yet to become a cultural weapon to fight and beat the colonial masters in a true nationalist sense. Hence, the efforts of Nagendra Prasad and the likes may be situated in the transition of Indian pursuit of British sports from imitation to competition. The ideas of 'subversion' and 'resistance' in the arena of football were yet to gain currency.[88] Despite that, the growth of Bengali clubs around Calcutta from mid-1880s onwards added a new dimension to Bengali socio-cultural life, and by the turn of the century football sunk deep roots in even the remote parts of Bengal.

Popular Adoption and Social Adaptation

It is an interesting question as to why the Bengali from amongst the Indians so readily took to the game of football, which became much more popular than other foreign sports. Swami Vivekananda's often-quoted remark 'playing football rather than reciting Gita will take one nearer to God' arguably might have had a far-reaching impact on the Bengali psyche.[89] From a more pragmatic point of view, however, the cheapness and simple laws of the game made it more popular than other sports. As for the babu patronage of football, probably it owed its existence to their anglicised behaviour. The Bengali youth, on the other hand, saw in football a worthwhile cultural weapon to reassert their hurt self-esteem and injured masculinity. While it is not known what was in his mind when Nagendra Prasad first initiated his countrymen to outdoor sports, it is certain that, in his mature days, his sole aim for conversion was to make his young countrymen physically fit so that in the field of competition they were

---

[88] For a brief but instructive analysis of these ideas in the context of colonial Calcutta football, see Majumdar, 'The Vernacular in Sports History', pp. 3069–75.

[89] Swami Vivekananda was a very celebrated Bengali spiritual leader whose address at the Religious Conference of Chicago in 1893 had a stirring effect on global public opinion and had earned him worldwide renown.

able to hold their own against aggression from any quarter. 'That was the nationalism', writes his biographer, 'which Nagendra Prasad preached and practiced in all his life.'[90] It was in fact a religion to Nagendra Prasad to find ways and means to uplift the physique of his country. That he extolled the virtues of physical prowess is evident from the following interaction at a social gathering in the Sovabazar palace:

> ... a young family member ridiculed Nagendra Prasad's powerful stature and stamina saying that a man only needed so much strength that he would be able to drink a glass of water by himself!! Surrounded by armed retainers the babus present broke into laughter at the comment. Nagendra Prasad not amused in the least stunned everyone present by lifting the fellow off the ground and asking 'now that I shall fling you down, what do you imagine you will require to escape that fate?' It was only after the man apologized that Nagendra Prasad set him down. He declared in disgust, 'those who speak like this — they are the ones who are afraid to step out on the streets with their wives and daughters; and when they do (they) are unable to safeguard their honour. Muslim drivers intimidate them before their wife and daughter, extract double the money due to them, and walk away with a swagger while the *babu* humours himself saying I can't stoop to being a *chotolok* with the *chotoloks*. Such behavior however is not becoming of a *bhadralok* but of a eunuch! The rate of female abductions from the homes of Bengali Hindus is unparalleled in any other community. Bengalis are effete, let them gain in physical strength, — with the return of masculine splendour, will come respect from others'.[91]

As a corollary and more importantly, perhaps, the sensitive Bengali mind assimilated football as a means of crossing swords with the British imperialist on a cultural battlefield:

> It was a time when Bengal was caught in a surge of the nationalist movement. The social antagonism, the battle between the 'whites' and the 'natives' on the political plane transgressed its boundaries and entered the social sphere or more specifically the world of sports. Historically speaking, the ills of an unequal political structure threw up contradictions, which quite naturally had a deep impact on the social psyche. The age of Swadeshi had celebrated the brawn and cult of physical fitness through numerous festivals, rituals and physical culture clubs.[92]

---

[90] *Memoir*, p. 1.

[91] *Kridasamrat*, pp. 180–81, quoted in Majumdar and Bandyopadhyay, *Goalless*, p. 19.

[92] Mitra, 'Babu at Play', pp. 45–46.

Failing to attain political power, the Bengali mind naturally searched for apolitical ways to avenge their socio-political humiliation at British hands. Football afforded Bengali society just one such opportunity.

By the end of the 19th century, football in Calcutta had come a long way. From being an occasional recreation of military men, a school sport and merely a leisure activity among other Europeans, football soon became an arena for competition and conflict between the British and the Indians.[93] To suggest that Bengali football clubs of the 1880s and 1890s from their very inception began to reflect or represent a purely nationalist instinct or ethos on the sports field is perhaps too bold. Football, however, may be said to have become a new and unique cultural force in Bengali society at the turn of the century, although the approach of different clubs to the game in Calcutta was not uniform. The football clubs that cropped up in different localities of Calcutta in the second half of the 1880s, formed mostly at the initiative of locally influential middle-class Bengalis and enthusiastic youths and patronised by aristocratic families or maharajas, represented certain distinct trends of socio-cultural expression since their inception. The Sovabazar Club, a creation of Nagendra Prasad under the aegis of the Sovabazar Raj family, representative of a declining feudal aristocracy, looked upon football as a useful medium of social intercourse with the British. The club had its tent in Calcutta maidan amid those of the Europeans. 'The grandeur associated with it was directed in showing the British that they also appreciated modern leisure activities. To them, football was more of a social factor, in trying to sociate with the new masters.'[94] Despite the best efforts of Nagendra Prasad, it remained more of an institution for merry-making for the decadent feudal family of Sovabazar and hence was not quite guided by any constructive disciplined ideology.[95] Also, despite Nagendra Prasad's best efforts to foster a sporting identity among players cutting across affiliations of caste, class, religion, or community, Sovabazar remained more an emblem of elitist soccer culture in Bengal. However, it set the trend of fighting against European teams without boots by participating in early tournaments like the Trades Cup and the IFA Shield. Although Sovabazar did not earn any worthwhile glory in the field of competition except its singular famous victory over a

---

[93] Soumen Mitra has elaborately discussed this transformation of football's social dimension in his unpublished M.Phil. dissertation, 'Nationalism, Communalism and Sub regionalism: A Study of Football in Bengal, 1880–1950', Centre for Historical Studies, Jawaharlal Nehru University, 1988, Chapter 3. Also see Mitra, *In Search of an Identity*, Chapter 2.

[94] Mitra, 'Babu at Play', p. 49.

[95] RB, *Kolkatar Football*, pp. 91–92.

regimental team in the 1892 Trades Cup, it was around Sovabazar's competition with British teams that the first stirrings of Bengali spectator culture could be discerned.

In sharp contrast, National Association founded by Manmatha Ganguly, a Kalighat school teacher, was disciplined and had a strict ideological motivation.[96] If Sovabazar under Nagendra Prasad adapted the game with a certain amount of indigenous priorities, Manmatha Ganguly's National Association was faithful to the British sense of fair play, discipline and sportsmanship to gain success on the field. Ganguly's overarching ideology of 'sport for sport's sake' made him a strict disciplinarian while rearing young Bengali footballers. Ganguly was unwilling to field his team against Europeans until and unless his players became fully prepared through vigorous training to offer a satisfactory response to European challenge. Though the club gradually attracted patronage from some feudal aristocrats,[97] Ganguly's disciplined ideology was not affected and continued to provide mental and physical strength to the members and players of the club. Preferring to play with boots, National became the first Indian team to put up a spirited show against European outfits from the late 1890s. National won the Coochbehar Cup first in 1894 and again thrice in a row from 1897 to 1899. In 1900 it became the first Indian team to win the Trades Cup.[98] National's success ensured football's potentiality as a viable social force in Bengal at the turn of the 20th century.

If Nagendra Prasad and Manmatha Ganguly remain the 'Father of Indian Football' and the ideologue of Bengali football-play respectively, it was Oomesh Chandra Majumdar alias Dukhiram Majumdar who became the popular idol of a guru to contemporary Bengali footballers and football fans. To him goes the credit of rearing a viable subculture of soccer both on and off the field. Dukhiram got his renown both as a coach and also as a player recruiter. In fact, he can be regarded as a predecessor of Bengali 'player catchers' who controlled the player transfer mechanisms of Calcutta's Big Three in the 1970s.[99] He was more radical than any other to break the shackles of social barriers in nurturing a band of class Bengali

---

[96] *Ibid.*, pp. 91–93.

[97] The most important of those aristocrats were the Rajas of Bhukailash, viz., Satyadhenu and Satyabhanu Ghosal, and Raja Jogindranath of Natore.

[98] *The Indian Daily News* (11 August 1900) gave prominence to this victory and noted that the match 'attracted a very large number of crowds'.

[99] Calcutta football's Big Three in the second half of the 20th century referred to Mohun Bagan, East Bengal and Mohammedan Sporting. However, from the late 1990s, Mohammedan Sporting's place came to be threatened by other clubs such as Tollygunj Agragami, Eveready, Chirag United, etc.

footballers for his beloved club, the Aryan. It is said that Dukhiram used to sacrifice a lot for the upkeep of potentially quality players.[100] He even took recourse to lies in order to help his players play in crucial matches. Once he asked Suroprasad Chatterjee, one of the important players of Aryan, to lie to his father to play for his club.[101] Dukhiram was realistic enough to teach his young brigade to play with boots so that they could match well with the heavily built booted Europeans, albeit without much success.

It was Mohun Bagan which rose from the Bengali clubs to symbolise the true nationalist response of the injured Indian/Bengali 'cultural self' against the British. Originally founded in 1889 by a few idealistic north Calcutta gentlemen at Mohun Bagan Villa, it proved, from its very inception, to be more than a club. It was an institution with the avowed objective to not only produce excellent sportsmen, but to impart in them impeccable moral and social values. The ideals that the founders had set before themselves were novel for Indians at that time:

> The ideals that the founders had set before themselves were high. At the inception, except for a limited few at the top it was the convention to accept only students as members. Each applicant for membership had to produce his guardian's permission for joining the Club. There was a probationary period of six months. The executives of the Club saw to it that each member combined the development of the body with the development of the mind. They prescribed a high moral code for the members. Some of the old members recall how J. N. Basu would suddenly line up younger members of the Club and test their educational progress in their schools and colleges. A young member was expelled from the club because he was found smoking.[102]

---

[100] Tradition has it that he had to change the identity of a few players like Samad, a Muslim, and Roopchand Dafadar, a Christian, in order to provide them permanent residence. It is also documented that he used to fetch drinking water of the tube well from Shyampukur to Baranagar on his bicycle for tuberculosis-affected Haridas, a player of the Aryan Club. For details, see Sibram Kumar (ed.), *RB Rachita Kolkatar Football*, Kolkata: Prabhatai Prakashani, 2002, pp. 173–74.

[101] As Chatterjee's father was completely against his son coming to Calcutta to play club football, Majumdar asked Suroprasad, nicknamed Bhola, to tell his father that he would attend his friend's marriage party and thereby come to Calcutta to play the match against Calcutta Football Club. This fascinating information is gathered from Dukhiram Majumdar's letter to Suroprasad Chatterjee, 29 May 1920, cited in Hariprasad Chattopadhyay, 'Sir Dukhiram', *Khelar Asar*, 20 May 1980, p. 25.

[102] *Mohun Bagan Club Platinum Jubilee Souvenir*, Calcutta: Mohun Bagan A.C., 1964 (hereafter *MB Souvenir*), pp. 2–3.

Thus while the Mohun Bagan Club was instituted with perceptibly high ideals and moral codes, the early pioneers of the club inspired by the Victorian ideals of fair play and discipline certainly looked upon modern sports like football as an important prop of character building. Moreover, as it seems from available evidences, the founders of the club maintained close relations with the local British authority and personnel.[103] This certainly helped them obtain suitable sports grounds or construct its tent in its infancy.[104] However, a large number of college students 'put their impress on the spirit animating the Club in the conduct of its games and affairs'.[105] In the early 1890s, the club used to play friendly matches with other local teams like Sovabazar, National, Town, Aryan, Kumartuli, Calcutta Medical College, Sibpur B.E. College, and Fort William Arsenal. It also began to take part in the Coochbehar Cup from 1893, albeit without any worthy success. The turning point in the club's history came in 1900 when Subedar Major Sailendra Nath Basu took over as the honorary secretary and the club acquired its ground in the Calcutta maidan. The latter move was important in view of 'the increase in membership and the growing activities in competitive football, which called for greater ground facilities'.[106] The club's meteoric rise as a strong soccer outfit in the following decade was largely due to the organisational acumen and team building ability of its new honorary secretary.[107] Little did the

---

[103] Prof. F. J. Rowe of the Presidency College presided over the meeting at the first anniversary of the club in 1890. When he learnt that the club's activities did not include such sports as shooting or fishing, he suggested the club's name should better be changed from 'Mohun Bagan Sporting Club' to 'Mohun Bagan Athletic Club'. And the suggestion came into immediate effect. The second anniversary of the club was presided over by an Englishman, Thomas Holland, a member of the Governor General's Council. *MB Souvenir*, p. 5.

[104] Shortly after the second anniversary in 1891 the club moved to the Shyampukur grounds which belonged to Maharaja Durga Charan Law and his brothers. It was through the efforts of Raja Joy Gobind Law and the cooperation of Harry Lee, the then chairman of the Calcutta Corporation, that the use of the ground was made available to the club. Later, with the opening of the Shyam Square, a public park under the Calcutta Corporation, the club was allotted space there too. *MB Souvenir*, p. 5.

[105] 'Early History', in *Mohun Bagan A.C. Golden Jubilee Souvenir*, Calcutta: Mohun Bagan Club, 1939, p. 10.

[106] *MB Souvenir*, p. 5.

[107] *Ibid.*

pioneers envisage, however, that the club would, through its epic victory over the East York Regiment in the 1911 IFA Shield final, bring about a national reawakening!

The Local Roots of the Growth of Football in Bengal

The increasing popularity of football in Calcutta reached its suburbs in no time. In Chinsurah, E. M. Wheeler, the then principal of Hoogly Mahsin College, took a leading role in popularising the game. The first football club of Chinsurah, the Town Club was established in 1883, even before the formation of any worthy Bengali club in Calcutta. It was followed by the foundation of the two most notable outfits of the town, that is, Ripon A.C. (1890) and Chinsurah Sporting (1893).[108] More importantly, the latter club took the initiative to organise an annual football tournament called Gladstone Cup from 1898, which became no less popular than the IFA Shield.[109] In Howrah, the Howrah Sporting Club (1889) led the way. There was regular exchange of footballers between the strongest outfits of Howrah and Calcutta in the 1890s.[110] It has been said, albeit without any viable evidence, that Nirmal Chatterjee, a footballer from Krishnanagar, Nadia, was an Oxford Blue and played club football in England without boots in the first decade of the 20th century.[111] He later excelled as a player of the Aryan Club. Young footballers from these different suburban regions used to come to Calcutta to play for big Bengali clubs like Mohun Bagan, National, Sovabazar, and Aryan. Thus the suburbs came to provide a rich supply line of able footballers for the Calcutta clubs.

The spread of football in the eastern and northern parts of Bengal was no less phenomenal than what happened in and around Calcutta at the turn of the century. In east Bengal, Dacca was the centre of football's growing

---

[108] Tathagata Moulik, 'Hoogly Jelar Oitihyapurna Kheladhulo' (Traditional Sports and Games in the Hoogly District), *Paschimbanga*, Special Number on Hoogly, 1998, p. 168.

[109] *Ibid.*

[110] For a detailed discussion of the growth and development of football in Howrah, see Kali Ray, *Howrah Jelar Football Khelar Itikatha* (History of Football in Howrah District), Calcutta: Bharati Book Stall, 1985.

[111] *Khelar Asar*, 13 June 1980, p. 32. Also see S. M. Badruddin, 'Nadia-r Kheladhulo — Atit o Bartaman' (Games and Sports in Nadia: Past and Present), *Paschimbanga*, Special Number on Nadia District, 1997, p. 178.

stature and popularity.[112] British officials, college and university teachers, Western educated Bengalis — all took earnest initiatives to promote the game in Dacca.[113] Players hailing from Dacca and adjoining regions used to come to Calcutta to gain wider recognition at the competitive level from around this time. Wari Club, the first sporting club to be founded in Dacca in 1898, was the premier football club of the age. Wari and its arch-rival Victoria Sporting (1903) had mastered considerable following in eastern Bengal in the first decades of the 20th century. Rai Bahadur Surendra Nath Roy, a landlord and an enthusiastic sportsman, took the initiative in 1898 to establish the Wari Club.[114] The club soon obtained a plot of land in the Paltan maidan where a modest club pavilion with necessary facilities was constructed. In 1910 Wari created a stir by defeating a star-studded Coochbehar Raj XI, which included 10 players of the Mohun Bagan team that was to win the IFA Shield in 1911.[115] This success encouraged the club authority to send its team to Calcutta to play friendly matches against the Calcutta Football Club and Dalhousie Athletic Club in 1912–13.[116] From 1912 Wari also became regular participant in the IFA Shield. Victoria Sporting Club, the arch-rival of Wari at that time, was founded in 1903 at the initiatives of five zamindari families.[117] It was named after the then

---

[112] For a brief but useful description of soccer's early growth in Dhaka, see Lutfar Rahman Ritan, *Football*, Dhaka: Bangla Academy, 1985, pp. 27–33.

[113] Among these early promoters, the names of Sir Fajlur Rahman and Dr Mahmud Hasan, two former vice chancellors of Dacca University, Ray Bahadur Satyen Bhadra, ex-principal of Dacca Jagannat College, Altaf Hossain, principal of Dacca Intermediate College, Sir B. C. Gupta, principal of Ahsanullah Engineering College, and Dr Jenkins and Dr Majharul Haq, professors of Dacca University, are worth mentioning. Among them Dr Mahmud Hasan, Dr Jenkins and Dr Majharul Haq along with a few other teachers of the university used to play for the university soccer team regularly.

[114] 'Our Club', in *Wari Club: Shatabarsho Smarani, 1898–1998* (Wari Club: Centenary Memoriam, 1898–1998), Dhaka: Wari Club, 2000; also see Mahmudur Rahman Momin, 'Wari Club a Big Name: A Reminiscence', in *Beximco Pharma Abul Hashem Table Tennis Championship 2004 Souvenir*, Dhaka: Wari Club, 2004.

[115] 'Our Club'; Momin, 'Wari Club a Big Name'; Ritan, *Football*, p. 29.

[116] 'Our Club'; Momin, 'Wari Club a Big Name'.

[117] These zamindars were: Babu Suresh Chandra Dham of Tejgaon and Kurmitola; the only son of Babu Nripen Roy Chowdhury of Zamindar of Baladhar; Roy Bahadur Keshab Chandra Banerjee, Zamindar of Murapara; Zamindar Dinesh Banerjee; and Babu Sunil Kumar Bhosh of the Bhosh family of Malkhan Nagar.

queen of England, Queen Victoria. The club at its birth had its clubhouse at the Paltan maidan.[118] Initially no subscription was raised for the club, and office executives were nominated. The then divisional commissioner was chosen as the president of the club while Babu Suresh Chandra Dham was assigned the post of general secretary. Later on both the teams became regular participants in the IFA Shield.[119] The First Division Football League started in Dacca in 1915.[120] In Rajshahi, Kumudini Bandyopadhyay, the principal of Rajshahi College, instituted the 'Kumudini Cup' for the promotion of soccer at the school level. The government immediately took the responsibility of organising the tournament.[121] From Dacca and Rajshahi the game quickly spread to other parts of eastern Bengal including Chittagong, Mymensingh, Narayangunj, Khulna, Barisal, and Faridpur.[122] It has been recorded that Calcutta club teams like Hare Sporting and National undertook 'annual tours to distant places like Dacca, Barisal, Pabna, Rajshahi, Berhampore, Bhagalpore, and other centres'.[123] As a result, football in colonial Bengal got a number of notable players and organisers from various parts of eastern Bengal: P. Dasgupta, Sirajuddin and Junior Rashid from Chattagram; Pakhi Sen, Rakhal Majumdar, Ajit Bose, and Paresh Mukherjee from Mymensingh; M. Dutt Roy, Alauddin Giyasuddin and Sirajul Haque from Narayangunj; Saiyad Abdus Samad, Mojammel Haque, Mohini Banerjee, and Rashiduzzaman from Rajshahi and Dinajpur; A. Sabur and Gostho Paul from Khulna and Faridpur; N. Majumdar and A. Ganguly from Barisal.[124]

Northern Bengal can also boast of a rich tradition of soccer culture from the last decade of the 19th century. Most important pockets where the game flourished at the initiative of enthusiastic locals were Coochbehar, Jalpaiguri, Balurghat, Dinajpur, and Rangpur. The Maharaja of Coochbehar certainly played an inspirational role as a great patron of modern sports in the region. In 1891 Mahraja Nripendra Narayan Bhup

---

[118] S. M. Shaheb Ali, 'Past History of Victoria Sporting Club, Dhaka', *Platinum Jubilee Souvenir*, Dhaka: Victoria Sporting Club, 1991.

[119] For a brief discussion on Wari–Victoria rivalry in Dacca, see Ritan, *Football*, p. 27–33.

[120] *Ibid.*, p. 31.

[121] Jiten Mahalanbis, 'Khelar Maathe' (On the Sports-field), in *Jalpaiguri District Centenary Volume*, Jalpaiguri, 1869, p. 386.

[122] Ritan, *Football*, p. 30.

[123] *The Statesman*, 8 July 1934.

[124] Ritan, *Football*, p. 30.

Bahadur declared at a students' meet at Jenkins School that 'should the Syndicate of the Calcutta University approve of the suggestion that physical education should be made compulsory, a rule of that effect would at once be introduced for benefit of the students'.[125] In fact, the school later became the chief recruiting ground of quality footballers who shined on the Calcutta maidan afterwards.[126] The maharaja also presented a beautiful silver cup called the Coochbehar Cup in 1893 to be controlled by the IFA for competition among Indian clubs only.[127] At a more popular level, however, it was in Jalpaiguri that soccer came to enjoy a formidable and organised mass following. Local British officials and the tea-planters of Duars were the early promoters of the game while football remained more or less an exclusively British leisure pursuit in the 1880s.[128] Watching the Europeans play and impressed by the game's attributes, local aristocrats as well as the educated middle class took keen interest to adopt football in an organised manner. The formation of the Jalpaiguri Town Club with a large sports ground of its own in 1898, which was the outcome of a joint initiative of the British and Bengali enthusiasts, constituted a major landmark in the development of the game in the district.[129] The club used to play friendly matches with the European tea-planters' XI and the police side quite regularly. Teams from Rangpur and Dinajpur too began to play with Town Club in inter-district competitions from 1902 onwards. Large crowds attended all these matches.[130] The resultant enthusiasm led to the birth of a series of *para* clubs throughout the town in the following decade — Victoria Club, Raikat Para Club, Ukil Para Club, Star Club, and Diamond Jubilee club.[131] In Balurghat, West Dinajpur, too, football became a popular cultural pursuit from the beginning of the 20th century. Some enterprising local youths started a football club at the premises of the

---

[125] Sorabji Jahangir, *Prince and Chiefs of India*, vol. 2, quoted in Niraj Biswas, 'Khelay Coochbehar' (Coochbehar in Sports), in *Madhuparni*, Special Number on Coochbehar, 1989, p. 467.

[126] Biswas, 'Khelay Coochbehar', p. 476.

[127] *The Statesman*, 8 July 1934.

[128] Mahalanbis, 'Khelar Maathe', p. 384.

[129] For further details about the formation of Town Club, see *ibid*. Also see Kamakhya Prasad Chakraborty, *Sekaler Jalpaiguri Sahar ebong Samajik Jibaner Kichhu Kotha* (The Town of Jalpaiguri of That Age and Some Aspects of Social Life), Jalpaiguri: Chakraborty Paribar, 2004, pp. 35–36.

[130] *Ibid*.

[131] *Para* refers small localities within a town.

palace of the zamindar in 1901 and named it Town Club. Rajendranath Sanyal, the zamindar, enthused by the huge interest of the young players, became an ardent patron of the club and brought a football from Calcutta to help them learn the rules of the game.[132] In the initial years, Kalidas Chakraborty, the first sub-registrar of Balurghat which was transformed into the sub-divisional town of Dinajpur in 1904, played an important role in soccer's popularisation among the locals.[133] Football, however, very soon became a most popular game among the schoolboys. The role of Balurghat High School in popularising the game at the school level was phenomenal indeed. The school football team under the inspiring leadership of its sports-loving headmaster Ananta Kumar Ray, became a formidable side in the town. Later, the team, as a mark of respect to its founder-guide, came to be known as the Ananta Sporting club.[134]

These local roots of the game, hitherto ignored in existing studies as well as in popular sporting chronicles, deserve careful attention if we desire to have a true understanding of the threads of popular culture both on and off the field that grew around this mass spectator sport throughout Bengal. Socio-historical researches on football in Bengal commonly suffer from a sweeping and long-standing generalisation. According to it, football in colonial Bengal is understood to be primarily a Calcutta-based phenomenon. In other words, a history of Bengali football is commonly identified with Calcutta football.[135] But this approach is mistaken. It is important to understand that without prior consideration of a sport's local origins, developments and specificities, construction of its wider regional history can be a flawed exercise. Furthermore, the local growth of the game also shows that the wider popularity of football throughout Bengal

---

[132] *Balurghat Town Club Centenary Souvenir*, Balurghat: Balurghat Town Club, 2001, p. 3.

[133] Bhabani Prasad, 'Harano Din: Kheladhular Itibritta' (Lost Days: Chronicle of Games and Sports), *Uttaradhikar Balurghat, Dadhichi*, Special Issue, 2000–2001, pp. 306–7.

[134] *Ibid*. Also see Swapan Majumdar, 'Kheladhulay Paschim Dinajpur' (West Dinajpur in Games and Sports), *Madhuparni*, West Dinajpur District Number, 1992–93, p. 544.

[135] Both Soumen Mitra and Paul Dimeo considered Calcutta football to be synonymous with Bengal football and, hence missed its local character completely. Mitra, 'Babu at Play'; Dimeo, 'Football and Politics in Bengal' and 'Colonial Bodies, Colonial Sport'. For such examples of popular writings, see Moti Nandy, 'Football and Nationalism', in Sen (ed.), *The Calcutta Psyche*; Rupak Saha, 'Banglair Football' (Bengali's Football), *Desh*, 28 August 1993, pp. 21–34.

Boot versus Barefoot

was by no means a post-1911 phenomenon, which most of the existing histories of the game would tell us.

Cultural indigenisation of soccer in late 19th-century Bengal has been a theme of major interest among Indian sports writers. The virtual universality of football in colonial Bengal went hand in hand with its unique character of cultural indigenisation. Since the inception of the game in Bengal, the majority of the Bengali players played the game without wearing boots. It has been stated proudly, if a little strongly, that 'Calcuttans and the rest of India in their trail, were the only people in the world to transform football skill and technique into their own indigenous ways, playing unshoed, as they did from the very beginning. The rest of the world played in the original British way, India alone, inspired by Calcuttans showing the way, imparted to the game a distinct racial touch.'[136] Nagendra Prasad himself never cared to don the boots, even though the play, which first inspired him, comprised kicking the ball not with the feet but with boots. Certainly, the Bengalis imparted to the game a distinctive Indian touch. As noted sports writer Rakhal Bhattacharya remarks: 'As a result, the foreign plant, transplanted in our soil, grew up a distinct Indian character.'[137]

Basically because of the Bengalis not being naturally fond of boots in their normal daily life, they preferred playing barefoot. Naturally therefore, they considered playing the game with tied-up shoes only as an imposition. However, there might have been another practical reason behind the Bengali's general aversion to boots. The majority of the Bengalis desirous of playing the game could not afford costly boots. Apparao, the mercurial East Bengal forward in the 1950s, is once said to have simply wailed that the cost of boots would rule out football for many boys of 'my poor country'.[138] Whatever may be the cause, except for a few individuals like Dukhiram Majumdar, P. K. Biswas, Sudhir Chatterjee, and Chhoney Majumdar, Calcuttans generally played barefoot. In fact, football play in its early days in Bengal ran through two distinct channels

---

[136] RB, 'Calcuttans Showed the Way', in *I.F.A. Shield Souvenir 1973*, Calcutta: IFA, 1973. This contention of RB, however, is not totally correct, as the Africans had also started playing football without boots.

[137] RB, 'Indian Football and Boots', *I.F.A. Shield Souvenir 1977*, Calcutta: I.F.A., 1977.

[138] *Ibid*.

to develop two different characteristics. The first stream flowing out of the Sovabazar Club preferred to adapt an Indian style of playing barefoot. The Sovabazar Raj family, patron of the club, despite its deep loyalty to the British Raj, displayed an unusual keenness to stick to the traditional way of Bengali living. This probably had something to do with Nagendra Prasad's insistence on playing barefoot and displaying masculine power on the field. In south Calcutta, on the other hand, the popular pursuit of the game emanated from Manmatha Ganguly, a school teacher. To Ganguly, football being a part of the new Westernised education had to be adopted in its original British form. Ganguly's National Association preferred to play booted football, because he believed that, without being properly equipped, Bengalis would not be able to match the booted and heavily built Europeans on the football field. However, this trend of booted play did not find much favour with the general Bengali public. Even Dukhiram Majumdar, the celebrated 'Sir' of Bengali football and a staunch champion of the cause of booted play, failed to convince most of his disciples except a few devoted lot like Chhoney Majumdar, of the utility of boots.

From the very beginning, Mohun Bagan played barefoot, keen on cashing in on barefoot speed and footwork, and despite abject failure against booted teams on rainy grounds, never thought of wearing boots. And the 1911 IFA Shield winning team had 10 players in its rank who played without boots.[139] It was extremely fortunate for them to have an unusually dry spell during the 1911 IFA Shield allowing them to reap the fullest rewards of barefoot skill. The club and the supporters bewailing for Mohun Bagan's failures on rainy grounds were mocked as coming to the battle with wet gunpowder. Still no one ever thought of taking wholesale to boots. In fact, the barefoot jugglery of Indian legends like Gostho Paul, the Bhaduris, Samad and Kumar against booted European teams even on slushy surfaces was later to become a constant source of a reconstructed masculine satisfaction for the nationalistic Bengali spectators. The barefoot genius of Indians made P. B. Clark, the captain of the visiting Islington Corinthians, an amateur British side, remark in 1938: 'Indians alone play real football, what they call football in Europe is after all only bootball.'[140]

Thus the Bengali footballers in a sense Indianised football technique by developing an uncanny barefoot jugglery in the dribbling art. The Bhaduris were the early masters of soccer jugglery, followed by Samad, Gostho

---

[139] Only Rev. Sudhir Chatterjee, the Mohun Bagan defender, played with boots.

[140] Cited by RB, in 'Indian Football and Boots'.

Paul, Abhilash Ghosh, Sarat Sinha, Mona Dutta, Umapati Kumar, Majid, Rashid, and other lesser celebrities. Ahmed Khan, perhaps the last best representative of the trend, charmed Mr Wolf Lyberg, one of the foremost European football promoters of the 1950s, so much so as to make him remark that 'money would rain on Ahmed if he would demonstrate his barefooted jugglery in Europe'.[141] While playing without boots allowed them to reap the fullest rewards of barefoot skill, success most often eluded Bengali clubs in major tournaments simply because the Bengali players had little chance of matching the heavily built and booted British on slushy and inundated grounds on rainy days. Yet the Bengali fans used to take pride in the fact that the Indian footballers with their barefoot jugglery sometimes got the better of the Europeans even on slushy surfaces.

More importantly, in the transformed political scenario of the first decade of the 20th century when Bengal was caught by the upsurge in the wake of the Swadeshi Movement, the Bengali cultural nationalists did not force their fellowmen to boycott football, a British cultural import.[142] Rather, the 'barefoot' style of Bengali football represented an attempt to Indianise the foreign game, which may be taken as a silent but curious protest of Bengali psyche against the Western construction of the 'effeminate Bengali'. Later there was even literary attempt to prove football's Indian lineage by referring to the *Mahabharata*.[143] Hence, the dichotomy of boot and barefoot can be explained in terms of a clash of cultural identities — or to be more general, a colonial-nationalist conflict. One commentator has even equated the uniqueness of barefoot play with the innovative styles of play introduced and popularised by Ranji in cricket and Dhyan Chand in hockey:

> ... there was a certain *Indianness* about it (barefoot style of play), which was as unique as the rope-trick or shall we say Ranji's leg glance! Ball control

---

[141] RB, 'Calcuttans Showed the Way'.

[142] While active resistance to British sports like soccer or cricket seems to have been fairly uncommon, there is evidence of limited but determined intellectual opposition to such modern games in Bengal. For an interesting observation on this matter, see Pramatha Nath Basu, *Swaraj — Cultural and Political*, Calcutta: Usha, 1929, pp. 222–27. In a few colleges a limited opposition to Western sports could be discerned. For example, in one mofussil college at Daulatpur in eastern Bengal games such as *buri chui* (catching game) were organised as against the more usual cricket and football. For details, see *University of Calcutta Reports on Mofussil Colleges*, 1908, p. 97.

[143] Nagendra Prasad Sarvadhikari, 'Football', *Desh*, no. 34, 14 July 1934.

was easier, because every Indian was more at home with the direct contact of foot, toes and instep with the ball. Wearing a boot immediately set up a mental barrier, because it was something foreign to an Indian footballer. After all, Ranji revolutionized cricket with the introduction of shots hitherto never seen on a cricket ground. They were uniquely Ranji — uniquely *Indian*. Similarly with Dhyan Chand, when it came to hockey.[144]

Gostha Paul, in an interview with sports journalist Rakhal Bhattacharyya, said that he had never been scared of heavily booted British forwards dashing up like wild bulls; rather, he had added, the booted forwards always feared him.[145]

Thus, during the course of football's popular adoption, the Bengali transformed it into a part of his pattern of life attaining therewith at times excellence at par with British military skill. The new brand evolved by the Calcuttans, which even though forsaken later, had given the Bengali as well as Indian soccer a charm of its own and made it a spectator's delight. This delightful soccer culture that Bengal could boast of pioneering in India also proved to be an apolitical arena where identities of racism, nationalism, regionalism, and communalism got reflected and reproduced through experiences on and off the pitch. It is to this transition in the Bengali's football culture in the first half of the 20th century that we shall turn our attention in the subsequent chapters.

---

[144] Melville de Mellow, *Reaching for Excellence: The Glory and Decay of Sport in India*, New Delhi: Kalyani Publishers, 1979, pp. 52–53; emphasis added.

[145] RB, 'Indian Football and Boots'.

2

From Imperialism to Nationalism: The Changing Culture of Soccer in Late Colonial Bengal

In the changed socio-political context of the early 20th century when Bengal was engulfed by a spate of nationalist fervour in the wake of the anti-Partition movement during 1905–8, football came to be increasingly looked upon as a novel instrument of cultural nationalism in Bengal. Transcending the hitherto boundaries of sociability and assertion of masculinity, the game became a cultural weapon to fight against the British on the cultural battlefield of the maidan and an emblem around which nationalist consciousness could be fostered. This spirit of nationalism affected the patterns of spectator culture and fan sub-culture in colonial Bengal to a great extent. As Amilcar Cabral commented aptly, 'national liberation is necessarily an act of *culture*'; the maidan became a prototype of cultural warfare.[1] Spontaneous effusion of nationalist sentiments found ready expression as and when a native team, especially Mohun Bagan, played against the British civilian or regimental sides in the first three decades of the 20th century. However, the formulation of this cultural nationalism around a modern Western sport in a colonial setting

---

[1] Amilcar Cabral, 'National Liberation and Culture', *Transition*, no. 45, 1974, p. 13; emphasis added. Cabral considered culture as 'an essential element in the history of a people'. According to Cabral, 'culture is, at any moment in the life of a society, . . . the more or less conscious result of economic and political activities, the more or less dynamic expression of the relationships prevailing in that society. On the one hand, between man (considered individually or collectively) and nature, and on the other hand, between individuals, groups of individuals, social strata or classes.' For him, 'the value of culture as an element of resistance lies in the fact that, in the ideological or idealistic context, it is the vigorous manifestation of the materialist and historical reality of the society already under domination, or about to be dominated'. Cabral, 'National Liberation and Culture', p. 13.

is neither simplistic nor linear. Its origin, growth, character, and impact need to be analysed in the context of the changing balance of intended British imperial designs and their unintended consequences via indigenous appropriation. This chapter charts as also explores the key moments, complex patterns and diverse responses in the evolution of soccer culture in the first three decades of 20th-century Bengal.

Modern Sport, Cultural Imperialism and Colonial Response: A Conceptual Framework of Study

In an important collection of essays entitled *Geopolitique du sport*, Claude Hurtebize has observed that the global diffusion of modern sports occurred at the same time as 'the constitution of world markets and colonial empires'.[2] Johan Galtung, in the same vein, notes suggestively that the 'massive export of [modern] sports' from developed to underdeveloped areas followed 'old colonial trade and control lines . . . into the last little corner of the world'.[3] The football or cricket grounds of Calcutta and Bombay are therefore as much the relics of British rule as much as the Victoria Memorial in Calcutta. However, Great Britain's dual success as an imperial power in seizing the lion's share of colonial booty as well as becoming the foremost country in the development of modern sports was not merely a coincidence but a result of what Allen Guttmann calls 'causation'. As he rightly argues, 'modern sports abetted the imperial expansion that carried them to the ends of the earth'.[4] In fact, the imperialists themselves emphasised causal connections. As Reverend J. E. C. Welldon, headmaster of Harrow School from 1881 to 1895, proclaimed: 'In the history of the British Empire, it is written that England has owed her sovereignty to her sports.'[5]

---

[2] Claude Hurtebize, 'Geopolitique de la genese, de la diffusion et des interactions culturelles dans la culture corporelle et le sport', in Borhane Errais, Daniel Mathieu, and Jean Praicheux (eds), *Geopolitique du sport*, Besancon: Universite de Franche-Comte, 1990, p. 87, cited in Guttmann, *Games and Empires*, p. 4.

[3] Johan Galtung, 'The Sport System as a Metaphor for the World System', in Fernand Landry, Marc Landry and Magdeleine Yerles (eds), *Sport: The Third Millennium*, Sainte-Foye: Presses de l'Universite Laval, 1991, p. 150, quoted in Guttmann, *Games and Empires*, p. 4.

[4] Guttmann, *Games and Empires*, p. 5.

[5] J. E. C. Welldon, 'The Imperial Purpose of Education', in *Proceedings of the Royal Colonial Institute*, vol. 26, 1894–95, p. 823, quoted in Mangan, *The Games Ethic and Imperialism*, p. 36.

Numerous scholars have taken the view of Welldon and his like at face value. Peter Rummelt, for instance, has characterised the spread of modern sports throughout Africa as nothing more or less than colonialism at work.[6] Other specialists in sports studies, influenced by the writings of Andre Gunder Frank and Fernando Henrique Cardoso or by those of Immanuel Wallerstein, see the global expansion of modern sports as a hitherto neglected aspect of the 'development of dependence' on the periphery of the 'world system'.[7] Still others, equally convinced that the displacement of traditional indigenous pastimes by modern sports has been a cultural disaster, have written in Gramscian terms of the 'hegemony' of Western sports.[8]

In the study of ludic diffusion of modern sports, however, most discussions have referred not to cultural hegemony but rather to cultural imperialism although both come very close in understanding the process of diffusion.[9] John Tomlinson usefully defines 'cultural imperialism' as 'a form of domination . . . not just in the political and economic spheres but

---

[6] Guttmann, *Games and Empires*, p. 5.

[7] *Ibid*. Guttmann refers to the following relevant works in this context: Andre Gunder Frank, *Capitalism and Underdevelopment in Latin America*, New York: Monthly Review Press, 1967; Fernando Henqique Cardoso and Enzo Faletto, *Dependency and Development in Latin America*, trans. Marjory Mattingly Urquidi, Berkeley: University of California Press, 1979; James D. Cockcroft, Andre Gunder Frank and Dale L. Johnson (eds), *Dependence and Underdevelopment*, Garden City: Double-day-Anchor Books, 1972; Immanuel Wallerstein, *The Modern World System*, 3 vols., New York: Academic Press, 1974–89; Alan Klein, 'Baseball as Underdevelopment: The Political Economy of Sport in the Dominican Republic', *Sociology of Sport Journal*, vol. 6, no. 2, June 1989, pp. 95–112.

[8] According to Gramsci, political relationships between the rulers and the ruled cannot be characterised as simply the result of absolute domination by the former and absolute submission by the latter. 'The most stable form of rule is one in which the strong (who are never all-powerful) have their way only after the weak (who are never completely powerless) have their say.' Guttmann, *Games and Empires*, p. 6. For details on the Gramscian notion of 'hegemony', see Antonio Gramsci, *Selection from the Prison Notebooks*, trans. and ed. by Quinton Hoare and Geoffrey Nowell Smith, New York: International Publishers, 1971. Also see Borhane Errais, 'La planete sportive', in Landry et al. (eds), *Sport: The Third Millennium*, p. 582; Minseok An and George H. Sage, 'The Golf Boom in South Korea: Serving Hegemonic Interests', *Sociology of Sport Journal*, vol. 9, no. 4, December 1992, pp. 372–84.

[9] In the present context, 'ludic diffusion' refers to a process of spontaneous transmission or dissemination of modern sports from Britain to the colonised countries of Asia and Africa more or less concurrently.

also over those practices by which collectivities make sense of their lives'.[10] The question which is being addressed here in a broader perspective of colonial response to the intrusion of modern sports in India is: can the diffusion of modern sports from Europe to the rest of the world be considered a form of cultural imperialism? Since team games like soccer seem to evoke an intense collective psychological identification, this chapter will later endeavour to show that the so-called diffusion of football met quick acceptance than prolonged resistance in colonial Bengal as it suited indigenous appropriation for nationalist purposes.

One of the chief factors that is commonly held responsible for the rapidity or slowness of the diffusion of modern sports from one nation to another is the relative political, economic, and cultural power of the nations involved. As Ruud Stoviks argues, the popularity of any given sport in any given country 'depends upon the development of the positions of economic and political power among the nations of the world system'.[11] It therefore follows that in general, the sports characteristic of wealthy and powerful nations 'will be adopted by the populations of other lands who fall within the spheres of influence of the mighty'.[12] But both political and economic models of ludic diffusion are not entirely adequate to understand the historical complexity of the process. Political motives mostly moulded by a concept of sport as part of a programme of political domination, as 'a useful instrument of imperial purpose' seem to be too unidirectional.[13] One influential economic model of ludic diffusion is drawn from Andre Gunder Frank's theories of the 'development of dependency'. This model, which insists that modernisation is impossible unless the 'peripheral' society breaks away from the capitalist 'world system', too

---

In the spread of Western sports into the colonies, the concept of cultural hegemony seems to establish the preponderance and domination of such sports over the traditional forms of indigenous sport, which began to feel the threat of extinction to modern sports.

The reference to cultural imperialism is because cultural imperialism gives the scholar a much wider canvas of understanding, helping to explore subtleties in the intentions and forms of domination and unintended consequences of reaction and resistance.

[10] John Tomlinson, *Cultural Imperialism*, Baltimore: Johns Hopkins University Press, 1991, p. 7.

[11] Quoted in Guttmann, *Games and Empires*, p. 173.

[12] *Ibid.*

[13] Mangan, *Games Ethic and Imperialism*, p. 18.

seems rigidly deterministic.[14] However, there can be little doubt that the history of modern sports has conclusively demonstrated the ability of the 'satellites' to surpass the 'metropolis'.

Sports, like other fields, investigated by scholars committed to 'cultural studies', are contested terrain in theory as well as in practice.[15] It is here that the Gramscian notion of 'cultural hegemony' again resurfaces as a useful formula of understanding. Gramscian theory correctly stresses the fact that the cultural interaction is something more complex than the domination of the totally powerful over the entirely powerless. In other words, it is important to emphasise the individual's capacity for active selection and selective retention. Hence, the ethnocentric assumption that non-Western societies simply accept, without selection or interpretation, whatever explicit or implicit messages the Western sports transmit, has long been discredited. In the analysis of sport as cultural imperialism and the resultant colonial response to it, one should neither credit the colonialists with diabolical powers nor deny all *agency* to the colonised. However, although both cultural imperialism as well as cultural hegemony imply intentionality, in fact those who adopt a sport are often the eager initiators of a transaction of which the 'donors' are scarcely aware.[16]

If we wish to understand, in all of its complexity, the process of cultural diffusion of soccer and colonial response to it, suggests Allen Guttmann, Thorstein Veblen's idea on emulation is as applicable as Gramsci on hegemony. 'Veblen, of course, wrote ironically of emulation in order to satirize the absurdly, pathetically imitative behaviour of men and women frantic to rise in the hierarchy of social prestige, but Veblen points to an important psychological truth: emulation is a powerful motivator.'[17] Guttmann goes further to assert:

---

[14] Gunder Frank, *Capitalism and Underdevelopment in Latin America*, pp. 3, 11. Not all the theorists of 'dependency' are as dogmatic as Frank about the utter impossibility of development within the capitalist system; see Cardoso and Faletto, *Dependency and Development in Latin America*, pp. 185–86.

[15] For the relevance to sports studies of Stuart Hall and the Birmingham Center for Contemporary Cultural Studies, see Richard Gruneau, 'The Critique of Sport in Modernity', in Eric G. Dunning, Joseph A. Maguire and Robert E. Pearton (eds), *The Sports Process*, Champaign: Human Kinetics, 1993, pp. 85–109; David L. Andrews and John W. Loy, 'British Cultural Studies and Sport', *Quest*, vol. 45, no. 2, May 1993, pp. 255–76.

[16] Guttmann, *Games and Empires*, p. 179.

[17] *Ibid.*

Culturally dominated groups have often had sports imposed upon them; but they have also — perhaps just as often — forced their unwelcome way into sports from which the dominant group desired to exclude them. To dismiss this kind of emulation as 'false consciousness' or 'colonization of the mind' is not persuasive.[18]

In Western sports like soccer, more often probably than in any other domain, the initially dominated have turned the tables on their erstwhile dominators. As Guttmann succinctly remarks:

> Once successful emulation has shattered the ludic monopoly, the literal or metaphorical colonials have a splendid opportunity to enhance their self-esteem, for nothing can be more delightful than 'beating them at their own game'. Simultaneously, one signals allegiance ('It's your game!') and superiority ('We're better at it than you are!').[19]

In the Indian context, Mohun Bagan's victory over British regimental teams in the 1911 Shield has been interpreted in these terms. It was an additional source of emotional satisfaction since the game was played on 'the vast expense of green just in front of Fort William which, since the days of Robert Clive, had symbolised the British military presence in Calcutta'.[20]

Joseph L. Arbena writes of the Cuban experience: 'Even the Cubans, for all their nationalistic and ideological rhetoric, prove the success of their Revolution, if only to themselves, by playing Anglo sport better than the Anglos.'[21] In fact, as Harold Perkin has suggested, 'a turnabout in the balance of ludic power can be the prelude to more significant shifts in political and economic power'.[22] In other words, spontaneous power implicit in the notion of 'sport as a tool of cultural imperialism' can generate ripples in the domains of political and economic power of the imperialist. Modern sports have sometimes functioned to crystallise anti-colonial sentiments and even to provide an organisational framework for a movement of national liberation. Arbena, surveying the diffusion

---

[18] *Ibid.*

[19] *Ibid.*

[20] Bose, *A History of Indian Cricket*, p. 17.

[21] Joseph L. Arbena, 'Sport, Development and Mexican Nationalism, 1920–70', *Journal of Sport History*, vol. 18, no. 3, Winter 1991, p. 362; also see Joseph L. Arbena, 'Sport and Revolution: The Continuing Cuban Experience', *Studies in Latin American Popular Culture*, vol. 9, 1990, p. 325.

[22] Perkin, 'Teaching the Nations How to Play', pp. 145–46.

of European sports throughout Latin America, concludes that 'imported sports had a partially imperialistic impact in that they helped to shape local elites and their values in ways at least initially beneficial to the Europeans', but he goes on to admit that these same sports became, in time, 'the agent of anti-colonialism and anti-imperialism'.[23] Later sections of this chapter will show how the emancipatory impulses were institutionalised in the Bengali soccer clubs in colonial India. This emancipatory potential of modern sports has become a parallel theme to the undeniable role of modern sports as means of social control and imperial rule. It also makes room for the argument that if nations are what Benedict Anderson's influential theory claims them to be, that is, 'imagined communities', then modern sports are 'an important and popularly accessible aid to this politically indispensable form of imagining, particularly in the colonial setting'.[24]

Traditionalists insist, however, that the talk of the possible contribution of sports to nation-building misses one important point. For them, modern sports are a form of cultural domination, and ludic diffusion is tantamount to the imperialist or hegemonic destruction of authentic native cultural forms.[25] The traditionalist argument has an initial plausibility, but as Guttmann has noted, it is seriously flawed. 'The notion that the adoption of another culture's sports is *ipso facto* a sign of lost authenticity ignores the fact that cultures are never static.'[26] As Joseph Maguire has argued, 'cultures and peoples are responsive and active in the interpretation of the global flow of people, ideas, images and technologies'.[27] Edward Said

---

[23] Joseph L. Arbena, 'The Diffusion of Modern European Sport in Latin America: A Case Study of Cultural Imperialism', *South Eastern Latin Americanist*, vol. 33, no. 4, March 1990, p. 6, cited in Guttmann, *Games and Empires*, p. 181.

[24] Anderson defined nation as 'an imagined political community'. It is 'imagined because the members of even the smallest nation will never know most of their fellow members, meet them, or even hear of them, yet in the minds of each lives the image of their communion'. It is imagined as a 'community' because, 'regardless of the actual inequality and exploitation that may prevail in each, the nation is always conceived as a deep, horizontal comradeship'. Benedict Anderson, *Imagined Communities: Reflections on the Origin and Spread of Nationalsim*, rev. ed., New York: Verso, 1991, pp. 15–16.

Guttmann, *Games and Empires*, p. 183.

[25] *Ibid.*, p. 184.

[26] *Ibid.*; emphasis in original.

[27] Joseph Maguire, 'Globalization, Sport and National Identities: "The Empire Strikes Back"', *Loisir et Societe*, vol. 16, no. 2, Autumn 1993, pp. 310–11.

too has made the same point forcefully: 'the history of all cultures is the history of cultural borrowings.'[28] While it is certainly true that a culture can be annihilated, it is also true that 'cultures can be resilient, adaptive and transformative — in sports as in every other domain'.[29] More important, however, as Jay R. and Joan D. Mandle once pointed out, 'is not where a cultural form originated but what happens to it upon its arrival'.[30] This chapter tries to understand what happened to football when it was adopted and adapted into the fold of Bengali culture in the first half of the 20th century.

Football and National Consciousness: The Context of the Swadeshi Movement

The nationalist football culture was certainly not born overnight. First stirrings of it could be discerned during the Swadeshi movement in Bengal.[31] In the wake of the vehement anti-Partition agitation Bengalis looked towards the game with a new eye. Any success against British teams on the football field began to be looked upon as a victory of the spirit of nationalism over the evil of colonialism. Incidentally, this was also the period when Mohun Bagan meteorically rose to prominence as the sole Indian club to earn a series of worthwhile successes in various tournaments beating, on many occasions, civilian European teams.

In terms of success on the football field, the 'Swadeshi age' seemed to have begun in 1900 when the National Association won the Trades Cup as the first Indian team. One local newspaper gave prominence to this victory and noted that the match 'attracted a very large number of crowds'.[32] However, the trend of barefoot on-field battle against European civil and military teams was set in the context of political agitation and social unrest that grew in response to the Partition of Bengal in 1905. The so-called Swadeshi age from 1905 to 1911 was incidentally the age of Mohun Bagan in Bengal football. The club came to prominence with successive wins in

---

[28] Edward W. Said, *Culture and Imperialism,* New York: Knopf, 1993, p. 217.

[29] Guttmann, *Games and Empires*, p. 185.

[30] Jay R. Mandle and Joan D. Mandle, *Grass Roots Commitment: Basketball and Society in Trinidad and Tobago,* Parkersburg, Iowa: Caribbean Books, 1988, pp. 19–20.

[31] The anti-Partition Swadeshi movement was waged against the unjust decision of the British government in 1905 to partition Bengal. For an authoritative discussion on the same, see Sumit Sarkar, *The Swadeshi Movement in Bengal: 1905–08,* Delhi: Peoples Publishing House, 1973.

[32] *The Indian Daily News,* 11 August 1900.

the Coochbehar Cup in 1904–5. In 1905, it won the Gladstone Cup as well. From 1906 to 1908, thrice in a row, the club won the Trades Cup — a rare feat in itself. This was in addition to winning the Gladstone Cup in 1908, the Coochbehar Cup in 1907 and 1908, and Lakshibilas Cup in 1909 and 1910. More importantly, Mohun Bagan achieved some stunning victories against the strongest of European sides during this period, stirring up mass imagination in terms that suggest a passionate and fruitful blending of nationalism and sport.

The first of these victories came in 1905 when Mohun Bagan thrashed Dalhousie A.C., winners of the IFA Shield that year, by a redoubtable margin of 6–1 in the final of the Gladstone Cup tournament at Chinsurah. This sensational victory came against the prevailing opinion which considered Mohun Bagan to be 'chicken-feed' for the Shield champions.[33] There is a fascinating oral tradition about this famous soccer victory of the club:

> Old members recall how the teams were traveling by the same train from Sealdah Station to Chinsurah (via Naihati) and how some of the playing members of Mohun Bagan were somewhat 'relieved' to find only seven members of Dalhousie's Shield-winning team in the train that afternoon, hoping that their remaining players would be drawn from the second team. One of the supporters of Mohun Bagan was curious enough to ask a player of the Dalhousie Club what happened to the rest of the players. The confident Dalhousie player was reported to have replied: 'Seven is good enough for Mohun Bagan.' The four other Dalhousie players, all of the Shield-winning team, had, of course, travelled to Chinsurah from Howrah by the E.I.R. route. But history was created that afternoon at Chinsurah when Mohun Bagan defeated Dalhousie by six goals to one! That victory was a landmark in the career of the Club.[34]

Mohun Bagan created another sensation in 1906 when it outclassed the formidable Calcutta Football Club (CFC) 1–0 in the Minto Fete Tournament. It is said, however, that the tournament committee had scratched Mohun Bagan for having fielded P. K. Biswas, who was a regular player of the National Association for that season. As the tournament, organised to serve a greater cause, was not a regular one, the inclusion of Biswas in place of an absent regular player never struck anybody to be

---

[33] *Mohun Bagan Platinum Jubilee Souvenir*, Calcutta: Mohun Bagan Club, 1964 (hereafter *MB Souvenir*), p. 7.

[34] *Ibid.*, p. 11.

irregular or unfair.[35] But when the decision of the committee to scratch Mohun Bagan due to this technical breach was informed to the CFC, its executive replied that 'the Calcutta Football Club was fully satisfied that it had been defeated fairly and squarely by "eleven players of Mohun Bagan, not twelve", and withdrew from the Minto Fete Tournament'.[36]

Mohun Bagan's consistently remarkable performances against strong European sides affected the crowd behaviour at the maidan too. Habul Sarkar, a Mohun Bagan regular those days as well as a prominent member of the 1911 Shield-winning team, later recalled an exemplary incident:

> There was an incident in the preliminary round of the Trades Cup probably in 1907 while playing against Dalhousie 'B'. When our opponents were losing by 3 to 2, they lost temper, began to play very rough and even used fists and kicks upon us indiscriminately. This enraged the spectators who rushed into the field and began to assault the offending players and even the members of that Club, and the game had to be abandoned. The spectators were so rowdy that the police had to intervene and as a result of this the Dalhousie 'B' was scratched.[37]

Mohun Bagan's victorious run in the Trades Cup made the club authority confident enough to participate in the IFA Shield in 1909, however, only to see the club lose to Gordon Highlanders by 0–3 in the second round on a slushy ground. Mohun Bagan, however, avenged this defeat by beating the same team in the final of the Lakshibilas Cup the same year after five drawn games. Oral tradition has it that 'in spite of the defeat, a few of the disappointed and enraged Highlanders snatched the Cup away from the victors, though only for a while!'[38] The incident certainly

---

[35] This tournament had been specially organised under the patronage of Her Excellency Lady Minto, wife of then viceroy Lord Minto, in aid of a fund for providing nurses to India.

The absent player was probably Donga Dutt, one of the regular full backs, who could not come down from Benares to play the match. *MB Souvenir*, p. 11.

There are no records available as to the specific rules of the tournament, which show that the committee could take such action in case of a player from a different team not participating in the tournament, who plays for another team.

[36] *MB Souvenir*, p. 12.

[37] Habul Sarkar, 'My Reminiscences', *Mohun Bagan Athletic Club Golden Jubilee Souvenir*, Calcutta: Mohun Bagan A.C., 1939, p. 65.

[38] *MB Souvenir*, p. 11. Habul Sarkar, in his reminiscence, also mentions this incident thus: 'the donor of the cup could not present it to us on the occasion as the soldiers got excited and chased after us to snatch away the cup.' Sarkar, 'My Reminiscences', p. 67.

reflects the prevailing European sentiment — a defeat at the hands of a native team was considered shameful and derogatory to their reputation as the ruling race.

The meteoric rise of Mohun Bagan to football fame before 1911 had an obvious impact on the involvement of the Bengali crowd with the game. The perceptions of the Bengali crowd gradually became enmeshed with the on-field tensions of a soccer encounter between a Bengali team (Mohun Bagan to be specific) and a European outfit. People all over Bengal appreciated these victories in the context of a surge of anti-British sentiments in the political realm, stimulated by the Partition of Bengal. Soon, the masses rallied behind the Mohun Bagan Club, which had become an emblem of nationalist pride.

Incidentally, for the Presidency College, one of the leading educational institutions of contemporary India, the first decade of the 20th century, a period when nationalist movement reached a peak, 'constitute[d] a great period of college football'.[39] The college won the Elliot Shield, the premier inter-college football tournament five times in a row from 1904 to 1908. Kanu Roy, a consistent performer of the team, was later to play a key role in Mohun Bagan's historic IFA Shield victory of 1911. Presidency's success as a major football force continued unabated till 1915 and the college magazine born in 1914 used to publish detailed reports on the success of the college in the game. According to one recent interpretation, such success of the college comprising Bengali students had nationalist connotations:

> ... the educated Indian subjects had successfully utilized the 'games ethic' to suit their nationalist needs. In fact, it would not be wrong to assert that the 'games ethic' was their only available means of resistance, opposition that did not incur the wrath of the colonial state. Belief instilled on the sporting field, that the Indians could defeat the British, contributed in no small measure to challenging British superiority in the political realm.[40]

Other college football teams too reflected such nationalistic ethos in gaining success on the football field. For example, the *Scottish Church College Magazine* lauded and congratulated Mohun Bagan for its famous Shield victory by defeating European teams and took deepest pride in the fact

---

[39] *Presidency College Centenary Volume*, Calcutta: Presidency College, 1956, pp. 195–96.

[40] Boria Majumdar, 'Imperial Tool "For" Nationalist Resistance: The "Games Ethic" in Indian History', *The International Journal of the History of Sport*, vol. 21, nos ¾, 2004, pp. 397–98.

that three current and former college students were in the rank of the Shield-winning team.[41] Incidentally, the college football team too won the Elliot Shield that very year. The achievement was reported in the college magazine in a fair bit of detail featuring a full-page photograph of the playing eleven, which clearly suggests how important such a victory was to the native crew of the college:[42]

> There has been no more enthusiastic body of footballers this season than they (of Scottish Church College), and we all feel justly proud of their achievements. It may be interesting to review what our college *eleven* have done.
>
> The greatest glory a Calcutta College can achieve on the football Field is to gain the Elliot Shield, and this year that very glory is ours. . . . Bishop's College A team entered the lists against us in the semi-final, and the battle this time was stiffer. All the same the S.C.C. *would* have its goals, and Bishop's College went home with a load of four on their minds and none on their *football boots*.
>
> Then came the tug-of-war — but it was a wonderfully easy tug-of-war after all. We did not expect to vanquish the Presidency College A team by more than one goal but our players that day behaved like little Oliver Twist. They asked for more — goals, and got them. Consequently they have got the shield, and it may be very difficult for any other College team to take it away again.
>
> Did they satisfy our *exorbitant* team? By no means. Only the day after they carried home the Elliot Shield, they were hugging as theirs the Marcus Square Cup. And now these two trophies will be given an honourable place in our College Hall. Long may it be before we have to relinquish them. Honour and congratulations are due to every member of the team, for they all struggled manfully.[43]

1911: The Moment of Departure

In July 1911 Mohun Bagan, comprising 10 barefoot Indian players in its ranks, created sporting history when it defeated the booted European

---

[41] Two students were Abhilash Ghosh and Ranjan Sen (mistaken for Rajen Sengupta) while Sudhir Chatterjee was a former student of the college. For further details, see *The Scottish Church College Magazine*, September 1911. Also see Asit Kumar Sen, 'Glimpses of College History', in *The Scottish Church College Ter Jubilee Commemoration Volume*, Calcutta: *The* Scottish Church College, 1980, pp. 140–41.

[42] *The Scottish Church College Magazine*, September 1911, pp. 63–64.

[43] *Ibid.*

civil and military teams one by one to lift the coveted Indian Football Association (IFA) Shield.⁴⁴ When the IFA Shield competition began in July 1911, Mohun Bagan was by no means considered even a 'dark horse', not to speak of it being the favourite.⁴⁵ When Mohun Bagan moved to the second round beating St. Xavier's College on 10 July, *The Englishman*, hailing Mohun Bagan as the best native team of Calcutta, made a caustic comment: 'great as the rejoicing was in the Indian camp after the last evening's victory, the lamentations on Friday may be much greater.'⁴⁶ It also noted that 'the supporters of the native team mustered in full force around the field . . . in spite of the excellent arrangements it was at times difficult to keep the hordes of Bengalis off the ground of play'.⁴⁷ The next Friday, 14 July, was scheduled for Mohun Bagan's second round match against the Rangers whom the club beat 2–1 on a heavy surface on a wet evening. The match was marked by 'excessive rough play' on the part of the European side who seemed to react to defeat at the hands of an Indian team most unsportingly. Yet the Anglo-Indian press found solace in a typical glorification of the notion of cultural imperialism. Tony Mason prefers *The Englishman*'s version of the event as succinct: 'the Bengali eleven appeared to have learned the lesson of British sportsmanship well, because the player against whom the foul had been committed intervened with the referee on his opponent's behalf and he was allowed to resume play.'⁴⁸ Mohun Bagan faced its first military opponent in the third round, the Rifle Brigade. This match was of particular interest in view of the presence of a huge crowd. The *Amrita Bazar Patrika* estimated it to be in between 35,000 and 40,000.⁴⁹ *The Statesman* depicted a neat picture of the scene on the maidan that day:

---

⁴⁴ Only Sudhir Chatterjee played in boots for the club.
Details on the results of all these matches can be found in *MB Souvenir*, pp. 15–17; also see Nandy, *Mohun Bagan 1911*, 1976.

⁴⁵ One week ahead of the Shield, *The Englishman* (4 July 1911) forecast that but for the determined fight of the local European outfits the Royal Scott would be most likely to clinch the Shield that year. Among local teams, the *Indian Daily News* (8 July 1911) found it logical to support the cause of the Calcutta Football Club as the most potential contender for the Shield.

⁴⁶ *The Englishman*, 11 July 1911.

⁴⁷ *Ibid*.

⁴⁸ *The Englishman*, 15 July 1911; Mason, 'Football on the Maidan', p. 145.

⁴⁹ *Amrita Bazar Patrika*, 20 July 1911.

As early as 4 o'clock excited Indian youths and men — some of whom had travelled twenty to thirty miles from small suburban stations — came and took their places and before half past five there was scarcely standing room left. A vast sea of eager, exciting faces thronged the galleries, tables and boxes and about 16 or 18 deep fringed on the ground. From it there arose a continuous crackle of chatter — mostly in the vernacular — and the crowd was an entirely different one from the crowds that generally witness other football matches, full of fire and enthusiasm with only one thought — the thought of victory.[50]

Mohun Bagan's progress into the semifinal created a sensation among the Bengali masses. Public interest to watch Mohun Bagan play and beat the Middlesex Regiment in the semifinal became obvious when by 3 o'clock in the afternoon on the match day thousands of spectators occupied the best positions around the ground. One English newspaper furnishes a vivid picture of the evening's excitement:

At 4 o'clock the field was lined by several rows of spectators and every minute saw the crowd growing denser and denser . . . from all sides the crowds poured in and the wonder was that at that early hour, so many of Calcutta's citizens were available. However, if the truth were known, many an ardent Bengali football enthusiast absented himself from work in order to see the game and the Clerks in almost every office in the city went so far out of their ordinary course as to clamour for early dismissal to witness the game. Indeed Bengali Calcutta had gone football mad. . . . Last evening the box wallahs and stool wallahs who ply their trade in furnishing stands and miscellaneous bric-a-brac from which latecomers view the game did a roaring trade, but even their resources were taxed to the utmost and many thousands had to leave the field disappointed at not being able to obtain a glimpse. . . . The trees around the field swarmed with spectators who climbed up to the very tops. Many a man came down and had a nasty fall and an immense branch of one of the trees behind the Dalhousie tent, unable to bear the strain, crashed to the ground with its load of human freight. Several persons were injured.[51]

In the same match when Mohun Bagan conceded the first goal owing to a disputed decision of the referee, the Bengali crowd lost patience and vehemently abused the referee and the linesmen.[52] As Mohun Bagan reached the final after its famous demolition of the regimental team in the replayed semifinal, *The Times of India Illustrated Weekly* observed:

---

[50] *The Statesman*, 20 July 1911.
[51] *The Englishman*, 25 July 1911.
[52] *The Indian Daily News*, 25 July 1911.

On Thursday and Friday every Bengalee carried his head high and the one theme of conversation in the tramcars, in offices and in those places where the Babus congregate most, was the rout of the King's soldiers in boots and shoes by barefooted Bengali lads.[53]

The enthusiasm that Mohun Bagan's march into the final created was unique. It may be perceived as 'the moment of departure'[54] in the history of Indian football, when an indigenous brand of Bengali nationalism started appropriating a Western sport to assert its distinctive identity. One indication of this new trend was the enthusiastic participation of the crowd in unprecedented numbers. The numbers that turned up were estimated in between 80,000 and 100,000. As one newspaper noted: 'The spectators who packed every inch of the maidan simply defied calculation. They might have been eighty thousand or they might have been more.'[55] The IFA declared the encounter between East Yorkshire Regiment and Mohun Bagan as a charity match with admission charges of Rs 1 and 2[56] and scheduled it to be played at 5 p.m. at the Calcutta ground. By 2 o'clock 'the crowd was of unmanageable proportions' as 'Bengalis turned out in their thousands'.[57] The phenomenal interest the match aroused among the natives also becomes clear from the black-marketing of tickets and betting on the result of the match — unprecedented in the history of soccer in colonial India. A 2-rupee ticket fetched as much as 15, as noted by a few newspapers.[58] Newspaper reports also hinted at gambling developing around the game in that context.[59] In the absence of any permanent galleries or seating accommodation, people helped themselves watch the match with devices such as wooden boxes for which fantastic rates were charged and paid.[60] A few hundred chairs were, however, arranged for

---

[53] Cited in Mitra, 'Babu at Play', p. 54.

[54] I have taken this term from Partha Chatterjee's celebrated work *Nationalist Thought and the Colonial World: A Derivative Discourse?* London: Zed Books, 1986, Chapter 3, pp. 54–84. Chatterjee, however, used the term in an entirely different context.

[55] *Amrita Bazar Patrika*, 31 July 1911, p. 8.

[56] The match realised a sum of 6,914.00 from the 'paying spectators'. See Ramesh Ghoshal, 'Calcutta's Frenetic Night of History: Soccer Victory that Galvanised a Nation', *MB Souvenir*, p. 202.

[57] *The Pioneer*, 31 July 1911, p. 4.

[58] *Ibid.* Also see *The Snapper* (monthly magazine of the East Yorkshire Regiment), no. 6, 9 September 1911, p. 158.

[59] *Hitabadi*, 4 August 1911; Nagendra Nath Gupta, 'Football Final', *Bharatbarsha*, vol. 1, no. 4, 1913, p. 484.

[60] *MB Souvenir*, p. 15.

the European spectators by way of a contract with B. H. Smith & Co., the cabinet-makers.[61] People came down from distant Assam and Patna as well as from the eastern districts of Bengal.[62] The kind of soccer fever that gripped the people of Calcutta on the day of the final is best explained by the fact that 'a special meeting called by an academic body like the Vangiya Sahitya Parishat for the same evening for condoling the death of Indranath Bandyopadhyay fell through, as recorded in the minutes, for poor attendance of members gone to see the football match'.[63]

In order to cope with the expected rush of spectators, the East Indian Railway ran a special train from Burdwan to Howrah and back while additional steamer services brought more people from Rajgunj and Baranagar.[64] Maidan-bound tramcars from Shyambazar and Chitpur were loaded to their 'utmost capacity'.[65] The area between the High Court and the Strand Road was choked with waiting carriages, hundreds more were parked on the two sides of the ground.[66] *The Empire*, an evening paper, brought about an 'unprecedented journalistic enterprise' by installing a temporary telephone connection with the CFC ground for relaying the different stages and the final result of the match instantly to the people all over Calcutta.[67] As the *Reuter*'s correspondent stated: 'there was a scene of extraordinary enthusiasm. . . . The vast majority saw nothing of the game.'[68] Yet they kept cheering as they got cues from watchers on the tree-tops and from willing volunteers who kept the multitudes 'informed of the progress of the match by flying kites of different colours' when one side or the other scored a goal.[69]

Thus when Mohun Bagan actually entered the final of the IFA Shield, signs of a great mass awakening in Bengal were quite visible. People became obsessed with the dream of beating the ruling British at their own national game. The European residents too became conscious of this psychological head-on collision. The dream became a reality when Mohun Bagan defeated the East Yorks 2–1 in that historic final of 29 July 1911.

---

[61] *Ibid.*

[62] *Amrita Bazar Patrika*, 31 July 1911.

[63] Ghoshal, 'Calcutta's Frenetic Night', p. 202.

[64] *Amrita Bazar Patrika*, 31 July 1911.

[65] Ghoshal, 'Calcutta's Frenetic Night', p. 202.

[66] *Ibid.*

[67] *Amrita Bazar Patrika*, 31 July 1911.

[68] *Reuter News Agency*'s cablegram to England, 29 July 1911.

[69] *Ibid.*; Ghoshal, 'Calcutta's Frenetic Night', p. 202.

Shibdas Bhaduri and Abhilas Ghosh scored the goals for the victorious team while Jackson netted one for the East Yorks. *The Empire* noted: 'All honour to Mohun Bagan! Those eleven players are not only a glory to themselves and to their club and to the great nation which they belong, they are glory to the game itself.'[70]

1911: The Moment of Arrival

With Mohun Bagan's historic Shield victory of 1911 against heavy odds sporting nationalism was at its 'moment of arrival'[71] as the win marked Indian football's coming of age. The tremendous excitement that prevailed and the rejoicing that followed the victory were unprecedented in Bengal's social life. Ganen Mallick, sports journalist of the *Amrita Bazar Patrika*, wrote:

> The scene that followed was beyond description. Hats, handkerchiefs, umbrellas and sticks were waved and the tremendous cheering shook heaven and earth. It was as if the whole population had gone mad and to compare it with anything would be to minimize the effect.[72]

As the paper pointed out: 'The victory is no doubt ours and that in line of the physical culture wherein the Bengalees at any rate were so long held to be lamentably deficient.'[73] It therefore thought it would be wise to 'excuse the wild enthusiasm in which almost every Indian lost himself on that memorable Saturday evening'.[74] *The Mussalman*'s comment was more revealing: 'The victory of Mohun Bagan, . . . has demonstrated that Indians are second to none in all manly games.'[75] In the wake of Mohun Bagan's success, *Nayak*, a European-owned newspaper, came up with the following interesting observation:

> Indians can hold their own against Englishmen in every walk of art and science, in every learned profession, and in the higher grades of the public service. . . . It only remained for Indians to beat Englishmen in that peculiarly English sport, the football. . . . It fills every Indian with joy and pride to know that rice-eating, malaria-ridden, barefooted Bengalis have got the better of

---

[70] Quoted in *MB Souvenir*, p. 15.
[71] This term too is borrowed from Chatterjee, *Nationalist Thought and the Colonial World*. For Chatterjee's elaboration of the concept, see pp. 131–66.
[72] *Amrita Bazar Patrika*, 31 July 1911.
[73] *Ibid.*
[74] *Ibid.*
[75] Cited in *MB Souvenir*, p. 25.

beef-eating, Herculean, booted John Bull in the peculiarly English sport. Never before was there witnessed such universal demonstration of joy, men and women alike sharing it and demonstrating it by showering of flowers, embraces, shouts, whoops, screams and even dances.[76]

The paper also acknowledged that the 'Bengalis have proved themselves to be possessed of uncommon power of success in every department of life'.[77] Yet, interestingly enough, the paper attributed the 'sterling qualities' of the Bengali mind vividly expressed in the victory to 'their religion, which has stocked their mind with such a perennial store of high and noble qualities'.[78] While it explained India's long subjection to foreign yoke in terms of the Hindus' fall from the religion, the paper also stated: 'The germ of Hinduism, however, still lurks in them, and so they still excel in many things.'[79] The 'Hindu' connotation of the victory was also highlighted by another leading native newspaper of Calcutta, albeit to strike an entirely different note:

> But if we are to be true to *Hindu* instinct and culture such triumphs should not at all be exploited for other ends than establishing the best of relations between the two races. These are divine events meant for facilitating the harmonious working of the two great peoples by curbing to a certain extent the pride of the one and contributing to the growing self-consciousness of the other.[80]

The physical aspect of the game was also recorded in the foreign press as one of the major factors leading to Mohun Bagan's victory. As one London-based newspaper commented: 'It was a notable victory, gained over the best British Regimental teams, and not even the sweltering heat of Calcutta, to which the Bengalees are better insured than the white man, can discount it.'[81] Another British newspaper argued that the victory should not be construed as a surprise since 'victory at Association football goes to the side with the greatest physical fitness, quickest eye, and the keenest wit'.[82] The joyful and proud celebrations of the Bengalis in the streets of

---

[76] *Nayak*, 30 July 1911.
[77] *Nayak*, 5 August 1911.
[78] *Ibid.*
[79] *Ibid.*
[80] *Amrita Bazar Patrika*, 31 July 1911. Emphasis added.
[81] *Daily Mail* (London), quoted in *MB Souvenir*, p. 17. But no date of publication is given.
[82] *Manchester Guardian*, 4 August 1911.

Calcutta and its suburbs seemed understandable and befitting in the light of this famous victory.

The victory, however, also brought some overreaction from the media in its trail. In describing the significance of the match, the plucky *Indian Mirror* opined that Japan's victory over the Russians did not stir the East half as much as did the match between the two said teams.[83] Criticising such a sweeping view, the vernacular periodical *Prabasi* forthrightly contended: 'We are pleased but not surprised . . . those who have sought to raise the episode of the Russo-Japanese war in this connection suffer from a pronounced lack of restraint and a sense of humour.'[84] Its English counterpart, *The Modern Review* asked: 'Why should we lose our heads over a successful football game, when we know that we are capable of much higher things requiring both manliness and the qualities of leadership and combination?'[85]

Since the inception of colonial rule in India, the British categorically degraded the Bengali as a 'non-martial' race and continued to ridicule him as 'feeble' and 'effeminate'.[86] The practical repercussions of the colonial construction of Bengali effeminacy and racial inferiority were visible in ruthless British attitude and behaviour in everyday social life. Bengalis had become used to bear the brunt of daily British discrimination, condescension and physical assault in all walks of life. From tramcars to offices, the British, until the end of their rule, practised a form of racial apartheid in India.[87] The Bengali always awaited opportunities to return

---

[83] *Indian Mirror*, 5 August 1911.

[84] Quoted in Ghoshal, 'Calcutta's Frenetic Night', p. 205.

[85] *Ibid.*

[86] This stereotype of physical effeminacy of the Bengali as a 'race' found most prolific expression in critiques offered by British officials and writers like Thomas Macaulay or G. W. Steevens already quoted and referred to in Chapter 1.

[87] Even as fervent an admirer of the British Empire and culture as Nirad C. Chaudhuri acknowledges this fact in his autobiographical *Thy Hand, Great Anarch! India: 1921–1952*, London: Chatto & Windus, 1987. Even as late as 1928, noted Chaudhuri, he was told off for walking on the wrong side of the Eden gardens, the side reserved for Europeans. Subhas Chandra Bose, too, depicts a neat picture of this daily British racial discrimination against the Indians in his unfinished autobiography, *An Indian Pilgrim: An Unfinished Autobiography and Collected Letters, 1897–1921*, London: Asia Publishing House, 1965, pp. 22–23, 64–66. According to him, 'this phenomenon was the psychological basis of the terrorist — revolutionary movement — at least in Bengal'.

the compliment by any means, however trivial. Calcutta's football maidan proved to be one apolitical space to hit back at the masters.[88] The Mohun Bagan victory was considered to be exactly such a 'hit back' or *palta mar* against British racism. European scholars like Tony Mason and Paul Dimeo find a self-contradiction in the rejoicing following the victory as it reinforced the success of the public school spirit.[89] But they fail to understand that the occasion also provided an inherent threat within that project to the colonial games ethic itself as the cultural-racist superiority of the West was surpassed and nullified by its so-called inferiors at its own standard. More so because Mohun Bagan played almost barefoot and even then proved better than booted regimental teams. It may be said to have added insult to injury. The 19th-century colonial construction of Bengali racist effeminacy was thus subverted in this context of football's cultural indigenisation in Bengal.

The depiction of the victory in racist colour was not, of course, uniform in the contemporary press. Though both English and vernacular press reports more or less allude to the event as of nationalist and political significance, they differ strongly on the question of its racist implications. The Anglo-Indian press — the European-owned newspapers — while handing out accolades to Mohun Bagan for the victory, strongly denied any racist implications in the adulation. The *Reuters News Agency* in its cablegram to England commented: 'The absence of all racial spirit was noted. The European spectators were good humoured and the Bengalees cheered the loosing team.'[90] The *Basumati* affirmed: 'They are greatly mistaken who seem to find race antagonism in this national victory. Race-antagonism had

---

[88] Bose succinctly sums up the essence of this 'reverse hit': 'In conflicts of an inter-racial character, the law was no avail to Indians. The result was that after some time Indians, failing to secure any other remedy, began to hit back. On the streets, in the tram-cars, in the railway trains, Indians would no longer take things lying down. The effect was instantaneous. Everywhere the Indian began to be treated with consideration. Then the word went around that the Englishman understands and respects physical force and nothing else.' Bose, *An Unfinished Autobiography*, pp. 65–66.

[89] For Mason and Dimeo, Mohun Bagan's victory seemed to reinforce the success of the assumed British notion of the civilising mission alias games ethic, which the public school system had tried to instruct through games and sports in India. See Mason, 'Football on the Maidan' and Dimeo, 'Football and Politics in Bengal'.

[90] *Reuter News Agency*'s cablegram to England on Mohun Bagan's success on 30 July 1911, quoted in *MB Souvenir*, p. 17.

nothing to do with it. There is nothing of meanness in the tide of patriotism that had rushed into the silted-up life stream of the Bengali.'[91] *The Telegraph*, too, sang from the same hymnbook: 'The victory of the former was well taken by the English population of Calcutta. . . . this is as it should have been for it was a fair contest, fairly and gallantly fought on both sides in a friendly spirit, without anything like race-hatred and rancour finding any place in the hearts of the combatants.'[92] Several of these newspapers highlighted the English quality of 'magnanimous equanimity' even in the face of defeat and urged the Bengalis to show gratitude to their masters for providing this rare opportunity to better them.[93] *The Statesman*'s suggestion that both communities had something to celebrate clearly pointed to the celebration of the cult of cultural imperialism:

> One great lesson that the English devotion to sports teaches is that defeat should be accepted with a good grace and the English people must have been bad pupils in the national school of good temper and chivalry if they did not welcome the triumph of the Mohun Bagan team and cherish a strong desire to defeat them at the earliest opportunity.[94]

The Empire went so far as to state that 'it is their gallant opponents who ought to feel most proud at this singular distinction of a batch of Bengalee athletes, because it is they, the former, who taught them the game as well as the method of achieving distinction in it'.[95] Its further comment is more revealing:

> That (Mohun Bagan's victory) is a subject for legitimate pride both on their (Bengalis') part, and on the part of the Britishers who have introduced them to the game and taught them how to acquire such proficiency in it. We see nothing in this evening's contest that need arouse any but the most friendly feelings, and whatever be the result, we trust that the losing side and their sympathizers will show a truly sportsmanlike and *British* temper.[96]

The Anglo-Indian press certainly showered praise on the victorious Mohun Bagan. Nevertheless, the defeat produced, it seems, widespread

---

[91] *Basumati*, 5 August 1911.
[92] *The Telegraph*, 5 August 1911.
[93] *Nayak*, 30 July 1911; *Indian Mirror*, 30 July 1911.
[94] *The Statesman*, 3 August 1911.
[95] Cited in *Amrita Bazar Patrika*, 31 July 1911.
[96] *Ibid.*; emphasis added.

European dejection. It was reported in one vernacular newspaper that in the immediate aftermath of the match the European parts of the city wore a dark and deserted look reflecting something very mournful.[97] *The Englishman*, too, reported that the 'Saheeb' localities of Calcutta were engulfed by gloom after the defeat.[98] Some Europeans, however, appeared to respond with bitterness. The humourist of the *Hitavadi*, writing under the nom-de-plume of 'an old man' reported that 'on the semi-final day, when an Englishman and a native Christian were travelling together in the same railway compartment, the latter, in all innocence, enquired of his companion the result of the day's contest, to which the only reply he received was a slap on the cheek'.[99]

Bengali emotion surged high at the sight of the Bengalis being repressed, humiliated and branded as inferiors in all spheres of life. Defeating the best European civil and military teams in their own game of soccer lifted Mohun Bagan like a colossal nationalist Himalaya on the sporting horizon.[100] The Bengalis were mentally prepared to see the British Raj in turn humiliated and brought to its knees. That is the measure of what Mohun Bagan achieved on the football field. For a brief moment, the nebulous desire in the subconscious of the Bengali people to come out winners in the struggle for self-assertion leading to independence was made a tangible reality.[101] The status of Mohun Bagan as the national soccer team made them a major fighting unit in India's wider battle against the imperialists. Mohun Bagan had become almost synonymous with the national battle cry of *Vande Mataram* ('worshipping the mother').[102] Their matches against

---

[97] For a lively narrative of this situation, see Nandy, *Mohun Bagan 1911*, pp. 3–4, 132. Also see *Amrita Bazar Patrika*, 31 July 1911.

[98] *The Englishman*, 31 July 1911.

[99] *Report on the Native Newspapers in Bengal* for the weeks ending 5 and 12 August 1911.

[100] The Himalaya is the great mountain that surrounds the Indian subcontinent in the north.

[101] According to the most enduring anecdote surrounding Mohun Bagan's Shield victory, immediately after Mohun Bagan's victory in the Shield final, an elderly Brahmin wearing a white dhoti and the sacred thread, pointing to the Union Jack fluttering on top of Fort William, the emblem of British military presence in Calcutta, asked Shibdas Bhaduri, captain of the winning team, 'Now as you have beaten the military side, when will you pull that down?' An amazed but emotional Shibdas replied: 'When Mohun Bagan will win the Shield next time.' Coincidentally, it was in 1947 when Mohun Bagan won the Shield again, that the Union Jack was replaced by the Indian tri-colour as India won freedom.

[102] Achintya Kumar Sengupta, *Kallol Yug* (The Kallol Age), Calcutta: M. C. Sarkar & Sons, 1950, p. 66.

European teams were perceived as campaigns to defeat the Raj and the match between Mohun Bagan and CFC came to be seen in that light. Thus Bengali nationalist instinct in the wake of such a perceived Indian national victory converged with the broader stream of Indian nationalism, thereby merging the two in the flow. That it created a tremendous stir among nationalists all over India also lends strength to this argument.

The victory fired the imagination of the whole nation. *The Englishman*'s comment on Mohun Bagan's win sums up its political importance: 'Mohanbagan have succeeded in what the Congress and the Swadeshiwallas have failed to do so far to explode the myth that the Britishers are unbeatable in any sphere of life.'[103] The Mohun Bagan success thus indirectly highlighted the political failures of the Indian Association and the Congress:

> There are no players today in the playroom of the Indian Association. The Congress playroom has been blown off by one blast like a house of cards. Revered leaders like Surendranath have not been able to unite their adherents by the tie of unity. In a country where union takes place only to dissolve, where repulsion is more powerful than attraction, you have been able to knit together so many hearts.[104]

A few years before this sporting victory of Mohun Bagan, Ranji's extraordinary success in a cricket field in England had provided Indian political leaders with a 'hero'. Dadabhai Naoraji commented that a 'rediscovery of India' had taken place through Ranji's performance.[105] Mohun Bagan's victory was greeted in the same spirit by the country. It destroyed the myth of British invincibility not only in the eyes of the Bengalis but in that of the Indians. People all over India began to appreciate the victory in the new light of anti-British nationalist resentment and rally behind the club as an emblem of nationalist pride.

More radical implications of the triumph lay in attempts — both contemporary as also recent — to politicise a sporting success in terms of nationalism. In praising the Bengali team, *The Englishman* could not resist having a fling at the Bengali agitators: 'Political agitators gnashed their

---

[103] *The Englishman*, 31 July 1911.

[104] *Basumati*, 5 August 1911.

[105] Moti Nandy, 'Football and Nationalism', in Geeti Sen (ed.), *The Calcutta Psyche*, New Delhi: India International Centre, 1990–91, p. 243. For the most recent consideration of Ranji's cricketing prowess and its relations to his political ambition, see Mario Rodrigues, *Batting for the Empire: A Political Biography of Ranjitsinhji*, New Delhi: Penguin, 2003 as well as its review by Boria Majumdar, 'On a Political Pitch', *Biblio — A Review of Books*, vol. 8, nos 7–8, 2003, pp. 21–22.

teeth in impotent rage to think that with all their fine fury they had never been able to collect such audiences as these.'[106] Referring to the socio-political morale of the victory, *Basumati* observed:

> We have seen Bengalis assembled on various occasions of danger, distress and sorrow, such as that of the Partition. . . . But never before did we witness such a vast concourse, such a demonstration of joy.
>
> Mohun Bagan has infused a new life into the lifeless and cheerless Bengali . . . (who) will never be able to repay the debt they owe you for infusing the revivifying nectar into their lifeless body . . .
>
> By your victory sport has been turned into a unifying force, an occasion of common rejoicing . . . [Mohun Bagan have] held up before the Bengali an ideal of striving in concert.
>
> The Bengali must ever remain indebted to those who have, in these dark days of disunion, found the secret of union.[107]

More recent observations on 1911 seem to confirm, of course with minor variations, the view that the victory had a deeper impact on Bengali society with redefined political/nationalist meanings. Ramachandra Guha, noted Indian sports historian, explores an interesting and overtly close relationship between sport and politics in the context of the 1911 Shield victory:

> Oddly enough, it was in the same year, 1911, that the British shifted the capital of the *raj* from Calcutta to Delhi. Recent memorialists of Mohun Bagan's victory have, alas, failed to notice this coincidence. *If* it is a coincidence, for it is highly likely that one was the cause of the other and that to pre-empt further humiliation the British adroitly and deliberately moved the seat of power from Bengal, away from its skillful footballers and its bomb-wielding nationalists. The link between sporting prowess and militant anti-imperialism was thus undermined, to be finally rent asunder by Gandhi and the Bombay capitalists.[108]

An equally interesting observation is offered by a scholar-turned-journalist:

---

[106] *Report on the Native Newspapers in Bengal* (week ending 12 August 1911), p. 993.
[107] *Basumati*, 5 August 1911.
[108] *The Telegraph* (Calcutta), 20 June 1998.

The victory seems, in retrospect, to have been a triumph of the moral force which Gandhi extolled and advocated in *Hind Swaraj*. For Bengalis who had seen only a few years ago their land partitioned and their young men and women imprisoned and punished during the Swadeshi movement, the win over a white team in football seemed a moment of national pride. It appeared as some sort of recovery of dignity and self-respect in the year that Calcutta was to lose its status as the capital. It was the inherent inequality of the encounter in which the apparently weak trounced the obviously strong that made Mohun Bagan's victory the stuff of legends.[109]

In contrast we find a more modest yet radically alternative tone in Mason's evaluation of the event:

Mohan Bagan's victory did not produce a bombardment of Fort William by Bengali athletes, nor did it provoke a military revolt against peace and order. It clearly injected some confidence into some of the native peoples of Calcutta and convinced them that they were as good as their masters. But it also seems to have reinforced admiration for those masters. Perhaps that is the essence of the mystery of hegemony.[110]

The best assessment of 1911 as a moment of nationalist resistance perhaps comes from one recent non-academic commentator:

Barefoot Bengali *babus* had battled with their British 'bosses' on equal terms, and had got the better of them. A subject race, humiliated by hauteur, ridiculed by so-called racial superiors and derided by a discriminating ruling class, had, at last, delivered a fitting reply. In a moment, Mohun Bagan Athletic Club was transformed from a Calcutta football team into a symbol of nationalist aspirations. The Bengalis had found their voice on a football field, and the voice echoed and re-echoed all over India.[111]

Mohun Bagan in 1911: Social, Cultural and Commercial Implications

The 1911 victory proved to be of immense significance towards the social popularisation of the game in Bengal. It also played a crucial role

---

[109] Rudrangshu Mukherjee, 'Elegy on the Maidan', *The Telegraph*, 5 March 2002.

[110] Mason, 'Football on the Maidan', pp. 150–51.

[111] Surapriya Mookerjee, 'Early Decades of Calcutta Football', in *An Economic Times Special Feature: Calcutta 300*, Calcutta: Bennett and Coleman and Co. Ltd, 1990, p. 151.

in shaping the future of football's progress and its potential impact as a social phenomenon in Bengal. The Shield victory and its immediate social aftermath also point to the game's importance as a potential bond of social unity and communal amity in Bengal. Football as a cultural idiom and Mohun Bagan as a cultural institution came to be perceived increasingly in this light after 1911. Football, in that context, provided a common language to Bengali people irrespective of class, caste, creed, community, or religion. It may therefore be said to have introduced a unique means of cultural self-expression in Bengali society. The gathering of a massive crowd on the days of the semifinal and final pointed to football's new social role as a mass mobiliser.[112] Although most of the people had very little idea about the game, what brought them to the maidan was 'a sense of oneness, a feeling of concern aroused for a fellow team pitted against the British Regimental teams in an unequal competition for strength'.[113]

The Mohun Bagan victory also provided an occasion for communal amity. When the victory procession of the team was on their way to Thanthania Kali Temple of Calcutta, the Muslims rushed to Dharmatala with a band party to join the same. In fact, they were allowed to lead the rally with their beating drums and bands. *The Mussalman* wrote:

> . . . although Mohun Bagan was a team composed of Bengali Hindus, the jubilation in consequence of its success was in fact a sense of universal joy, which pervaded the feeling of the Hindus, the Mohammadans and the Christians alike. The members of the Muslim Sporting Club were almost mad and rolling on the ground with joyous excitement on the victory of their Hindu brethren.[114]

Another Muslim journal, *The Comrade*, of which Maulana Mohammed Ali was the founder and editor at the same time, said: 'We hereby join the chorus of praise and jubilation over the victory of Mohun Bagan. The team did remarkably well throughout the tournament and won the Shield by sheer merit.'[115] This remarkable amity in the realm of sports, one must note, was in striking contrast to contemporary political rift between the Hindus and the Muslims, which followed the strained relations between the

---

[112] Whatever be the actual figure of spectator presence on the day of the final, even the minimum claim suggests that it was unprecedented in the history of public gatherings in colonial India.

[113] Mitra, 'Babu at Play', p. 56.

[114] *MB Souvenir*, p. 25.

[115] *Ibid.*

two communities during the Swadeshi age. In this sense, football proved to be great leveller in contemporary Bengali society.

More important, however, was the impact of the Shield triumph on social power relations in contemporary Calcutta. During the two decades that preceded the 1911 event, Bengali football clubs failed to display the unity necessary to fight the discrimination exercised by the British on the sports field. With the growing number of Bengali clubs, unfortunate trends of jealousy, conflict and humiliation raised their heads over the question of control, organisation and competition of clubs. In fact, this trend was in tune with the then Congress politics characterised by ideological, personality or power conflicts. Mohun Bagan especially had to always bear the brunt of jealousy and anguish of other Bengali clubs during its early years of success. When the club first obtained a plot of land and a tent on the maidan, the Bagbazar Club resorted to the age-old doggerel: 'Ants fly only to die.'[116] When Mohun Bagan secured its first entry into the IFA Shield in 1909, previous Indian participants like Sovabazar, Town, Chinsurah Sporting, and Hare Sporting sneered at its progress and began to ridicule the club when it lost 0–3 to Gordon Highlanders in the second round.[117] They even published 'some very humourous pamphlets' and circulated those among the sporting public of Calcutta 'to point out the folly of "aiming too high"'.[118] This selfish and uncompromising attitude of its elder clubs to Mohun Bagan's success on the eve of the 1911 IFA Shield illustrates the divisive and competitive nature of social power relations — a unique feature of the contemporary urban society of Calcutta.

Mohun Bagan of course reacted to this insult aptly when it won the Shield in 1911. Mohun Bagan's victory, however, radically altered this power equation in Calcutta's footballing society. As already argued, it acted as a great leveller for all the people associated with the game in any way. The new status of Mohun Bagan as a national sporting institution, to a great extent, wiped out the previous trends of jealousy and ill-feeling among the Bengali clubs of Calcutta. The club became an emblem not only of a cultural nationalism but of a unitary social identity. The victory inspired other Bengali clubs to fight spiritedly against the colonisers on the sporting fields of Calcutta maidan. Mohun Bagan, of course, remained for the next two decades the undisputed leader in that cultural battle.

---

[116] Shantipriya Bandopadhyay, *Cluber Naam Mohun Bagan* (The Name of the Club is Mohun Bagan), Calcutta: New Bengal Press, 1979, p. 45.

[117] *MB Souvenir*, p. 11.

[118] *Ibid.*

Again, the psychological and moral impact of the event in Bengali society is more or less overlooked in prevalent interpretations. The win certainly 'played a vital role in injecting confidence in the "native" and disproving the invincibility of the British race'.[119] But what is completely ignored is the moral impact of the victory on the social psychology of the Bengali people. Mohun Bagan's success gave birth to a redefined status of the game in Bengali society. The public image of the players, club members and spectators underwent a dramatic change almost overnight. It led to a notable rise in the social respectability of the footballing public and provided momentum for the emergence of many new clubs all over Bengal.[120] Football began to be identified with something very akin to fighting the colonial masters. The game was perhaps even preferred by Bengali parents and guardians as a better and more viable means for the youth to associate with nationalist activism and show anti-colonial resentment than to indulge in Swadeshi or revolutionary activities with which ran the risk of intimidation, repression and even death.

Finally, a look at the social composition of the victorious Mohun Bagan team reveals certain neglected truths about the social impact of football as a mass spectator sport in contemporary Bengal. If newspaper reports following the memorable win as well as the rich vernacular sporting chronicles that grew around the same are to be believed, the combination provided interesting evidence of cross sections of Bengali society playing for honour and pride, transcending barriers of social status, class/caste hierarchy or professional commitment.[121] To one sports commentator, the team seemed a 'strange combination' in view of 'the social strictures

---

[119] Mitra, 'Babu at Play', p. 59.

[120] The impact of the victory reached as far as Malda when, inspired by Mohun Bagan's football glory, some enterprising locals at the initiative of Sripati Banerjee founded the Malda Town Club in August 1911. It is also recorded that some of the Mohun Bagan players including the Bhaduri brothers, Rajen Sen, Abhilas Ghosh and Kanu Roy used to play quite regularly for the Cooch Behar 'A' team. This certainly helped popularise the game in the area to a great extent. For details on this, see Biswas, 'Khelay Cooch Behar', p. 476.

[121] To be specific, as for newspapers, *Amrita Bazar Patrika*, 31 July 1911. Most important of the vernacular chronicles are: Nandy, *Mohun Bagan 1911*, pp. 154–71; Kumar (ed.), *RB Rachita Kolkatar Football*, pp. 123–30; Rupak Saha, *Ekadashe Suryoday* (Sun-Rise in 1911), Calcutta: Karuna Prakashani, 1990; Chirakaaler Mohun Bagan Prokashona Committee, *Chirakaaler Mohun Bagan* (Mohun Bagan For Ever), Kolkata: Amal Kumar Sen, 2003, pp. 326–27; Jaydeep Basu, *Stories from Indian Football*, New Delhi: UBSPD, 2003, pp. 14–16.

and taboos that prevailed in the Indian society at that period of time'.[122] Three of them were students of renowned colleges — Rajen Sengupta and Abhilas Ghosh of the Scottish Church College and Kanu alias Jatindranath Roy of the Presidency College.[123] Goalkeeper Hiralal Mukherjee who came from a poor lower-middle-class family could not continue his studies in the university due to financial insolvency and used to do a job with the Martin Brick Company at a meagre remuneration.[124] A. Sukul, a young businessman of Calcutta, had a partnership trading concern called Messrs Sukul & Bhaduri with Bijoydas Bhaduri, another player of the team.[125] Reverend Sudhir Chatterjee, a Bengali Christian, was a staff of the L.M.S College, Calcutta although his reputation as a professor depended more on his expertise as a footballer.[126] Four other stars of the victory were all government servants or private officials — Nilmadhab Bhattacharyya was a clerk of Bengal National Bank; Srish Chandra alias Habul Sarkar an undergraduate clerk in the Calcutta Corporation; Shibdas Bhaduri a veterinary inspector and Manmohan Mukherjee a clerk in the PWD.[127] It can therefore be argued that football by then had already fostered a kind of sporting identity among the Bengalis irrespective of existing social or professional affiliations. More importantly, some of these players came from places outside Calcutta — Manmohan Mukherjee from Uttarpara, Hoogly; Nilmadhab Bhattacharyya from Srirampur, Hoogly; Abhilas Ghosh from Mymensingh, Dacca; and the Bhaduri brothers from Faridpur, Dacca.[128] This certainly makes room for the argument that the game had already attained a considerable level of popularity as also maturity in several districts of Bengal. It also posits that football's growth as a mass spectator sport throughout Bengal should not be mistaken as a post-1911 phenomenon.

Mohun Bagan's IFA Shield victory also sent ripples through the cultural world of Calcutta. The most enduring effect was felt in the field of sports journalism. The historic final led to what was then 'a novel kind of journalistic enterprise'.[129] The entire tournament including especially

---

[122] Basu, *Stories from Indian Football*, p. 14.

[123] *The Scottish Church Magazine* of September 1911 and the *Presidency College Centenary Volume* mention their names with deep pride.

[124] Nandy, *Mohun Bagan 1911*, pp. 158–59.

[125] *Ibid.*, pp. 160, 170. Also see *Amrita Bazar Patrika*, 31 July 1911.

[126] Nandy, *Mohun Bagan 1911*, p. 161; *Amrita Bazar Patrika*, 31 July 1911.

[127] *Amrita Bazar Patrika*, 31 July 1911.

[128] Nandy, *Mohun Bagan 1911*, pp. 157–71.

[129] *MB Souvenir*, p. 25.

Mohun Bagan's winning run was covered widely by almost all the leading newspapers of Bengal, while the final drew large columns in the newspapers from other Indian states and abroad.[130] The event provided a real booster to the development of vernacular sports journalism in Bengal. The day-by-day build-up to the Shield final reversed the pre-1911 insignificance of football reporting in the sports pages of the contemporary press. In the aftermath of the victory was born a new genre of nationalist sports journalism. Boria Majumdar draws our attention to the discrepancy between English and vernacular reports on the significance of the victory in 1911, which, according to him, 'lay at the root of a concerted move on the part of the Bengali intelligentsia to establish Bengali sports journalism on a firm footing from the 1930s'.[131] In fact, the press reports after the final clearly show that the sports pages of newspapers became divided on nationalist and imperialist lines.[132] Mason has argued that both sides treaded cautiously, but he frankly confesses his inability to read the local language press.[133] Finally, it is noteworthy that Bengali periodicals, which had hitherto attached very little importance to sports, suddenly began to take up sports like football as important issues for writing.[134]

The literary world of Calcutta, however, remained somewhat indifferent to the glory of Mohun Bagan's football victory. Although the victory celebrations brought in their wake poems and songs nationalist in

---

[130] Almost all the newspapers published from Bengal covered the tournament. To mention a few of them, *Amrita Bazar Patrika, The Statesman, The Englishman, The Indian Daily News, The Telegraph, Nayak, Hitavadi, Basumati, The Mussalman, Comrade, The Empire, Bengalee,* and *Bandemataram* are the most important.

The reports of *The Pioneer* of Allahabad and *The Times of India Illustrated Weekly* of Bombay testify to the immediate impact of the event on sports journalism in other Indian states. Among foreign press reports, worthy of mention are the *Reuters News Agency, Daily Mail, Manchester Guardian, London Times,* and *The Singapore Free Press*.

[131] Majumdar, 'The Vernacular in Sports History', p. 3073.

[132] The *Amrita Bazar Patrika, Bengalee, Bandemataram, Manasi, Prabasi,* and *Hitavadi* reflected the nationalist ethos of the sports page. Ganen Mallick, the renowned sports journalist of the *Amrita Bazar Patrika* was the most fervent protagonist of this nationalist spirit. British-owned or -influenced newspapers like *The Englishman, The Empire, The Statesman, Nayak,* and *Basumati* on the other hand represented the imperial line of sports reporting.

[133] Mason, 'Football on the *Maidan*', pp. 149–50.

[134] Bengali periodicals like *Probasi, Manasi* and *Masik Basumati* started to publish pieces on sports-related matters after 1911. Two new Bengali periodicals, viz., *Balok* and *Bharatvarsha* which emerged respectively in 1912 and 1913 used to have regular columns on sports, especially football, from their first issues.

tone,[135] the victory could not excite eminent literateurs of the age including Rabindranath Tagore and Satyendranath Dutta to write anything about it. However, a rich genre of Bengali sporting literature has cropped up around Mohun Bagan's historic victory in post-colonial West Bengal, to which we shall turn our attention in a subsequent chapter.[136]

---

[135] One such poem published in *The Bengalee* on 30 July 1911 is as follows:

> 'Thanks my friends of football renown,
> For bringing the British teams down.
> A victory grand to behold
> Serene and noble — bright and bold.
> — The Mohan-bagans.'

A very captivating popular song composed by Karunanidhan Bandopadhyay was published in the September–October (corresponding to Bengali month of *Aswin*) 1911 issue of *Manasi*. The first few lines of the song go like this:

> *Jegechhe aaj desher chhele pathe loker bhir*
> (The sons of the soil have awakened: the streets are crowded)
> *Antapure futlo hasi Banga rupasir*
> (The Bengali women have broken out in smiles)
> *Goal diyechhe gorar gole Bangalir aaj jit*
> (We have scored against the whites; it's a triumph of the Bengalis)
> *Akash chheye uthchhe udhao unmadonar geet.*
> (The air is filled with songs of rejoicing)
> *Aajikar ei bijoy bani bhulbe na ko desh*
> (The motherland will never forget today's victory)
> *Sabash sabash Mohun Bagan khelechho bhai besh*
> (Hail! Hail! Mohun Bagan; you have played very well).

> For a translated version of the full poem, see Majumdar, 'The Vernacular', p. 3074.

[136] Most notable contributions in this regard are: Nandy, *Mohunbagan 1911*; Sibram Kumar (ed.), *Mohunbagan Omnibus*, Calcutta: Prabhabati Prakashani, 1983; Bandyopadhyay, *Cluber Naam Mohunbagan*; Jayanta Dutta, *Victorious Mohunbagan*, Calcutta: Sahitya Prakash, 1979; Rupak Saha (ed.), 'Mohunbagan: Prathom Eksho Bachhar' (Mohun Bagan: First Hundred Years), *Ananda Bazar Patrika*, 24 and 28 November, 1990; Saha, *Ekadashe Suryoday*. Apart from this literary output, one interesting audio cassette, released to commemorate the centenary of Mohun Bagan Club, contains lively narration and nostalgic recollection of the event by many former players. For details, refer to *Shotoborsher Mohun Bagan* (Mohun Bagan in its Centenary), produced by Tutu Basu and directed by Sankar Banerjee, Calcutta: UD Industries, 1999.

The reception of the news of Mohun Bagan's victory and its immediate impact in the cultural world of Calcutta remains an unnoticed phenomenon to date. Emotional outbursts and cultural effusion characterised the post-victory reaction. The prize-giving ceremony after the final match was followed by an impressive victory procession through the heart of the city with the women blowing conch shells and showering flowers. The procession ended at the residence of the club secretary's house at Shyambazar where the celebrations continued throughout the night with a public banquet, magic show and musical performances. The Adi Arya Saraswat Samaj staged a free and open show of their contemporary play *Vismavijaya* in honour of the club.[137]

The club began to receive standing ovation everywhere. It was but natural that supporters and admirers of the club should have wanted to fete Mohun Bagan and requests to that effect, both directly to the club and through the press, were not few. *The Times of India* invited the club to play a friendly match with the Harwood League champions in Bombay to promote interest in football. There were those who even offered to send the team to England at their own expense.[138] But the club, while appreciating this enthusiasm, was unwilling to accept such offers. In fact, it did not entertain the idea of being lionised for a victory won in a sport. Even so, requests were insistent and persistent. In the end, S. N. Bose, the then honorary secretary and one of the chief architects of the club, wrote to *The Statesman* to that effect:

> ... it is the decision of the Management of the Club that it is not desirable to make a fuss over last Saturday's success, as the Club in general and the players in particular look upon it as the result of practice and study of the science of the game under the guidance and with the help of their numerous friends both European and Indian.[139]

Despite the sentiments expressed by the management of the club, invitations continued to pour in from all quarters spontaneously till at last the club had to accept a few that included the ones from Mr Eardley Norton, barrister-at-law and from Dr Thornhill, chief judge of the Small Causes Court.[140] In that situation a rumour, though baseless, spread

---

[137] Ghoshal, 'Calcutta's Frenetic Night', p. 203; also see Nandy, *Mohun Bagan 1911*, p. 149.

[138] *MB Souvenir*, p. 27.

[139] *The Statesman*, 2 August 1911. The newspaper appreciated Mr Bose's point of view in its editorial paragraph on 3 August 1911.

[140] *MB Souvenir*, p. 27.

that Mohun Bagan would receive precious monetary rewards from the Indian princes. The *Amrita Bazar Patrika* even conducted an enquiry into the potential of such rewards in their columns.[141]

The people of Calcutta also offered numerous proposals to greet the victorious team. One such proposal desired to start a competitive football tournament in the name of 'Mohun Bagan Challenge Shield'. The replica of the 11 players of the victorious team was to be engraved at the middle of the shield. Another proposal intended to name one 'great recreation park' of north Calcutta as 'Mohun Bagan'. A group of north Calcutta intelligentsia also suggested arranging a grand public reception at Town Hall to honour the club and install a group photograph of those 11 players there. *The Bengalee*, on the other hand, started collecting contributions from people to offer substantial monetary rewards to the club. The latter, however, immediately acted on its own to stop that venture.[142]

The cultural implications of the Shield victory thus highlight an element of spontaneity in the immediate response to the event in Calcutta. While it nearly changed the orientation of football-reporting in English and vernacular newspapers and periodicals, it could not create much stir in the contemporary literary world. The event, however, aroused huge enthusiasm among the public, who became keen to celebrate the victory and showed eagerness to greet the Mohun Bagan team in different ways. What is certain is that, after 1911, football became an integral part of Bengali popular culture.

---

[141] Ghoshal, 'Calcutta's Frenetic Night', p. 204. There is evidence to show from letters to the editor in the readers' column in the newspaper that such an enquiry was requested and urged upon by the interested readers. For example, one Prokash Chandra Chatterjee wrote to the Editor:

Sir,
The great victory of the Mohun Bagan Football team has given birth to a host of rumours. Among the sundry others that are prevalent just now one is, that besides what they have already got in the shape of rings, watches etc. from persons of note, the "immortal eleven" are still to get princely presents, in money, from most of the Indian Chiefs by way of encouragement.
Has the report really any legs to stand upon? I hope that someone amongst your readers, perhaps the Secretary of the Club himself, will come forward and let us know through the columns of your paper whether this has any foundation, in truth or not.' (*Amrita Bazar Patrika*, 5 August 1911).

Prokash Chandra Chatterjee
Salkia, Howrah.

[142] Ghoshal, 'Calcutta's Frenetic Night', pp. 204–5.

The commercial importance of Mohun Bagan's IFA Shield victory has been no less fascinating either. Black marketing of tickets in Indian sport may be said to have begun with the historic IFA Shield final of 1911. As one Allahabad-based newspaper noted, the demand of tickets was so much that a 2-rupee ticket fetched as much as Rs 15.[143] One newspaper also hinted at gambling on the game's outcome and expressed some concern over the issue.[144] The commercial world of Calcutta too could not remain unaffected by the feat of Mohun Bagan. Calcutta-based businessmen and commercial firms widely used the magic of the club's name as a brand to promote their businesses and enterprises. The Standard Cycle Company (59, Harrison Road) distributed halftone photographs of the victorious team in collaboration with the *Amrita Bazar Patrika* along with the latter's issues on 31 July 1911. The firm later distributed a further 1,000 photographs from their shop. Messrs Hald & Chat (79, Ahiritolla Street), the leading dealers in musical instruments in Calcutta, declared on the occasion of an Indian team's Shield victory to offer their harmoniums at 10 per cent discount for two months. Messrs S. Roy & Co., another renowned Calcutta firm of sports goods, offered footballs at a cheaper rate from Rs 4 to 12 to encourage the youth to play football and thereby get a chance to play for Mohun Bagan. In fact, the football alias sports goods industry got a great fillip by Mohun Bagan's heroic success. The most attractive commercial utilisation of Mohun Bagan's victory was done by the Great National Theatre (9/3, Beadon Street) that advertised their latest production 'Baji Rao' with the by-line: 'Mohun Bagan has won the Shield! Baji Rao has gained the victory.'[145]

The commercial implications of the 1911 victory clearly point to the sound commercial sense of Bengali businessmen to utilise the market potential of a sporting success even during that age of colonial rule. This fruitful equation of sporting success and marketisation again became operative after a break of more than two decades when commercial concerns began to use individual players of the Calcutta League leaders Mohammedan Sporting Club and their potential Indian contender

---

[143] *The Pioneer*, 31 July 1911, p. 4.

[144] The *Hitabadi* (4 August 1911) remarked that 'betting has commenced in connection with football. It would be most sad if an innocent sport like football and the one that is mostly attended by boys and young men be converted into a subject of gambling. It is hoped that Government will attend to the matter.' *Report on Native Newspapers in Bengal* week concluding 5 and 12 August.

[145] Nandy, *Mohun Bagan 1911*, pp. 149–50 and Ghoshal, 'Calcutta's Frenetic Night', p. 205.

East Bengal Club for commercial advertisement.[146] The lull in commercial utilisation of football after 1911 can be easily explained in terms of the lack of success on the part of Bengali teams in open competitions. While the potential of sport's commercialisation, created by the 1911 victory, could not be fulfilled at that time, the victory may definitely be said to have set the trend. This trend of commercialisation of sport in the first half of 20th-century Bengal disproves the existing notion that commercialisation of sport started in India only in the 1980s. Moreover, it also challenges the conventional contours of the economic history of colonial India, which regard sport as unimportant from the perspective of economic history.

Racialism and Nationalism: The Changing Face of Bengali Football Culture

Football's appropriation for overtly nationalist purposes went hand in hand with an attempt to establish the credibility of the indigenous pursuit of the game against racist discrimination on the football field. While some British took the game to the locals, many others organised it so as to exclude them, using 'sport as a means of establishing "Indian" separateness or inferiority and of offering British-style strategies for improvement'.[147] However, the British did not ignore the sports field in their efforts to assert imperial control and racist discrimination and imposed over-arching constraints on the organisation and control of the game. This is in congruence with Brian Stoddart's cogent argument:

> Given the social significance and responsibility placed upon games, then, it follows that their introduction into the colonial system was a *natural development*. But it was not an uncontrolled development, because it also follows that the type of sports to be introduced would be *monitored closely* so that desirable rather than undesirable social characteristics would be engendered amongst the subject populations.[148]

---

[146] In 1939, the Indian Tea Market Expansion Board used Jumma Khan, a Mohammedan Sporting full back in a press advertisement for their product. The advertisement was published in *The Statesman*, 31 July 1939. Similarly, P. Chakraborty, an East Bengal player, was used by the same concern for an advertisement in 1948 in the inside page of Satya Kumar Roy's edited *Illustrated Olympic Number: Indian Footballers*, 1948. In fact, from the late 1930s Indian footballers often featured in commercial advertisements of the Indian Tea Expansion Board.

[147] Dimeo, 'Football and Politics in Bengal', pp. 61–66.

[148] Brian Stoddart, 'Sport, Cultural Imperialism and Colonial Response in the British Empire', *Comparative Studies in Society and History*, vol. 14, no. 3, Winter 1987, p. 656; emphasis added.

Since football's inception in Calcutta as an organised game, the British had owned, managed and dominated the game. Like other walks of socio-political life, they followed a systematic policy of discrimination against the Bengali clubs in sports. This practice began with the IFA, which from its foundation in 1892 was completely non-Indian. An Indian had been recruited as joint secretary at the turn of the century but he was nothing better than the European honorary secretary's 'personal clerk'.[149] The affiliated clubs were classified as European and Indian, the former enjoying predominance on the IFA Governing Body and in the Council. The Indian teams always felt cornered and suffered numerous disadvantages at the hands of the European majority in the first four decades. On the other hand, Bengali teams were allowed limited participation in the IFA Shield from its inception mainly to maintain its 'open' character in comparison to tournaments such as the Durand Cup (Simla) and the Rovers Cup (Bombay) that remained totally confined to, and dominated by British Regimental teams until the mid-1920s. Membership of the IFA League from its start (1898) was denied to Bengali clubs and the same was true of the Second Division, which was added to the League in 1904.

The Calcutta Football League remained a more or less 'white' competition until 1914 when only two Bengali teams were allowed to join. Even in the so-called open IFA Shield tournament, Bengali teams other than Sovabazar had a very restricted entry. The Maharaja of Coochbehar, Raja Rajendranarayan Bhup Bahadur, aggrieved over the proscription of Indian teams, organised an open football tournament called the Coochbehar Cup.[150] Besides a few open tournaments, apartheid was planned through institution of separate tournaments. At college level, the British introduced two tournaments — the Cadet Cup for European and Anglo-Indian students and the Elliot Shield for Indian students.

It was Mohun Bagan who reacted to this repressive sporting imperialism in great style. The injured self-esteem of Bengali club officials, players and spectators found ready expression in the determined struggle of Mohun Bagan against European sides on the football field. It is important to note that Mohun Bagan's entry into the IFA Shield was unbelievably hard earned. The real force of European discrimination against the Bengali teams commenced after the shock-victory of Mohun Bagan.

---

[149] RB, 'Indian Football before and after Independence'.

[150] From the beginning, this tournament drew enthusiastic participation from native teams such as Town Club, Sovabazar, National Association, Fort William Arsenal, Mohun Bagan, and Mohammedan Sporting.

Surprisingly, this series of discriminations in the aftermath of the Mohun Bagan victory mostly go unnoticed in the writings of Mason and Dimeo.[151]

In the aftermath of the 1911 victory, as we follow the native vernacular press reports, such discrimination became appalling. The two decades following 1911 are replete with examples of either the white referee's partisan conduct or the IFA's unjust policy or the European team's highhanded attitude leading to obvious suffering of the Bengali sides.[152] In the 1912 competition, the European referee of Mohun Bagan's first round match against Calcutta Football Club (CFC) disqualified two genuine Bagan goals on the grounds of off-side.[153] In 1922 one native vernacular newspaper expressed great alarm at the white referee's partiality during Mohun Bagan's League encounter against the Calcutta Football Club.[154] Such discrimination came to cross all proportions when in the IFA Shield final of 1923 Mohun Bagan was forced to play against the same European side on a slushy inundated unplayable surface only to lose by three goals to nil.[155] As Hiren Mukherjee, a renowned historian, recalled later: 'Just out of school, we had waited for victory which normally should have come but for over two days it rained — not cats and dogs but "lions and tigers" — and while all expected postponement of the fixture, the powers that be (mainly British) decided, on the report, expectedly, of the referee R.R. Clayton, enormously competent but unashamedly partisan, that the slushy, still inundated ground, was fit for football.'[156] No doubt Mohun Bagan had to bear the most frequent brunt of British apathy on the football field. However, it is not that Mohun Bagan remained the singular victim of

---

[151] Mason, 'Football on the Maidan'; Dimeo, 'Football and Politics in Bengal'.

[152] For a fuller discussion of the prominent examples of such racist discrimination, see Kausik Bandyopadhyay, '1911 in Retrospect: A Revisionist Perspective on a Famous Sporting Victory', *International Journal of the History of Sport*, vol. 21, no. 3–4, 2004, pp. 369–72.

[153] This match was of particular interest because it was the first football match in India of which motion pictures had been taken by the famous pioneers of the film industry in India, Messrs J. F. Madan & Co. merely as a cinematic interest. It may be noted here that one or two Mohun Bagan goals that had been disallowed on the plea of offside were, according to the film, when projected on the screen, found not to be so. *MB Souvenir*, p. 29.

[154] *Ananda Bazar Patrika*, 18 May 1922.

[155] *Ananda Bazar Patrika*, 31 July 1923. Also see Hirendranath Mukhopadhyay, *Nirbachita Probondho*, Kolkata: Mitra & Ghosh, 1998, p. 200.

[156] Hiren Mukherjee, 'Playing for Freedom', *The Statesman*, 9 August 1997.

British discrimination those days. Other Bengali sides including Kumartuli or Aryan too suffered the same fate at times.

The Bengalis firmly believed that biased refereeing was to frequently blame for defeats. Bengali views about the football injustices in the 1920s and 1930s are made explicit in Achintya Kumar Sengupta's autobiographical *Kallol Yug*:

> In those days, it was a monopoly of the British to be referees and obdurate referees repeatedly caused trouble for Mohun Bagan. An indisputable goal by Mohun Bagan — and the whistle blows for an offside. The CFC is guilty of a foul — it is ignored or blamed on Mohun Bagan. When there is no other way to undermine Mohun Bagan, like a bolt from the blue, without a warning, comes a penalty charge.[157]

A concession was made to the Bengali teams in 1914 allowing participation in the Second Division League to two teams, Mohun Bagan and Aryan. It was, however, also ruled that even if promotion were won, not more than two native sides would be accommodated in the First Division League. Mohun Bagan earned a promotion in 1915 and Aryan next year. But when Kumartuli qualified for the First Division for the next three years and in 1919 as the first Indian team to win a League championship, the First Division was barred to them each time. Kumartuli's enthusiasm remained high until the following year when they reached the IFA Shield final. However, they proved ultimate victims of racial discrimination. Kumartuli, which could have become a notable team in Calcutta soccer, in consequence, remained only a junior team.

Many among the Bengalis attributed the white referees' partisanship to their overtly racist anti-Indian attitude.[158] Achintya Kumar Sengupta's eyewitness account succinctly sums up the matter:

> In those days, Bengali people whose eye witnessed gross injustice against Mohun Bagan on Calcutta maidan could not help become furiously anti-British both in blood and word. And this fire of blood and word sharpened the edge of determination to fight for freedom. . . . A player beating a referee is no doubt a grievous offence. But Balai Chatterjee slapping Clayton on the Dalhousie ground out of sheer disgust remains a memorable history for all.[159]

---

[157] Sengupta, *Kallol Yug*, pp. 66–67; translation mine.

[158] Mukherjee, *Nirbachita Probondho*, vol. 1, p. 200.

[159] Sengupta, *Kallol Yug*, pp. 66–67; translation mine.

The kind of 'hit back' Sengupta hinted at was also a weapon, albeit non-violent, for both Bengali footballers as well as spectators to give a befitting reply to British discrimination both in social life and on the football field. As Sengupta connects the two plausibly, 'There is no exaggeration to say that it was Mohun Bagan's battle on the football field that incited Bengali nationalism. It provided the much-needed match-tick to flame the powder barrel of anti-British Bengali sentiments'.[160] He, however, sounds too radical when he asserts that the 'terrorism' that grew out of helplessness of the oppressed 'perhaps first raised its head on the football field'.[161]

Amidst soccer's cultural growth as a nationalist tool, evidence of limited intellectual opposition to it is on record. In the mid-1920s the *Amrita Bazar Patrika* published a series of articles urging the government to give full play to the revitalisation of the Bengali's physical prowess. This move aroused a new-found interest in indigenous games in certain circles. The way modern games like football displaced all other indigenous games from their position of popularity was a cause of some concern to a few conservative nationalists. An example of such sentiment could be found in Pramatha Nath Basu's espousal of cultural and political Swaraj:

> There are various sporting clubs among school boys in our town. They send the hat round for subscriptions and donations which one seldom has the heart to refuse. On the last occasion, however, I had the hardihood to smother my feelings and held the following conversation with the boy who came round on such an errand.
>
> Q. Do you know of indigenous outdoor games which without entailing any expense give as good exercise and afford as much amusement as tennis, cricket, football &c.?
> A. I have heard of such games, but never played any.
> Q. Are you aware that a large number of your fellow students are too poor to afford sufficient nourishing food?
> A. That is true.
> Q. Are not then the costly sports of richer communities a luxury to us?
> A. They are.
> Q. Is it consistent with one's self-respect that he should beg for luxuries? And might not the money spent upon them be more advantageously devoted to wholesome nourishing food?
> A. It might.
> Q. Why do you not then take to the inexpensive native out-door games?

---

[160] *Ibid.*, p. 66.
[161] *Ibid.*

A. Because they have gone out of fashion, and European sports are encouraged by the heads of our schools.

The heads being Europeans or Europeanised Indians naturally encourage the sports they have been used to. I told the boy, that if he and his associates went in for Indian games, I would be very pleased to give them a good feed. I do not know whether he took this as a joke. Any how, this was more than a year ago, and I have not yet heard that any party of schoolboys has gone back to native games as yet in this town.[162]

Lady Picketers on the Maidan: Football and Nationalist Politics in Colonial Bengal

The relationship between football and nationalist politics in late colonial Bengal, however, requires greater attention. It may be stated on the basis of available sources that the Bengali footballing community was always responsive to the call of the nationalist movement. For example, during the intense political awakening in the wake of the Civil Disobedience movement of 1929–31, the Calcutta football maidan could not remain indifferent.[163]

Direct expressions of nationalism were discernable at the maidan when the Football League had to be abandoned due to the political boycott of lady picketers on 24 May 1930.[164] The *Amrita Bazar Patrika* wrote:

---

[162] Basu, *Swaraj — Cultural and Political*, pp. 222–24.

[163] Major historical studies on the first Civil Disobedience Movement in India include C. V. H. Rao, *Civil Disobedience Movement in India: Or, The Indian Struggle for Freedom*, Lion Press, 1946; D. G. Tendulkar, *Mahatma: Life of Mohandas Karamchand Gandhi*, Delhi: Ministry of Information and Broadcasting, Government of India, 1960; Judith M. Brown, *Gandhi and Civil Disobedience: The Mahatma in Indian Politics*, Cambridge: Cambridge University Press, 1977; Christopher Baker, 'Gandhi and Civil Disobedience: The Mahatma in Indian Politics 1928–34', *Modern Asian Studies*, vol. 11, no. 3, 1977, pp. 469–73; Sumit Sarkar, 'The Logic of Gandhian Nationalism: Civil Disobedience and the Gandhi-Irwin Pact, 1930–31', *Indian Historical Review*, vol. 3, July 1976; Irfan Habib, 'Civil Disobedience, 1930–31', *Social Scientist*, vol. 25, nos 9–10, September–October 1997, pp. 43–66. For civil disobedience in Bengal, see Leonard Gordon, *Bengal: The Nationalist Movement, 1876–1940*, New York: Columbia University Press, 1974.

[164] *Amrita Bazar Patrika*, 25 May 1930, p. 3. This was in striking contrast to the Swadeshi Movement (1905–8) and the Non-cooperation Movement (1920–21) in Bengal, when football, instead of being boycotted by the nationalist Bengalis, was looked upon as a nationalist weapon to contest the British on the sports field.

> For the first time in the annals of Calcutta Football, games had to be abandoned on Saturday last owing to lady picketers making their appearance at club tents.
>
> The Mohun Bagan tent was practically besieged by the picketers from the Nari Satyagraha Samiti who numbered about fifty.
>
> They blocked all entrances to the club enclosures and filled in the tent itself including the dressing room.
>
> The picketers arrived in motor cars and buses as early as 4.30 P.M. The party comprised of principally Guzerati and Bengali ladies who appealed to club officials and players to abandon the games in view of the present situation of the country. The picketers stayed at the maidan till 6-15 P.M. — till the time for a start was practically over.[165]

Rumours that women picketers would attempt to interfere with football had been current since the arrest of Mrs Sarojini Naidu, and her conviction persuaded the Bengal Congress Provincial Committee to put their intentions into effect.[166] As *The Statesman* noted:

> The league match between Calcutta F.C. and Mohun Bagan — undoubtedly the most popular game of the season — had been fixed for the C.F.C. ground.... The Indian section, which usually gathers between 10,000 and 12,000 at its game, was smaller than usual in consequence of propaganda during the day.
>
> The Calcutta team was ready for the game but the Indian side did not turn up. Meanwhile, an unusual scene was being enacted at Mohun Bagan tent close by, for a crowd of several dozen Bengali ladies, shepherded by Congress volunteers, practically invaded the tent.[167]

It was also noted that the women picketers, being ladies of respectable families, gently persuaded the members of the Mohun Bagan club not to play.[168] A cyclostyled appeal bearing the signature of the secretary of the Bengal Provincial Congress Committee was posted on the walls of the Mohun Bagan enclosure and freely circulated to the crowd. It stated that 'as the "war" of independence was in progress and as their "leaders" Mahatma Gandhi, ... Jawaharlal Nehru, Mrs. Sarojini Naidu, Subhas Chandra Bose and J.M. Sengupta were in the hands of the enemy',

---

[165] *Ibid.*
[166] *The Statesman*, 25 May, p. 11.
[167] *Ibid.*
[168] *Ibid.*

they appealed to all Indians to forsake all sports and take up the cause of their country.[169] So the sports field was also taken into the fold of non-cooperation espoused by the Civil Disobedience Movement. This *exclusivist* non-cooperation was thus a departure from the process of *inclusive* appropriation of football in Bengal till the 1920s.

The lady picketers had been successful in stopping all the games fixed on the day at the maidan. On the Dalhousie ground where the home team were to meet the Aryans, 'a similar disappointment awaited a large crowd of Europeans and a few Indians'.[170] The ladies had picketed the Presidency College tent, used by the Aryans, very effectively, and the Aryans consented not to play. Other important matches including East Bengal vs Bhowanipur, Mohammedan Sporting vs Loyal Regiment 'B' and Camerons 'B' vs Headquarters of the Loyal Regiment were all abandoned due to crowd invasion.[171] An official of one of the leading Indian clubs said he hoped that 'by the next week the present feeling would pass away but he thought that the situation would only improve if the political situation improved'.[172] However, taking careful note of the situation, the Indian Football Association convened a special meeting and postponed all the League matches for the time being.[173] Meanwhile, encouraged by the political stance of the Bengali sporting clubs, other Indian clubs like Chinsurah Town Club, the Sporting Club and the Central A.C. decided to suspend their games in view of the 'present political situation'.[174] They also proposed to abandon the Football League for that season. Finally, on 31 May 1930, at a special meeting of the Calcutta Football League Committee, the Indian clubs unanimously resolved to withdraw from playing their League fixtures for the season, 'without affecting their respecting positions in the Leagues'.[175] The decision came after the negotiation of the Indian football club officials with the members of the Nari Satyagraha Samiti. The Indian football clubs were eager to continue football provided there be no picketing, and they were strongly against playing the League games under police protection. They stated that they 'would withdraw should their participation bring about any riot in which

---

[169] *Ibid.*

[170] *Ibid.*

[171] *Ibid.* See also *Amrita Bazar Patrika*, 25 May 1930, p. 11.

[172] *The Statesman*, 25 May, p.11

[173] *Amrita Bazar Patrika*, 27 May 1930, p. 3.

[174] *Amrita Bazar Patrika*, 29 May 1930, p. 3.

[175] *Amrita Bazar Patrika*, 1 June 1930.

the obstructionists, male or female, might be involved'.[176] This proved that the Indian football clubs in Bengal were even ready to abandon the pursuit of sport in situations of *national* crisis.

The European quarter of the city condemned the action of the picketers for linking sporting activity to political movement. *The Statesman* clearly reflected this sentiment:

> A Statesman reporter was told yesterday that every effort is being made to come to a settlement with those who are organizing the picketing movement. As a body footballers are very anxious to resume at once. The reporter was told that there are *other ways of serving their country* than by putting a stop to the *healthy recreation* which they have enjoyed with Europeans for so many years.[177]

The Indian clubs thought of sending another representation to the members of Nari Satyagraha Samiti for resolving the crisis. But, meanwhile, the political situation of the country took a new turn with the government's press announcement of fresh ordinances on picketing. In such circumstances, the Indian club members became unanimously resolved that 'the exigencies of the political situation in the country, particularly after the promulgation of the Ordinance on picketing, were all against the continuance of league football by Indian teams'.[178]

The participation of women was nothing new in the contemporary national movement of early 20th-century India.[179] Women had begun to take an active interest in the national movement as well as nationalist politics since the Swadeshi movement of 1905–8. By the time civil disobedience became the exhortation in 1930, particularly in Bengal,

---

[176] *Ibid.*

[177] *The Statesman*, 28 May 1930, p. 11; emphasis added.

[178] *Amrita Bazar Patrika*, 1 June 1930.

[179] For considerations of women's role in Indian nationalist movement, see: Suruchi Thapar-Bjorkert, *Women in the Indian National Movement: Unseen Faces and Unheard Voices, 1930–42*, paperback edition, New Delhi: Sage, 2006; Radha Krishna Sharma, *Nationalism, Social Reform and Indian Women: A Study of the Interaction between Our National Movement and the Movement of Social Reform among Indian Women, 1921–1937*, Delhi: Janaki Prakashan, 1981; Anup Taneja, *Gandhi, Women, and the National Movement, 1920–47*, New Delhi: Har Anand, 2005; Geraldine Forbes, *Women in Modern India*, paperback edition, Cambridge: Cambridge University Press, 1998, pp. 121–56. For an interesting treatment of women in the nationalist movement in Bengal, see Niranjan Ghosh, *Role of Women in the Freedom Movement in Bengal, 1919–47: Midnapore*, Kolkata: Firma KLM, 1988.

Sarojini Naidu became a charismatic figure inspiring a new voice among Bengali women. It was in such a context that women picketers stopped football-play in Calcutta as a mark of protest against the arrest of their leader Sarojini Naidu. It is interesting to note that even on the sports field, an arena completely dominated by men in the colonial period, male nationalist leaders of Bengal thought it wise to allow the female members of the Nari Satyagraha Samiti to stage the picketing.[180] However, this decision could also have been prompted by an apprehension that male protesters would have to face police wrath, and therefore, the object of peaceful satyagraha would have been defeated.[181] Yet this singular event of women's protest on the football field, which definitely had an element of sensation and drama, should be regarded as an important landmark in the history of sporting nationalism in India.

In 1935, Mohun Bagan, led by Gostho Paul, waged a unique satyagraha on the field by 'throwing untypical tantrums and inviting goals' during the course of a League match to protest against the deliberate partiality of the European referee, which was seen as a political stance.[182] *The Statesman*, in its usual style, reported the incident in the following way:

> Mohun Bagan discredited a very fine record yesterday, when, as a protest against the rulings of the referee, C.Q.M.S. Manzie (Black Watch), they made a farce of the last ten minutes of their Football League match against Calcutta F.C. on the Calcutta Club's ground.
>
> In the opinion of Paul, Mohun Bagan's full back and a former captain of the side, Calcutta's third goal was scored by a man in an offside position. Taking their lead from Paul, Mohun Bagan, for the remaining ten minutes of the game, strolled about the field or rested on the ground, making no attempt to play football.

---

[180] Interestingly enough, the late 1920s and early 1930s constituted the very period which witnessed a growing antipathy and hostility towards women's soccer in Bengal. Braja Ranjan Ray, a journalist with the *Ananda Bazar Patrika*, noted this trend in his unpublished manuscript 'Banglay Krida Sangbadikatar Adiparba' (Early Phase of Sports Journalism in Bengal). For details, see Majumdar and Bandyopadhyay, *Goalless*, pp. 182–85.

[181] Satyagraha was a unique means of political passive resistance propagated and employed successfully by Gandhi first in South Africa and later in India. Literally meaning the 'force of truth', it implied, in Gandhian terms, a non-violent non-cooperation involving peaceful violation of specific laws.

[182] *Amrita Bazar Patrika*, 12 May 1935.

Twice the ball was handled in a most deliberate manner in the penalty area. Paul going so far as to catch it above his head with both hands, with the consequence that Calcutta won by six goals to *nil*.

This was extraordinary behaviour in a man who has played in Calcutta football for the past twenty years and who had earned a reputation, forfeited by a reckless impulse, as one of the leading sportsmen among the Indian footballers. [183]

It also noted the European reaction to the incident: 'The spectators on the Calcutta members' stands expressed their disapproval of Mohun Bagan's "satyagraha" tactics by hooting deliberate infringements and by loudly applauding their own team when they walked in at the end of the match.'[184]

The League Committee, heavily dominated by the members of the European clubs, too defended the referee and exonerated him of any partiality. H. N. Nicholas, vice-president of the IFA and president of the Calcutta Referees Association even went so far as to put the onus on native teams: 'But the trouble is that players will not play to the whistle and the supporters of the Club hoot and jeer at the referees, with the result that it is hopeless to expect the referees to give of their best, and unless we do something to remedy this state of affairs we shall have trouble always.'[185] However, it seems quite clear from the media reports that Gostha Paul, the legendary Mohun Bagan player, became so aggrieved over the issue of the white referee's bias and partiality that he found no other alternative but to wage such a unique satyagraha on the ground along with his fellow teammates. It thus transpires from this incident that, in the tense political situation during the Civil Disobedience Movement, sporting grievances merged with nationalist grievances.

Appropriating the Game: Nationalism, Subversion and Resistance

In summary, football in late colonial Bengal came to be looked upon as an apolitical avenue for expression of the colonised against the colonialist.

---

[183] The report went with the byline 'Mohun Bagan Spoil Good Football Record: "Satyagraha" on C.F.C. Ground — Indian Team's Protest Against Referee's Rulings'; *The Statesman*, 12 May 1935.

[184] *Ibid*.

[185] *The Statesman*, 13 May 1935.

It leapt from its sporting boundaries to become a cultural weapon to fight the imperialist. Playing and watching the game cut across the affiliations of indigenous caste, class or community in Bengali society and provided a social bond for the nationalist-minded Bengalis. Football as a cultural weapon to fight and defeat the British added a new dimension to the anti-British national consciousness of the Indians, particularly in Bengal. Thus, parallel to the political struggle against an oppressive colonial power, there began a social struggle of national liberation over a specific cultural component. The success of Bengali footballers playing for an Indian team against a European team representative of the colonial rulers led to a nationalisation of their mind. In that context, the football maidan as a national cultural territory began to reflect a Bengali alias Indian nationalist impulse that found heroic expression in the efforts of the footballers.

In the aftermath of the Mohun Bagan success, football as an outlet for aggression gradually came to reflect the 'pent-up nationalism' of Bengali professionals and students. A large section of the Bengali community were affluent, educated, practical and decent, but were hesitant to actively take part in the freedom struggle. They considered the football field an ideal place to confront the British. Similarly, the political events of the first decade of the 20th century had a stirring effect on the Bengali youth. Nevertheless, many of them were reluctant to participate in the politics of direct confrontation. Hence football came to be a potent nationalist gesture and beating the British produced a sort of immense emotional satisfaction for them. The urban and suburban middle-class Bengalis, who served the British as officials, clerks or professionals, and could not show their anti-British resentment in public, and the working-class people, who were not drawn into the fold of nationalist politics until the late 1920s, could express their nationalism freely only at the maidan. The 'pent-up' nationalism of the Bengali middle and working classes thus found prolific expression through emotional outbursts during playing or watching a match when a Bengali team got the better of a British side. Moreover, on the football field it was considered to be an act of great courage to shove an elbow or a fist into the face of a Sahib or a soldier, or kick him under the guise of tackling. Those who could get away with it were respected as great players.[186] Footballers like Gostho Paul, Abhilash Ghosh and Balai Chatterjee earned glamour and fame in Bengali society for their reputation to execute successfully this 'reverse hit' or *palta mar*. In sporting

---

[186] Nandy, 'Football and Nationalism', p. 245.

encounters, it is also said, some Bengali spectators would deliberately pick up quarrels with the 'superior' British. Sometimes these encounters would turn violent and afford the Bengalis the opportunity of giving the *gora* Sahibs a 'sound beating'.[187]

Thus, what the nationalist politicians and native representatives in the British Indian administration could not do, the footballers were expected to do. They were required to be ideal cultural nationalists and in this role, 'freedom fighters', who would get the success that eluded others in politics and economy, the more crucial spheres of national life. Football heroes like the Bhaduris and Abhilash Ghosh, became, for the common Bengalis, the ultimate remedy for all failures — moral, economic and political — of the country.[188] If India, according to these sporting Bengalis, was constantly losing to its imperial rulers in politics and economics, football was to ameliorate the nation's feelings of inefficacy and emasculation.[189]

John Plamenatz, in one of his most influential yet less celebrated articles, has considered nationalism as 'primarily a cultural phenomenon'.[190] In his discussion of the two types of nationalism, 'Western' and 'Eastern', Plamenatz stresses the importance of a common set of standards to measure the state of development of a particular national culture. For him, as for Benedict Anderson, it was the West that provided this common set of standards to the Eastern nations.[191] However, he finds an inherent contradiction in the attempt of the 'Eastern' type of nationalism to 're-equip' the nation culturally for transforming it. As he goes on to suggest: 'It is both imitative and hostile to the models it imitates . . .' Partha Chatterjee clarifies the first projection neatly: 'It is imitative in that it accepts the value of the standards set by the alien culture.'[192] But it is the

---

[187] *Ibid.*

[188] Sibdas Bhaduri and Abhilas Ghosh were the goal scorers for Mohun Bagan in the Shield final of 1911.

[189] I have taken this particular construction from Ashis Nandy, who elaborates on a similar role cricket might have played in late 20th-century India, though in a different context. See Nandy, *The Tao of Cricket*, Preface, p. xix.

[190] John Plamenatz, 'Two Types of Nationalism', in Eugene Kamenka (ed.), *Nationalism: The Nature and Evolution of an Idea*, London: Edward Arnold, 1976, pp. 23–36, quoted in Chatterjee, *Nationalist Thought and the Colonial World*, p. 1.

[191] Anderson, in his *Imagined Communities*, too, talks about a set of 'modular forms' provided by the historical experience of nationalism in the West and in Russia for the nationalist elites of Asia and Africa to choose and adopt.

[192] Chatterjee, *Nationalist Thought and the Colonial World*, p. 2.

hostility to that model involving two ambivalent rejections, which seems to attract larger attention: 'rejection of the alien intruder and dominator who is nevertheless to be imitated and surpassed by his own standards and rejection of ancestral ways which are seen as obstacles to progress and yet also cherished as marks of identity.'[193]

Plamenatz's conceptual model of 'Eastern' cultural nationalism is useful in understanding the character of footballing nationalism in late colonial Bengal. The football field provided a cultural space where the Bengali adopted the British game and then tried to beat the master at their own standard. This of course necessitated and in fact resulted in downplaying (if not complete rejection) of traditional Bengali sports while football was indigenised especially through an essentially Bengali style of play without wearing boots. For European scholars like Mason and Dimeo, Bengali/Indian victory over their colonial master on the football field was nothing but a success story of British cultural imperialism.[194] They read Indians' unwitting admiration for, acceptance of, and submission to such cultural imperialism in such football victories. Richard Cashman raised a pertinent question as to whether we can analyse the spread of colonial sports solely in terms of the ideology of colonialism and games ethic or not.[195] For him, the indigenous appropriation (domestication) of modern sport (cricket in his case) calls for more logical explanation.[196]

According to Cashman, there are two major differences of interpretation and approach in this regard.[197] First, there are those, Mangan, Mason and Dimeo in particular, who stress the power of football and its associated ideology to indoctrinate colonial subjects.[198] In the words of Cashman, 'because it was *wrapped up* in the garb of a compelling and fascinating game, it was a very powerful imperial weapon'.[199] However, for those who look

---

[193] Plamenatz, 'Two Types of Nationalism', quoted in Chatterjee, *Nationalist Thought and the Colonial World*, p. 2.

[194] Mason, 'Football on the Maidan', pp. 150–51; Dimeo, 'Football and Politics in Bengal', p. 71. For a most authoritative discussion of British cultural imperialism on the sports field, see Guttman, *Games and Empires*.

[195] Richard Cashman, 'Cricket and Colonialism: Colonial Hegemony and Indigenous Subversion', in Mangan (ed.), *Pleasure, Profit, Proselytism*, pp. 259–60.

[196] *Ibid*.

[197] *Ibid*.

[198] Mangan, however, has also pointed to the complex nature of indigenous responses to colonial purpose of using sport as an imperial tool.

[199] Cashman, 'Cricket and Colonialism', p. 259; emphasis added.

at football and colonialism more 'from below', or from the perspective of the recipients of the game's ideology, there are significant problems with the perspective which concentrates exclusively on the proselytiser. As Cashman brilliantly argued in the context of colonial Indian cricket:

> Where does the promoting hand of the colonial master stop and where does the adapting and assimilating indigenous tradition start? Is it merely adaptation and domestication or does it go beyond that to constitute resistance and even subversion? And how far can the colonial acceptance of cricket be seen as superior colonial salesmanship or a successful exercise of social control using the highly developed ideology of games and colonialism? Or was it that many colonial subjects chose to pursue a game, because of the ideology, or even in spite of it, because it suited them to take up cricket for their own reasons? Or was the ideology of colonialism the starting point for the adoption of cricket but once the game was launched other factors came to bear which led to its spread and consolidation?[200]

Cashman's conclusion, too, sounds historically cogent: 'while games are an effective vehicle for proselytisation in some circumstances, they can be subverted in others.'[201] The appropriation of football in colonial Bengal for nationalist purposes, as this chapter has shown, is definitely proof to a colonial reformulation of the imperial model of games ethic. It points to football's transformed role as an instrument of reaction, resistance and subversion.

A few European scholars like J. A. Mangan have hinted at the complexity of interpreting indigenous responses to imperial projects of games ethic. That Mangan is unsure of the reality and character of indigenous response is evident when he says: 'the legacy of the game in the region (Kashmir) hints at a more complex story once the game has been adapted and adopted by Indian groups.'[202] Boria Majumdar also has emphasised this potential of indigenisation and subversion of a colonial sport in course of time, and on its 'becoming' 'an area for the articulation of an indigenous brand of nationalism'.[203] He rightly remarks: 'Inverting the colonial ideology on its head, resistance and subversion were often dominant in the second phase of the histories of these games in the colonies.'[204]

---

[200] *Ibid.*, p. 261.
[201] *Ibid.*
[202] Mangan, 'Soccer as Moral Training', pp. 49, 54.
[203] Majumdar, 'The Vernacular in Sports History', p. 3071.
[204] *Ibid.*

In fact, what most of the European scholars miss out completely in analysing the relational complexities of football, imperialism and nationalism in colonial Bengal is the conscious indigenous attempt to overturn the imperial ideology to suit an overtly nationalist purpose of shattering the so-called British cultural/racial/masculine superiority. Nothing could provide greater satisfaction to the masses than the fact that the allegedly inferior natives would defeat the racially proud imperialists in direct physical/masculine confrontation. Ashis Nandy's analysis comes very close to deciphering the psychological underpinnings of this cultural nationalism in a colonised society. He talks about the victim's construction of the West, a West that would make sense to the non-West in terms of the non-West's experience of suffering. 'However jejune such a concept may seem to the sophisticated scholar', says Nandy, 'it is a reality for the millions who have learnt the hard way to live with the West during the last two centuries'.[205] This 'non-West' of Nandy constantly invites one to be Western and to defeat the West on the strength of one's acquired Westernness. Beating the West at its own game is the preferred means of handling the feelings of self-hatred in the modernised non-West.[206]

Thus footballing nationalism in colonial Bengal was not only a subversion of colonial games ethic or cultural imperialism. But, arguably, it informed a more serious subversion of colonial masculinity. And here also Nandy's construction about the psychology of the colonised for an entirely different context is succinctly applicable:[207]

> They (*Indian footballers and spectators*) sought to redeem the Indians' masculinity by defeating the British, often fighting against hopeless odds, to free the former once and for all from the historical memory of their own humiliating defeat in violent power-play and 'tough politics'. This gave a second-order legitimacy to what in the dominant culture of the colony had already become the final differentiae of manliness: aggression, achievement, control, competition and power.[208]

Nandy's construction, as applied to footballing nationalism in colonial Bengal, also resembles Cabral's earlier espousal of *culture* as a harbinger of protest:

---

[205] Ashis Nandy, *The Intimate Enemy: Loss and Recovery of Self under Colonialism*, Oxford: Oxford University Press, 1983, p. xiii.

[206] *Ibid*.

[207] Nandy specifically referred to 'many pre-Gandhian protest movements' in that context.

[208] Nandy, *The Intimate Enemy*, p. 9.

The study of the history of liberation struggles shows that in general, they are preceded by an increase in cultural phenomena which progressively crystallize into an attempt, successful or not, to assert the cultural personality of the oppressed people in an act of *rejection* of that of the oppressor. Whatever may be the state of subjection of a nation to foreign rule and the influence of economic, political, and social factors in the furtherance of this domination, it is generally in culture that the seeds of protest, leading to the emergence and development of the liberation movement, is found.[209]

The wider perspective into which anti-colonial nationalism around the masculine game of football needs to be contextualised concerns the processes by which the promotion, acceptance, and incorporation of the game occurred. As Brian Stoddart has rightly suggested:

> For the most part, however, the real power of sport did not come from being laid out formally by colonial masters to be studied by colonial subjects. Instead, it perhaps belonged more in the realm of what the Annales school of historiography has identified as *mentalites*, a set of beliefs acquired subconsciously.... It was largely this subconscious element, outside the bounds of formal policy making, which rendered sport so powerful a factor in the maintenance of and *reaction* to British control throughout the empire.[210]

Football in colonial Bengal certainly provided the ideal space for *reaction* to British control. This constituted one immediate problem for the imperial power. 'Having encouraged the measurement of social progress by comparing colonial against British achievements in sport, there would always come the day of a colonial victory that might be interpreted as symbolic of general parity.'[211] And when such colonial victory came at a time of intense political unrest, as it did happen in colonial Bengal, 'the victory was widely regarded as a sign of Indian development, equality, and even superiority'.[212]

---

[209] Cabral, 'National Liberation and Culture', p. 13; emphasis added. In case of football as a cultural instrument of national liberation in colonial Bengal, the rejection is conceived in terms of that of the so-called superiority of the oppressor alias the coloniser.

[210] Stoddart, 'Sport, Cultural Imperialism and Colonial Response in the British Empire', pp. 660–61. First emphasis in original, second emphasis added.

[211] *Ibid.*, p. 667.

[212] *Ibid.*

3

Communalism on the *Maidan*: Community and Identity in Bengali Football

That modern sports can be divisive despite their apparent integrative impact, that they can exacerbate conflict and jeopardise social structures, no one doubts. A new trend in Bengali football of the 1930s was soccer's burgeoning communal encounter which began to erode football's overwhelming status as an instrument of cultural nationalism. This trend can be meaningfully explained only in terms of the socio-political and economic life of Bengal in the 1930s. In the changed socio-political atmosphere of Bengal, the binary of Indian versus British in football came to acquire a new dimension: Hindus representing the *majority* versus Muslims representing the *minority*. The unhealthy clash between the Hindu bhadrolok-dominated Indian Football Association and the Mohammedan Sporting Club, representative of the Indian Muslim community, who began to suffer from a minority syndrome under the influence of representative political parties and personalities, often played a critical role in creating possibilities of communalisation of sport in the 1930s and 1940s. This chapter explores and analyses the key factors precipitating such communal conflict in Bengali football. It shows how this communal clout overshadowed Mohammedan Sporting Club's five straight Calcutta Football League titles between 1934 and 1938, with the result that Mohun Bagan Club's victory against East Yorkshire Regiment in the IFA Shield final in 1911 is still perceived as a much greater nationalistic triumph than Mohammedan's feat.

Representing Community in Football: Early History of the Mohammedan Sporting Club

Muslim representation in Calcutta football began in the last decade of the 19th century when Mohammedan Sporting Club gained in prominence thanks to the efforts of some Muslim individuals.¹ Mohammedan Sporting, established in 1891, was an institution of the progressive Muslims and was gradually carving out a niche in Calcutta's football scene. The initiative of some Muslim youths, both of Calcutta and the mofussil, who felt the need of the Muslim youth to have their own sporting club founded the Crescent Club in 1889.² It is, however, said that the club had its predecessor in the Jubilee Club founded in 1887 in Calcutta at the initiative of Khan Bahadur Aminul Islam, Maulavi Abdul Ghani of Malda and Maulavi Muhammad Yasin of Burdwan.³ In 1890, the club's name was changed again into Hamidia Club. In 1891, finally, the club came to be transformed into the Mohammedan Sporting Club. Nawab Syed Amir Hossain, the then Presidency magistrate and Nawab Nasirul Momaleque Mirza Sujat Ali Beg were elected president and vice president of the club respectively while Abdul Ghani and Nur Muhammad Ismail became respectively secretary and assistant secretary.⁴ Nawab Sujat Ali Beg gave the club a donation of ₹300 on behalf of Her Highness Samsuzzoha Begum of Murshidabad to start the 'Nawab Begum Football Cup' in her honour.⁵ A monthly subscription of ₹200 used to be collected at that time.

The first annual meeting of the club was held in 1894 under the presidentship of Justice Sir Syed Amir Ali at the Calcutta Madrasa premises. Abdus Salam, a retired BCS, delivered a lecture on the physical culture of the Mohammedan youths. This speech was later published in book form and was dedicated to Sir John Woodburn, the then lieutenant governor of Bengal.⁶ Shortly afterwards, a monthly journal called *Calcutta Monthly*, was started under the auspices of the members of the club as a club magazine. Leading Muslim gentlemen of Calcutta were regular contributors to

---

¹ The Jubilee Club was established in 1887, a sporting organisation for the Muslims in Calcutta. The club changed its name twice in the next few years, first to the Crescent Club and then to the Hamidia Club. Finally, in 1891, the latter culminated into the Mohammedan Sporting Club. *Mohammedan Sporting Club Records*, Mohammedan Sporting Club, Calcutta.

² 'History of the Club', *Mohammedan Sporting Club. Calcutta League Champions 1934–35. A Souvenir*, Calcutta: Mohammedan Sporting Club, 1935 (hereafter *MSP Souvenir*), pp. 27, 35–39.

³ Ritan, *Football*, p. 17. Also see Narayan Dasgupta, 'Kibhabe tinbar naam badle holo aajker Mohammedan' (How Today's Mohammedan Came into Being Changing its Name Thrice), *Khela*, 18 September 1998; Ajay Basu, 'Tumko lakho selam' (Salute you Million Times), *Desh*, 22 December 1990.

⁴ 'History of the Club', p. 27.

⁵ *Ibid*.

⁶ *Ibid*.

the magazine. The magazine, however, continued for only three years. The management of the club also started a reading room for Mohammedan students in Calcutta, which came to be known as the 'Diamond Jubilee Reading Room'.[7]

The Mohammedan Sporting Club had no playground of their own when the club was founded. However, at the insistence of its president Amir Hossain, the club obtained permission to play on the ground of the Calcutta Boys' School on each alternate day.[8] Subsequently, when the members of the club increased in number and other games were introduced into the club, three days in a week proved insufficient and the need for a regular ground was felt. Mr Lambert, the police commissioner, gave permission for the whole week while the Calcutta Boys' School was provided another plot of land as their playground.[9] In its early days, Mohammedan's greatest triumph was the winning of the Coochbehar Cup in 1909.

As the Annual Report of the club in 1928 noted, when S. A. Rashid and I. G. H. Arif took over charge of the club in 1924, they found the affairs of the club in a poor state.[10] There was only ₹9 to the credit of the club as a balance, while the outstanding bills of the different sports firms were not less than ₹3,600. There were 208 members on the roll but the majority of them were free and the monthly collections under the head of membership were never more than ₹25 or 30. The arrears of the servants' pay alone amounted to ₹460. Not to speak of other games, even football did not remain a matter of interest to most of the members. The club was not even represented on the major sports councils of Bengal including the IFA.[11]

In two years, however, working in excellent partnership, the joint secretaries succeeded in putting the state of things in good order. Most importantly, they put the club on a sound financial basis and effected a noticeable improvement in the club's interest and performance in all games. In 1927, the club came into prominence as it was promoted into the second division of the Calcutta Football League. Moreover, it came to be represented through S. A. Rashid on all sports bodies.[12] As for the attempt to redress the financial bankruptcy of the club, an annexure to

---

[7] *Ibid.*
[8] *Ibid.*
[9] *Ibid.*
[10] *Annual Report*, Mohammedan Sporting Club, 1928.
[11] *Ibid.*
[12] *Ibid.*

the Annual Report of 1928 mentions that the joint secretaries of the club made an appeal to all concerned 'to support a scheme of the club, *extending its activities in the social sphere for Muslims*'.[13] They also requested 'for donations amounting to ₹3500 to ₹4000'.[14] Although the response to this appeal was not sufficient enough to give effect to the scheme for that time being, the financial assistance that ultimately came through helped the club to retrieve itself from its sinking financial position.[15]

It would be a mistake to argue that the club reflected communal overtones from its inception. But that it was anti-Congress even in the mid-1890s has been a reality. The object of *Calcutta Monthly*, started in 1896 under the auspices of the club, was 'to discuss and ventilate literary, scientific, educational, social, moral, sporting and other cognate subjects of interest'.[16] Reacting to criticism by a Muslim Congress leader of the hostile Muslim attitude towards the Congress, the *Calcutta Monthly* in its editorial of December 1896 wrote:[17]

> We wish we could induce Mr. Sayani to live for sometime in Bengal and see with his own eyes how Mohammedans fare at the hands of their Hindu friends in every matter . . . and when he shall have done that, we have no doubt in our mind that he will pause thrice before committing himself to the espousal of a cause, the success of which will mean the gradual, but inevitable, extinction of his co-religionists as a political unit in India.[18]

---

[13] Emphasis added.

[14] *Ibid.*

[15] *Ibid.* Also see, Dasgupta, 'Kibhabe tinbar naam badle holo aajker Mohammedan', p. 26.

[16] *Calcutta Monthly*, July 1896.

[17] Even years after the establishment of the Indian National Congress, the majority of the Muslim community had not changed their attitude towards the national movement. In 1896 Rahmatullah Sayani of Bombay presided over the Congress session held at Calcutta. Sayani was a leading Muslim from Bombay; honorary magistrate; president of the Municipal Corporation; and member of the Legislative Council of Bombay. In his presidential speech, he criticised the hostile attitude of the Muslim community towards the Congress and urged that 'the Mussalmans, however, instead of raising puerile and imagery objections from a distance, should attend Congress meetings and see for themselves what is going on in such meetings'. His speech provoked protests from the Bengali Muslims. For Sayani's speech, see *Report of the Indian National Congress*, 1896, pp. 1–39, especially p. 24. Also see Sufia Ahmad, *Muslim Community in Bengal: 1884–1912*, Dacca: Asiatic Press, 1974, pp. 191–92.

[18] *Calcutta Monthly*, December 1896.

Even with this generally anti-Congress tilt, the club showed, despite its apparent failure as a good football outfit, its sporting spirit in the truest appreciation of the game since its inception. In the aftermath of Mohun Bagan's Shield victory, the members of the club, wrote *The Mussalman*, 'were almost mad and rolling on the ground with joyous excitement on the victory of their Hindu brethren'.[19] Another Muslim journal, *The Comrade*, of which Maulana Mohammed Ali was the founder and editor at that time, said: 'We hereby join the chorus of praise and jubilation over the splendid victory of Mohun Bagan. The team did remarkably well throughout the tournament and won the Shield by sheer merit.'[20] Such reports were of course in tune with the general trend of the Muslim journals till the late 1920s, which speak more of amity than of conflict amongst the two communities. Recounting Mohun Bagan's status as a team beloved to both the communities, Achintya Kumar Sengupta wrote:

> Till then communalism had not entered the sports-field. Mohun Bagan then belonged to both the Hindus and the Muslims. The green galleries that burnt in the football stadium of the Calcutta that day carried the mark of both Hindu and Muslim hands. One brought the petrol and the other the matches.[21]

Revival and Success of the Mohammedan Sporting Club

Until 1934, the year that marked the beginning of Mohammedan Sporting Club's glorious League victories, five in a row, Calcutta football remained more or less free from any communal overtones. It was, however, quite unfortunate that the Bengalis' anti-British footballing identity came to be fractured from the mid-1930s on communal lines.

It was only natural, however, for the Muslim community to find in Mohammedan Sporting a club that they could really call their own, when it emerged as a powerful team in Calcutta football in the early 1930s. Although the achievements of Mohammedan Sporting Club were Indian success stories, the Hindu football-lovers felt only a mixture of respect and fear and no sensation of joy at all.[22] The Muslim League, by then a force

---

[19] Quoted in *Mohun Bagan Club Platinum Jubilee Souvenir*, Calcutta: Mohun Bagan Club, 1964, p. 25.

[20] *Ibid.*

[21] Sengupta, *Kallol Yug*, p. 66, translation mine.

[22] Comments of Muhammad Nasiruddin, the editor of *Saugat*, a periodical published from Dacca, quoted in Ritan, *Football*, p. 21.

hostile to the Congress, was also the ruling party in Bengal and had the support of the British. Even the Muslim nationalists held the Congress flag in one hand and the black-and-white banner of Mohammedan Sporting in the other, while the Muslim League itself used the club as an obvious example of Muslim superiority in Bengal. This was certainly a definitive indication of the club's growing popularity in Bengal. Actually, from the second half of the 1930s, rivalry in Bengali football was no longer confined to the British versus the Indians, but had extended to include the Hindus versus the Muslims, adding definite communal overtones to sport. This new trend in Bengali football, however, needs to be understood in the changed socio-political scenario in Bengal from the middle of the 1930s.[23]

It was in the year 1932 that 'a group of young, energetic, patriotic and progressive men' in Calcutta formed the New Muslim Majlis.[24] The spearhead of this drive was Khwaja Nooruddin, cousin and brother-in-law of Khwaja Nazimuddin, who later played a heroic part in making the Mohammedan Sporting Club a premier football club. One of the main and immediate aims of the Majlis was to capture the Mohammedan Sporting Club and to develop it into the nation's premier club. The socio-political successes of the Majlis went hand in hand with the success on the football field achieved by the Mohammedan Sporting Club for which Khwaja Nooruddin deserves laurels. It was he who, as the secretary general of the club, brought to life a dying organisation and made football history not only in Bengal but in the rest of India. A. K. Aziz, secretary of the club in 1932–33 recorded:

> The season was the most successful in every sense. For the first time in the history of our club we could fulfill our long cherished desire to earn the right of playing in the first division of the Calcutta Football League. Though we started the season rather tamely we finished it brilliantly, winning the last eight matches consecutively.[25]

When the club went on to win the First Division League on its first appearance, the repercussions were overwhelming. The club souvenir published in 1935 noted:

---

[23] For details on this, see Shila Sen, *Muslim Politics in Bengal*, New Delhi: Impex India, 1976.

[24] M. A. H. Ispahani, *Qaid-E-Azam Jinnah — As I Knew Him*, Karachi: Forward Publications Trust, 1966, p. 4; Kenneth Mcpherson, *The Muslim Microcosm: Calcutta, 1918–1935*, Wiesbaden: Franz Steiner Verlag, 1974, p. 121.

[25] *Annual Report, 1932–33*, Mohammedan Sporting Club.

In the 44th year of its existence we find the club not only makes its own history but history in Indian Football by winning the championship of the Calcutta Football League. When the Calcutta League, 1934, opened, the Mohammedan Sporting team were styled as the babes of the League owing to their promotion from the second division. From babes through the evolution of victory after victory and holding the top place on the League table they became the giants of the League and earned the coveted and unique distinction of being the first Indian team to win the League.[26]

The club souvenir also pointed to enormous enthusiasm that the victory brought in its wake:

> With their progress in the League there was unbounded enthusiasm among the Muslim public of Calcutta and the team were responsible for increasing the gates at whichever match they played fourfold. But not only in Calcutta was this enthusiasm manifested. In the mofussil, thousands followed each game with the greatest of interest, so much so that many used to walk miles to the railway station to meet incoming trains with Calcutta newspapers in order to get the results as soon as possible.
>
> After their victory, the team was lionized in the city of Calcutta and it was not for some weeks after that they could call an evening their own without having to attend some function in their honour. They were given a civic reception at the Town Hall when an address was presented to them by the Mayor of Calcutta.[27]

Though the year 1934 was one of great success for the club, the financial position of the club since 1931 had not been satisfactory despite contributions of, and advances made by a few people including Qazi Ashraf Ali, the financial secretary of the club. As the records of 1934 declared:

> As there had been signs of dissatisfaction shown by the public at the past management of the club and as rumours were in circulation owing to party feeling in the club the present Executive Committee decided to do their best themselves and not to go to the public for donations unless they could prove to the public that with all their difficulties they could set their house in order. Thanks are due to Mr. Zakaria, Mr. N. Anis, Mr. Qazi Ashraf Ali, Khan Sahib Rashid, Maulavi Gafur, members of the Committee who advanced large sums of money and saved an awkward situation.[28]

---

[26] 'History of the Club', p. 36.
[27] *Ibid.*
[28] *Ibid.*

S. A. Rashid took upon himself to enlist prominent Muslims as life members and in such ways obtained the support of many to relieve the club of its financial difficulties. These first life members included Sir Nazimuddin, KCIE; Khan Bahadur Azizul Haque, minister for education; I. G. H. Arif, bar-at-law; and K. Sudderuddin. His Excellency John Anderson, governor of Bengal, became the patron of the club.[29] The club also built an iron-fencing around the club pavilion with the permission of A. D. Gordon, commissioner of police, and the financial assistance of Muslim merchants of Chandni, Calcutta.[30]

Another step towards stability of the club was the establishment of a Board of Trustees to find ways and means of raising funds for the club. Many eminent Muslims agreed to serve on the Board. This was in accordance with the declaration made by the club souvenir in 1935:

> While the club is today on a very business-like footing, it is by no means clear of financial anxiety and it is surely up to the Muslims, who are today so proud of the achievement of the club team in football, to come forward and support their club in a greater measure. Funds are the mainstay of any club and brilliant and excellent performances on the field of play are prone to have a serious setback if the club is unable to maintain itself and is hampered with financial difficulties.[31]

In 1935 when Mohammedan Sporting won the League for the second consecutive time, it was deemed to be a great achievement by the Calcutta Muslims. The club souvenir thus recorded the immediate reaction to the victory:

> Tumultuous scenes were witnessed on the Calcutta ground after the match. The joy of the crowd was unbounded and each of the players was carried shoulder high while their bus was escorted in triumphant procession by thousands of Mohammedans wild with joy.[32]

One major factor precipitating Mohammedan Sporting Club's revival and success was the socially and financially influential base of its patronage in terms of members and players in the 1930s. The most important names in this regard were: Khwaja Sir Nazimuddin, ex-minister of education of Bengal; Sir Syed Sadullah, an ex-finance member of the Assam

---

[29] *Ibid.*
[30] *Ibid.*, p. 39.
[31] *Ibid.*
[32] *Ibid.*

government; Subid Ali, a leading Calcutta merchant; Khan Sahib Syed Ahmed Rashid, the first Mohammedan appraiser; Syed Ahmed Afzal, a public accountant and auditor; Ishanul Huq, a zamindar and a merchant; K. Habibullah Chowdhury, a celebrated Muslim journalist; S. M. Yakub, deputy mayor of Calcutta; and K. Nooruddin, a councilor of the Calcutta Corporation and the secretary of the Majlis.[33]

There were other major sporting reasons for Mohammedan Sporting's success in overpowering all other Bengali as well as British teams in the Calcutta League and other worthy tournaments outside Calcutta.[34] One major reason for Mohammedan's spectacular success was the formation of a strong team by collecting ace Muslim players from around the country. This gave them a definite edge over their Bengali Hindu counterparts to fight against the mighty British teams and to win the Calcutta Football League five times in a row. Other Bengali clubs like Mohun Bagan or East Bengal till that date did not think of such an effective player recruitment policy. However, more significant was the club's decision to play wearing boots especially on the rain-affected ground. The club took this pragmatic decision even before its promotion to the First Division League in 1933. The club authorities studied the reasons of failure of the Indian teams 'despite their being rather superior to the European players in India in basic football skill'.[35] S. A. Aziz, the person in charge of building the club's football team, therefore decided to recruit booted players for the side in 1933. The result was instantaneous: six booted players in the team, recruited from Sandemarians, enabled Mohammedan Sporting to trounce the barefoot Nebubagan side 16–0 on a rainy ground in the Second Division League.[36]

The initial success encouraged Aziz to try experimenting with a fully booted side. Yet 'he was practical enough not to fully lose the advantage of barefooted play by the terribly fast players with uncanny footwork he had in the ranks of the club'.[37] So he conceived and experimented with the Fort William Cobblers to devise a form of light and soft boot, 'beyond, however, the knowledge of anybody else, lest storm of objection would upset his plans'.[38] Aziz's plan was fulfilled, as he was able to persuade

---

[33] For details on these personalities, see *MSP Souvenir*, pp. 29–30.

[34] These included Rovers Cup and Durand Cup, both of which Mohammedan won as the first Bengal club.

[35] RB, 'Indian Football and Boots'.

[36] *Ibid.*

[37] *Ibid.*

[38] *Ibid.*

Mohammedan's new recruits to wear the desirable type of boots on a wet ground. Thus he pioneered the new two-in-one system in Bengali football, that is, playing barefoot on a dry ground, but quickly donning boots, kept ready just beyond the sidelines, as soon as the rains came. It was proved, noted one sports journalist, that the same player, who excelled in his own style of play when the weather was fair, could be equally effective with boots on a rainy turf without losing much of his basic efficiency.[39]

Impact of Mohammedan Sporting's Successive League Victories

The unprecedented success of Mohammedan Sporting in winning the Calcutta Football League for a record five times in a row had a visibly mixed impact on Bengal's footballing society. For many irrespective of their caste, creed or community, it was a worthy victory for the Bengalis as also Indians on the sporting field. As the *Star of India* wrote:

> The incentive for a team to win the Second Division of the Calcutta Football League is that they will be promoted to the First Division, even though they have to bear for the first year the label of 'Babes'. But in the first year of promotion to win the championship in the First Division is to hope for the impossible.
>
> The 'Babes' came; they saw; they conquered. And their victory is doubly creditable inasmuch as they have the distinction of being the first *Indian* team to win the League. Mohammedan Sporting has thus written history in Calcutta football.[40]

The Statesman noted the enthusiasm in the wake of the victory: 'There were unprecedented scenes of enthusiasm when, with a final flourish that dazzled Kalighat, one of the season's poor relations, Mohammedan Sporting became the first *Indian* team to win the League since its inception in 1898. The reforcing were transferred from the Maidan to the city, where noisy but good tempered demonstration were the order.'[41] The supremacy the club began to master over British sides came to be hailed as an Indian victory in many quarters. It was expected to encourage the other Bengali clubs to follow in the footsteps of Mohammedan Sporting Club. The newly elected nationalist mayor of Calcutta, Nalini Ranjan Sarkar, called the occasion 'a great unifier . . . a matter of pleasure and

---

[39] *Ibid.*

[40] *Star of India*, 6 July 1934; emphasis added.

[41] *The Statesman*, 6 July 1934; emphasis added.

gratification to all citizens'.⁴² Such was his enthusiasm that he spent ₹1,000 on a lavish civic reception organised to greet the players and management. By contrast, a mass rally the previous week in Calcutta for Mahatma Gandhi only warranted Rs 10 from the mayor's purse.⁴³ For the Muslims in particular, Mohammedan's wins were seen in terms of the community's success to prove its mettle on the field of sport and were expected to inject confidence amongst them to gain similar victories in *other spheres of life*.⁴⁴ For some, a section of Hindus to be particular, however, the development was of otherwise concern as it represented a victory of Muslim confidence and superiority. An overview of the responses and tributes the club received on the occasion of its second straight League triumph in 1935, as gathered from the club's souvenir, reveals this mixed lot of repercussions of the club's successes.

The secretary of East Bengal Club, one of Mohammedan Sporting's biggest rivals in the Calcutta League, wrote: 'This is indeed a glorious achievement of your club and for all the *Indian* clubs to take a legitimate pride in.'⁴⁵ The tribute from Aligarh University was on similar line: 'The Mohammedan Sporting Club has done great service to India in general and Mussalmans of Calcutta in particular.'⁴⁶ A report of a particular newspaper is more revealing on this count:

> The Mohammedans have created a new history in Indian football, being the first *Indian team* to achieve the league honours. Their success is no doubt a glory to *Indian football* which is but another name for speed and nippiness. The rapid advancement which the game of soccer has made among the Indians, presents another problem to the foreign oppositions who will find it none too easy to solve.⁴⁷

The Nawab of Murshidabab, Wasif Ali Meerza, too regarded the club's victory as an 'Indian' one and urged 'all lovers of sport' to acknowledge their splendid performance.⁴⁸ The Maharaja of Santosh, then president of the Indian Football Association, also struck a similar chord of comment:

---

⁴² *Amrita Bazar Patrika*, 1 August 1934.

⁴³ *Forward*, 12 July 1934.

⁴⁴ These *other spheres* included, amongst others, mainly education, government service and different professions.

⁴⁵ *MSP Souvenir*, p. 28; emphasis added.

⁴⁶ Secretary of the university, F. Noor Muhammad, sent this congratulatory message to the club. Quoted in *ibid*.

⁴⁷ *Amrita Bazar Patrika*, n.d., quoted in *MSP Souvenir*, p. 11; emphasis added.

⁴⁸ *MSP Souvenir*, p. 16.

> I fervently hope that you (Mohammedan Sporting) will keep your flag flying. Like Mohan Bagan and East Bengal you, too, have enhanced the reputation of *Indian footballers*. You naturally occupy a very warm corner of Bengal's heart and I am sure you will continue to do so as long as your efficiency is not impaired and your methods remain clean.[49]

Some even expected that Mohammedan Sporting's success would have a greater impact on social relations and augur social amity. As the sheriff, Abdul Halim Ghuznavi, maintained: 'In conclusion, I wish the club, its organizers and its players every success, and hope and expect that they will do everything to raise the standard of sports all round and increase a brotherly feeling amongst all classes and communities interested in outdoor games.'[50] Hassan Suhrawardy greeted the club for its great success and wished for greater success in 'a wider sphere of activities'. He, too, did not fail to take note of the potential of social amity on the occasion: 'In the healthy atmosphere of sports and manly games you will make friendships and understandings, irrespective of class, creed and colour, which will last through out your life time.'[51] Finally, R. Ahmed, the principal of Calcutta Dental College and Hospital, commented admirably on the far-reaching consequences of a recreational victory:

> There are reasons for believing that the pioneer Muslim sporting club of Bengal will keep up the lead and thus encourage the growth of healthful recreation amongst the masses. For after all, the greatest object lesson a sporting club can offer is the raising of a physique and health of the people in general. I hope the Mohammedan Sporting Club may continue to do so and thus help the country in a most tangible way.[52]

However, there were tributes and messages which clearly hailed Mohammedan's victory in terms of the success of a particular community. The Muslim Leader, A. K. Fazlul Haque, commented on the occasion: 'The marvelous achievements of the Mohammedan Sporting Club on the football field have earned a name and fame for *Muslims* in the sporting world, of which *the community* may justly be proud.'[53] Syed Abdul Hafeez, a member of the Council of State, wrote in his message: '*The Muslims* of the sporting world take pride in the initiation taken by the Mohammedan

---

[49] *Ibid*; emphasis added.
[50] *Ibid.*, p. 18.
[51] *Ibid.*, p. 19.
[52] *Ibid.*
[53] *Ibid.*, p. 12; emphasis added.

Sporting Club of Calcutta. The club came into existence to fulfil a long felt want of the sporting spirit of *the community*.'[54] Another Muslim gentleman, M. Rafique, spoke of the importance of the club's success in terms of a great community service:

> Games and sports play a vital part in moulding and shaping the character and ultimately the destinies of individuals, no less than that of communities. The success of the Mohammedan Sporting Club will be a harbinger of greater successes in the *self-realisation of our great community in other branches of human endeavour*.[55]

That even only after the second year of its League success, Mohammedan Sporting Club had already become a symbol of Muslim identity and confidence all over India was clear from the congratulatory messages it received from different corners of Bengal and the whole of India.[56] As K. Nooruddin, one of the revivers of the club in the 1930s, remarked: 'Their spectacular performance, in recent years, is the turning point for the Mussalmans of Bengal in the field of sports.'[57] More importantly, as to how the Muslim fans supported the club's cause throughout the years, the club souvenir recorded the following:

> Ever since their (the club's) chances were rosy (in clinching the League) in the League last year and throughout this year, they have had the solid backing of thousands of supporters who — rain, cloud or sunshine — have mustered to a man to see them play and encourage them.
>
> Club football fans would be amazed to see who some of these supporters are. Businessmen who leave their firms and shops to witness the games, old men who have lost interest in football for years, but who have had it resuscitated with the enthusiasm for Mohammedans.[58]

Recording Mohammedan Sporting Club's huge fan following those days, Mohammad Nasiruddin, editor of *Saogat*, wrote:

---

[54] *Ibid.*, p. 25; emphasis added.
[55] *Ibid.*, p. 26; emphasis added.
[56] Hundreds of messages came from Muslim clubs and organisations of different parts of India including Shillong, Sylhet, Dacca, Rangpur, Tippera, Dinajpur, Jalpaiguri, Darjeeling, Purnea, Cuttock, Benares, Bombay, Bangalore, and Calcutta. For details, see *MSP Souvenir*, p. 28.
[57] *Ibid.*
[58] 'Tribute from the Green Stands', in *ibid.*, p. 34.

Calcutta *maidan* used to witness large gathering on the days of Mohammedan Sporting's match. The crowd comprised educated and uneducated youth and old men along with maulavis and maulanas. When space on the sidelines of the ground proved insufficient, diehard fans climbed upon trees and sat on the branches to witness the matches of their favourite club. Kaji Nazrul Islam, the famous Muslim bard, called these over-enthusiastic fans 'branch-monkeys'.[59]

Consequent to the success of Mohammedan Sporting Club, a number of Muslim sporting clubs were established in the districts and sub-divisional towns. As *The Statesman* noted: 'The Mohammedan Sporting is as popular in the mofussil as in Calcutta and stories are current of crowds in Bengal towns collecting of an afternoon round wireless loudspeakers and echoing the cheers of its supporters from the Calcutta maidan.'[60] Thus the Muslims of Dhaka were inspired to form Dhaka Mohammedan Sporting Club in 1936.[61] This was, however, preceded by two more Muslim clubs: Muslim Sporting Club (1927) founded at the initiative of some of the members of Dhaka's nawab family at Dilkhusha House, and Kumilla Mohammedan (1928). While the first club was disbanded only after two years, the latter still exists.[62] The first president and general ecretary of the Dhaka Mohammedan were Khwaja Md Azmal and Khwaja Md Adel respectively.[63]

When Mohammedan Sporting won the League title in 1938 to make it five times in a row, the jubilation went beyond description.

> There was spontaneous demonstration after the match and also on the Mohammedan Sporting ground and finally around the Subid Ali Mansions. Thousands of Muslim supporters marched in procession with band and rent the skies with tremendous shouts of jubilation. . . . Till late in the evening it was impossible to enter the Mohammedan Sporting tent, there were thousands around it. A spontaneous Kabuli dancing recital was held under the skies of their ground. Led by buglers, the players returned to the

---

[59] Comments of Mohammad Nasiruddin, quoted in Ritan, *Football*, pp. 20–21; translation mine.

[60] *The Statesman*, 6 July 1937.

[61] *Dhaka Mohammedan Sporting Club er Sankhipta Itihas* (A Brief History of the Dhaka Mohammedan Sporting Club), Dhaka: Mohammedan Sporting Club, 2004, p. 2.

[62] *Ibid.*, pp. 2–3.

[63] *Ibid.*

club tent from the CFC ground and as they reached the club the flag was hoisted on the pole. The players were profusely congratulated from all round for bringing respect to the club and the Indian football.[64]

Muslim poets also felt the need to greet the club's success by writing poems in the club's honour. The poems of Nazrul Islam and Golam Mostafa on this theme became very popular among Bengali Muslims. The poems and songs composed by Mostafa on that occasion were popularised by the Gramophone Record Company when they brought on sale records of those songs sung by the famous singer Abbasuddin.[65]

The huge impact of Mohammedan Sporting's victories on Muslim society needs to be analysed in the larger socio-political context of Hindu–Muslim relations of the 1930s. However, the commotion raised by the consecutive victories of the club in Hindu–Muslim circles, as has already been shown, was mixed. While the success of the club was regarded as a *Muslim* victory against the Hindus by many among both communities, many others considered it as an *Indian* victory to end British supremacy on the football field. But, in the long run, it must be added, the actual impact of the club's popularity seems to be immense, especially in generating confidence among the Muslim masses and lending strength to the political cause of the Muslim League in Bengal.

Mohammed Salim: A Lost *Indian* Icon of the Mohammedan Sporting Club

Incidentally, the first Indian footballer to play in Europe was Mohammed Salim, a player of distinction of the Mohammedan Sporting Club in its days of glory in the 1930s, who played for the well-known Celtic FC in Scotland in pre-independence India.[66] Celtic, Mihir Bose mentions, 'was not only the first British club to win the European Cup, they were also the first European club to play an Indian and, what is more, he performed

---

[64] *Amrita Bazar Patrika*, 14 July 1938.
[65] Ritan, *Football*, pp. 24–25.
[66] Salim has got a minor mention in the works of Phil Vassili, *The First Black Footballer*, London: Frank Cass, 1998 and Paul Dimeo, '"With Political Pakistan in the Offing . . .": Football and Communal Politics in South Asia, 1887–1947', *Journal of Contemporary History*, vol. 38, no. 3, July 2003, pp. 377–94.

Celtic FC is a legendary Scottish football club. Rivalry between Celtic and Rangers is one of the best-known football rivalries in the world.

in bare feet'.⁶⁷ However, the extraordinary story of Mohammed Salim has not been given due recognition in the existing works on the history of Indian soccer until recent times.⁶⁸ It is interesting to note that the reason why Salim faded into oblivion has something to do with the changing socio-political situation of Bengal in the 1930s affecting the Bengali football culture, rivalry and administration of the time.

Salim delivered some extraordinary performances for the Celtic.⁶⁹ Salim, during his brief stint at Celtic, had established himself as a key member of the team. Although the club authorities requested him to stay for another season in 1937–38, Salim returned to India to help his favourite club Mohammedan Sporting to continue with their famous run in the Calcutta Football League in the 1930s.⁷⁰ Commenting on his extraordinary skill, the *Scottish Daily Express* had declared:

> Ten twinkling toes of Salim, Celtic F C's player from India hypnotized the crowd at Parkhead last night in an alliance game with Galston. He balances the ball on his big toe, lets it run down the scale to his little toe, twirls it, hops on one foot around the defender, then flicks the ball to the center who has only to send it into goal. Three of Celtic's seven goals last night came from his moves. Was asked to take a penalty, he refused. Said he was shy. Salim does not speak English, his brother translates for him. Brother Hasheem thinks Salim is wonderful — so did the crowd last night.⁷¹

On his arrival at London, the Celtic manager agreed to give Salim a trial. However, he emphasised the need to seek special permission from the Football Federation for someone playing with bare feet. If the Federation gave their nod, he would give Salim a trial. Permission was eventually granted and Salim was asked to demonstrate his skill before 1,000 club members and three registered coaches. He had never faced a trial like this before and was understandably nervous. The coaches took him to

---

⁶⁷ *The Daily Telegraph*, 22 May 2003. This article was the outcome of a long discussion between Boria Majumdar and Mihir Bose, the *Daily Telegraph* sports writer and author of numerous books on sport.

⁶⁸ Very recently a work on Indian football has redressed this imbalance. See Majumdar and Bandyopadhyay, *Goalless*, Chapter 5.

⁶⁹ For details, see *Scottish Daily Express*, 29 August 1936.

⁷⁰ *Khelar Ashar*, 8 June 1979.

⁷¹ *Scottish Daily Express*, 29 August 1936. Given his exceptional barefoot style of play and staggering display of dribbling, the newspaper had no other words but to call him a 'juggler'.

different corners of the ground and asked him to demonstrate his skill in six different ways. When Salim finished his demonstration, they were astonished. Salim, the shy Indian, then stunned them by displaying three further styles of play with distinction. Eventually, they were convinced that an exceptional talent had arrived in Scotland. They decided to include him in the playing 11 for the forthcoming match against Hamilton. Thus began his short stint at Celtic FC.[72]

In his first match for Celtic against Hamilton, he was in great form. In fact, he was exceptional and Celtic won the match 5–1. In his second match against Galston, Celtic won 7–1 and his performance led the *Scottish Daily Express* of 29 August 1936, to carry the headline 'Indian Juggler — New Style'.[73] Salim was also offered a professional contract to play in Germany.[74] However, he was determined to return to India in time for the 1937 Calcutta Football League.

When after a few months in Scotland, Salim began to feel homesick and was determined to return to India, the Celtic Football Club pleaded him to play for one more season. Celtic tried to persuade him to stay by offering to organise a charity match in his honour, giving him 5 per cent of the gate proceeds. Salim did not realise what 5 per cent would amount to and said he would give his share to orphans who were to be special invitees for the match. Five per cent came to £1,800 (colossal money then) but although he was astonished, he kept his word. In doing so, Mohammed Salim earned a unique recognition for himself and his country in the eyes of the Westerners. Alongside, his performances for Celtic in the limited number of matches that he played demonstrated that barefoot Indians could match the British on an even keel.[75] This belief may have inspired his colleagues in Mohammedan Sporting to win five straight Calcutta Football League titles (1934–38) defeating leading European teams in the process.

Many years later, Rashid, his second son, wrote to Celtic stating that his father was in distress and that he needed money for his father's treatment. Amazingly, the club sent a bank draft for £100 as financial assistance.

---

[72] *Khelar Ashar*, 8 June 1979.
[73] *Scottish Daily Express*, 29 August 1936.
[74] *Khelar Ashar*, 8 June 1979.
[75] *Junior Statesman*, 11–24 September 1976; In this issue a photograph was published that shows a European feeling Salim's feet to check what magic they contained. In colonial India a white person touching an Indian's feet was an extremely rare occurrence.

Rashid was delighted, not because he received the money but because his father still holds pride of place in Celtic.[76]

In colonial India, trying to challenge British superiority was the most difficult task of all. Both Salim and his club, Mohammedan, had achieved this seemingly impossible task through their performances on the football field. In a nation plagued by social tension, religious violence, political and economic uncertainties, Salim's football on foreign soil 'served a purpose that went beyond the football field'.[77] 'It helped colonized Indians *reinvent* themselves' by showing to the world that an *Indian* could display superior skill than a European in a manly Western game.[78] While on earlier occasions, achievement in sport helped colonised Indians capture the imagination of the West and bind the nation into a feeling of unity, Salim's feats on the sporting field were never highlighted as nationalist success, and had gone mostly unmentioned at his time as well as after independence. This happened probably because the success story of Salim and his club was a victim of the unhealthy contest between the IFA and Mohammedan Sporting Club in the late 1930s, having consequent repercussions on the society and polity of Bengal.

Conflict between the IFA and Mohammedan Sporting Club: Context, Growth and Aftermath[79]

Coincidental to the changes in the political equation in Bengal in the mid- and late 1930s, Mohammedan Sporting had a continuous tussle with the IFA. Despite their gallant performances against leading European teams, they were not given due recognition anywhere near that accorded to Mohun Bagan after their victory in the IFA Shield in 1911. The Muslim community always found the IFA to be discriminatory against Mohammedan Sporting,

---

[76] Transcript of Boria Majumdar's interview with Rashid Ahmed, Calcutta, 20 January 2002. I am grateful to Boria Majumdar for providing me this transcript.

[77] Bengal in the 1930s was plagued by political turmoil. Increased communal tension in the wake of migration from East Bengal and shifts in the economic balance of power in the wake of Marwari influx from UP had affected the politico-economic life of the province.

Quote from Majumdar and Bandyopadhyay, *Goalless*, p. 88.

[78] *Ibid.*; emphasis added.

[79] This section resonates some of the arguments and media extracts which I shared with my co-author Boria Majumdar in *Goalless*, Chapter 5.

their club. This so-called discrimination, as the most recent study on the subject suggests, was a response to the Muslim political ascendancy in West Bengal in the 1930s.[80] According to this study, the Bengali bhadralok began to feel threatened by the Muslim political ascendancy in Bengal in the middle of the 1930s.[81] It was also accompanied by Bengal's marginalisation in national/Congress politics as the central Congress leadership had started displaying a growing apathy towards the bhadralok who dominated the Bengal Congress.[82] Along with this, there also occurred a minimisation of the bhadralok's regional hegemony, an outcome of what Joya Chatterji has called 'the emergence of the mufassil in Bengal politics'.[83] Chatterji shows how the metropolis, which had dominated Bengal politics till the end of the 1920s, increasingly became less significant from the early 1930s, as political fortunes began to be determined by the Muslim vote concentrated in rural and small town Bengal.[84] This transformation, an outcome of the Communal Award of 1932 and the Government of India Act of 1935, which enlarged Muslim representation in the provincial assemblies at the expense of the Hindu vote, culminated in the accession of the Krishak Praja Party-Muslim League ministry led by Fazlul Haq in 1937.[85] The new ministry soon set in motion a series of reforms that affected the interests of the Hindu bhadralok. As Chatterji enumerates:

---

[80] *Ibid.*

[81] *Ibid.*

[82] Bengal's marginalisation in Congress-led nationalist politics was well-discussed in John Gallagher, 'Congress in Decline: Bengal, 1930–1939', *Modern Asian Studies*, vol. 7, no. 3, 1973: pp. 589–645. For details on the Bengal Congress's growing rift with the central leadership, see Joya Chatterji, *Bengal Divided*, Cambridge: Cambridge University Press, 1994, pp. 18–54, 103–49. In his two-volume autobiographical work published at the beginning of the 1930s, the famous scientist, Prafulla Chandra Ray, noted, 'The Bengali is now awakening to the fact that his leaders are very old men, that no one is taking their place, and that whether in Delhi or inside the Congress his representatives have little influence. The political centre of gravity is shifting northwards and westwards.' Prafulla Chandra Ray, *Life and Experiences of a Bengali Chemist*, Calcutta: Chuckervertty, Chatterjee & Co., Ltd., 1932, vol. 1, p. 471.

[83] Chatterji, *Bengal Divided*, pp. 55–102.

[84] *Ibid.*

[85] Led by Abdul Kasem Fazlul Haq, the Krishak Praja Party drew its strength from the mass following it enjoyed among Bengal's Muslim peasantry and intermediate shareholders.

In 1938, the Fazlul Haq ministry changed the rules about police recruitment so that 'while enlisting Bengali constables the Superintendent of Police must see that not less than 50% of the recruits are Muslims'. In the same year, the ministry passed legislation that stipulated that 60 per cent of all Government appointments be reserved for Muslims. In 1939, the Government instructed local bodies 'not to propose for appointment to local bodies persons who were known to be actively opposed to the policy of the Ministry', and slapped administrative controls on nominations to the Union Boards, which accounted for one-third of their total membership.[86]

Thus in almost every domain of public sphere from higher education to administrative and political appointments, the Hindu bhadrolok preserves were under threat. It was in such a situation, it has been argued, that Muslim ascendancy led them, leading patrons of sport, to look favourably upon British rule. In football they were opposed to the dominance of Mohammedan Sporting and tried their best to thwart it.[87]

The growing tension between the club and the IFA reached a climax in 1937 over a controversial incident during a League match between Mohammedan Sporting and East Bengal. In this match on 11 June 1937, it was reported, one influential member and player of the Mohammedan Sporting Club kicked at the face of one East Bengal official, who had run to the assistance of Rahamat, an injured player of the Mohammedan Sporting Club.[88] It was known to all concerned that the IFA would take appropriate action against him. The match was followed by disgraceful scenes. Immediately after the game, there were several cases of stabbing outside the ground, the most unfortunate victim being a boy of 13.[89] As one newspaper correspondent noted:

> Tempers ran riot and the gentleman who previously used to stroll about the Maidan under the name of 'sporting spirit' was shot dead outright and buried. Bitter partisan feelings of a none-too-specific type strode about menacingly like a moody child bent on mischief. Quiet lovers of the game had no other alternative but seek the first available vantage-point of safety. The C.F.C. members had to extend hospitality to the distressed. There were assaults here and there and in a few cases dangerous weapons were used.[90]

---

[86] Chatterji, *Bengal Divided*, pp. 107–8.
[87] Majumdar and Bandyopadhyay, *Goalless*, p. 94.
[88] *Amrita Bazar Patrika*, 15 June 1937, p. 11.
[89] *Amrita Bazar Patrika*, 12 June 1937, p. 9.
[90] *Ibid.*, p. 11.

A section of the Muslims with over-the-top behaviour were blamed for the post-match violence:

> We have not the least doubt that none regrets more the disgraceful conduct of some of the Muslims among the spectators than the Mohammedan team. We trust the Muslim press will forget its communalism and condemn the conduct of those who had come to witness a first class sport, but exhibited a mentality that was as remote from sportsmanship as hell is from heaven. What can be more horrible than that people should come with daggers concealed in their person to use them against innocent spectators? These people no doubt belong to the class of goondas . . . who flourish in this city despite the Goonda Act. We wish it had been possible to dismiss the incidents as the hard work of a few desperados who really belong to the lawless class. But it is common knowledge that communal partisanship often finds very disgraceful expression in language whenever a Muslim player comes to the grief at the hands of his Hindu opponent. . . . Calcutta football maidan is no longer the respectable place that it once was. The invasion of communalism of sports has invested it with bad odour to decent people.[91]

The controversy arose over the identity of the Mohammedan Sporting Club player who committed the wrong. The club as well as the newspapers representing Muslim sentiments such as the *Star of India* claimed that it was Sattar who actually hit at the face of Girin Ghosh, an East Bengal official.[92] The IFA, however, instead of taking stern action against Sattar, suspended Habib, one of the best players of the Mohammedan Sporting side.[93] The IFA, in its Governing Body meeting held on 14 June, took the following resolutions:

(1) Habib, the Mohammedan Sporting player, was unanimously found guilty of having assaulted Girin Ghosh, an official of East Bengal Club, during the match between East Bengal and Mohammedan Sporting on the C.F.C. Ground last Friday. He was suspended for three years.
(2) A committee consisting of Messrs. Nagle, Pepper, S.N. Banerjee, Sushil Sen, H.M. Hafeez, and both the joint honorary secretaries, was appointed to enquire whether Mohammedan Sporting was responsible for the Habib-Ghosh incident and whether the Club tried to shield Habib, and whether any action should be taken.

---

[91] *Amrita Bazar Patrika*, 13 June 1937, p. 8.
[92] *The Statesman*, 16 June 1937.
[93] *Star of India*, 16 June 1937.

(3) A committee consisting of Messrs. G.C. Fletcher, A.K. Basu, K. Nooruddin, G.H. McIntyre, G.M. Habib and Inspector Ford, with the two joint honorary secretaries was appointed to devise ways and means to prevent, if possible, a recurrence of the incidents that followed last Friday's match.[94]

The Maharaja of Santosh, president of IFA, was however against placing the blame on 'the Mohammedan Club for the lawlessness of the vast crowd of their supporters'.[95] While he admitted that 'every club should do its best to check its supporters from behaving badly', he also strongly argued that 'it would be stretching their (IFA's) rules to tell Mohammedan Sporting that they would be suspended if there was a recurrence of lawless incidents among the bad characters on the slopes of the Fort outside the ground'.[96] The Maharaja suggested that the club 'should form a set sort of volunteer corps from among their members to sit among the spectators on the green stands and use their influence, with the help of the police, in keeping order'.[97] It was also suggested elsewhere that 'Mohammedan Sporting could print leaflets in Urdu appealing to the members of the Mohammedan community to refrain from acting in such a way as would bring their *national* club into disrepute'.[98]

After deliberating on these suggestions, the Executive Committee of the Mohammedan Sporting Club notified the IFA that the suggestions were totally unacceptable. According to it, 'one of the resolutions passed at the meeting of the I.F.A. was humiliating to the Mohammedan Sporting Club, and the club regret they will not be able to play any more league matches until the resolution is rescinded and erased from the books of the I.F.A.'.[99] The meeting also considered the Habib incident, and found after enquiry that Sattar, and not Habib, was responsible for the assault upon Girin Ghosh, and forthrightly suspended Sattar indefinitely.[100] Commenting on the humiliating suggestions of the IFA, the club authorities declared: 'A serious crisis appeared inevitable and the Governing Body of the IFA created a situation that caused great resentment not only amongst the members of the club but among the entire Muslim public

---

[94] *The Statesman*, 15 June 1937.
[95] *Ibid.*
[96] *Ibid.*
[97] *Ibid.*
[98] *Ibid.*; emphasis added.
[99] *The Statesman*, 16 June 1937.
[100] *Ibid.*

of Bengal.'[101] When the club's secretary, K. Nooruddin, protested against this arbitrary decision-making, the apex body decided to ban him from attending its Governing Body meetings for the next three years. As a mark of protest, Mohammedan Sporting Club withdrew from the League on 16 June 1937.[102] The Executive Committee of the club also condemned 'the malicious and one-sided propaganda of a section of a press, and particularly of the "Statesman" against the Mohammedan Sporting Club' and urged the Muslims 'to boycott the "Statesman" which has clearly deviated from its policy of impartiality and assumed the role of a propagandist in favour of anti-Islam Zionism in Palestine and of the champion of the anti-Mohammedan forces in the I.F.A., Calcutta, which have made an unholy alliance against the Mohammedans on purely communal grounds'.[103]

These actions generated considerable ill-feeling among the Muslims, evident from the following editorial published in the *Star of India*:

> The inevitable has happened. The irresponsible and vindictive manner in which the Governing Body of the IFA had dealt with the situation created by false and malicious propaganda against Mohammedan Sporting has resulted in a deadlock, which may ruin Calcutta football forever. In our leading article yesterday, we pointed out the uncalled for insult which the IFA Governing body had offered the Mohammedan Sporting Club by the spiteful and shameful resolution appointing a committee to enquire into the conduct of the club itself in order to find out whether it had shielded Habib, the player wrongly punished by the IFA in the same meeting. We knew that the only answer, which the Mohammedan Sporting Club could give the IFA, consistent with self respect, was to decline to play any more games conducted by that Association. But yesterday we deliberately wrote with restraint because we had faint hopes that a good night's sleep might help the Maharaja of Santosh and his colleagues on that governing body to realize the lengths to which they had been led on the evening previous. We had hoped that at least the Maharaja of Santosh would soon realize the mistake made and would use his influence to bring his erring colleagues to their senses and scrap the offensive, entirely uncalled for, petty minded and absurd resolution ... entirely unworthy of grown up men who are expected to be reasonable and unbiased.

---

[101] *Mohammedan Sporting Club Souvenir*, Calcutta: Mohammedan Sporting Club, 1939, p. 62.

[102] *The Statesman*, 17 June 1937.

[103] *Amrita Bazar Patrika*, 17 June 1937, p. 11.

> But wisdom has not yet dawned, and the infamous decision to hold an inquest on the conduct of a club managed and controlled by men, many of whom are held in higher esteem by the public than the more boisterous gentleman on the IFA Governing Body still stands. The Mohammedan Sporting Club has refused to stand this act of cold-blooded insult and deliberate injustice. If the men who voted for this monstrous resolution in the IFA meeting on Monday, despite protests from several other members, had any idea how men with any sense of self respect react to such insults as they were offering the Mohammedans, they would have hesitated a hundred times before mooting so unmannerly, so revengeful and so unprecedented a proposal before the meeting. But it is clear that the majority present on the occasion had gone there determined to punish the Mohammedans. The Mohammedans had in their eyes merited punishment not because of what happened or did not happen on Friday last; that was but the excuse of the Tiger to the Lamb.[104]

It went on to assert that,

> the Mohammedans merited the severest punishment in their eyes for other reasons. They had driven out of the picture the 'Premier' Indian team and all teams, in fact, which had held supremacy before the advent of the all-conquering Mohammedans. They had taken the glory out of Hindu football, and had fought their way to a glory never before achieved by Indians. In this year of grace, the Mohammedans seemed to be once more on the high road to the same achievement — and if for the fourth year in succession the league honors went to them, would not this fair land of Indians be overcast with the clouds of ignominy? The very idea of so much glory to the Mohammedans seemed to have destroyed appetites and stolen sleep from the eyes of the thousands of the only loving children of Mother India.[105]

The Editorial concluded thus:

> The tricks that were played to trip up the victorious Mohammedans on their onward march to victory, the accidents that robbed them of advantages on the field of play and the confused judgements of referees at the most crucial moments in the movement of the leather — all these and many things are too well known to tens of thousands of Muslims . . . who have regularly watched the contests on the Calcutta *maidan*.
>
> But we ourselves never took notice of these little ways or little men; we had confidence that as long as the Mohammedans played the splendidly

---

[104] *Star of India*, 20 June 1937.
[105] *Ibid.*

efficient and commendably clean football which they alone can play at present, laurels would come to them despite all intrigue, impediment and controversy.

And now some of the men whom both chance and design have placed in a position wherefrom the strangler's rope can be fastened round the neck of the unloved Mohammedans, have created an opportunity to "feed fat the ancient grudge." It may be further noted that the Mohammedans are to have from next year a better field and an enclosure of their own in a part of the *maidan* which would make their club territorially the second best to Calcutta FC. Could there be a more bitter gall and wormwood for the unhappy nationalist who has invaded the field of sport? But the nationalist is a clever stage manager and plotter. He realized that if the Mohammedans could be driven to an intolerable position, if on some pretext or other, they could be subjected to an insult, which they could not and would not brook, if a situation could be created in which the only alternative for the Mohammedan Sporting Club would be to cut themselves adrift from the IFA, then the unwanted Club and its unconquerable eleven could be effectively prevented from acquiring such permanent importance in the world of Indian football. That intolerable position has been created, that pretext has been invented, that situation has been engineered. And now is the exit of the Mohammedans awaited with hope and joy.

The indecent haste with which the Governing Body of the IFA arrived at their decisions on Monday, was further proved when it was found that they had punished the wrong man. The Mohammedan Club executive after the enquiry have ascertained that it was their reserve player Sattar and not Habib who had assaulted Girin Ghose, and they have promptly suspended the guilty person, and naturally demanded that the IFA's wrong and slanderous act against Habib, the innocent, must be rescinded.[106]

Noting that public opinion had been mobilised against the IFA, the Maharaja of Santosh, president, hastened to find a peaceful solution to the controversy.[107] As a result, the IFA and the Mohammedan Sporting Club arrived at a temporary truce after K. Nooruddin, secretary of the club, met the Maharaja of Santosh at his residence.[108] At this meeting an agreement with the following decisions was signed between the two bodies:

(a) That time be given to the Mohammedan Sporting Club to reconsider the situation.

---

[106] *Ibid.*
[107] *Amrita Bazar Patrika*, 17 June 1937.
[108] *Amrita Bazar Patrika*, 18 June 1937.

(b) That the Mohammedan Sporting Club shall lodge an appeal with the Indian Football Association in accordance with its rules and the Governing Body (of the IFA) will do all that is just and reasonable to redress the grievance of Mohammedan Sporting Club, if any.
(c) That in view of the understanding and in order to keep the doors of negotiation open, Mohammedan Sporting's matches were to be postponed as requested by the club.[109]

As per the terms of the understanding, Mohammedan Sporting Club appealed to the IFA on 19 June 1937, urging the Governing Body to reconsider decisions against the club.[110] Rather than softening their stand in view of the club's appeal, the IFA imposed a fresh series of conditions upon the club declaring that only if the conditions were met would their appeal be considered.[111] The primary condition given by the IFA was that the club would have to unconditionally withdraw all the resolutions and letters sent to the apex body. After its meeting of 6 July, the IFA asserted that the Maharaja of Santosh, president, had already notified the Mohammedan Sporting Club that if their letter of 16 June was not withdrawn their appeal would not be considered.[112] At this meeting, the IFA also decided that no more time would be given to the club and rejected the appeal by Mohammedan Sporting. This decision came only four days after the club registered its record fourth triumph in the Calcutta League on 2 July 1937. In doing so, the IFA also ignored the wishes of some of the European members of its Governing Body. G. C. Fletcher, a key member of the Governing Body, had moved a resolution whereby the Mohammedan Sporting Club was to be given a further 48 hours to withdraw their letter.[113] But the Indian members, mostly Hindus representing other clubs, were determined not to give the club any further time and wanted their appeal to be rejected immediately, as was eventually done:

> there was a feeling in many quarters in Calcutta that the IFA have been surrendering its legitimate right to control football in Calcutta and it looked as if there would be one body left to rule football that is either the IFA or the Mohammedan Sporting Club.[114]

---

[109] *Ibid.*
[110] *Amrita Bazar Patrika*, 20 June 1937.
[111] *Amrita Bazar Patrika*, 1 July 1937.
[112] *Amrita Bazar Patrika*, 7 July 1937.
[113] *Ibid.*
[114] *Ibid.*

Accordingly, Lt. Henson of the Army Sports Control Board strongly urged that 'the matter should be dealt with then and there and no further adjournment should be given, and if the Mohammedan Sporting Club be given any further opportunity to re-consider this point, Mr. K. Nooruddin on behalf of the club should straightaway withdraw the letter and revoke the resolution adopted at the meeting'.[115] As against this, the Mohammedan Sporting Club authorities asserted: 'We submit that the Governing Body cannot reasonably take exceptions to our opinion expressed with regard to suggestions, which affects not only our club but also the good name of our community.'[116] Even when the club pleaded for a reconsideration of their appeal, the plea was rejected. Finally the IFA decided to forward to the club the following letter drafted by the president, the Maharaja of Santosh: 'I am directed to regret that under the rules of the Association they are unable to go out of their way to reopen the issue.'[117] Criticising the IFA's stand, the *Star of India* stated:

> We tell the Maharaja of Santosh that the terms of an agreement to which he put his solemn signature have been violated and that he has himself been a party to that violation. Mr. Nooruddin did not give any 'assurance' over and above what was put down in writing and signed by him jointly with the Maharaja. When later there was a vague talk of 'assurances given by Mr. Nooruddin', the Mohammedans Secretary, we understand, several times protested against the suggestion that he had given any other assurances and asked for permission to contradict the reports. That permission was refused by the President of the IFA although Mr. Nooruddin was never told what the assurances he was supposed to have given were. And even if there were assurances, which there were not, the Maharaja of Santosh and the 'able lawyers' who are on the IFA should know very well that after two parties in dispute put down their agreement in writing and specify certain terms and conditions thereof, any subsequent understanding has no validity in law.[118]

Despite such criticisms, the IFA refused to alter its stance. Habib was under suspension for three years and the censure against secretary Nooruddin, who it was alleged, 'did not behave in a candid manner before the general body at its meeting held on 14 June and attempted to shield

---

[115] *Ibid.*
[116] *Ibid.*
[117] *Ibid.*
[118] *Star of India*, 7 July 1937.

Habib', stood unaltered.[119] Thus even after much deliberation, the conflict between the IFA and the Mohammedan Sporting Club did not abate and the situation remained unchanged.

Interestingly, in the midst of this atmosphere of continuing hostility, the club went on to register their fifth straight League triumph on 13 July 1938. 'The club had the proud distinction of winning this match and yet another record was set by winning the league for the fifth year in succession.'[120] Despite this performance, tensions escalated between the IFA Governing Body and the club, and in 1938 the club again came to a serious tussle with the IFA authorities. The climax was reached when the question of the Australian tour came up. The suggestion of the club to postpone the tour until the end of the IFA Shield was ignored. However, the players rose to the occasion and showed their great love for the club and refused to join the Australian touring team till the end of the IFA Shield. By this time the members were exasperated, and a general demand was made that the time had now come when the club, once and for all, should decide its line of action and withdraw from the Shield as a mark of protest. However, the Executive Committee eventually decided to continue to play in spite of all opposition.[121]

According to the souvenir of the club published in 1939, the central grievances of the club were 'maximum punishment for minimum offences, repeated bad referring, arbitrary decision with regard to the venue of matches and generally the tyranny of the majority of the council of the IFA against our club'.[122] Even though Mohammedan Sporting competed in the 1938 IFA Shield under extreme duress, its continuous rift with the IFA had finally taken its toll and forced the Mohammedans to withdraw from the Calcutta Football League in 1939. On the eve

---

[119] *Ibid.*

Commenting on this injustice the *Star of India* wrote, 'At a stormy meeting of the Governing Body held last night, with the Maharaja of Santosh in the chair, at which the representative of the Mohammedan Sporting Club who is not a lawyer, had a rough time having repeatedly to seek the protection of the chair, which too was not always readily forthcoming. The Mohammedan Sporting Club was hanged, quartered and drawn for what? — for having, as luck would have it, created another piece of history in British empire soccer, that of annexing the league championship for four years in succession.' *Star of India*, 7 July 1937.

[120] *Mohammedan Sporting Club Souvenir*, p. 66.

[121] *Ibid.*

[122] *Ibid.*

of its second leg League match against Mohun Bagan to be played on 24 June 1939, the club, already much aggrieved over poor supervision in most of their matches that season, decided to lodge a protest with the IFA against 'the manner in which the game has been supervised this season in the matches in which the Mahomedan Sporting Club has played'.[123] Then, on 5 July Mohammedan Sporting, along with East Bengal, Aryan and Kalighat made it public that they would refrain from participating in any of the remaining games except East Bengal's charity fixture against Mohun Bagan on 8 July 'unless their grievances as set forth in their letter to the President of the I.F.A. are redressed forthwith'.[124] The Aryan, however, revised its decision overnight and rejoined the scheduled fixture immediately. The IFA, on its part, considered the action of the other three clubs to be a violation of its decision, 'tantamounting to flouting the authority of the Association' and, in an emergent meeting of the Governing Body, took an unprecedented decision to suspend the three clubs till 31 December 1939.[125] In response, the Executive Committees of the three 'rebel' clubs decided at a joint conference on 9 July to work towards an honourable settlement of their grievances with the IFA.[126] However, the meeting also resolved 'to take steps for the initiation of a separate football league, in the event of an honourable settlement not arrived at'.[127] It was also decided to term the league as the 'Brabourne League'. The clubs played a number of exhibition matches between themselves at different venues throughout Bengal in July and August, which attracted large crowds on every occasion. Finally, a counter Bengal Football Association was born on 11 August 1939 with Nailini Ranjan Sarkar, finance minister of the Bengal government, as the president.[128] The Association organised a knock-out tournament called 'Brabourne Cup' in September. Although a temporary truce was once again arrived at in 1940, resulting in the re-entry of these clubs into the Calcutta Football League, 'the temporary parting of ways', particularly between the IFA and the Mohammedan Sporting, 'did have a lasting effect'.[129] The root of this ill-treatment meted

---

[123] *Amrita Bazar Patrka*, 23 June 1939, p. 14.
[124] *Amrita Bazar Patrika*, 6 July 1939, p. 14.
[125] *Amrita Bazar Patrka*, 7 July 1939, p. 14.
[126] *Amrita Bazar Patrika*, 10 July 1939, p. 12.
[127] *Ibid.*
[128] *Amrita Bazar Patrika*, 12 August 1939, p. 14.
[129] Majumdar and Bandyopadhyay, *Goalless*, p. 101.

out to Mohammedan Sporting and the resultant rift between the IFA and the club, as has already been shown, had its roots in the changes in the balance of socio-political power in Bengal.

From *Community* to *Communal*: Football and Communalism in Bengal

Thus a potential situation of extreme social tension was created in Bengali football in the course of the 1930s, when peaceful coexistence of the two communities in challenging British supremacy on the soccer field gave way to serious rift between the Hindus and the Muslims. This transition from *community* to *communal* in Bengal football had several delicate moments, subtle shifts and points of convergences. It is to this transition of Bengali football from nationalist force to communal identity that the last section of the chapter pays attention.

There are ample evidences available in contemporary periodicals to show that the Mohammedan Sporting Club started representing purely community interests from the late 1930s. In 1934, a letter to the editor of a newspaper pointed out:

> Any lover of sports or any Indian who has the good of his or her country at heart cannot but be shocked to see how Calcutta football matches are spreading communalism among the masses. A match between Mohammedan Sporting Club and any other team draws tens of thousands of Mussalmans who want only the success of the said team, which they think glorifies the name of their community only and not of the whole Indian nation.[130]

The way football came to be interlinked with communalism also drew criticism from the press:

> What is football coming to in Calcutta? From sports it is definitely veering round to communalism and politics from which it should be thoroughly divorced. . . . The Mohammedan Sporting Club . . . have earned all the praises bestowed on them from all parts of India. But to earn plaudit is one thing and to retain mentioning this fact had they not succumbed to the temptation of winning cheap clapstraps from their communal coreligionists. And in doing so they have ruined and are fairly in the way of still ruining their enviable record of non-stop victories.[131]

---

[130] Letter to the Editor by Beni Madhab Choudhury, *Amrita Bazar Patrika*, 4 July 1934.
[131] *Amrita Bazar Patrika*, 6 June 1938.

In the aftermath of the controversial Mohammedan-East Bengal match of 11 June 1937, a *Statesman* editorial argued:

> In India one community hates another virulently for the love of the game. If a side and its supporters cannot take a beating without showing the savagery seen on Friday it were better that inter community games be forbidden by some Criminal Law Amendment Act: A Communal Award could hardly rouse worse passions. . . . Calcutta football seems to be not a pale, but a highly coloured reflection of Bengal politics.[132]

The attempt of the Muslim press to exonerate the Mohammedan Sporting Club was criticised in the leading newspapers of Calcutta:

> What blood is to leopard, the football incident has been to the Muslim communalists, one shudders as one reads the onthrusts in a section of Calcutta's Moslem Press on the action taken by the IFA. . . . It (IFA) has by that decision become one of the 'tube of Paramanandas' and its members have become 'Hindu Mahasabites'. It is 'revengeful' and 'spiteful' and its whole purpose is to deprive 'all conquering Mohammedans' of the glory that it knew was awaiting them even after their defeat at the hands of East Bengal. . . . Do we not know that continued indulgence from certain quarters has resulted in producing the mentality that a Moslem, in the right or in the wrong, must be defended? This mentality has been created for political reasons. . . . How to cure this mentality?[133]

In 1938, for example, *Bharatbarsha*, a Bengali periodical, appreciated the club's decision not to play against the incoming Burmese national team at the Calcutta ground to protest the discrimination with regard to seat allotment of spectators. But it condemned Mohammedan Sporting's action to stop all its supporters from going to the ground on the match day:

> Special efforts were made to ensure that no Muslim fans visit the ground to watch the Burma team play. Muslims were stopped from going to the ground either by distributing handbills or by issuing orders to that effect. While Mohammedan's decision not to play can be defended for the sake of its opinion, the club's effort to withdraw its supporters from the match is by no means supported.[134]

---

[132] *The Statesman*, 13 June 1937.
[133] *Amrita Bazar Patrika*, 18 June 1937.
[134] *Bharatbarsha*, Asadha 1345 B.S. (1938), p. 150; translation mine.

In the same year, the club authority also felt aggrieved over the issue of the distribution of charity funds realised from Mohammedan's matches. It argued that while the realised fund from the charity matches in 1936–37 amounted to ₹70,000, only ₹4,300 was donated to Muslim voluntary organisations.[135] Consequently, a meeting of the Muslims was organised at the maidan on 31 July 1938. The meeting urged for more representation of Muslim members in the IFA Governing Body and requested the IFA to look after the basic amenities of the Muslim players in Calcutta.[136] However, as it seemed to the reporter of *Bharatbarsha*, these grievances and demands discussed in the meeting had no direct link with the Mohammedan Sporting Club as the Muslim leaders of the meeting threatened to boycott not only Calcutta football but the club if their demands were not properly considered by the authorities concerned.[137]

The victory of the Muslims against strong European and also Hindu teams on the football field instilled a spirit of self-confidence and pride in the Muslims of Bengal in particular, a vast majority of whom, through years of persecution and humiliation, had lost confidence in themselves and in their future.[138] It may therefore be argued that the contribution of the Mohammedan Sporting Club in making the Muslim League popular in Bengal was not insignificant.[139] The series of victories achieved by the club, even in the all-India competitions, considerably increased the prestige of the party. Its effect on Muslim fans 'was electrifying', and a number of Muslim sporting clubs were established in the districts and sub-divisional towns.[140] On the other hand, the fact that the Muslim League was in power helped the club in getting government patronage.[141] Nazimuddin allotted plot no. 41 at Calcutta maidan solely to the club in violation of the existing rules prescribed for it, and also stood surety on the club's behalf to the extent of ₹12,000.[142] Such a policy, though on the pattern of the

---

[135] *Bharatbarsha*, Bhadro 1345 B.S. (1938), pp. 487–88; translation mine.
[136] *Ibid*.
[137] *Ibid*.
[138] Ispahani, *Qaid-E-Azam Jinnah*, p. 12.
[139] Abul Kalam Shamsuddin, *Atit Diner Smriti* (Memories of Olden Days), Dacca, 1968, pp. 154–58.
[140] Humaira Momen, *Muslim Politics in Bengal: A Study of Krishak Praja Party and the Elections of 1937*, Dacca: Sunny House, 1972, p. 72.
[141] Sen, *Muslim Politics in Bengal*, pp. 110–11.
[142] A number of applications for allotment of football grounds were lying with the government when the Muslim League came to power. Immediately, the secretary of the Mohammedan Sporting Club wrote a letter for allotment emphasising that

normal 'spoils system' of all democratic governments, had the effect of consolidating the Muslim League's hold over the administration and also of creating the image that the League was alive to the interests of the Muslims. As these measures were meant for the exclusive benefit of Muslims, Hindus raised the cry of 'communal overtone' against the ministry.[143]

Suranjan Das's hint at Muslim 'self-mobilisation' around the Mohammedan Sporting Club in the context of the 1946 Calcutta-riots was not confined to the Muslims only.[144] Such self-mobilisation efforts were also noticeable among the Hindus under the aegis of the Hindu Mahasabha. In fact, one strand of nationalist activities from the 1920s, as Tanika Sarkar points out, which reinforced a sense of insecurity among the Muslims, was the crop of physical culture associations or *akhras* for Hindu youth in Calcutta and mofussil towns.[145] The presence of Hindu centres of *lathi* and dagger-play made the Muslims nervous and stimulated similar preparations among them. In the early 1940s when Hindu volunteer groups proliferated in Calcutta, smaller *para* ('neighbourhood') groups such as the 'Yuva Sampradaya' of Behala started by Nirmal Kumar Chatterjee in 1943 included in their functions a 'football section' apart

---

this 'will remove the long-standing grievances of the Muslim community'. The sanctioning officer proposed to give plot no. 41 to the Mohammedan Sporting Club and the Kalighat Club as according to the existing rules a ground had to be shared by two clubs. However, Nazimuddin interfered and ordered the allotment of enclosure 41 exclusively to the Mohammedan Sporting Club and guaranteed ability to pay ₹12,000 required for the development of the plot. At that time all the European and the Indian football clubs like the Dalhousie, Rangers, Mohun Bagan, and East Bengal were sharing grounds in the Calcutta maidan. See *Government of Bengal, Home-Police*, File 7-M of 1936, and File 7-M (1–3) of 1937; proceedings A 1–3 May, 1940.

[143] With the advent of Mohammedan Sporting Club, the sporting situation in Calcutta maidan underwent a change. In the mid-1930s just as the Congress was branded by the Muslim League as the Hindu organisation, Mohun Bagan came to be called by the Muslims the Hindus' national team. The bitter political animosity then raging between the two communities was reflected in the soccer ties between Mohammedan Sporting and Muhun Bagan, which became the annual classic of the new era.

[144] Suranjan Das, *Communal Riots in Bengal*, New Delhi: Oxford University Press, 1991, p. 170.

[145] Tanika Sarkar, 'Communal Riots in Bengal', in Mushirul Haasan (ed.), *Communal and Pan-Islamic Trends in Colonial India*, New Delhi: Manohar, 1985, p. 309.

from usual *bratachari* and dagger-play, drama section and organising Durga Puja and Saraswati Pujas.[146] On the other hand, the Muslims, who were 'rolling on the ground with joy' in 1911 at the victory of their Hindu brothers on the football field, had all disappeared, and been replaced by a new breed who came to watch the game carrying knives and bottles of soda water. Bengalis had never displayed such aggressive spirit on the Calcutta sports field before. Das remarks of this communal situation on the maidan aptly: '. . . reverses suffered by the Mohammedan Sporting Club in football matches enraged Muslim feelings which were expressed in sporadic violence against the Hindus.'[147] Or, as another writer comments, 'with each victory, a communal wedge was driven deeper into Calcutta football if not into Calcutta society'.[148] Thus the decade between 1937 and 1947 saw a fundamental change of vision of football in the nationalist discourse of both the Hindus and the Muslims.

The Quit India movement of 1942, the economic insecurity generated by the Second World War, the panic evacuation of Calcutta caused by the fear of Japanese bombs, the famine, restlessness among the youth, and the communal riots that broke out on the day of the call for 'direct action' by the Muslim League — the stress of all these events gradually wiped out any enthusiasm for football in Calcutta.[149] Because of the riots, there was no competition for the Shield in 1946 and the League was not played in 1947. Unfortunately, the advantages of building a successful club entirely on the patronage of rich businessmen and political leaders from a particular community were offset with associated problems. As Moti Nandy writes: 'Who knows then their selfish needs would be over, when their largesse would come to an end? Immediately after the partition of August 1947, having finally achieved their heart's desire, the patrons of Mohammedan Sporting Club left for either East or West Pakistan.'[150] The club's flame of success was thus extinguished, never to be revived again.[151] Since independence it has been League champion on only three occasions.

---

[146] Note on Volunteer Organisations dated 11 September 1946. GB SB 'PM' Series. File No. 822/46II, quoted in Chatterji, *Bengal Divided*, pp. 235–36.

[147] Das, *Communal Riots in Bengal*, p. 170. Also see *Amrita Bazar Patrika*, 8 July, 1946, p. 4; File-5/27/46 Poll (I), the IB Daily Summary Information of 8 July 1946, referred to in Das, *Communal Riots in Bengal*, p. 170.

[148] Nandy, 'Calcutta Soccer', p. 318.

[149] *Ibid.*

[150] *Ibid.*

[151] Sultan Ahmed, present secretary of the Mohammedan Sporting Club, has argued that the club's representative character always acted as a bar in any

Thus the meteoric rise of the Mohammedan Sporting Club in the Bengal as well as Indian sporting scenario in the early 1930s and its continuous clash with the IFA in the late 1930s and 1940s shows how football's role as a unitary nationalist force gave way to a divided sense of loyalties in Bengal. It also explains why a rich history of football in India around the club has been overshadowed by the politics that grew around the game. A study of contemporary socio-political realities of the late 1930s and the resultant communal strife in the 1940s demonstrates why, despite winning five straight Calcutta Football League titles defeating leading European sides, Mohammedan Sporting did not usher a new wave of sporting nationalism in colonial Bengal. As a result, Mohun Bagan's solitary IFA Shield triumph in colonial India continues to be regarded as a greater success of Indian nationalism on the sporting field.[152] The factors influencing the gradual marginalisation of Mohammedan from Bengali sporting scenario in the 1940s also throw light on the association between politics, communalism and sport in the Indian context. However, it was not simply 'the Bengali bhadralok's failure to come to terms with the spectacular success of Mohammedan Sporting that led to the erasure of a rich chapter of Bengal's sporting history'.[153] Rather, it was the oppositional perception of identity of the two communities in the tense socio-political context of Bengal, which led to the fracture of footballing nationalism from the 1930s. This chapter has attempted to consider football as an integral component of 'Bengali' political and social life, thereby drawing attention to the relationship between sport and identity in the colonial context. It thus tries to widen the conventional historical understanding of community, communalism and identity in colonial India, using soccer as a lens in Bengal in the 1930–40s.

---

long-term efforts to revive its fortunes. Giving a contemporary example, he pointed out that the club could not find a viable sponsor since the late 1990s because it represents the Muslim community, and in effect a Muslim identity. Following Ahmed's argument, it can be inferred that most of the better Hindu Bengali footballers in the post-colonial period might not have preferred to play for the club for its exclusively *Muslim* character until the 1980s when the club offered them a lucrative financial package. Interview with Sultan Ahmed, 15 July 2004.

[152] The club next won the IFA Shield in 1947.
[153] Majumdar and Bandyopadhyay, in *Goalless* (p. 102), argue on this line.

Plate 1
Dukhiram Majumdar
Source: Courtesy of Mona Chowdhury

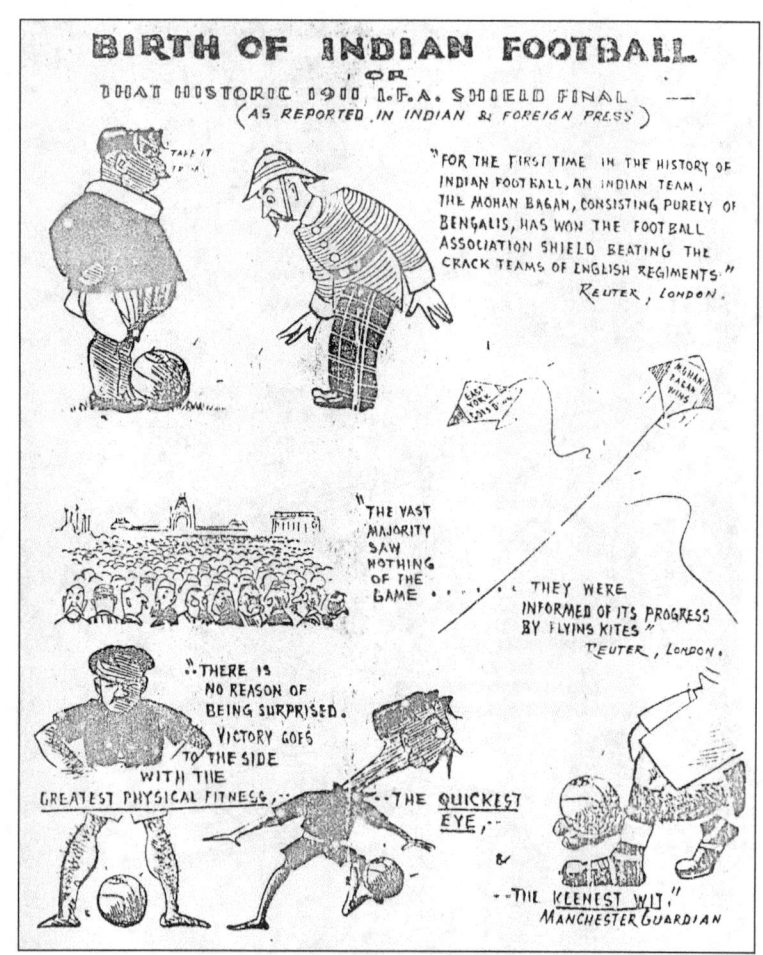

Plate 2A
Birth of Indian Football or that Historic 1911 IFA Shield Final
Source: Courtesy of *Mohun Bagan Club Platinum Jubilee Souvenir*.
Calcutta: Mohun Bagan A. C., 1964

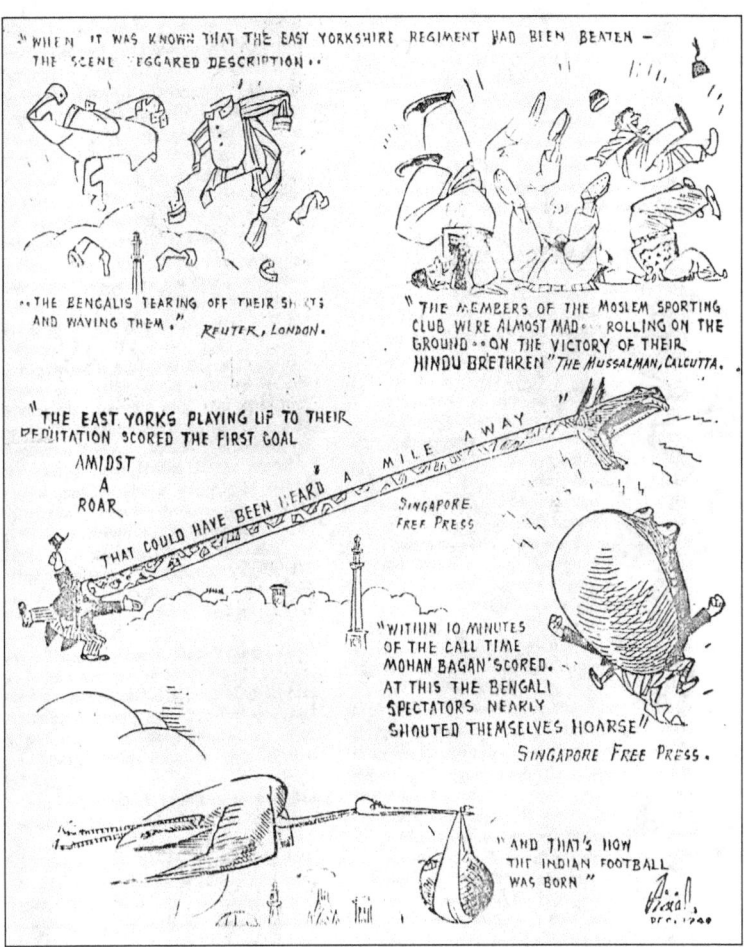

Plate 2B
Birth of Indian Football or that Historic 1911 IFA Shield Final
Source: Courtesy of *Mohun Bagan Club Platinum Jubilee Souvenir*.
Calcutta: Mohun Bagan A. C., 1964

Plate 3A
Mohun Bagan Match: A Study in Expression
Source: Courtesy of *Mohun Bagan A.C. Golden Jubilee Souvenir.*
Calcutta: Mohun Bagan A.C., 1939

Plate 3B
Mohun Bagan Match: A Study in Expression
Source: Courtesy of *Mohun Bagan A.C. Golden Jubilee Souvenir*.
Calcutta: Mohun Bagan A.C., 1939

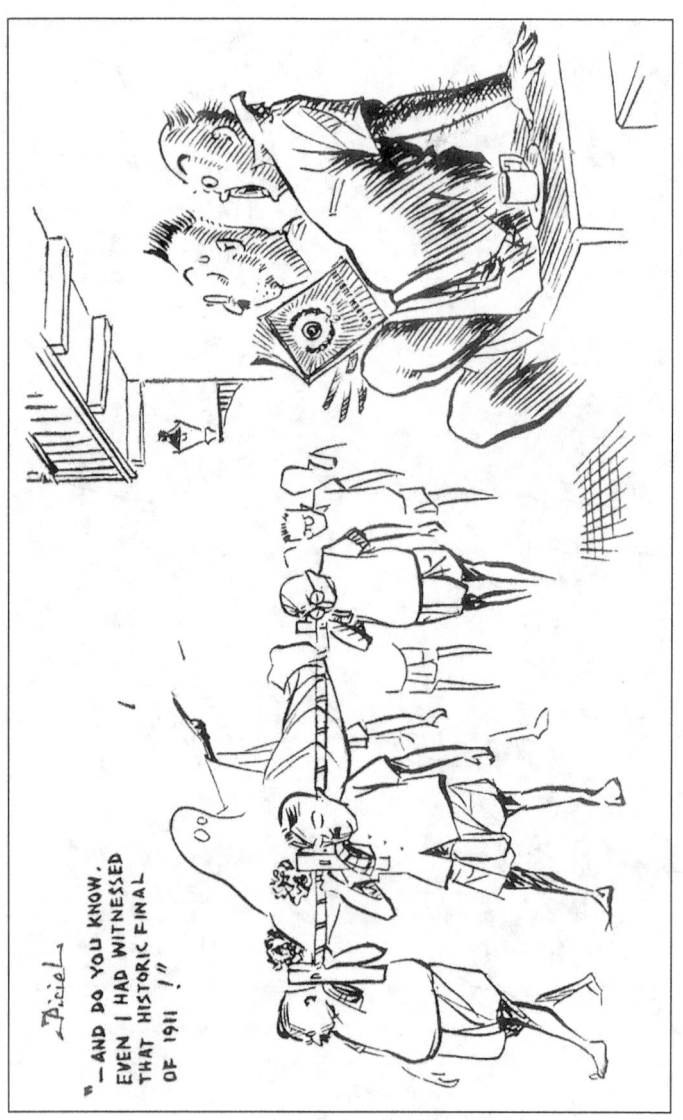

Plate 3C
Mohun Bagan Match: A Study in Expression
Source: Courtesy of *Mohun Bagan A.C. Golden Jubilee Souvenir*.
Calcutta: Mohun Bagan A.C., 1939

Plate 4
The Victorious Mohun Bagan Team with the IFA Shield in 1911
Source: Courtesy of Mona Chowdhury

Plate 5
Mohun Bagan Captain Shibdas Bhaduri and Honorary Secretary S. N. Bose with the IFA Shield in 1911
Source: Courtesy of Mona Chowdhury

Plate 6
IFA Shield Winning Aryan Team in 1940
Source: Courtesy of Mona Chowdhury

Plate 7
Queue for Tickets at a Match in Calcutta First Division League in the 1960s
Source: Courtesy of Mona Chowdhury

Plate 8
Mounted Police Trying to Discipline the Spectators in Queue for
Tickets Outside the Ground
Source: Courtesy of Mona Chowdhury

Plate 9
Football Fans Sitting atop a Monument to View a Match
Source: Courtesy of Mona Chowdhury

Plate 10
Effusion of the Fans Behind the Goalpost after Their Favourite Club Scored a Goal
Source: Courtesy of Mona Chowdhury

Plate 11
Referee and Linesmen being Cordoned by Police after the League Match between Mohun Bagan and East Bengal in 1975
Source: Courtesy of Mona Chowdhury

Plate 12
One Mohammedan Sporting Player Hitting the Referee during a League Match
Source: Courtesy of Mona Chowdhury

Plate 13
Mohun Bagan Footballer Prasun Banerjee being Garlanded by a Woman Fan
during the Course of a Match
Source: Courtesy of Mona Chowdhury

Plate 14
Dead Body being Taken from Upper to Lower Tier of the Eden Gardens
during the Tragedy on 16 August 1980
Source: Courtesy of Mona Chowdhury

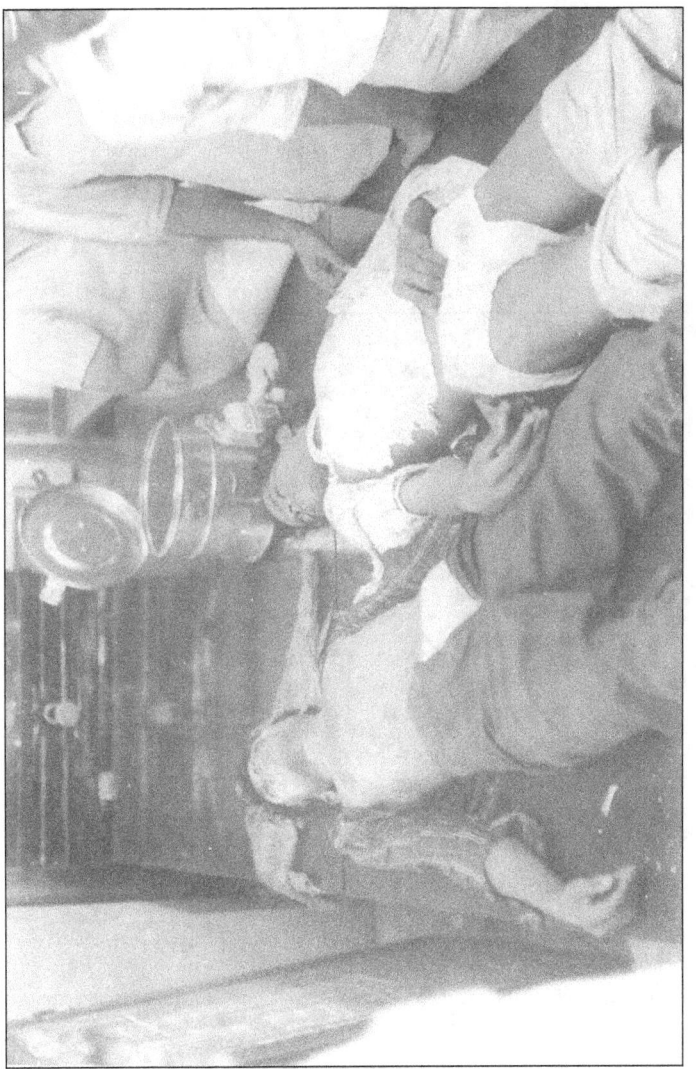

Plate 15
Dead Bodies of the Victims of 16 August 1980 Tragedy Kept at the Club House of the Eden Gardens
Source: Courtesy of Mona Chowdhury

Plate 16
Statue of Gostho Paul, the Legendary Mohun Bagan Footballer, at Kolkata Maidan
Source: Courtesy of Sabyasachi Mallick

4

Tussle in Football Administration: Bengal and the Regional Politics of Soccer in Colonial India

The rise of Mohammedan Sporting Club and the communal tension in Bengali football coincided with serious rifts in the administration of the game at the central level. The Indian Football Association, hitherto considered to be the sole arbiter of football in the country, began to face stiff challenge from new contenders like Bombay and Delhi, which tried to mobilise the support of other regional soccer associations to form a new all-India apex body to control the game in the country. The IFA contended the challenge by emphasising its tradition, contribution and all-India character and tried to evolve out of its own constitution a restructured all-India organisation. This regional politics of soccer reached its height in the mid-1930s when both Bengal on the one hand and other regional associations on the other tried to draw the support of the Football Association (FA) of England and the Army Sports Control Board (ASCB) of India to ensure their power and position. While this tussle over power and control of Indian soccer administration clearly reflected a regional power rivalry among the Indian states, as this chapter argues, it also pointed to the continuing importance of the British in the control and management of the game in India despite their apparent marginalisation as a football force in the Indian competitions. The resultant cultural politics of soccer forced Bengal to adapt to the changing priorities of football administration against the backdrop of provincial power rivalry in colonial India.

Regional Politics of Soccer in Colonial India: The Historical Debate

Paul Dimeo and James Mills argue that 'the British had stopped being a significant presence in Indian football by the 1930s and that Indians had adopted the game and played amongst themselves since they had first picked it up in the nineteenth century'.[1] Furthermore, Dimeo maintains:

> Bengal is the traditional powerhouse of Indian football precisely because the game and its institutions became a powerful vehicle for the energies that emerged during the history of the period. Once these energies turned towards organizing communities to compete for the spoils in the event of British de-colonization, football took on communal significance, and by 1930s it seems that a consideration of the place of football in Indian society and politics required no focus on the British at all.[2]

While it is true that the British teams gradually began to be marginalised as a strong football force in Indian football from the mid-1930s, especially with the rise of native clubs led by Mohammedan Sporting, their importance as arbiter of Indian football continued to remain vital. As Boria Majumdar has argued, British recognition and support was pivotal in shaping the development of Indian soccer in the 1930s and 1940s.[3] The IFA, in its bid to play its role as a governing body in the development of football in the whole country, counted upon the support of the British authority. Such dominating intentions of the IFA faced challenge from other state soccer associations, which formed the All India Football Association (AIFA) in 1935.[4] The formation of the AIFA in September 1935 triggered the beginning of a bitter struggle between the Indian states — Bengal on the one hand and the western and northern Indian states on the other — for assertion of supremacy over the control of the game.[5] In this struggle, as Majumdar has tried to show, Bengal at every stage drew upon British support, especially that of the ASCB of India and the FA of England, a factor that, according to him, eventually contributed to the success of the Maharaja of Santosh, the president of the IFA, in combating efforts to establish a parallel governing body, the AIFA, to rival the IFA with its headquarters in Calcutta.[6] According to a contemporary

---

[1] Dimeo and Mills, *Soccer in South Asia*, p. 6.

[2] Dimeo, 'Football and Politics in Bengal', p. 71.

[3] See Boria Majumdar, 'The Politics of Soccer in Colonial India, 1930–37: The Years of Turmoil', *Soccer and Society*, vol. 3, no. 1, 2002, p. 22.

[4] The All India Football Association came into existence at Darbhanga on 20 September 1935.

[5] *Amrita Bazar Patrika*, 20 September 1936.

[6] Majumdar, 'The Politics of Soccer in Colonial India', p. 23. All the leading newspapers of the country, *Amrita Bazar Patrika*, *The Statesman*, *Ananda Bazar Patrika*, *Star of India*, carried detailed reports about this ongoing tussle through the 1930s.

newspaper referred to by Majumdar, in soccer, faced with challenge from other Indian states, the Bengalis, trying to retain their supremacy over the control of the sport, fell back on the support of the British Football Association.[7] Recognition granted by the British Football Association to the IFA was garnered by the Maharaja of Santosh to impress that the IFA was the only internationally recognised governing body for soccer in India.[8]

James Mills, on the other hand, argues that the story of the conflict clearly reveals that 'all the actors are Indian and the dispute concerns which group of Indians would control the game'.[9] Indeed, he further points out, 'when the British did get involved in his (Majumdar's) story they were dismissed as simply representing European opinion and therefore of little bearing, while the English FA was dragged into the dispute only as a makeweight by one group of Indian disputants'.[10]

These views have their useful points as well as unreasonable extremes. Although Bengal drew upon British support in its fight to retain dominance over other provinces in soccer, this chapter tries to argue, the IFA-AIFA conflict reflected more a power rivalry between Indian regional states for the control of the game, with the British FA playing the role of a mere legitimating authority. Rather, at crucial junctures of the conflict it was the European-controlled ASCB, which came to play a decisive role in shaping and resolving the dispute. The chapter further argues that both Bengal and its rivals tried to mobilise the support of the ASCB in strengthening their position vis-à-vis the other. That the Maharaja of Santosh ultimately could not persuade the ASCB in following his line of proposals in forming an all-India body by reforming and remodelling the IFA clearly shows that his rivals in the north and west were more successful in convincing the ASCB of their point of view. As a result, even after continuously invoking the support of the FA of England, the Maharaja had to give up and comply with the ASCB's proposals, which resulted in the formation of the All India Football Federation (AIFF) in 1937.

---

[7] *The Orient Illustrated Weekly*, 11 October 1936.

[8] *Amrita Bazar Patrika*, 14 May 1936.

[9] James Mills, 'Introduction', in James Mills (ed.), *Subaltern Sports: Politics and Sport in South Asia*, London: Anthem Press, 2005, p. 9.

[10] *Ibid.*

Provincial Football Associations in Colonial India

While football had already become a popular spectator sport in Bengal at the turn of the 20th century, most regions in the country adopted the game in the 1920s and 1930s. Bombay, well known for its cricketing prowess at the time, did not lag far behind. The third oldest tournament of India — the Rovers Cup — was inaugurated in Bombay as far back as 1891.[11] Some British military soccer enthusiasts got together in 1890, formed the Rovers Club, and brought into being this tournament.[12] The Bombay Football Association was formed in 1902 to run a local league. Seven teams participated in the first year.[13] As Col. Harwood, the president of the Association, donated the cup, the league later came to be known as the Harwood League. In 1911, the two bodies, the old Rovers Club running the Rovers Cup and the Bombay Football Association managing the League were amalgamated to form the Western India Football Association (WIFA). Hon. Mr Justice Russell, president of the Rovers was elected president and P. R. Cadell, president of the League, vice-president. The respective secretaries, Mr F. Hogan and Mr J. B. Linn, became joint honorary secretaries.[14] Russell and Hogan were associated with the organisation of football in Bombay since 1902 and were pillars of soccer-promotion in the city.

Besides Bombay, the states from the south promoted football in an organised manner in colonial India. The list begins with Mysore (present Karnataka), which became the third centre to establish a football association, that is, the Mysore Football Association (the former name of the Karnataka Football Association) in 1908.[15] The Madras Football Association (present Tamil Nadu Football Association) was founded in 1934 while the Hyderabad Football Association was formed in 1939–40.[16]

---

[11] The oldest football tournament — the Durand Cup — was held at Simla in 1888. It was followed by the Trades Cup in Calcutta in 1889.

[12] J. C. Maitra, '50 Glorious Years: W.I.F.A.'s Unique Achievement', *WIFA Golden Jubilee Souvenir*, Bombay: Western India Football Association, 1961.

[13] These seven teams were: Oxford Lt., R.A., Bombay Rovers, Bombay Gymkhana, Telegraphs, Bombay Volunteer Artillery, and H.M.S. Magdala. Oxford became the champions that year.

[14] Maitra, '50 Glorious Years'.

[15] *34th National Football Championship: Official Souvenir*, Calcutta: IFA, 1977.

[16] *Ibid*.

The latter was founded at the initiative of S. M. Hadi, the first secretary of the All India Council of Sports, and his brothers Col. Ali Raza, Nawab Mahmood Yar Jung, S. A. Rahim and Ahmed Mohiuddin.[17] In fact, the 1930s was an important decade for the organisational progress of soccer in India. It opened with the formation of a controlling body for soccer in Bihar — the Bihar Olympic Association — in 1931.[18] This association was one of the founder-members of the AIFF and took part in the Santosh Trophy from the very first year. The North-West Football Association was founded in 1932 at Lahore, capital of undivided Punjab. After the partition of Punjab in 1947, the East Punjab Football Association came into existence, to be soon replaced by the Punjab Football Association, which was affiliated to the AIFF in 1951.[19] The Rajputana Football Association was established in 1934. It later became the Rajasthan Football Association after the change in the name of the state.[20]

Two other central sports bodies that took active interest in the development of soccer in both colonial and post-colonial India were the ASCB and the Railways Athletic Association. The former, which was established in 1919 to control sports for the services personnel in the army, navy and the air force, as this chapter will show, played a crucial role in the foundation of the AIFF in 1937. The board was reconstituted as the Services Sport Control Board in 1945.[21] The apex body for the control and coordination of sports activities of the staff of the Railways was set up in 1928 as the Indian Railways Athletic Association. On its reconstitution in 1959, the Association adopted its present name — the Railways Sports Control Board.[22]

---

[17] In 1959 Shiv Kumar Lal, vice-president of the All India Football Federation, brought about the amalgamation of the Andhra and Hyderabad Football Associations to form the Andhra Pradesh Football Association.

[18] The soldiers and the indigo planters carried the game to the barracks at Dinapore in Bihar in the late 19th century. The general public, however, took up the game at the turn of that century. In its early years, Patna, Jamshedpur, Danapur, Dhanbad, and Darbhanga were the centres where football acquired popularity.

[19] *34th National Football Championship: Official Souvenir.*

[20] *Ibid.*

[21] *Ibid.*

[22] *Ibid.*

Bengal versus Other States: The Birth of the All India Football Association

The troubled relationship between the various state soccer associations was a unique feature of Indian football by the middle of the 1930s.[23] Till the 1920s, the dominance of Bengal over the sport was unquestioned. This state of affairs, however, underwent a radical transformation from the close of the decade as other provinces, hitherto averse to soccer, emerged as active patrons of the sport. This in turn marked the onset of a phase of crisis in Indian soccer that was to culminate in the formation of the All India Football Federation (AIFF) in 1937.[24]

Interestingly enough, this changing equation in the arena of sport was a reflection of what had already happened in the field of politics. Since the rise of Gandhi in Indian politics and particularly after the death of Chittaranjan Roy, Bengal gradually began to lose its prominence in the nationalist movement led by the Indian National Congress. Even in the central Congress politics as well as in its leadership, Bengal began to be marginalised from the mid-1920s. And by the early 1930s, especially with the launch and spread of the Civil Disobedience movement, central and western India came to hold the major sway over nationalist politics in India.[25] It is an interesting historical coincidence that states like Delhi or Bombay, which had taken over Bengal's lead in the nationalist movement as also in Congress politics so successfully, also began to challenge Bengal's supremacy in soccer administration.

By the early 1930s, Bombay, which had already taken a lead over Bengal in cricket, was gradually shifting its interest to soccer. Growing apprehension among the Bengali sports patrons about a possible challenge from Bombay led them to formulate a series of proposals to restructure the IFA, in an attempt to make it more representative.[26] This scheme, guided by the assumption to safeguard Bengal's supremacy over the control of soccer in the country, proposed the setting up of an all-India body, one that would still be controlled by the IFA:

---

[23] Misunderstanding and mistrust between the associations that existed from the beginning of the 1930s came to the fore after the formation of the AIFA.

[24] This body eventually came into existence in May 1937 at Simla.

[25] For Bengal's marginalisation in Congress-led nationalist politics and its growing rift with the central leadership, see Gallagher, 'Congress in Decline', pp. 589–645; and Chatterji, *Bengal Divided*, pp. 18–54, 103–49.

[26] *Advance*, 18 November 1933.

The present situation has given rise to two things. Time has come to form an All India Federation — the name of which must be the IFA and Bengal must take the lead in the matter being the home of best football in the country. The present administrative body in Calcutta should clearly define their jurisdiction as in the coming federation the areas have to be settled in a manner by which Bengal's interests may not be side tracked as now the case in the Indian Hockey Federation, Indian Olympic Association and Board of Control for Cricket.[27]

Provincial football associations of Delhi and Bombay started their venture to make themselves affiliated to the Football Association of England from 1934. However, the FA, respectful of its traditional patronage of the IFA, the only affiliated unit of the FA in India, asked both Delhi and Bombay to negotiate through the IFA.[28] Delhi and Bombay were in no mood to bow their heads to the IFA for such purposes. They strongly reminded the FA that the IFA was only representative of the province of Bengal and that it had no jurisdiction whatsoever over other provinces. As the secretary of the Delhi FA wrote to the FA secretary:

> I am to state that the IFA, Calcutta, is not an All India Football Association as the name suggests. It is no doubt the oldest FA in India but its jurisdiction extends over the province of Bengal only. At present all the members of the Calcutta Association are representative of football clubs of Bengal. So long as an All-India Football Federation is not formed, my committee as well as the representatives of military teams of Delhi think it is essentially necessary that Delhi FA should be affiliated to the Inter-National FA of London.[29]

Mr A. C. Hinrichs, president of the WIFA, too, expressed similar sentiments:

> While it may be the case that the Rules of the IFA afford other Provincial Associations the opportunity of affiliating, we are not aware that any of these, of which there are several, have done so, for, ... the IFA is *not* accepted as the 'mother' association of India.... from every other point

---

[27] Interview with Pankaj Gupta, *Advance*, 18 November 1933.
[28] See FA secretary Stanley F. Rous's letter to the secretary of Delhi FA, 27 December 1934, and FA secretary Stanley F. Rous's letter to A. C. Hinrichs of WIFA, 28 December 1934, *Private Papers of Maharaja of Santosh* (hereafter *MSPP*), File 4-I, pp. 20–24.
[29] Letter of the secretary of Delhi FA to the secretary, FA, 14 February 1935, *MSPP*, File 4-I, p. 23.

of view the I.F.A. is a provincial one with no jurisdiction whatsoever over other provinces. Therefore, may I on behalf of my committee ask you to be good enough ... to accept my assurance that what the IFA is to the province of Bengal the W.I.F.A. Ltd. is to the presidency of Bombay, and as you have accepted direct affiliation from the I.F.A. and Burma, you will be equally prepared to recognize the importance of our organisation in football activities in Western India and, therefore, our strong desire to be affiliated with the parent body.[30]

But the FA, too, was not ready to entertain such pressures and sent strong messages to both the Delhi FA and the WIFA. It wrote to the Delhi FA: 'We suggest that you at once commu-nicate with the IFA and cooperate with that Association in forming an All-India Football Association.'[31] To the WIFA, the FA Secretary urged similarly: 'In our opinion, it is advisable for all Associations in India to unite into one governing body and we hope that you will cooperate with the IFA in forming an All-India Football Association.'[32]

To implement the scheme of forming a new all-India governing body for soccer in India, the president of the IFA, the Maharaja of Santosh, convened a conference of the provincial soccer associations of the country at Darbhanga in September 1935.[33] However, the delegates representing Delhi and Bombay were determined to keep Bengal out of the body and therefore sternly opposed to accept him as the chairman.[34] Even before the Maharaja's arrival at Darbhanga, they had already drafted the constitution of the all-India body. In such a situation, as the Maharaja decided to abandon the conference and return to Calcutta,[35] the All India Football Association (AIFA) came into existence at Darbhanga on 21 September 1935.[36] The Maharaja of Santosh was utterly dismayed at the actions of the delegates of other states:

---

[30] Letter of the president, WIFA to the secretary, FA, 6 February 1935, *MSPP*, File 4-I, p. 22.

[31] FA secretary Stanley F. Rous's letter to the secretary of Delhi FA, 27 February 1935, *MSPP*, File 4-I, p. 23.

[32] FA secretary Stanley F. Rous's letter to A. C. Hinrichs of Western India Football Association, 27 February 1935, *MSPP*, File 4 I, p. 22.

[33] *Amrita Bazar Patrika*, 15 September 1935.

[34] *Amrita Bazar Patrika*, 22 September 1935.

[35] *Forward*, 22 September 1935.

[36] The *Amrita Bazar Patrika*, 22 September 1935 reported: 'The twenty first of September 1935 will go down to history as a memorable day in the formation of

I am going away from Darbhanga sorely disappointed over the question of the formation of an All India Federation. I found the provinces of India hopelessly divided on this front. *Internal suspicion and provincial jealousies retarded progress of the country in almost every department of public life.* I find that even the field of sport is unable to rise above these elements. There is no chance for a federation worth the name until we grow more patient and tolerant and learn to set high premium on co-operation and premium trust. Bengal had stretched out the hand of friendship and had come with an open mind but found it curtly refused.[37]

Later, the Maharaja ventilated his grievances more clearly to Colonel Majendi, the president of the ASCB:

That conference, in my considered opinion, was not a representative one and its doors were deliberately shut against me as the President-elect of the Conference and other Bengal delegates. It was held by a certain number of provincial delegates in a room of the Darbhanga Guest House, where they were living, in spite of the fact that the Indian Football Association which had invited the Conference called it off and the Maharaja-Kumar of Darbhanga, exercising *ipso facto* the functions of a Reception Committee, as the recognized host, prohibited the holding of the said conference in his Palace which had been officially announced as its venue. I may be permitted to say, with all the emphasis that I can command, that these two determining factors are not negligible and the proceedings of the so-called conference must be considered as wholly irregular, unconstitutional, and *ultra licitum*.[38]

Other Bengali soccer administrators including S. N. Banerjee of Mohun Bagan Club and Pankaj Gupta, both of whom had represented the IFA at Darbhanga considered the conference to be a farce.[39] In fact, the decision to form the AIFA excluding the IFA was unacceptable as the IFA was

---

the AIFA despite efforts by the IFA to complicate matters at Darbhanga. Different provincial delegates excepting Bengal held meeting this morning at the Raj Guest house under the Presidentship of Mr. Moinul Haq, OBE (Bihar) and unanimously resolved that an All India body be formed to control Association football in India and it be named the All India Football Association.'

[37] *Forward*, 22 September 1935; emphasis added.

[38] Maharaja of Santosh's letter to the president of ASCB, 15 January 1936, *MSPP*, File 4-I, pp. 31–32; emphasis in orginal.

[39] Pankaj Gupta was a renowned sports administrator in colonial India, who served as a Governing Body member of the IFA for a long time. *Advance*, 29 September 1935.

the biggest and oldest soccer association of the country, and was the only association affiliated to the British Football Association and FIFA.[40]

IFA versus AIFA: The Critical Role of ASCB

Despite its dramatic beginning with an independent and separatist flair, it was tough going for the newly formed AIFA to function smoothly without Bengal for long. With Bengal opposed to the body, it was difficult for the AIFA to raise necessary funds for its maintenance. Further, with the Maharaja of Santosh leading the opposition against it, it was quite natural for many other princes, mostly allies of the Maharaja, to stay away from according patronage to the newly formed body.[41] Even the Maharaj Kumar of Darbhanga, deemed to be the president of the AIFA, intended to maintain his connection with football in India solely through the IFA.[42] Moreover, confusion for the AIFA was further aggravated by the growing tension among the delegates of the Western India Football Association. J. C. Maitra, representing the Indian Football League of Bombay at the Darbhanga convention, alleged that the Western India Football Association led by Mr Turner at Darbhanga could at best represent the European opinion of Bombay.[43] He too expressed clear dissatisfaction at the exclusion of the IFA from the all-India body.

The ASCB, however, from the very beginning of the tussle, seemed to be firmly committed to a position that provided a sort of legitimisation to the AIFA. In a communication to the president of the IFA, it clearly said:

> As football in India depends very largely on the ready cooperation of teams from military units, my Board feel that it would be doing no service to football generally by standing aloof from an All India Association, to which the majority of Provincial Associations have already affiliated in order to promote the better control of football throughout the country.[44]

And the ASCB categorically warned the IFA that 'should the A.S.C.B., India, affiliate and your Association not do so, my Board, much against its will, would under the rules of the All India Football Association, have to forbid the participation of military teams in the I.F.A. Shield competition

---

[40] *Advance*, 24 September 1935.

[41] *Advance*, 28 September 1935.

[42] *Ibid.*

[43] *Ibid.*

[44] Letter of the president, ASCB to the president, IFA, 18 December 1935, *MSPP*, File 4-I, p. 26.

and in any other leagues or competitions controlled by your Association'.⁴⁵ This closeness of ASCB to AIFA seemed to be largely because of the former's composition (representing the army, largely recruited from northern India) and the latter's main location (northern India).

As the administrative problems and financial crisis of the AIFA got more and more compounded, the IFA took the opportunity to denounce the authority of the new association and offered to form a compromise All India Federal Council under its aegis to unite the soccer associations of the country.⁴⁶ The IFA's position was consolidated by media reports, which described the formation of the AIFA as 'the staging of Hamlet without the Prince of Denmark'.⁴⁷ The object of the Federal Council, it was declared, was to promote soccer in India by the organisation, management and control of inter-provincial football leagues, tournaments and matches. It also aimed to create football zones in the country and exercise control over the provincial associations affiliated to the IFA.⁴⁸ The Federal Council was to be constituted on an all-India basis, consisting of two representatives from Bengal proper, two representatives from the erstwhile province of Eastern Bengal, and two representatives each, from all the other provinces. The ASCB and the Indian Railways were also to be represented in the council.⁴⁹ The headquarters of the body was to be at Calcutta with a permanent office maintained by the IFA. It was also stipulated that all meetings of the Federal Council were to be held at the headquarters.⁵⁰

According to Boria Majumdar, the decision of the ASCB to support the IFA also strengthened the position of the IFA vis-à-vis the AIFA.⁵¹

---

⁴⁵ *Ibid.*

⁴⁶ *Advance*, 15 March 1936. This proposal was sent to the secretary of the ASCB and the AIFA apart from others.

⁴⁷ *Amrita Bazar Patrika*, 14 March 1936. It wrote: 'The Indian Football Federation was formed last year after the Darbhanga convention. But it has ever remained an isolated organization in which the IFA, the oldest and greatest corporate soccer body of India and the only Association which has been recognized by the FA of England, never joined. In fact the whole procedure can be compared to the staging of Hamlet without the prince of Denmark.'

⁴⁸ *Amrita Bazar Patrika*, 14 March 1936.

⁴⁹ *Ibid.*

⁵⁰ *Ibid.*

⁵¹ Majumdar, 'The Politics of Soccer in Colonial India', p. 27. Surprisingly, he also seemed to have come to such a conclusion on the basis of contemporary newspaper reports and the private papers of the Maharaja of Santosh.

This support, he argues, 'starkly disproved the sovereignty of the AIFA'.⁵² Majumdar's contention, however, seems to be based on partial reading of newspaper reports. The official correspondences between the IFA and the ASCB, reveal an altogether different story. In striking contrast to what Majumdar tries to prove, the ASCB was quite critical of the Federal Council proposal put forward by the IFA. Its president, General Majendi, considered the proposed All India Federal Council to be 'merely an off-shoot' of the Indian Football Association.⁵³ He further argued:

> ... there does not appear to be the slightest chance of the other presidency and provincial associations accepting the proposals put forward by the Indian Football Association. The latter in my opinion are based on the faulty assumption that an All-Indian Federation must be built up round the I.F.A. There can be no doubt, if the interests of India as a whole are considered and a long view of football in India is taken, that an All Indian Federation with its governing body must come into being as a new organization to which the existing associations can be affiliated.⁵⁴

The president also urged the IFA to become realistic and wake up to the call of the hour:

> The time has come to recognize the situation which now exists. The All India Football Association is in being and is holding a meeting in Delhi on the 12th of April. Every presidency and provincial association in India of any importance, with the exception of Bengal, has now affiliated to this body. *It seems quite out of the question that this newly constituted All Indian Association will agree to its own dissolution and its replacement by an alternative built up round the I.F.A.*
>
> I have reason to suppose that at the meeting on the 12th of April the All Indian Association will express a strong desire for the co-operation of Bengal, and in order to obtain it may be prepared to offer to the I.F.A. a larger representation on the Council than any other body and to change its name to the All Indian Football Federation in order that the I.F.A. may not run any risk of losing its identity. If this offer is made, it would be fair and reasonable, and in my opinion one which should be accepted by the I.F.A., both in its own interests and in those of India as a whole.⁵⁵

---

⁵² *Ibid.*

⁵³ Letter of the president, ASCB to the president, IFA, 21 March 1936, *MSPP*, File 4-II, p. 26.

⁵⁴ *Ibid.*, p. 27.

⁵⁵ *Ibid.*, p. 28; emphasis added.

This letter clearly indicated that the ASCB was in no mood to accept any proposal of the IFA to the formation of a restructured old body. More importantly, its sympathy with the AIFA and its anticipation of fresh AIFA proposals towards accommodation of the IFA into an all-India body hinted at the existence of a continuous cordial relation between the ASCB and the AIFA since the latter's birth. The Maharaja of Santosh was probably late in understanding the gravity of this link and wasted much time to convince the ASCB of his good intentions. In this process, Santosh always tried to make use of the support and sanction of the British FA the IFA was enjoying: 'To us, the difference (difference between a new and an old organisation) is material because we have an all-India body recognised as such by the F.A. in England and we lose much if it is relegated to the background as a mere provincial Association and cut off from its great history for no fault of ours.'[56] Moreover, the Maharaja used his close relations with the British Indian civil administration to garner support for the IFA from the high officialdom of the governor-general's establishment with strong arguments:

> You might have heard of the Football Federation Conference which was held at Darbhanga in September last and how the doors of that Conference were deliberately shut against me, as its President-elect and other Bengal delegates. I was able to convince Lord Willingdon that the proceedings of that Conference were irregular, unconstitutional and *ultra licitus*.
>
> Lord Willingdon did not become their Patron; but I dare say an attempt will now be made to persuade His Excellency the new Viceroy to give his patronage to the so-called All-India Football Association. I am not acquainted with His Excellency's Military Secretary who is supposed to deal with such matters and I am writing this to you in the hope that you may be pleased to put him on his guard. The important facts of the case have been given in this letter to enable him to proceed on cautious lines and also to enlist his sympathy on behalf of the old Association of which I am the President.[57]

The AIFA, as anticipated by the ASCB, strongly disapproved of the new scheme, because it clearly established the supremacy of the IFA

---

[56] Letter of the Maharaja of Santosh to the president, ASCB, 12 April 1936, *MSPP*, File 4-1, p. 13.

[57] Letter of Maharaja of Santosh to one high English official called Sir Eric, 28 April 1936, *MSPP*, File 4-I, pp. 54–55.

over the control of soccer in the country.⁵⁸ Echoing more or less the line of arguments that the ASCB had already communicated to the IFA, the AIFA, in its meeting at Delhi on 12 April 1936, rejected the Federal Council proposals for two reasons:

1. That the proposed All-India Federal Council appears to be merely an 'offshoot' of the I.F.A.
2. It was considered that the formation of an All-India Football Association with its governing body must come into being as a new organisation to which the existing associations can be affiliated.⁵⁹

After rejecting IFA's proposals, the association offered its compromise scheme, urging the IFA to join hands with the AIFA.⁶⁰ The AIFA also agreed to recognise the importance of the IFA and reconsider its suggestions in the administration and control of the game throughout the country. The media too became optimistic about the prospect of the settlement: 'Give to Ceasar what is due unto him. The All India Football Association, who at one time thought that they could build up their association without the IFA left out of it is slowly coming to their senses.'⁶¹

Yet the IFA could not accept the compromise scheme, as it would relegate the former into a mere provincial association. Hence, agreeing to make further revisions in the Federal Council proposals, it urged both the ASCB and the AIFA to consider the formation of an all-India body out of the IFA.⁶² The ASCB, however, remained firm to reiterate its earlier position:

> I cannot disguise from the fact that in my opinion the attitude adopted by the AIFA is entirely reasonable and that the offer made to the IFA is fair

---

⁵⁸ Letter of the general secretary, All India Football Association to Maharaja of Santosh, president of IFA, 1 May 1936, *MSPP*, File 4-II, p. 50–51. Also see *The Statesman*, 13 April 1936.

⁵⁹ Resolution of the All-India Football Association meeting of 12 April 1936, *MSPP*, File 4-II, p. 51.

⁶⁰ Letter of the general secretary, All India Football Association to Maharaja of Santosh, president of IFA, 1 may 1936, *MSPP*, File 4-II, pp. 50–51.

⁶¹ *Forward*, April 1936, quoted in Majumdar, 'The Politics of Soccer in Colonial India', p. 27.

⁶² Letter of Maharaja of Santosh to the president, ASCB, 30 April 1936, *MSPP*, File 4-I, pp. 39–43; Letter of Maharaja of Santosh to the general secretary, AIFA, 19 May 1936, *MSPP*, File 4-I, pp. 63–67.

and just.... I feel that the IFA would be ill-advised to refuse this offer and by so doing would be acting in a manner which would adversely affect the future of football in India.[63]

The exchange of letters between the Maharaja and the president of the ASCB continued unabated for the next three months, with both remaining committed to their respective positions. While both were optimistic about convening a joint conference in the winter of 1936 to resolve the matter, the ASCB sternly made the IFA aware that 'the A.S.C.B. in India has never been affiliated to the I.F.A., as we have always regarded it as a provincial association for Bengal and not as an All India one'.[64]

IFA, AIFA and the Importance of British Support

Faced with an uncompromising attitude from the ASCB that seemed to have full sympathy towards the cause of AIFA, the only glimmer of hope for the IFA was the continuing support of the FA of England, which continued to press the AIFA to move through IFA for affiliation with that international body. Things, however, seemed to start changing from July 1936 as the FA president Stanley Rous urged the Maharaja to 'abandon the idea of having an All-India Federal Council' and suggested: 'You should arrange for a special meeting to be held to discuss the reconstitution of the IFA and at the same time approve the new constitution and rules of the AIFA.'[65] Yet the Maharaja appropriated the letter of the FA president to convince the ASCB of its efforts to reform its constitution and convene a conference.[66] He also sought wholehearted support from the FA in its fight against the AIFA to establish credibility as the true representative of Indian football:

> But it is to you that we mainly look for support as we have always treated the Football Association of England as our patron body and have carried

---

[63] Letter of the president, ASCB to Maharaja of Santosh, 15 May 1936, *MSPP*, File 4-II, pp. 23–25.

[64] Letter of the president, ASCB to Maharaja of Santosh, 3 July 1936, *MSPP*, File 4-II, pp. 17–19.

[65] Letter of Stanley Rous to Maharaja of Santosh, 29 July 1936, *MSPP*, File 4-II, pp. 8–9.

[66] Letter of Maharaja of Santosh to the president, ASCB, 2 August 1936, *MSPP*, File 4-I, pp. 149–52.

on our works all these years under your flag. In respect of the dispute which now lies between the Indian Football Association and so-called newly formed All-India Football Association, for supreme control of football in this country we look to you alone for your guidance and support. The All India Football Association, like all institutions of mushroom growth, has struck up a defying attitude.... I *have no manner of doubt that any institution, which may claim to represent India in the domain of Football, must abide by your decision.*[67]

More importantly, being anxious to retain the support of the apex international body, he urged the FA to restrain the ASCB in the latter's favourable equation with the AIFA:

> *as we are placed far away from the Army Headquarters, whereas those who are responsible for the formation of the so-called All-India body, have their strong holds in Delhi and Simla, I am not surprised to find the Army wavering.* The coterie is out to rob Bengal of its supremacy in Football and to relegate the I.F.A., which was born in Bengal, to the background as a mere provincial association, in spite of its great history which chronicles the Association's typical inter-provincial and international activities. But it is my belief that the ASCB in England being affiliated to the Football Association of England, the A.S.C.B. in India cannot break away from us until our affiliation is cancelled by that supreme body, or the new All India Football Association is allowed to be affiliated with you. What I fear is that if the ASCB in India is won over by the other side, it may ultimately exercise its influence with you to change your present favourable attitude towards us. I, therefore, appeal to you to take such step as you may think fit, at your earliest convenience, to safeguard the long standing connection which exists between the Army in India and the Indian Football Association.[68]

---

[67] Letter of Maharaja of Santosh to the president, FA, England, 20 August 1936, *MSPP*, File 4-I, p. 120; emphasis added.

[68] *Ibid.*, pp. 117–18; emphasis added. The Maharaja could realise the defection of the ASCB towards the AIFA as early as 19 May 1936 as he wrote to Colonel R. B. Butler, military secretary to His Excellency the governor of Bengal: 'The real difficulty is that the so-called All-India Body is nearer to the A.S.C.B. than ourselves and I am afraid they are gaining grounds with the Board in their attempt to relegate the I.F.A. to the background as a mere provincial association. If the A.S.C.B. affiliate themselves to the new body next year, the I.F.A. is bound to be humiliated as without the Army its historic Shield Competition must lose its all-India importance.' Santosh's letter to Colonel Butler, 19 May 1936, *MSPP*, File 4-I, pp. 61–62.

Santosh also wrote a similar letter to Colonel H. H. Stable, military secretary to His Excellency the viceroy, urging him to save the IFA's connection with the FA.[69] His letter to John Anderson, the governor of Bengal, too voiced the same concern: 'Everything will be alright if the Army in India do not break away.'[70] His call for support to the top British officialdom is thus clear proof of the determining role played by the ASCB in deciding the future of Indian football administration in the 1930s.

The IFA, acting on the FA's suggestions, in a circular letter dated 28 August 1936, invited the soccer associations of the country to set up an all-India body at a conference at Calcutta in December 1936 with the promise to enlarge its present constitution by giving adequate representation on its council to all provincial associations of soccer in India.[71] It was also declared that the scheme had the sanction of the Football Association of England. The circular letter also stated that the idea of a representative conference had the approval of the president of the ASCB.[72] The Maharaja of Santosh also communicated this circular to Sir Nripendra Nath Sircar, Law Member of the Government of India, asking for his help to persuade the viceroy and the commander-in-chief to become the patrons of the IFA instead of its rival AIFA.[73]

The AIFA, led by the representatives from Delhi and Bombay, stubbornly questioned the merit of the scheme. For them, the scheme was nothing but a revived plan to re-establish IFA's dominance over the administration of soccer in India by dissolving the existing AIFA.[74] Their main objection was against the inclusion of four representatives from Bengal (two from Bengal and two from Calcutta proper) in the governing body.[75] S. C. Banerjee, secretary of the Delhi Football Association, made the point amply clear:

---

[69] Letter of Maharaja of Santosh to Colonel Stable, 18 August 1936, *MSPP*, File 4-I, pp. 109–13.

[70] Santosh's letter to John Anderson, 18 August 1936, *MSPP*, File 4-I, pp. 128–31.

[71] For the draft of the circular letter, see *MSPP*, File 4-II, pp. 34–36. Also see *Amrita Bazar Patrika*, 10 September 1936.

[72] *Ibid.*

[73] Santosh's letter to Nripendra Nath Sircar, 10 September 1936, *MSPP*, File 4-I, pp. 153–55.

[74] See the letter of the honorary secretary, AIFA to the president, IFA, 2 October 1936, *MSPP*, File 4-II, pp. 46–47.

[75] *Ibid.*

In the circular letter which has been addressed to all provincial associations, the Maharaja of Santosh says that the Football Association of England and the International Football association has recognized the IFA as the only All India body throughout the British empire. Armed by this authority, he had asked other associations to consider his pet scheme, which appeared in the papers some time back and to attend a conference to be held in Calcutta in December next. *This definitely indicates that he is not prepared to accept the offer, which was made by the AIFA to the IFA at the suggestion of the ASCB.*[76]

Mr Turner, spokesperson for the Western India Football Association, also echoed similar sentiments:

We, in Bombay, will not affiliate to a body, which is only a provincial organisation like ourselves. The Maharaja of Santosh talks glibly of being authorized by the Football Association of England to put certain proposals before the rest of the provinces, but he does not inform the provinces of the contents of his letter to Mr. Rous, Secretary of the Football Association of England. *This circular is a last minute attempt to secure for Bengal domination in the sphere of football in India.*[77]

The representatives of Assam, Lucknow, Orissa, Jamshedpur, Ranchi, Patna, Jamalpur, Hazaribagh, and the UP, on the other hand, were in favour of putting an end to the long-drawn quarrel and hence ready to accept Bengal as the leader in forming the all-India body.[78] However, the secretary of the North West Indian Football Association, Mr Soofi maintained that it was necessary that the controlling body for the whole of India be called 'all-India' and therefore it was desirable that a conference to settle any outstanding points should be called by the AIFA at Delhi, which was more central and more convenient than Calcutta.[79] The Maharaja of Santosh, while criticising the cynical attitude of Delhi and Bombay, was still hopeful that under the guidance of the Football Association of England and with the potential cooperation of the army in India, the IFA, with its resources, experience and tradition, would be able to build a greater sporting fraternity in the East.[80]

---

[76] *The Statesman*, 12 September 1936; emphasis added.
[77] *Ibid.*; emphasis added.
[78] *Amrita Bazar Patrika*, 14 September 1936; *The Statesman*, 15 September 1936.
[79] *Amrita Bazar Patrika*, 15 September 1936.
[80] *The Statesman*, 15 September 1936.

Formation of All India Football Federation (AIFF)

The hope of resolving the critical points of dispute between the IFA and the AIFA was further aggravated by the positions taken by the ASCB as well as the FA in response to the circular letter issued by the IFA. The FA, which always stood by the IFA throughout the dispute, by now, took a careful view of the AIFA's objections to the IFA's stand. It, therefore, asked the IFA to explain the issues of trouble between the two bodies.[81] The response of the ASCB, on the other hand, was rather harsh:

> you were perhaps ill-advised to address this circular letter to Provincial Associations which are affiliated in fact to the All India Football Association.... I cannot believe that any goodwill result from endeavouring to ignore the existence of the AIFA which is actually in being.... Your suggestion therefore that the present constitution of the I.F.A. should be so remodelled as to bring together all the provinces of India seems somewhat at variance with the actual facts of the existing situation.[82]

Colonel Majendi, the president of ASCB, also objected to the venue of the proposed conference selected by IFA, that is, Calcutta, and suggested Delhi to be a more suitable place for the same. More importantly, he showed circumspection at the Maharaja's claim that his scheme was prepared at the instance of the Football Association of England.[83] Although he assured the Maharaja to adopt 'an attitude of impartial neutrality' until an all-India body was formed, he also warned the IFA of ASCB's future course of action: 'The day may, however, come if this unhappy controversy continues, when we shall be compelled to decide which of the two rival bodies has to be considered the more representative of All India, but I sincerely hope that such action will not be forced on us.'[84] The letter provided a rude shock to the IFA president as it clearly revealed the close connection between the ASCB and the AIFA and the former's sympathy with the latter's cause. As the Maharaja of Santosh admitted: 'it has pained me very much to find that the enemies of the Indian Football Association have succeeded

---

[81] Letter of the secretary, FA, England to the Maharaja of Santosh, 18 September 1936, *MSPP*, File 4-II, p. 4.

[82] Letter of the president of ASCB to Maharaja of Santosh, 24 September 1936, *MSPP*, File 4-II, pp. 11–16.

[83] *Ibid.*

[84] *Ibid.*

in persuading you to drift away from the position which was unmistakably indicated by the message of hope which you were kind enough to vouchsafe to me at Major General Lindsay's Luncheon Party.'[85] However, in his reply to the ASCB president, the Maharaja remained firm in asserting his association's tradition, pride and all-India character:

> I am afraid I cannot admit that the Indian Football Association is a provincial association representing only Bengal and I have the authority of the Football Association of England and the Federation Internationale de Football to oppose such an idea, apart from the historical proofs which I am able to produce in justification of our contention. I am still of opinion that the inter-provincial and inter-national activities of the Indian Football Association cannot be ignored by the hardest of its critics.
>
> Any way, I must tell you that we cannot accept the so-called All-India Football Association as the supreme Football Body in India. It should not be allowed to supersede the claims of the older body. What has it done uptil now?
>
> Finally, taking everything into consideration my advice and request to you is that you should direct the ASCB to participate in the works and competitions of both the associations and patiently await the survival of the fittest.[86]

The impasse over the issue of settling the outstanding issues between AIFA and IFA continued unabated as the proposed conference to compromise the interests of the parties at Calcutta was abandoned thanks to the opposition of Delhi and Bombay. The IFA also decided not to accede to any demand advanced by the AIFA. Moreover, it was suspected that the AIFA was trying to manoeuvre disintegration in the ranks of the IFA.[87] In response, the Maharaja of Santosh, the IFA president, took the matter to his Council and asked their full support to explore 'all possible avenues for an amicable settlement':

> The Secretary of the A.I.F.A. is unfortunately trying to bring matter to a head through all possible channels. He has started writing to individuals and clubs with a view to effect, if possible disintegration in our ranks. I do not

---

[85] Letter of Maharaja of Santosh to Colonel Majendi, president of ASCB, 29 September 1936, *MSPP*, File 4-I, pp. 166–71.

[86] *Ibid.*

[87] Santosh's speech addressed to the 'Gentlemen of the Council', Indian Football Association, n.d., *MSPP*, File 4-II, pp. 37–43.

know if the announcement which he made in Bombay and Mysore to the effect that the I.F.A. is ready to join the A.I.F.A., is the outcome of any reply which he might have got from any individual or club in Bengal. I hope to carry the Council with me when I record my emphatic protest against this unconstitutional procedure and when I appeal to our members and clubs not to cut the ground under my feet when negotiations are in progress.[88]

The tussle between Bengal and the other regions over the control of football administration continued even in the early 1937 without any signs of abatement. In such a situation, the ASCB, a key player in the whole controversy, proceeded to bring the dispute to an end by calling a meeting of all soccer associations of India at Simla in May 1937. Its plan was apparently to work out a compromise between the two bodies and form the All India Football Federation, a body, which would give considerable importance to the IFA. Boria Majumdar argues, 'while this solution was not something Bengal would have coveted, it was the best result under the circumstances'.[89] One needs to note, however, that, given the ASCB's constant support to the AIFA in this long-drawn-out tussle, it was only expected that the ASCB would have forced this solution upon the IFA at some point of time. Moreover, the ASCB had already warned the IFA to take the case to the FA through their London War Office in view of the continuing puzzle on the issue. As Bengal could not take the risk of alienating the ASCB, whose support was key to the survival of the IFA, it tried to defer the meeting further on different pretexts. The ASCB, however, became too adamant to entertain IFA's pretensions any more. Colonel Majendi, the president of ASCB, in a personal letter to the Maharaja of Santosh, made his intentions very clear:

> I am sorry to say that it is quite impossible to accede to your request that the meeting, to be held next month at Simla and at which we hope to bring into being the All India Football Federation, should be postponed till July. As you know, the original date has already been put back one month to suit the I.F.A. with considerable inconvenience to the other parties concerned, and any further postponement would, I know, cause great offence to them and upset all their arrangements.... I regret that the present date is not very convenient for the I.F.A., but I am sure that you will agree that any postponement is out of the question for the reasons stated. I hope very

---

[88] *Ibid.*
[89] Majumdar, 'The Politics of Soccer in Colonial India', p. 32.

much that you will find it possible to send a suitable representative to the meeting.[90]

Finally, the ASCB president issued a warning to the IFA in case of a failure of the meeting:

> I must confess that I find the last few lines of your letter rather perturbing as they imply that even at this late stage in the proceedings you may find it impossible to accept the A.I.F.F. or to co-operate loyally with such a body.... I have, however, decided that if the meeting at Simla next month is unsuccessful and does not result in the formation of the A.I.F.F. to be loyally supported by all concerned, I shall be forced to refrain from any further participation in this football controversy. *In such a contingency, I will be forced to forward to the F.A. in England a report on the happenings of the last few months and on the reasons for the breakdown of negotiations, and thereafter events in India would have to follow their normal course.*[91]

Faced with this stern ultimatum from the ASCB, the Maharaja of Santosh had no other alternative but to support the formation of the AIFF. This was because he could not risk the alienation of the British FA that always remained sympathetic to it as its sole affiliated body in India. The members of the AIFA including Delhi and Bombay, too, had to accept the formation of AIFF because it satisfied their central demand, that is, the creation of a new all-India body to control football affairs in the country in which Bengal would no longer retain its position of dominance. As a sequel, the All India Football Federation was born in May 1937.

Regionalism in Indian Soccer: The End of Bengal's Administrative Monopoly

Indian football till the 1930s more or less centred on Bengal. Just as Bengal led the nationalist movement and the Bengali politicians dominated the Indian National Congress till the early 1920s, it was the Bengali clubs like Mohun Bagan, Aryan, Mohammedan Sporting, and East Bengal that represented the Indian challenge against the British on the football field in open competitions while the IFA of Calcutta remained the only viable organisation to control and organise the game in the country till the mid-1930s. The IFA was also the only Indian association affiliated to the FA

---

[90] Letter of Colonel Majendi to the Maharaja of Santosh, 29 May 1937, *MSPP*, File 4-II, pp. 1–3.

[91] *Ibid.*; emphasis added.

of England and recognised by the Federation Internationale de Football Association (FIFA). Moreover, it used to make a worthy contribution to the cause of charity every year. Yet it was difficult for the IFA to claim the sole controlling authority over all other regional associations once the latter started taking active interest and proper measures in the organisation and management of the game in their respective regions. In that context, the IFA, apart from drawing the attention of both the regional associations as well as the British sports bodies to its contributions towards the growth and development of the game in India, constantly appropriated the affiliation of the FA as a means of legitimisation of its authority as the apex body of Indian football. It also tried to convince the ASCB of its authority to reorganise the soccer administration to accommodate the interests of the other regional associations, albeit without any long-term success. Rather, the other football associations led by Delhi and Bombay seemed, from the very beginning of this tussle, to enjoy the sympathy and moral support of the ASCB. Encouraged by this support, they first formed the AIFA, disputing the domination of Bengal alias IFA in relocating the future of Indian soccer and then rejected, one by one, all the proposals the IFA put forward to restructure itself into an all-India body. And finally, when things came to a deadlock, the ASCB, strongly upholding the viewpoint of the newly formed AIFA, forced the IFA by recurrent warnings to join the meeting leading to the formation of the AIFF.

The view of Paul Dimeo and James Mills that the British ceased to play any worthy role in Indian football by the 1930s is thus seriously flawed. As this chapter has tried to show, it was British recognition and support that proved decisive in shaping the future of Indian soccer in the 1930s. Mills's further attempt to explain the dispute over the control and organisation of the game as merely in-fighting among Indian groups, and British involvement in the dispute including that of FA as 'of little bearing' is also misleading. While the main combatants of the controversy were the Indian groups, that is, the regional soccer associations, the key player that controlled the fate of the dispute was the ASCB, a British association. That was why the IFA made a frantic attempt to enlist the support of that organisation in its fight to stem off the challenge posed by the AIFA. So, that the British opinion was of 'little bearing' is an entirely faulty assumption. Second, even when the support of the British FA was invoked by one group, that is, the IFA, it was appropriated not as 'a makeweight' but as a chief instrument of legitimisation of the IFA's authority. More importantly, when the ASCB decided to force the IFA to enter into a settlement in early 1937, it warned the IFA to refer the case to the FA through its War Office in England in case the IFA did not comply with the formation of the AIFF. This clearly shows the importance of the FA's possible intervention in the dispute concerning the regional politics of soccer in India.

Boria Majumdar, on the other hand, asserts that the British FA became a 'key player' in determining the fortunes of Indian soccer in the 1930s.[92] While the IFA always tried to invoke the support of the ASCB and impress upon the other associations by dint of its affiliation with the FA, it did not bear much fruit. This was because the position of ASCB was most crucial in resolving the dispute between the two warring Indian parties, and the ASCB could always influence the mind of the FA authority through its War Office in London. So the FA was an important player, but not the 'key player' to determine the future of Indian football of the time. Majumdar also argues that the position of the IFA vis-à-vis the AIFA was strengthened further when the ASCB decided to support the IFA.[93] This view is not borne out by the existing documents and private correspondences of the Maharaja of Santosh, the then president of the IFA. Rather, it becomes quite clear, especially from the personal communications between the Maharaja and the president of the ASCB that the latter was in full sympathy with the cause and concern of the AIFA since its inception in September 1935. That was the reason behind the IFA's ultimate compliance with the proposal to form the AIFF. By implication, therefore, the tussle in Indian football administration in the 1930s reflected a regional politics of soccer in which Bengal had to face serious challenges from other rising states like Bombay and Delhi and ultimately agree to the demand of a central apex body in 1937. But the key to resolving the dispute remained in the hands of the British power represented mainly by the ASCB and partly by the FA.

---

[92] Majumdar, 'The Politics of Soccer in Colonial India', p. 28.
[93] *Ibid.*

5

Mohun Bagan vs East Bengal: Social Conflict, Club Rivalry and Supporters' Culture in Bengali Football

◻

In the Prologue to *Football Culture: Local Contests, Global Visions*, Gerry Finn and Richard Giulianotti maintain:

> no matter how football clubs do change, they must always represent some sort of difference in relation to social identity. The evolution of football clubs will not lead to conformity, let alone uniformity. Without some framing of difference in association with football clubs, there can be no contest: without some social difference there would be no social significance to this match between two opposed teams. The issue is not social difference as such: the issue is how we conceptualize social difference, how it evolves, and then how we sport social identities when we come together to compare how we match up.[1]

Football in Bengal started as a marker of a unitary social identity and progressed as an emblem of nationalism, which constituted the focus of the second chapter. The third chapter sought to highlight the social *difference* expressed through communal overtones, premised upon which football thrived as a mass spectator sport in colonial and post-colonial Bengal. The notion that 'football is about social differentiation' becomes more evident when we take into account Bengal's most fascinating rivalry in football: Mohun Bagan versus East Bengal, best popularised as *Ghoti-Bangal* rivalry on the football field. A number of popular sporting traditions and

---

[1] Gerry P. T. Finn and Richard Giulianotti (eds), *Football Culture: Local Contests, Global Visions*, London & Portland, OR: Frank Cass, 2000, p. 8.

anecdotes have grown around this eternal football rivalry.[2] Even though such anecdotes may not be always too reliable, they convey a simple truth in spirit: enmity between these two clubs mirrors the oppositional identities, social differences and emotional commonalities inherent in Bengali society and culture. This chapter seeks to suggest that while the roots of the origin and concretisation of this football rivalry lay in socio-cultural and sub-regional differences rather than in any ethnic polarisation of colonial and post-colonial Bengali society, its evolution in the third quarter of the 20th century can only be meaningfully explained in terms of club loyalty and supporters' culture.

Ghoti-Bangal in Bengali Football: The Social Context

Paul Dimeo, one of the few scholars to have written about this rivalry, in a recent intervention on the history of club-conflict in Calcutta football, has argued that this most fascinating rivalry in India's club football between

---

[2] Two most popular anecdotes surrounding the two clubs may be recalled here:

'In a League match in the late 1970s Mohun Bagan won by a big margin. After the match the jubilant crowd rushed towards Esplanade to board buses and trams for home. A few bare-bodied young lads were standing on the rod of a tram's wheel hanging on to the windows of the same by one hand. They were waiving their sweated shirts like Mohun Bagan flags. As the tram suddenly stopped at a road signal, one of the lads got thrown onto the street. His feet seemed to be run over by the wheels of the tram. However, as the tram started to move, the lad ran and jumped onto the rod to catch the tram. After the tram left the place, a severed toe was found amidst a few drops of blood while a thin red line stretched along the tramline. The pain got lost in the euphoria of victory.'

'It was an unimportant match between East Bengal and some other local team in the late 1970s. The match was just about to start. A small crowd was gossiping at the main gate. Suddenly a middle-aged man with messy hair, red eyes and a worn out look appeared at the gate. While entering into the ground, he anxiously asked the gateman whether the match had begun or not. The gateman replied in the negative. A few other members who knew the man came to him and asked as to why he was so late to arrive that day. The man said: "My younger son passed away in the morning. I am directly coming from the crematorium."' For the anecdotes, see Rupak Saha, 'Bangalir Football' (Bengali's Football), *Desh*, 28 August 1993, pp. 21–23; translation mine.

Mohun Bagan and East Bengal can be interpreted in terms of an ethnic conflict between the Hindu residents of West Bengal called the Ghotis and the Hindu residents of East Bengal (later East Pakistan and Bangladesh) called the Bangals (who later migrated to West Bengal). The conflict was heightened in the aftermath of the Partition of 1947, in the wake of immigration of a large number of Bengalis from East Pakistan.[3] In other words, the rivalry between the host West Bengalis and the immigrant East Bengalis was seen in ethnic terms. But this rigid ethnic polarisation, probably emanating from the writer's lack of awareness about the fluidity of cultural identities of the two groups of people sharing more or less a broadly common language, religion, region of origin, and cultural past, seems not only over-simplistic but also flawed.

It has been stated that ethnicity provides a sense of peoplehood or we-feeling shared by members of a group.[4] In India, ethnicity operates on four major premises: caste, language, region of origin, and religion.[5] An ethnic group consists of a group of people having a common descent, name, language, norms, values, beliefs, practices, manners, customs, rules and regulations, unity, and integrity. The distinguishing physio-cultural features of an ethnic group make it unique, and distinguish it from other groups. According to Urmila Phadnis, an ethnic group can be defined as a historically formed aggregate of people, having a real or imaginary association with a specified territory, a shared cluster of beliefs and values, connoting its distinctiveness in relation to similar groups and recognised by others.[6] This definition thus has five components: (i) subjective belief in real or assumed historical antecedents; (ii) a symbolic or real geographical centre; (iii) shared cultural emblems such as race, language, religion, dress, or diet, or a combination of some of them which though variegated and flexible, provide the overt basis of ethnic identity; (iv) self-ascribed awareness of distinctiveness, belonging to the group; and (v) recognition by others of the group differentiation. As Cornell and Hartman have argued: 'Ethnicity, then, is identification in ethnic terms.... A population

---

[3] Dimeo, 'Team Loyalty Splits the City into Two', pp. 96–107.

[4] E. K. Francis, 'The Nature of Ethnic Groups', *American Journal of Sociology*, vol. 52, no. 5, March 1947, pp. 393–400; M. M. Gordon, *Assimilations in American Life: The Role of Race, Religion and National Origins*, New York: Oxford University Press, 1964.

[5] K. S. Nair, 'Structural Pluralism and Ethnic Boundaries: An Empirical Analysis in an Indian City', *Ethnic and Racial Studies*, vol. 6, no. 4, pp. 410–38.

[6] Urmila Phadnis, *Ethnicity and Nation-Building in South Asia*, New Delhi: Sage Publications, 1990, p. 14.

or social collectivity may be simply an ethnic category, assigned an ethnic identity by outsiders. Once that objective becomes subjective — that is, once that population sees itself in ethnic terms, perhaps in response to the identity outsiders assign to it — it becomes an ethnic group.'[7] Judging by all this criteria, the West Bengali (Ghoti)-East Bengali (Bangal) conflict does not seem to fall in the category of an ethnic rivalry. This is because the so-called differences between the two people are only cultural (for example, dialect, manner, dress, food habit, rites, and rituals) as well as very fluid in nature. Rather, the Ghoti-Bangal binary can be meaningfully interpreted in terms of a perceptional cultural clash between sub-regional sentiments.[8] Thus, in the sense an ethnic group has a sense of relatedness and feeling of alliance, the Ghoti-Bangal conflict did not represent any ethnic connotation as such.

The terms *Ghoti* and *Bangal* commonly refer to the people with their respective original habitats in the western and eastern parts of Bengal. However, while the term Bangal has found a place in most standard Bengali lexicons as a meaningful word, Ghoti is not included in any of them. Reference to the people of eastern Bengal as Bangal has been available in Bengali literature since the 12th century.[9] That Bangal became a butt of ridicule in western Bengal, especially in Calcutta in the 19th century, was evident from Dinabandhu Mitra's memorable drama *Sadhabar Ekadashi* where he depicted this attitude perfectly.[10] Famous Indian

---

[7] S. Cornell and D. Hartman, *Ethnicity and Race: Making Identities in a Changing World*, London: Pine Forge Press, 1998, p. 21.

[8] Soumen Mitra, in his M.Phil dissertation, 'Nationalism, Communalism and Sub-regionalism: A Study of Football in Bengal, 1880–1950' (Centre for Historical Studies, Jawaharlal Nehru University, 1988), comes close to this argument.

[9] *Sadukti Karnamrita*, a 12th-century text, mentions the word meaningfully. Mukundaram Chakrabarty's *Chandimangal*, a 16th-century text, also mentions the word in a derogatory sense. Another contemporary text, *Chaitanya Charitamrita*, clearly reveals that the Bangal of eastern Bengal became a comic figure in western Bengal for his style of pronounciation.

[10] Dinabandhu Mitra was a noted Bengali playwright of the late 19th century. His most famous piece was *Neel Darpan* that depicted the story of exploitation and oppression of Indian peasants by the European indigo planters in the middle of the century. The staging of the play created a stir among the Bengali populace in the wake of the Indigo Revolt of 1859.

For more layers on *Ghoti-Bangal* conflict, see Mansur Musa, 'Ghoti-Bangal er Birodh Nispatti', in Nitish Biswas and Mukulesh Biswas (eds), *Banga Sanskritir Sanhatir Oitihya* (Tradition of Cohesion in Bengali Culture), Kolkata: Oikotan Gobeshona Samsad, 1995, pp. 235–42.

sports writer Moti Nandy succinctly sums up the essence of this derisive attitude of the people of western Bengal towards the Hindus of eastern Bengal since the 19th century:

> Right from the beginning of the nineteenth century, people who came from East Bengal were treated with condescension by the original settlers of Calcutta, who took them for country bumpkin. On the stage and on the screen, East Bengalis appeared invariably as comic figures. To express their contempt, the Calcutta Bengalis called them *Bangal*.[11]

It is, however, difficult to determine as to how the word Ghoti appeared in that context. Moti Nandy refers to a letter in the *Ananda Bazar Patrika* in the late 1980s, which attempted an explanation:

> In the nineteenth century when water taps were unknown in every home in Calcutta, each household had its own well. The pots and buckets would often fall into the well. In the afternoon some men would do the rounds of the neighbourhood with a rope and a hook, shouting 'Ghoti tulben? Ghoti tulben?' 'Want the pots taken out?' Finally, they abbreviated their call to just shouting 'Ghoti! Ghoti!' in front of the houses. The East Bengalis who lived in these areas at that time heard this daily uproar and assumed that the locals of Calcutta were referred to as 'Ghotis'.[12]

Rupak Saha, a noted sports journalist of *Ananda Bazar Patrika* and the latest historian of the East Bengal Club, offers a different point of view. According to Saha, the word, unlike Bangal, has been of recent vintage, and it first came into use in the 19th century. He thinks the Bangal students of Calcutta, overturning the slur labelled against them by the West Bengalis, probably introduced the term to ridicule them. Since the West Bengalis used to make use of a 'ghoti' (a small pot) for all their household works from morning to night, the term was purposely taken as synonymous to their identity by the East Bengalis.[13] There is another popular explanation of the origin of the word:

> Once a person from Gaur went to visit the house of one of his relatives in eastern Bengal. But he forgot to take his 'Ghoti' with him. On arrival to the relative's place, he could not concentrate on anything for that mistake, i.e. for not having his essential 'Ghoti' with him. Ultimately he stole one from a neighbour's house, but was caught subsequently. For his heinous act, the

---

[11] Nandy, 'Football and Nationalism', pp. 249–50.
[12] *Ibid.*
[13] Saha, *Itihase East Bengal*, pp. 12–13.

image of the people of Gaur, i.e. West Bengal, was permanently tarnished. And henceforth they came to be called as the 'Ghotis'.[14]

Whether or not this is the correct explanation, neither community is apt to lose its temper when identified as Ghoti and Bangal today.

The trend of reciprocally derisive attitude aside, the difference between Ghoti and Bangal was discernable in terms of dialect, manner, dress, food habit, rites, and rituals and even appearance, transcending wider similarities of religion, language, region of origin, and a common cultural past. These mostly *cultural* differences, although not rigid by any means, had the potential to create sharply distinctive *social* identities in times of heightening socio-political tension. The Partition of Bengal in 1947 followed by a massive influx of East Bengali Hindu refugees into West Bengal provided the occasion for a sub-regional socio-cultural conflict to flourish.

In the aftermath of the Partition of Bengal that accompanied Independence, large-scale Hindu immigration from East Bengal/Pakistan (now Bangladesh) to West Bengal created a new socio-demographic tension whereby a distinct socio-cultural conflict ensued in Bengali society. The sub-regional cultural identity of the East Bengali Hindus clashed with that of the established Hindu Bengali residents of West Bengal. To the West Bengali Hindus, who used to call the former derisively as Bangals, the new immigrants caused an upset in their local life. Hence, they strongly disapproved of according them any worthy place in local society, culture, economy, and polity. The Bangals, with their common memory of everyday culture and a shared experience of suffering and migration fought hard to earn their living, economic strength, social position, and cultural recognition to ensure survival in a hostile environment. They, too, in their turn, returned the compliment by calling the locals as Ghotis. While the Ghoti-Bangal conflict certainly epitomised a social rivalry in Bengal, the identities, however, seemed more 'instrumentalist', that is, constructed than 'primordialist', that is, fixed and ascribed.

As such, the appropriation of modern sport to promote the cause of immigrant communities has been a useful ploy in many a 20th-century nation state. In colonial Bengal, the Bengalis employed football to express nationalist or communal identities. The turnover from colonialism to Independence, however, added a further fragmentary dimension to

---

[14] *Ibid.*

Bengal football. As Paul Dimeo argues: 'Football has the capacity to unite communities, produce and reproduce identities, maintain and shape social formations, and to create identities of a specific nature that draw upon wider social issues in diverse and sometimes contradictory ways.'[15] The Ghoti-Bangal social conflict sent its ripples to the football field as well. As the immigrants sought to preserve their cultural identity and integrity in a new society, they searched for avenues to prove that point. Football, in this context, was taken by the East Bengali Hindus as a useful tool to establish their social identity and cultural excellence. Consequently, the maidan became a cultural space where the opposed identities of Ghoti (settlers) and Bangal (immigrants), acquiring new meanings, came to be produced and reproduced through a bitter rivalry between Mohun Bagan, the club of the Ghotis and East Bengal, the club of the Bangals. The East Bengali refugees found in the East Bengal Club a club of their own representing their cultural 'self' to fight and win against the 'other', that is, the West Bengali Hindus. As the latter mockingly named East Bengal 'the club for Bangals', they, in their turn, renamed Mohun Bagan as 'the club for Ghotis'. Consequently, the Ghoti-Bangal rivalry on the maidan divided the Bengali Hindu society into two camps during every football match of either side. Interestingly enough, as Moti Nandy writes: 'These two communities even divided the aquatic population in a symbolic manner — the prawn for the Ghotis and the hilsa for the Bangals. In the evening after a football derby, the prices of prawn and hilsa used to rise or fall depending on the result of the match.'[16] This socio-cultural polarisation, according to Amitabha Das Sharma, 'is best mirrored in the annual league encounter'.[17] He rightly says: 'football remains a unique phenomenon, one that binds and divides the city. While almost all are together in their love for sport, team loyalty splits the city into two. One need not be a student of sociology to seize the palpable partisanship surrounding the two teams.'[18]

While this arch football rivalry struck another blow to Bengali footballing nationalism, it contradictorily played an important role in assimilating the immigrants into the host community. With time, however, this fluid sub-regional football culture proved ephemeral and a more virulent club rivalry between Mohun Bagan and East Bengal based on

---

[15] Dimeo, 'Team Loyalty Splits the City into Two', p. 96.
[16] Nandy, 'Football and Nationalism', p. 249.
[17] *Sportstar*, 22 September 1998.
[18] *Ibid.*

intense team loyalty and fan culture overtook the erstwhile sentiment at national-level competitions throughout India.

Origin and Growth of the East Bengal Club

The rivalry between the two clubs in socio-cultural terms began when the East Bengal Club was founded in 1920 in an unusual context of social difference. The East Bengal Club was started originally as one to be managed for East Bengali players by East Bengali people to ameliorate their sporting grievances born out of continuous discrimination waged against them by Calcutta's Bengali clubs.[19] The birth of the club can only be meaningfully explained in the context of this sub-regional polarisation in contemporary Bengali society. In fact, the club was born as a mark of protest against the injustice, bias and discrimination meted out to sports organisers and players who came from East Bengal. At the turn of the 19th century, football spread from Calcutta to strike deep roots in other districts of eastern and northern Bengal. In East Bengal, Dacca was the centre of football's growing stature and popularity. Players hailing from Dacca and adjoining regions used to come to Calcutta to gain wider recognition at competitive levels from around this time. That they performed well and sometimes even excelled greater than their West Bengali counterparts is borne out by the fact that eight of the 11 players of the victorious Mohun Bagan team in 1911 originally came from eastern Bengal.[20] More importantly, the legendary Mohun Bagan defender Gostho Paul also came

---

[19] Historians of the East Bengal Club have all noted this aspect of discrimination waged against the East Bengali players and people and unanimously pointed to the exclusively regional character of the club at its birth and its impressive beginning in Calcutta football. For details, see Bandopadhyay, *Cluber Naam East Bengal*; Jayanta Dutta, *Glorious East Bengal*, Calcutta: Sahitya Prakash, 1975; Nandy, *East Bengal Club, 1920–1970*; Pandit Mashai (Ramesh Chandra Goswami), *East Bengal Cluber Itihas* (History of the East Bengal Club), Calcutta: Book Garden, 1963; Saha, *Itihase East Bengal* (all in Bengali).

[20] Among these eight players, goalkeeper Hiralal Mukherjee and right back Rev. Sudhir Chatterjee came from Faridpur district; the famous Bhaduri brothers of the team, Sibdas and Bijoydas, were from Rajshahi; winning scorer of the final, Abhilash Ghosh, right winger Kanu Roy and half back Rajen Sengupta from Dacca; while another half back, Nilmadhab, Bhattacharyya, hailed from Barisal.

from a village of Faridpur district.[21] Despite this noticeable excellence of East Bengali players, a large number of them frequently became victims of discrimination at the hands of West Bengali club organisers, officials and players.[22] The foundation of the East Bengal Club was a direct outcome of such an incident.

In 1919 Sailesh Basu, a footballer from Vikrampur pargana of Dacca, became a reputed player of Jorabagan Club. The following year Basu faced an unusual exclusion from the team in a crucial tie in the Coochbehar Cup.[23] He realised that his East Bengali identity cost him the exclusion. He complained to the club's vice-president Suresh Chaudhuri, however, without any avail. As a result both severed their relations with the club. Chaudhuri, a rich and influential businessman of Calcutta, was originally the zamindar of Nagarpur of Mymensingh district, East Bengal. With his injured self-esteem, he decided to form a club by mobilising purely East Bengali players and football enthusiasts in and around Calcutta in order

---

[21] Incidentally, Gostho Paul is the only Bengali player to be honoured with a statue in the Calcutta maidan. Paul's early career, his rise to sporting fame and the legend that grew around his striking personality are well delineated in his two biographies: Rupak Saha, *Chinese Wall*, Calcutta: Hemlata Prakashani, 1979; Jayanta Dutta, *Footballer Mahanayak Gostho Paul* (Gostho Paul: The Superstar of Football), Calcutta: Anima Prakashani, 1986.

[22] It was hard for the East Bengali players to get a berth in the rank of well-known Bengali teams of Calcutta in the 1910s while those few who obtained the chance used to experience exclusion from the final playing 11 on different pretexts on the days of crucial matches.

[23] According to Shantipriya Bandopadhyay and Paresh Nandy, this match between Jorabagan and Mohun Bagan was played on 28 July 1920. For details, see Bandyopadhyay, *Cluber Naam East Bengal*, pp. 28–29; Nandy, *East Bengal Club*, pp. 28–30. Another club historian, Rupak Saha, thinks two East Bengali players, viz., Sailesh Basu and Nosa Sen, faced exclusion in Jorabagan's semifinal match against Calcutta Football Club in the Coochbehar Cup. When Jorabagan made it to the final and faced Mohun Bagan, both the players featured in the match at Suresh Chaudhuri's instance. Jorabagan, however, lost the game, and the onus fell on the poor performance of the two Bangal players. Insulted and hurt by the incident, Chaudhuri, along with them left the club. Saha, *Itihase East Bengal*, pp. 15–16. Yet a few others like Pandit Mashai and Shukharanjan Ghosh have argued that Sailesh Basu faced the discrimination of the club management not in a football match but in a cricket match against Calcutta Cricket Club during the 1919–20 season. Pandit Mashai, *East Bengal Cluber Itithas*, pp. 1–2; Shukharanjan Ghosh, *Bharatiya Footballe Tin Protidvandi* (Three Rivals in Indian Football), Calcutta: Manju Prakashani, 1986, pp. 79–80.

to give a befitting reply to the insult. Sailesh Basu, along with another East Bengali player, Nosa Sen, assisted him in founding the East Bengal Club in August 1920. The very name of the club was important as it clearly appealed to the discriminated East Bengalis in West Bengal for support. It gained immediate patronage from renowned peoples from different walks of life — Taritbhushan Roy, Raibahadur of Bhagyakul; Saradaranjan Roy, principal of the Metropolitan College (present Vidyasagar College); and Pankaj Gupta, one of the greatest sports administrators India has produced. The organisers of the club could form a modest team of East Bengali players within a few days and emerged champions in a six-a-side tournament called Hercules Cup held at Shyam Park in north Calcutta. One of its matches in the tournament was reported in a local newspaper which noted with surprise the presence of a big enthusiastic crowd to cheer for the newborn club.[24] In view of the background of the birth of the club, this was quite but natural. Since its inception the very name of the club may be said to have ensured it a reasonable support base all over Bengal.

A review of the club's history in the next five years points to a complex equation between social power relations and mechanisms of sports administration in contemporary Bengal. Suresh Chaudhuri and Taritbhushan Roy, the two joint secretaries of the club, both being socially influential in Calcutta and having good relations with the British officialdom, utilised their power and position to earn the club's affiliation to the IFA as well as a berth in the Second Division League and to obtain a ground on the maidan.[25] The meteoric rise of such an infant club as East Bengal to a

---

[24] *Amrita Bazar Patrika*, 13 August 1920.

[25] It was quite unusual those days for a club like East Bengal to earn a berth to play in the second division of the League in the very first year of its existence. It was again due to Suresh Chaudhuri's influential ties with the European members of IFA and his personal relations with other East Bengali social magnates that the club achieved this end. East Bengal filled the vacuum created by the withdrawal of Tajhat Club from the second division. In this case, too, Chaudhuri reaped the harvest of his friendly relations with the Raja of Tajhat in East Bengal, who owned the club. Moreover, the East Bengali players of the erstwhile Tajhat Club joined East Bengal. For details see Bandyopadhyay, *Cluber Naam East Bengal*, pp. 33–35; Nandy, *East Bengal Club*, pp. 37–40; Saha, *Itihase East Bengal*, pp. 20–21.

According to the existing rule of the maidan, two clubs used to share one common ground. Tarirbhushan Roy came to learn that Mohun Bagan shared its ground with National Association which by that time had ceased to exist. He referred this discrepancy to the police authorities and subsequently demanded the share for East Bengal. The then police commissioner Charles Tegart ordered

position of respectability, however, was not well taken by its sister clubs in Calcutta. The subsequent controversy over East Bengal's promotion to the First Division of the Calcutta Football League in 1925 would serve to clarify this point.

In 1924, the club shared a controversial first position in the Second Division League with Cameron Highlanders B.[26] Since the latter's A team was already in the First Division, it could not claim a promotion. Hence, it was East Bengal's turn to earn a promotion to the first division. However, according to the existing rule, not more than two Indian teams could be allowed to play in the First Division. The club initiated a movement to do away with this practice of injustice and partiality. Manmatha Nath Roy Chowdhury, the Maharaja of Santosh and president of the club, played an important role to press East Bengal's cause before the IFA Governing Body. As a result, despite the IFA secretary Medlycott's strong opposition, the club obtained majority support in the IFA Council and earned a much-deserved promotion to the First Division in 1925 amidst hot debate and constitutional controversy within the rank and file of the IFA. Medlycott subsequently resigned from his post.[27] Most of the historians of the East Bengal Club argue that the deadlock relating to the promotion of East Bengal was ultimately dissolved through the initiative of the Maharaja of Santosh, who was then the president of the club.[28] According to them, in

---

Mohun Bagan to share its ground with East Bengal. This sudden decision certainly enraged the Mohun Bagan people against the newborn Bangal club. Saha, *Itihase East Bengal*, p. 20; Nandy, *East Bengal Club*, pp. 47–48.

[26] The controversy arose from a misrepresentation of the final League table published by Messrs S. K. Lahiri & Co. Ltd on behalf of the IFA. According to this table, Police A.C. and Cameron B were placed at the first and second positions while East Bengal occupied the third spot. However, most contemporary newspapers published from Calcutta maintained that East Bengal and Cameron B shared the first position with equal points, and on goal average East Bengal came second. For a complete League table, see *The Statesman*, 3 July 1924, p. 4.

[27] Medlycott's role in the entire episode of East Bengal's promotion seemed to be very critical. Why he opposed East Bengal's promotion against the will of most of the European members of the IFA is not known. He might have been apprehensive that any relaxation in the existing rule and concession to native teams might open the door for greater concession or removal of bar in the near future. That he could not accept the ultimate decision to promote East Bengal becomes clear from his resignation from the IFA.

[28] Bandopadhyay, *Cluber Naam East Bengal*, p. 45; Dutta, *Glorious East Bengal*, pp. 10–11; Pandit Mashai, *East Bengal Cluber Itihas*, pp. 17–18; Saha, *Itihase East Bengal*, pp. 22–23.

October 1924 the members of the League Committee, at a special meeting held at the residence of the Maharaja, decided to abolish the existing rule that restricted only two Indian teams to play in the First Division League and introduce in place the standard rule of promotion and relegation. The decision ensured East Bengal its deserved promotion. Interestingly enough, all of them point out, while the European club representatives of the committee strongly supported the motion in East Bengal's favour, the two Indian members representing Mohun Bagan and Aryan strenuously opposed the move.[29]

A thorough look at the newspaper reports on the issue in 1924–25, however, points to a rather different course of events that eventually led to the club's success in earning the promotion. This engaging story clearly shows how the Bengali clubs led by Mohun Bagan and Aryan opposed East Bengal's promotion to the First Division. The League Committee's decision that accorded East Bengal the promotion in its annual general meeting on 15 April 1924 was reversed in its special meeting a week later mainly under strong pressure from other Indian clubs.[30] The Indian clubs had their own points, though facile, to tread such a course of action:

> Regarding Tuesday's football sensation, an impression seems to have gained ground that the majority of the Indian clubs are against the promotion of East Bengal to the First Division. On enquiry into the matter we are in a position to state definitely that this impression is absolutely groundless. It is understood that all the Indian clubs who voted for the annulment of the proceedings of the annual meeting, did so on account of the bigger issues involved in the case. They are out for a total removal of the 'colour bar' and appear not to be content with the 'petty concession' in the shape of the temporary promotion of an Indian team to the First Division. In this laudable endeavour, they are sure to have the sympathy of all the sportsmen.[31]

---

[29] Shukharanjan Ghosh, *Bharatiya Footballer Tin Protidvandi*, p. 81.

[30] Three leading newspapers of Calcutta — *The Statesman*, *The Englishman* and *Amrita Bazar Patrika* — published detailed reports on this meeting on 16 April 1925. For reports on the special meeting, see *The Englishman*, 22 April 1925.

[31] *Amrita Bazar Patrika*, 23 April 1925. It was as if the other Bengali clubs were out to do away with the 'colour bar', i.e., the longstanding rule of allowing not more than two Indian teams to play in the First Division League. They therefore considered the mere promotion of East Bengal, only one Indian club, as a 'petty concession', and demanded that any Indian team that would top the Second Division League should qualify automatically to play in the First Division.

When, to protest against this unjust decision, all the European clubs withdrew from the League one by one, Mohun Bagan and Aryan remained the only teams to play in the next year's League.[32] On the withdrawal of European clubs and their deadline to the League Committee, the Indian clubs condemned their action to support East Bengal.[33] Against such allegations, a representative of one of the European clubs argued in *The Statesman* that the Europeans only wanted the progress of Indian football.[34] He was certain that East Bengal's presence and participation in the First Division of the Calcutta League would substantially enhance the competitive edge as also the glamour of the tournament:

> Our action, strictly speaking, may not be quite constitutional, but we are out for the good of the game, and we contend that the admission of East Bengal will stimulate football in Calcutta very considerably. Surely the rules can be amended when it is found that they do not meet with conditions which were not perhaps contemplated when they were drawn up.[35]

Pankaj Gupta probably played a major role at this juncture to promote the cause of East Bengal. Gupta himself later narrated the story:

> I was approached by East Bengal Club to help them in their mission to be promoted to the first division.
>
> Late Mr. Thomas Lamb (later became Sir Thomas Lamb) was then the key man of the Calcutta Football Club.... I approached Thomas Lamb and he joined hands with me in our fight to delete such restrictions in regard to promotion in the first division.... Although I was not a member of the East Bengal Club for the sake of sporting justice I took a lead on this issue, and the late Mr. A. B. Rosser joined hands with us and helped us in a great way. Late Mr. Medlycott of the Customs opposed our move but ultimately we succeeded and restrictions were removed. Late Mr. Medlycott left the

---

[32] The big European four of Calcutta football, viz., CFC, Dalhousie, Rangers, and Cameron A withdrew from the League in protest against this injustice meted out to East Bengal. They demanded East Bengal's promotion, a permanent revision in the act that restricted Indian teams' entry into the First Division League and Medlycott's resignation. Even Medlycott's own team, Customs, followed suit leaving him in utter disgrace. *The Englishman*, 24 April 1925.

[33] *The Statesman*, 22 April 1925.

[34] *The Statesman*, 23 April 1925.

[35] *Ibid.*

meeting in a hurry and subsequently resigned from the Hon. Secretaryship of the IFA.[36]

The newspaper also expressed deep surprise at the other Indian teams' (especially Mohun Bagan and Aryan) hostile attitude towards East Bengal's cause. The most probable reason for such hostility, according to the newspaper, was the two leading Indian clubs' anxiety over the potential challenge East Bengal would pose to them in terms of both popularity and player collection.[37]

> To many people the most surprising feature of the situation is the fact that European clubs are making a strong bid for the inclusion of another Indian team, while Indian clubs have so far adopted a policy, rightly or wrongly, which tends to their exclusion. As a possible explanation of this, many do not hesitate to state the Indian clubs now competing in the First League fear that, with the advent of such strong rivals as East Bengal are likely to prove, their popularity may wane and their choice of players may be restricted.[38]

East Bengal's victory to break the organisational shackles in the IFA led, in the next few years, to the abolition of a series of biased conventions and rules in the IFA that had been used to act as bulwark against the rise of indigenous clubs.[39]

The club, however, by the 1930s, lost its exclusive East Bengali character and could field no more East Bengali players than Mohun Bagan or any

---

[36] Pankaj Gupta, 'Story on Calcutta Customs Club', *Platinum Jubilee: Calcutta Customs Club, 1892–1967*, Calcutta: Calcutta Customs Club, 1967.

[37] *The Statesman*, 23 April 1925.

[38] *Ibid.*

[39] For instance, in 1929, over the question of spectator violence during a League match between Mohun Bagan and Dalhousie, the European-dominated IFA Council put the entire blame on the hooligan behaviour of rowdy Indian spectators and suspended the Mohun Bagan custodian Santosh Dutta for two years for his foul play. The Indian clubs protested against this unjust verdict by withdrawing from the IFA and threatening to form their own Indian Sports Association. Finally, a compromise was reached at the mediation of Nripendranath Sircar, the then advocate general of Bengal. The suspension was annulled. More importantly, the composition of the IFA Council was completely changed. It was decided that henceforth both European and Indian clubs would have equal representations in the Council. Thus the long-standing domination of British authority in Indian football's premier controlling body was mitigated.

other Bengali club.⁴⁰ But the name and banner of the club continued to inspire among the East Bengali population in West Bengal an emotional attachment to the club. This particular emotional set-up, hardened more by the West Bengalis' discriminatory remark and attitude, was an extension of the social conflict between Ghoti and Bangal. And it lay, along with the communal tinge in Bengal football, at the root of fragmentation of Bengali sporting nationalism from the 1940s onwards.

Ghoti-Bangal Conflict on the Football Field: Colonial Bengal

Paul Dimeo has stated: 'Before partition, East Bengal and Mohun Bagan had a friendly relationship, ... and, until the cataclysmic political changes of 1947, the two clubs saw each other as siblings.'⁴¹ The evidences he provides in support of his view, however, are not substantial enough. According to him, that the clubs shared a common ground, and that Mohun Bagan hosted a celebratory tea party for their 'younger brothers' at the latter's first ever League triumph in 1942 are sufficient to prove his point.⁴² He further suggests: 'The main difference at this time [the 1930s–40s] was that while Mohammedan Sporting's rivalry with several Hindu clubs prompted serious communal violence, the two most successful Hindu clubs were on friendly terms.... Hindu clubs [mainly Mohun Bagan and East Bengal] cooperated in opposition to Muslim clubs, and in opposition to the last remnants of competitive British clubs.'⁴³ Dimeo's chief concern seems to situate what he calls the *ethnic* football rivalry between the two clubs solely in the context of post-Partition immigration. Dimeo, however, confuses his own position by furnishing contradictory evidence: 'Yet, an exhibition match in 1942 between the "Bengalees" — a term referring to the West Bengalis — and the Rest, took players' individual ethnicity as relevant: the Rest including Muslims, Europeans and East Bengalis.'⁴⁴

---

⁴⁰ A number of worthy footballers from eastern Bengal played for Mohun Bagan throughout the first half of the 20th century. The list includes names such as Nagen Kali, Hemango Basu, Rabi Basu, Bagha Som, Sanmatha Datta, and K. Datta. For details, see Sachin Sen, *Kheladhular Bichitra Kahini* (Numerous Stories of Games and Sports), Calcutta: R. M. Gupta/Geetanjali Book Centre, 1983, pp. 21–29.

⁴¹ Dimeo, 'Team Loyalty Splits the City into Two', p. 100.

⁴² *Ibid.*

⁴³ *Ibid.*, p. 101.

⁴⁴ *Ibid.*

Dimeo's views defy the contemporary realities of Bengal football. First, sharing of a common ground was not to become a factor precipitating friendship, but a source of discord as the bhadralok-dominated Mohun Bagan resented this choice forced upon them by the police authorities. Mohun Bagan's hosting of a tea party at East Bengal's first League win in 1942 may have been a rare occasion of goodwill. Such gestures have been shown mostly to impress the public about the concerned club's versatility rather than to honour the rival's success. It was, however, more the occasions of virulent enmity that proved vital in the 1930s. As has already been pointed out, Mohun Bagan strenuously opposed East Bengal's promotion to the First Division in 1925. This certainly waged a long-term bitterness between the two clubs. Their first meeting in any first class competition saw the infant club beating their more renowned rival 1–0 in the final of the Coochbehar Cup.[45] In their first encounter in the League, East Bengal's 1–0 victory over their opponent was another sweet revenge on all counts.[46] In the same year, East Bengal raised an objection on the legality of one of the Mohun Bagan players, J. Sen.[47] This move, needless to say, led to further hardening of their relations. The enmity continued unabated in the 1930s. For example, the League Council was forced to transfer the match between the two clubs in 1932 to the CFC ground to abort possible hooliganism. An unprecedentedly large number of policemen had to be employed to control law and order in and around the ground on that day.[48]

More importantly, Dimeo's conception of Mohun Bagan-East Bengal cooperation in opposition to the Muslim club, that is, Mohammedan Sporting is a grossly flawed one. Two specific instances would suffice to prove the point. During the 1939 League competition, Mohammedan Sporting, East Bengal and Kalighat jointly withdrew from the Calcutta Football League in protest against the IFA's cynical attitude towards them.[49] At this

---

[45] *The Statesman*, 24 August 1924.

[46] *The Statesman* of 29 May 1925 reported that although Mohun Bagan enjoyed larger spectator support, East Bengal too could count upon the support of a sizeable section of the same.

[47] *The Englishman*, 30 May 1925.

[48] *The Statesman*, 6 July 1932.

[49] For a complete view of Mohammedan Sporting's grievances, see *Mohammedan Sporting Club Souvenir*, Calcutta: Mohammedan Sporting Club, 1939, pp. 66–68. East Bengal Club's rancour towards the IFA mainly resulted from the latter's continuous partiality to Mohun Bagan Club. For an instructive discussion on the course of events, see Nandy, *East Bengal Club*, pp. 84–87; Saha, *Itihase East Bengal*, pp. 39–43.

juncture, J. C. Maitra, a contemporary reputed Bombay-based journalist, while expressing his full sympathy with the IFA's decision to suspend the 'recalcitrant clubs' and strong condemnation for the unsporting action of the clubs, maintained:[50]

> The association of East Bengal and Kalighat with Mohammedan Sporting may seem a little strange at first sight. Because they are not Muslims, though they have a sprinkling of them in their composition. Their affinity lies in a different direction.... They are the strongest supporters of importation of players from outside. It is a well-known fact that Mohun Bagan have sternly set their face against this move.... Evidently club rivalry and jealousy, which are much deeper and stronger than we see on the surface, have made strange bed-fellows.[51]

Maitra's comments and his unwitting reference to Mohun Bagan clearly bring out the realities of club rivalry in Calcutta football. The clubs went further to form a rival football association called the Bengal Football Association on 11 August 1939 and start a new tournament called the Brabourne Cup.[52] Although the crisis was averted through amicable negotiations in early 1940, the episode clearly points to the fact that East Bengal was in no mood to *cooperate* with Mohun Bagan in opposition to Mohammedan Sporting. The joint venture of East Bengal and Mohammedan Sporting to upset the IFA's decision, according to Maitra, was 'backed by persons who hold high offices in the Ministry of Bengal'.[53] This again, in direct contradistinction to Dimeo's view, points to a fruitful cooperation between the two clubs against IFA's favouritism of Mohun Bagan.[54]

Even at the height of communal tension in Bengal on the eve of the Partition, the IFA became very much alarmed at the increasing spectator

---

[50] This has already been discussed in detail in Chapter 3.

[51] *Bombay Chronicle*, 9 July 1939.

[52] *Amrita Bazar Patrika*, 12 August 1939, p. 14. The association had Hon'ble A. K. Fajlul Huq, Maharajadhiraj Bahadur of Burdwan and Nawab Bahadur of Murshidabad as its patrons, while Khwaja Nazimuddin, Maharajkumar of Burdwan, Maharaja of Cossimbazar and Nawab Bahadur of Dacca were amongst the vice presidents of the association. *Amrita Bazar Patrika*, 15 August 1939, p. 14.

[53] *Bombay Chronicle*, 20 August 1939. The most prominent amongst such persons was Mr Nalini Ranjan Sarkar, finance minister of the Bengal government and president of the East Bengal Club.

[54] For a discussion on how the two clubs cooperated with each other during the football crisis of 1939, see Chapter 3.

violence on the maidan on the occasion of every Mohun Bagan-East Bengal match. For example, the return League match between the two teams that ended in a goalless draw leading to East Bengal's League triumph in 1946 witnessed rampant hooliganism and violence after the match. The supporters on their return from the ground not only exchanged hot words but also threw bricks, stones and soda bottles at each other. One newspaper reported the incident thus:

> The partisan spectators fell out after the conclusion of the match on the C.F.C. ground but it did not stop there altogether. The players, members and supporters of the rival clubs moved to their respective tents with bad blood infused in their veins and almost after their arrival a free fight was waged in which bricks, stones and soda water bottles were freely used. Some of the members and a few players of Mohun Bagan received injuries, while casualty cases numbering twenty-eight were sent to the Medical College in the ambulance cars by the Indian Red Cross after the first-aid had been given to them.[55]

The Mohun Bagan tent was raided and ransacked either by dejected club supporters or at the hands of rival supporters.[56] The club lodged a complaint with the IFA against East Bengal for the incident, which the latter strongly denied.[57] The IFA president Major Stanhope urged the two clubs to move jointly to mitigate such unfortunate happenings in the future.[58]

Partition of India, Refugee Influx and Football Rivalry in West Bengal

The degree of social sensitivity and cultural divergence evidently visible in the Mohun Bagan-East Bengal rivalry before Partition, however, should not be exaggerated either. This bitter and fanatical rivalry between supporters of the two clubs shifted from a fluid to a rigid/exclusive state only after the Partition of Bengal in 1947. Hindu refugees started to arrive in droves in West Bengal from East Bengal/Pakistan. Moti Nandy catches the tragedy of this refugee exodus brilliantly:

> Searching for a roof over their heads in the city and its surrounds and a fistful of rice twice a day, they began their struggle for survival under conditions of

---

[55] *Amrita Bazar Patrika*, 8 July 1946.
[56] *Ibid.*
[57] *Amrita Bazar Patrika*, 10 July 1946.
[58] *Amrita Bazar Patrika*, 13 July 1946.

unbearable hardship. Lost and impoverished in an unknown territory and hostile environment, faced with severe adversities, they would sometimes lose the battle and fall back, then return once more to dream of settling down to a secure and normal existence.[59]

A more recent observation by a subaltern historian may be of more value here:

> The experiences of the refugees after being uprooted and upon their arrival in West Bengal were far from pleasant. They were forced to live in cramped government-run relief camps. There small sums were handed out to them as doles and they were given meagre family rations. In overall terms they were treated no better than beggars. No efforts were made to create employment opportunities to enable them to eke out a living.[60]

It was under the stress of such plight in everyday life that the Hindu refugees discovered a football club called East Bengal which was waging another battle on the sportsfield and surprisingly enough, winning! 'For these

---

[59] Nandy, 'Football and Nationalism', pp. 249–50. The experience of suffering, deprivation and impoverishment of the East Bengali refugees in the aftermath of the Partition has been vividly delineated in a rich crop of Bengali literature. Historically most important and memorable of these novels, dramas and short stories are: *Arjun, Atmaprakash* (Sunil Gangopadhyay); *Nonajal Mithemati* (Prafulla Roy); *Aranyadandak, Bakutala P L Camp, Balmik* (Narayan Sanyal); *Sona Fasoler Pala, Meghe Dhaka Tara* (Shaktipada Rajguru); *Notun Ihudi* (Salil Sen); *Ranipalangka, Gotrantar* (Bijan Bhattacharyya); *Epar Ganga Opar Ganga* (Jyotirmoyi Debi); *Madhab o tar Pariparshik, Jaal* (Sirshendu Mukhopadhyay); *Nilkantha Pakhir Khonje, Abad, Manusher Gharbari, Iswarer Bagan, Aloukik Jaloyan, Mrinmoyi* (Atin Bandyopadhyay); *Sthaniya Sambad* (Sankar); *Suchander Swadeshjatra, Adab* (Samaresh Basu); *Hasubanu* (Probodh Kumar Sanyal); *Lalmati, Bidisha, Maryada* (Narayan Gangopadhyay); *Shada Ghora* (Ramesh Chandra Sen); *Badwip, Swaralipi* (Sabitri Ray); *Sanko, Dalil* (Hritvik Ghatak); *Ei Swadhinata* (Sachindranath Sengupta); *Gar Srikhanda, Nirbas* (Amiyabhushan Majumdar); *Ghoorni* (Sambhu Mitra); *Gosthabiharir Jibanjapan* (Amalendu Chakraborty); *Ora Aajo Udbastu* (Dulalendu Chattopadhyay); *Manaskanya* (Jarasandha); *Nischitpurer Manush* (Jyotirindra Nandi); *Panchaparba* (Banaful); *Bipasha* (Tarasankar Bandyopadhyay); *Sarbajanin, Upay, Subala* (Manik Bandyopadhyay); *Duekti Ghar Duekti Swar* (Loknath Bhattacharyya); *Doorbhashini* (Narendranath Mitra); and *Nil Agun* (Saroj Kumar Roychaudhury).

[60] Gyanesh Kudaisya, 'Divided Landscapes, Fragmented Identities: East Bengal Refugees and their Rehabilitation in India, 1947–79', in D. A. Low and Howard Brasted (eds), *Freedom, Trauma and Continuities: Northern India and Independence*, New Delhi: Sage, 1998, p. 118.

ravaged and embittered masses', remarks Nandy, 'the one source of hope, pride and victory lay in the triumphs of the Club named after their abandoned homeland'.[61] In fact, a spell of five years (1949–53) in the immediate aftermath of the Partition and the refugee influx witnessed the spectacle of a dazzling display of football by the famous 'Five Pandavas' of the East Bengal forward-line — Vengkatesh, Apparao, Dhanraj, Ahmed Khan, and Saleh — leading to the club's series of successes in all national-level tournaments.[62] These victories, for the uprooted Bangal migrants, leapt from the boundaries of the sports field to become a cultural weapon to fight against settlers' discrimination. In other words, the Ghotis being identified as antagonists in their subconscious, the club's victory over Mohun Bagan on each occasion instilled a new confidence into their hearts. Naturally, they all began to assemble under the club's red-and-yellow banner. The city of Calcutta as also the entire West Bengal thus came to be divided into two clearly defined camps in football. As Berry Sarbadhikary noted in 1951:

> If a gallop-poll in the matter of football partisanship were taken today it would reveal a Calcutta split into two distinct camps, one for Mohun Bagan and the other for East Bengal; Mohun Bagan for their premiership amongst Indian football clubs, their hoary tradition and a uniformly high standard of play, and East Bengal for their solid, nearly all-conquering performances in recent years not only in Calcutta but all over the country. And so, if one half of Calcutta is glad, the other half inevitably becomes sad. Joy and sorrow constitute the pattern of life itself and are all in the game as long as these are tainted with fun-warranted boastfulness on the one side, and bitterness and malice on the other.[63]

It has been argued with some justification, if 'Mohammedan Sporting Club had brought with it hatred through its aggressive communalism born of a minority's natural instinct for self-preservation', 'East Bengal brought anger through regional, cultural and language differences in the backdrop

---

[61] Nandy, 'Calcutta Soccer', p. 319.

[62] Thanks to this legendary forward-line, during this period East Bengal won both the IFA League and Shield thrice (League — 1949, 1950, 1952 and Shield — 1949, 1950, 1951); Durand Cup and DCM Trophy twice (Durand — 1951–52 and DCM — 1950, 1952); and the Rovers Cup once (1949).

[63] Berry Sarbadhikary, 'Sports Commentary', *Amrita Bazar Patrika*, 11 June 1951.

[64] Nandy, 'Football and Nationalism', p. 250.

of a hostile social, economic and political environment'.[64] Press reports of the matches of the two clubs in the 1950s–60s either in the Calcutta League and Shield or in national-level tournaments like the Durand Cup in Delhi and Rovers Cup in Bombay confirm the presence of massive crowds on match days. The IFA Shield final between East Bengal and Mohun Bagan in 1947 had to be abandoned on the first occasion due to spectator violence. The situation became so rowdy that the police had to use teargas and ultimately fire bullets to disperse the invading crowds armed with stones and soda water bottles.[65] According to one communiqué, issued by the West Bengal government: 'police fired 22 rounds. Eleven were injured, two by bullets. Twenty-eight police personnel were injured, some seriously.'[66] In the Shield final between the two clubs in 1950, too, a huge police force had to be stationed at the ground to avert spectator violence.[67] These spectator skirmishes gradually extended to engulf the whole of the Calcutta maidan next year, so much so that the IFA decided to conduct the League with regular assistance from Calcutta Police in 1951.[68] East Bengal, however, objected to this decision and a bitter rivalry ensued between the club and the police. In fact, behind most of the spectator troubles lay the problem of accommodation and control of gates. The matter assumed such controversial dimensions that the chief minister had to intervene to settle matters.[69] Dr B. C. Roy, the chief minister, called a meeting of the representatives of all the First Division clubs at his office to devise ways and means for a satisfactory solution of the problem.[70] On his advice, the aggrieved clubs including East Bengal accepted 'the terms of settlement offered by the IFA authorities in consultation with the police'.[71]

The chief minister again expressed serious concern over the question of the organisation and control of the game in 1955. Disappointed with the IFA's role in the process, he proposed the formation of a central organisation to control the game in the city of Calcutta.[72] The same year the first-leg League match between the two clubs witnessed a spell of brick-batting on the ground over a decision of the referee.[73] The very next year

---

[65] *The Statesman*, 6 October 1947.
[66] *Ibid*.
[67] *Amrita Bazar Patrika*, 17 September 1950.
[68] *Amrita Bazar Patrika*, 31 May 1951.
[69] *Amrita Bazar Patrika*, 22 and 23 June 1951.
[70] *Amrita Bazar Patrika*, 21 June 1951.
[71] *Amrita Bazar Patrika*, 25 June 1951.
[72] *Amrita Bazar Patrika*, 29 June 1955.
[73] *Ananda Bazar Patrika*, 19 June 1955.

East Bengal, along with a few other clubs, lodged a petition to IFA for biased refereeing in the League matches.[74] The referee's bias, according to the petition, was simply intended to favour one particular club:

> The signatories of the letter further alleged that there appeared to be a method in the vagaries of the decision indulged in by the referees and such decisions had invariably gone in favour of one particular club, whose opponents had suffered directly in the matches against them or whose more serious rivals had suffered through adverse decisions in other games.[75]

They urged the IFA to change the scenario within a week.[76] Needless to say, the favoured club hinted here was none other than Mohun Bagan. However, J. C. Guha, the honorary secretary of the East Bengal Club, diplomatically stated that 'the club had no complaint against any club, much less the great Mohun Bagan. And even in case the indifferent supervision had actually benefited them, he was sure, that Mohun Bagan was in no way responsible for that.'[77] Throughout the 1950s–60s, thus, the arch rivalry between Mohun Bagan and East Bengal continued to prosper more or less on such sub-regional and cultural lines. There occurred a series of comically serious incidents to testify to this arch-rivalry over these years. One such example may be worth mentioning. A newspaper report in the mid-1950s revealed this comic incident with the title 'Mohun Bagan — East Bengal Mars Marital Peace' in the following way:

> While Calcutta's giant teams — Mohun Bagan and East Bengal clashed for a decisive game on Saturday last, little did the players know that they were causing a domestic brawl in a far-flung village under Bandipur Union near Barrackpore.
>
> The husband, an enthusiastic supporter of the Mohun Bagan Club, listened to the radio commentary on the game and in a jubilant mood came home with a few friends after his favourite team had won: 'Come on, I shall give you a feast.'
>
> Tea was served and other dishes were on the table when the wife entered the room in a rage. She was a patron of the losing team. Bewildered friends left the room in a hurry without touching the food. Temper of the hostess was too hot for them.[78]

---

[74] Other clubs included Aryan, Mohammedan Sporting and Rajasthan.
[75] *Amrita Bazar Patrika*, 23 June 1956.
[76] *Ibid.*
[77] *Amrita Bazar Patrika*, 28 June 1956.
[78] *Amrita Bazar Patrika*, 27 July 1955.

The refugees coming out from East Bengal/Pakistan 'were subjected to all kinds of pressure to agree to move out of West Bengal for rehabilitation in Dandakaranya. This pressure was coupled with threats by officials of stopping rations and doles and shutting down camps in an attempt to force them to go to Dandakaranya.'[79] More importantly, the refugees' move to Dandakaranya was hampered by the persistent campaign by the communists who urged them not to go out of West Bengal but to take recourse to agitation to urge for resettlement within Bengal.[80] The influx of refugees and their concentration in and around Calcutta had transformed the configuration of politics in West Bengal. The communists had strongly taken up the cause of the refugees. Communist cadres encouraged the refugees to occupy public spaces for shelter, colonise land in the villages, and resist the stopping of doles and the closure of camps by the government. They also opposed government plans for the dispersal of these refugees to neighbouring states. Donald S. Zagoria draws attention to this close link between the refugees' agitations and the ascendancy of the communists in West Bengal politics:

> In the urban areas of West Bengal, Communist strength does not appear to be based on any particular caste or community. Rather, one of the main bases seems to be the several million 'declasses' Hindu refugees who fled their homes in East Bengal after partition. These refugees constitute about one-fourth of the West Bengal population and a substantial portion of the Calcutta population. They apparently vote for the Communists overwhelmingly.[81]

A more recent study by Prafulla Chakrabarty also presents substantial evidence which shows that the political ascendancy of the Left in West Bengal owed a great deal to the refugees and their struggle for rehabilitation in the 1950s.[82] Chakrabarty argues that, while the communists provided the

---

[79] Gyanesh Kudaisya, 'Divided Landscapes, Fragmented Identities', p. 118.

[80] This was, however, not the sole cause of the refugees' reluctance to go outside West Bengal. The unwillingness to go to culturally unfamiliar areas for resettlement must be understood in terms of the state of the mind of the refugees themselves.

[81] Donald S. Zagoria, 'The Social Bases of Indian Communism', in Richard Lowenthal (ed.), *Issues in the Future of Asia: Communist and Non-Communist Alternatives*, London: Praeger, 1969, pp. 97–124.

[82] For a useful study of the relationship between communist political ascendancy in West Bengal and refugee politics, see Prafulla K. Chakrabarty, *The Marginal men, The Refugees and the Left Political Syndrome in West Bengal*, Calcutta: Lumiere Books, 1990.

refugees with leadership in their struggle for rehabilitation, the refugees, in turn, became the striking arm of the communists and provided them with the mass support which enabled them to penetrate into the city of Calcutta. According to Chakrabarty, it was the refugees who performed the 'vanguard function' in West Bengal in catapulting the communists to power and that 'the refugee movement coalesced in a broad movement of the left and democratic process which reached a point of crystallisation during the general elections of 1967'.[83] As refugees were largely centred around the Calcutta area, they tended to provide potential vote banks to the Left parties. As Kudaisya maintains: 'This is plausibly borne out by the electoral performance of the Left parties between 1951 and 1967, when it was the city of Calcutta, rather than the Bengal countryside, which was their stronghold — a trend which has been reversed since 1967.'[84]

While the refugees, backed strongly by the communists, waged a pitched battle against the Congress-led West Bengal government on the political plane, East Bengal led the onslaught on the cultural space, that is, the football field. The situation on the maidan became so alarming in the late 1950s that Dr B. C. Roy, the then chief minister of West Bengal, suggested a change in those club names which carried communal and regional overtones.[85] Speaking with reference to it, Dr Roy said that 'the Government should take a serious view of the situation and that it was their duty to check the growth of localism, provincialism and communalism among the people by disallowing such names as Mohammedan Sporting, Rajasthan Club or East Bengal etc.'.[86] He felt 'in a democratic country conditions unfavourable for the development of such communalism and localism through clubs should be created'.[87] Football's politicisation in the context of increasing spectator violence in the 1950s was a major source of discord between the IFA on the one hand and clubs like East Bengal, Mohammedan Sporting or Aryan on the other. The Ghoti-Bangal war on the football field and the political war on the streets of Calcutta thus merged in the 1950s–60s to produce a fruitful identification of sport with politics. However, one needs to remember that cultural and political factors in this case are qualified. The resultant craze and euphoria for this arch rivalry between the two clubs was to dominate the culture of Bengali football in the next decade as well.

---

[83] *Ibid.*, p. 405.
[84] Kudaisya, 'Divided Landscapes, Fragmented Identities', p. 118
[85] See *The Statesman*, 17, 18 and 24 July 1957.
[86] *The Statesman*, 17 July 1957.
[87] *Ibid.*

From Ghoti-Bangal Conflict to Club Rivalry

The configuration of Bengali football in terms of a social conflict between Ghoti and Bangal on cultural lines took on a rather aggressively violent turn in the 1970s. The war of liberation in East Pakistan and the emergence of Bangladesh in 1971 led to fresh immigration of Hindus into West Bengal. This certainly added substantially to East Bengal Club's support base as the club served as a rallying point of the immigrants' hurt sentiments embodying a shared memory. Strikingly enough, the first half of the 1970s was a glorious age of success for the club.[88] More importantly, during the six years from 1970 to 1975, the club conceded only one defeat at the hands of Mohun Bagan.[89] Naturally therefore, the supporters of the club dominated the maidan throughout this period.

The Bangladeshi immigration of the early 1970s coincided with a period of intensive social tension and political turmoil in West Bengal in the wake of the anti-establishment Naxalite movement that used violence and terror as a means to achieve its end. The football field could hardly escape this propensity of violence. The expression of spectator behaviour, in that context, began to undergo qualitative changes. As Surojit Sengupta, the footballer-turned-sports journalist, has remarked: 'In the context of Naxal Movement in the early 1970s, political uncertainty and social depression often turned Calcutta's football ground hot and violent.'[90] Emotional commonality towards a club rapidly acquired a violent temper, aggression became more pronounced, win or loss produced spontaneous euphoria or retaliation. Spectators used to stand in queues throughout the day and night to obtain their cherished ticket to watch the match.

---

[88] East Bengal won the League title six times in a row from 1970 to 1975 — still a record. It won the IFA Shield in 1970 and then with a gap of a year continued to clinch it every year from 1972 to 1976. The club bagged the Durand Cup in 1970 and 1972; Rovers Cup in 1972, 1973 and 1975; DCM Trophy in 1973 and 1974; and Bardoli Trophy in 1972 and 1973.

[89] This sole occasion when Mohun Bagan got the better of their arch-rivals was in the 1974 Durand Cup semifinal. Mohun Bagan won the match by a solitary goal.

[90] Interview with Surojit Sengupta, 25 August 2002. For Sengupta's fuller views on football culture that grew around the East Bengal-Mohun Bagan rivalry in India, see Surajit Sengupta, *Back Center*, Calcutta: Sunny Publishers, 1986. Incidentally, Sengupta, who was a classy right winger of the East Bengal team in the 1970s, left his job in a state bank to take charge as the sports editor of *Khela*, the foremost vernacular sports magazine of Bengal.

Skirmishes and feuds were quite common during the course of the long wait for tickets. People also got injured or fell ill at times. It was reported that before the League match between the two teams in 1975 two persons lost their senses and four got wounded in the overcrowded queue of tickets. All of them had to be taken to the nearby SSKM Hospital.[91] The same report noted that the queue comprised about 40,000 fans while the maximum number of tickets on sale was less than 10,000. In 1976 one fan named Shaktipada Nag was killed during feuds that broke out in the queue for tickets before the Mohun Bagan-East Bengal League match.[92] In the 1975 Shield final, East Bengal defeated Mohun Bagan 5–0. After the fourth goal was scored, one East Bengal supporter had a heart attack out of sheer ecstasy and had to be taken to hospital immediately.[93] For a 25-year-old young Mohun Bagan supporter named Umakanto Palodhi, the ignominious defeat aroused so much dejection that he committed suicide in the night on that day. The suicidal note he left is revealing: 'By becoming a better footballer of Mohun Bagan, I wish to take revenge of this defeat in the next birth.'[94] Subrata Bhattacharyya, a player of that Mohun Bagan team recounted later:

> Three hours passed since the match had ended. It was 9 o'clock in the night. Finding through the curtain of the tent that thousands of supporters still surrounded the tent, I fled through the back door along with Prasun Banerjee [another player of the team] and took refuge at a restaurant by the side of the river Ganges. It was only at 2.30 after midnight that Sailen Manna [a veteran and most revered Mohun Bagan footballer] came in a police jeep and rescued us to a mess at the Elliot Road.[95]

Again, when East Bengal defeated a much favourite Mohun Bagan at a 1977 League encounter, a young Mohun Bagan supporter poisoned himself by devouring a bottle of pesticides.[96] The post-match report also pointed to the extremely unruly behaviour of the crowd and mentioned

---

[91] *Ananda Bazar Patrika*, 11 July 1975.

[92] *Ananda Bazar Patrika*, 25 July 1976.

[93] *Ananda Bazar Patrika*, 30 Sept. 1975.

[94] *Amrita Bazar Patrika*, 1 October 1975; translation mine. Also see Manas Chakrabarty, 'Mohun Bagan-East Bengal Reshareshi' (Mohun Bagan-East Bengal Rivalry), *Anandamela*, 19 July 2000, p. 118.

[95] Chakrabarty, 'Mohun Bagan-East Bengal Reshareshi', p. 118; translation mine.

[96] East Bengal won the match 2–0. *Ananda Bazar Patrika*, 10 July 1977. The report said that the person was taken to the PG Hospital in a very critical condition.

that the joyous reaction of the East Bengal supporters after the match became quite uncontrollable.[97] Instances of such overtly excessive crowd reaction are galore in contemporary press reports. These signs of crowd behaviour indicate that behind the façade of eternal enmity between the two clubs probably lay some remnants of a deep-seated cultural conflict and more intense force of club loyalty.

In modern society, sporting rivalry inflamed by club loyalty breeds social *difference* while social divisions based on affiliations of race, ethnicity, community, or religion inform and reinforce such rivalries.[98] On this premise, social polarisation of supporters' culture has the capacity to produce recurrent spectator clashes often assuming violent forms. Bengali football, too, witnessed such a series of clashes around the Mohun Bagan-East Bengal rivalry during the three decades following Independence. In the late 1970s, as a columnist of a leading sports magazine of Calcutta noted, the transformation in the character of spectator behaviour during the two years of 1978–79 was sudden and unprecedented.[99] The matter came to a head in 1980 when, during a rather unimportant League match between the two teams at the Eden Gardens, Calcutta on 16 August, clashes between two supporter groups led to widespread violence in the stadium resulting in a stampede that cost the lives of 16 diehard fans.[100]

The Tragedy of 16 August 1980

The immediate issue that sparked off widespread violence was an ugly tackle by Dilip Palit, a tough East Bengal defender, against Bidesh Basu, a

---

[97] According to the same newspaper report, 'total disorder resulted in the streets and different quarters of the city as the euphoric supporters ran in wild joy with *mashals* (fire torch) in their hands from one place to another. There were several complaints against jubilant crowd who stopped private cars and scooters on the streets. Bricks were thrown into the ground and on another club's tent resulting in the injury of at least two dozens of people, three of them being rushed to Shambhunath Pandit Hospital. According to the police source, eight persons were arrested on that evening.' *Ananda Bazar Patrika*, 10 July 1977; translation mine.

[98] For a most recent consideration of these issues, see J. A. Mangan and Andrew Ritchie (eds), *Ethnicity, Sport, Identity: Struggle for Status*, London: Frank Cass, 2003.

[99] *Khelar Asar*, 3 July 1979, p. 38.

[100] The pre-match press reports suggested possibilities of chaos and violence on the match day. In fact, in the same year, the Federation Cup final between the two teams on May 8 witnessed extremely unruly behaviour of not only the fans but also the players and club officials and envisaged more violent outbursts in the near future. See *Ananda Bazar Patrika*, 15 August 1980; *Khelar Asar*, 16 May 1980.

mercurial Mohun Bagan forward, and the latter's spontaneous retaliation by kicking the former 10 minutes into the second half. The referee showed both red cards for the offences they committed. However, after initially awarding a free-kick in Mohun Bagan's favour, the referee resumed the game by dropping the ball. The supporters of the clubs in a particular stand of the gallery, enraged by the incident, became involved in a free-for-all while the police remained mere spectators.[101] Apart from shouting abuses and throwing missiles, rampant brickbatting ensued. Once the missiles which had been carried into the ground were exhausted, fans found 'replenishement' by 'pounding the concrete seats with shoes and rods'.[102] The resultant hail of concrete missiles caused spectators to swarm towards the exits, which they unfortunately found locked. As one newspaper reported later:

> Play continued even when the imprisoned spectators shouted for help and for water. But nobody responded. The police who were sitting at the base of the stadium on the ground, seemed absorbed in the match. When the police who had remained passive almost all through stormed the gallery swinging lathis, after the final whistle, the spectators started running in panic, knocking each other in the melee. A regular stampede was on. Some of those who had collected near the gates turned back and ran for the lower tiers of the stands hoping to escape to the ground. That was not easy. There was a ten foot drop to the lower tier concrete benches. Undeterred many took the plunge; some fail to survive the fall. The streams of people cascading through the narrow gates knocked down some who were trampled. The Mohun Bagan supporters being in a minority were more in panic. Amidst the confusion, the survivors started bringing the dead to the Club House. First a teenage boy — dead. Then another. One by one ten bodies — all without life — were placed on the floor of the Club House. The wounded and the dead covered the whole floor. The tragedy slowly sank into the consciousness of a benumbed public.[103]

Thirteen fans kissed the dust while several others were seriously injured. Three more succumbed to death at the hospital later on. Next day the leading Bengali daily *Ananda Bazar Patrika* began its match report on the

---

[101] At that time, there was no formal system of dividing access of the supporters of the big clubs into different stands. The flags they used to carry and the voices of their support were the common markers of their club identities.

[102] *Hindustan Standard*, 23 August 1980.

[103] *Ibid.*

first page with the by-line: 'Football: the New Killer in Calcutta! Thirteen Died, Hundreds injured. Pathetic Outcome of the Derby Match.'[104] As Paul Dimeo rightly argues: 'This was a tragedy indeed, the result of numerous factors specific to the day in question — police inaction, corrupt ticket sales, insufficient safety procedures, the violence of the players — but fundamentally the result of a deeply-felt rivalry.'[105]

Vengeance to the event found eloquent expression in an open letter Amal Dutta, a renowned football coach of Indian club teams, wrote to Jyoti Basu, the then chief minister of West Bengal:

> You have done the right thing by not coming to see the match. In that case, you will have to bear the pain of watching the last breathes of a number of young lives simply due to inaction on the part of your police.... This accident surely disproves your worth whatsoever as ministers for Home and Sports.... You won't be excused even if you immediately appoint an enquiry commission as mere eyewash. You must have realized the extent of decline of moral values among the youth during the course of Federation Cup football played early in the year. It must be well known to you that football is now more than a game to the Bengali — it is an *entity* to them. To sustain this entity a large section of the unemployed, aimless and reckless young society take drugs before and during a match like this. This information is well known to the police department and should have been reported to you by them. Besides this, in the last few years, spectators have got used to carry arms such as blade, razor, knife, brick and iron-rod while watching the matches of their favourite clubs especially in the 60 paise gallery. Whether your police have made any sincere attempt to stop this hooliganism or arrest the culprits is not known. It is really surprising as to how your government could take the responsibility of organizing such an important match without having made any attempts to avert clashes and arrange sitting allotments of rival supporters to two different blocs. In that case, how can you evade the responsibility for the disaster?[106]

This tragedy provided a jolt to the ever-rising fervour of Indian football enthusiasm. It indeed cast a heavy shadow on Bengali footballing society and ironically envisaged unfortunate changes in Bengali football.

---

[104] *Ananda Bazar Patrika*, 17 August 1980; translation mine. For a very insightful coverage of the tragedy, see *Khelar Kagoj*, 1 and 16 September 1980; and *Khelar Kotha*, 1 and 16 September 1980.

[105] Dimeo, 'Team Loyalty Splits the City into Two', p. 104.

[106] 'Open Letter to Jyoti Basu' (Editorial), *Khelar Kotha*, 1 September 1980; translation mine.

Mohun Bagan vs East Bengal: The Changing Nature of Rivalry

Although the social conflict between the East Bengali and the West Bengali existed even in the colonial period, it was only after the Partition and the resultant refugee immigration that the conflict took on a confrontational character sending its ripples onto the football field as well. Especially, for the uprooted East Bengali immigrant, the East Bengal Club became an emblem of pride and confidence and the Calcutta maidan an ideal place to show his worth and superiority. Yet, one has to admit, while the supporters of the two clubs took the matter of cultural and temperamental differences so seriously, players of the clubs never conformed to this perceptional equation of Ghoti-Bangal. Ghotis like Arun Ghosh earned fame playing for East Bengal while Bangals such as Gautam Sarkar rose to prominence as players of Mohun Bagan.[107] Both admitted that identification of the clubs as of Ghotis or Bangals was entirely the caricature of a section of loyal supporters and sometimes of a few club officials; footballers hardly played any role in it.[108] Since 1980 the supporters' rivalry on sub-regional and cultural lines, too, began to fade away, as memories of the Partition and the old homeland itself grew weaker. Intermarriages between Ghotis and Bangals during the three decades after Independence probably played an important role in this process of assimilation. Dimeo makes the point more apparent:

> By the 1980s, though, identity markers were becoming less distinct. The memory of East Bengal as 'home' was the preserve of a fading generation of migrants, their sons and daughters more at home in West Bengal. Intergroup relationships became more common, dialects less pronounced, and cultural traditions passed away. There are cases of fans with East Bengali parents supporting Mohun Bagan. Thus, a liminal, in-between space developed that contravened the polarity of previous years.[109]

Thus Bengal's eternal club rivalry, which had its beginnings in the 1920s with the birth and growth of the East Bengal Club, got concretised on the

---

[107] Arun Ghosh never felt that the Ghoti-Bangal conflict played any worthy role in the minds of the footballers of Mohun Bagan and East Bengal. 'It was rather a section of the club officials and supporters', he argued, 'who really made it an issue that created crowd disorder and violence in Calcutta maidan'. Interview with Arun Ghosh, 15 June 2000.

[108] Tanaji Sengupta, 'Nirapade Bhinna Clube' (Safely in the Other Club), *Desh* (Binodon sankhya), 1988, pp. 184–89.

[109] Dimeo, 'Team Loyalty Splits the City into Two', p. 106.

basis of cultural differences between the West Bengali hosts or the Ghotis and East Bengali immigrants or Bangals in the aftermath of the Partition in 1947 and the subsequent refugee influx from East Pakistan into India. The intensity of club loyalty and fan rivalry surrounding the two clubs steadily increased in the three decades following the Partition and ultimately reached a peak in the late 1970s. The political and social tension of this period also precipitated this social rivalry on the football field. The tragedy of 16 August 1980 marked the culmination of this process. However, as I have already argued, the Ghoti-Bangal rivalry gradually dissipated by the 1980s as the confrontation between the host and immigrant communities gave way to assimilation. Moreover, the 1980s was a most critical age when Indian football experienced recurrent fluctuation in terms of standard, popularity and professionalism.[110] Yet, the enmity between the two clubs continued unabated due to a variety of factors: the tradition of a long-term rivalry, consolidation of an oppositional sporting identity, convention of a fan culture, and intensification of modern club loyalty.

Binary of club rivalries is not uncommon in other centres of soccer excellence in India. Dempo vs. Salgaonkar in Goa, Air India and Mahindra United in Bombay, or Punjab Police vs. JCT Mills in Punjab — all these rivalries attracted or still attract a modest support base, but by no means can they claim to have the continuity or tradition of intense enmity that exemplifies the relations between Mohun Bagan and East Bengal.[111] Their rivalry is rightly compared to the ones between Brazil

---

[110] Despite radical changes in the Indian sporting map in the 1980s — the organisation of the Asian Games at Delhi (1982), India's World Cup victory in cricket (1983) followed by Mini World Cup triumph two years later (1985), live telecast of World Cup football since 1982 and of European and Latin American league and cup matches (since 1987), organisational laxity of the All India Football Federation, and most important of all, utter failure of the national and regional football bodies as well as the two great Calcutta clubs to adapt to the challenge of globalisation, commercialism and professionalism till the mid-1990s — the intensity of rivalry between Mohun Bagan and East Bengal showed no signs of abatement. However, the rivalry faced a real challenge in 1997 when both the clubs came to be sponsored and marginally controlled by the same company, viz., the United Breweries Group. After this sponsorship deal there arose a large apprehension among the supporters of the clubs that their age-old enmity would come to an end. Yet what still continues to dominate Indian football is a desperate rivalry between the two Bengali outfits.

[111] In the Federation Cup semifinal of 1997 an unprecedented 131,000 spectators watched the match between the two — a world record at any club level first class match. East Bengal won the match 4–1. For details see *The Statesman* and the *Ananda Bazar Patrika*, 14 July 1997.

and Argentina, Flumenitz and Flamengo (Brazil), River Plate and Boca Juniors (Argentina), Barcelona and Real Madrid (Spain), AC Milan and Inter Milan (Italy), Manchester United and Arsenal (England), Bayern Munich and BFC Leverkussen (Germany), and Ajax Amsterdom and PSV Aindhoven (the Netherlands).[112] What still differentiates this rivalry from other Indian club rivalries is an intense emotional attachment of supporters towards *their* club and vehement opposition to the *others'* club.[113] However, the opposed cultural identity of *self* and *other* signified by the clubs represented different fluid categories — individual, group, community, sections of community, culture, and club — changing according to shifting social and political priorities from time to time since Independence. Yet it is this oppositional perception of *self* and *other*, albeit in a much diluted form, which continues to shape the future of the most fascinating club rivalry in Bengali football.

---

[112] East Bengal supporters always seem to be more aggressive in temper and more violent in reaction while Mohun Bagan supporters look sober and moderate. For such comparisons, see Chakrabarty, 'Mohun Bagan-East Bengal Reshareshi', pp. 114–17; Saha, 'Bangalir Football', pp. 21–34, especially p. 25. However, this kind of comparison was offered as early as 1965, if not earlier. For details see *Ananda Bazar Patrika*, 19 July 1965.

[113] A more recent incident is conclusively revealing on this point: In late May 2003 Mohun Bagan Club, bogged down by internal strife and court cases, could not arrange for the money to retain its star players including the club's heartthrob Jose Ramirez Barretto, the Brazilian forward. Learning this from newspaper reports, one ardent supporter of the club decided to sell off his ancestral house and came to the club authority to know the formalities of payment. The club officials understandably refused the offer but take pride in it as a reflection of the club's continuing tradition and glory. As East Bengal, the foremost enemy of his club won all the five tournaments they participated in in the previous season including the all-important National League title with a nearly all-win record against Mohun Bagan, the fan could not bear the thought of a repeat of the same story next year. Hence, to retain the star forward who, he believed, could only ameliorate the plight of the club against their arch-rival, he committed his only asset for the sake of the club. For details, see *Ananda Bazar Patrika*, 3 July 2003; translation mine.

Rupak Saha narrates a similar incident of 1991 when an East Bengal fan mortgaged his house and took his wife's gold ornaments to rope in a few good players for the club in times of the club's financial crisis. For details, see Saha, 'Bangalir Football', pp. 23–24.

6

Open Space, Stadium Imbroglio and Spectator Culture: Ground Realities of Bengali Soccer

India may rank very low in the current FIFA ratings, yet Indian football merits high esteem in terms of its culture, tradition and mass following. The rich heritage of regional/local football culture in India is fascinating enough to invite comparison with those of Brazil, Argentina, Italy, or England. Importantly, the uniquely myriad patterns of India's regional/local football culture defy any simplistic homogenisation. Football in Bengal can boast of the most unique and diversified cultural glow in India. While the changing culture of the game in colonial Bengal mirrored the influence of the underlying forces of imperialism, nationalism and communalism, football in post-colonial West Bengal has been a powerful vector of new forces like social conflict, sub-regional tension, club rivalry, hooliganism and violence, ground redevelopment, stadium imbroglio, and semi-professionalism. These apparently disjointed facets of Bengali football culture such as development of football grounds or evolution of spectator culture have been rather neglected domains of research, which the present chapter seeks to redress. Drawing upon J. A. Mangan's suggestion, it also seeks to address the pertinent question of 'the autonomy of sport as a manifestation of indigenous popular culture, and local, regional and national negotiation and resistance in the face of global movements'.[1]

Development of Football Grounds and Problems of Open Space: From Colonial to Post-colonial Bengal

In the modern world, sport and environment are often stated as complexly interrelated phenomena. While environment usually plays a vital role in

---

[1] J. A. Mangan, 'Series Editor's Foreword', in Finn and Giulianotti (eds), *Football Culture*, p. viii.

the shaping of sport's incidents and cultures, the physical geography of sport, in particular its relationship with the local environment and microclimate, remains a decisive factor in sport's popularisation and commercialisation.[2] This internal geography of Indian sports in general and of football in particular has been mostly ignored by social scientists. Football ground/stadia development/redevelopment, largely and continuously influenced by environmental factors like weather patterns or nature of the local landscape, also reflects the emotional attachment, social control, political design, and economic transformation of the Indian nation. In the context of football in Bengal, however, one comes across a different kind of geographical and environmental factor, which shaped the pursuit of the game over the ages. This refers to the complex equation between the development and problems of *open space* utilisation and the question of football's popularity and decline in urban Bengal.[3]

Like a particular sport itself, a sports ground may claim to have its own history. The availability, opportunity and utilisation of a sports space/ground can have a deciding sway on the growth, popularity and decline of a particular sport at a particular place. More importantly, the growth, development and problems of sports grounds are intimately related to wider socio-economic, political and cultural processes. The history of football grounds in urban Bengal in the 20th century helps us unmask the relational complexities between open space utilisation, sports grounds development and popularisation of sport on the one hand and the broader issues of politics, economy, society, and culture on the other. Hence the process of growth, development and problems of open space vis-à-vis football grounds in 20th-century urban Bengal can be analysed only against

---

[2] The internal physical geography of sport includes the local landscape and the spatial dimension of the sports ground or stadium as also the impact of local climate and environment on that space. For an authoritative discussion of sports geography, see John Bale, *Sports Geography*, London: Spon, 1989. Also see John Bale, *Sport, Space and Society*, London: Routledge, 1992. A path breaking study on this subject has been published recently. Andrew Hignell in his work *Rain Stops Play: Cricketing Climates*, London: Frank Cass, 2003, examines the physical geography of English county cricket, in particular its interrelationship with the local environment and microclimate, and looks ahead to the likely impact global warming and the altered weather patterns will have on the county game.

[3] The term *open space* refers to a sizeable plot of plain wasteland lying in between urban agglomerations, which is not specifically used for any civic or commercial purpose.

the backdrop of political tension, social unrest, economic challenge, and cultural conflict.[4]

Conventional urban history of late colonial Bengal does not offer any concrete ideas about the evolution of open space and its utilisation as sports grounds.[5] It may seem, however, that open space remained in abundance in early 20th-century Bengal. This was, of course, not without exception. Given the density of population in north Calcutta, for example, the pressure on appropriating unused land for civic purposes was not unusual.[6] However, greater availability and easier reclamation of open space in general provided a suitable option for its use as a sports ground.[7] Football as the most popular sport of contemporary Bengal required open grounds for Bengalis' indigenous pursuit of the game. In fact, football's social popularisation as a mass spectator sport in the first two decades of the 20th century was well complemented and facilitated by the acquisition of green open spaces for the purpose of football-play throughout the cities of Calcutta and Dacca and their outskirts. Vast open spaces in the suburbs of Calcutta, too, gradually attracted the youth towards playing the game. It was from these suburban towns that the Bengali clubs of

---

[4] Here 'football ground' includes both the organised sector of sports ground, i.e., stadiums or enclosed grounds owned and maintained by state authority, sports bodies, maidan clubs or schools and colleges as well as those unorganised pieces of open grounds in the urban area, which are either occupied by local clubs or remain in abeyance without any viable proprietor. It is important to remember that football grounds maintained by the organised sector also had a connection with the general availability of open space and its use. 'Urban' Bengal, in the context of the present chapter, implies Calcutta and its extended outskirts (presently Greater Kolkata) as well as its neighbouring suburbs from where Calcutta gets a rich supply of footballers.

[5] A useful example on this point is Pradip Sinha, *Calcutta in Urban History*, Calcutta: Firma KLM, 1978. In many such other works, despite recurrent reference to the maidan, open space or sports ground as such hardly finds a place of worth.

[6] It is said that Mohun Bagan Club had to leave its original ground situated at Kirti Mitra's Mohun Bagan Villa in north Calcutta in the late 1890s since the land fell in the covetous eyes of contractors who bought the whole estate and sold the land in plots. For details, see Chirakaaler Mohun Bagan Prokashona Committee, *Chirakaaler Mohun Bagan* (Mohun Bagan Forever), Kolkata: Amal Kumar Sen, 2003, p. 124.

[7] In many cases, however, the use of unused landscape as sports ground was not legally authorised.

Calcutta used to get a rich supply of footballers since the turn of the century.[8] Moreover, football began to enjoy a reasonable edge over other sports like cricket and hockey in the aftermath of Mohun Bagan's historic IFA Shield victory in 1911. Thus competing claims of other sports were far less. This universal popularity of football made it the staple sport played on those grounds.

In view of abundance of open space, acquisition, maintenance, and consolidation of claims on different sports grounds did not seem to be a very complex process in urban Bengal during the late colonial period. The clash between de jure ownership and de facto possession was scarce indeed. Rather, the question of control over these open spaces used as playgrounds might have been a source of conflict among locally influential people.[9] Open space availability, of course, did not necessarily imply its suitability as football ground everywhere. In Calcutta, for example, public voice for a stadium began to be raised from the 1930s onwards.[10] Increasing popularity of football-play as a daily popular pursuit, however, certainly owed quite a bit to greater availability of open space and its utilisation as football grounds in the first half of the 20th century. This is not to deny at all the importance of football as a cultural nationalist force that really played the most crucial role in its social popularisation in contemporary

---

[8] These suburban towns are situated in the surrounding districts of Calcutta, viz., the 24 Parganas currently divided into two districts of the same name earmarked South and North respectively, and the districts of Howrah, Hoogly and Nadia.

[9] This conflict may have some resonance with the elite conflict or *daladali* in 19th-century Calcutta. S. N. Mukherjee has elaborated on the nature and forms of this *daladali* in his *Calcutta: Myths and History*, Calcutta: Subarnarekha, 1977, pp. 60–85. However, he does not take into consideration the sporting dimensions of this particular conflict in his work. Presumably, two kinds of *daladali* may be identified in this context: first, one between groups who wanted development of football grounds on open spaces nominally owned by private bodies, and the groups who did not; second, the one for the control of these football grounds and the clubs behind them. Another interesting study on the bhadralok in late 19th-century Calcutta with the same lax is John McGuire, *The Making of a Colonial Mind: A Quantitative Study of the Bhadralok in Calcutta, 1857–1885*, Canberra: Australian National University, 1983, especially Chapter 2, pp. 21–41. For an instructive analysis of the nature of elite conflict in early 20th-century Bengali society see J. H. Broomfield, *Elite Conflict in a Plural Society: Twentieth Century Bengal*, Los Angeles: University of California Press, 1968, which too sails in the same boat.

[10] A series of articles on the need for a stadium published in the IFA Shield souvenirs of the late 1930s bear ample testimony to this fact.

Bengal.[11] But, that the favourbale balance of open space in the physical environment of late colonial Bengal also played its part in the same process also merits careful attention.

When India achieved freedom from British yoke, football had already become an integral part of Bengali popular culture. Yet freedom also brought in its wake the unfortunate reality of Partition. In that context, football in Bengal came to acquire a sub-regional dimension through the Ghoti-Bangal conflict on the maidan.[12] As a result, the decades of the 1950s and the 1960s witnessed intensive massification of football in Bengal. This period also experienced major changes in Bengal's urban landscape. These changes emanated mostly from a radical population explosion, hectic industrialisation and rapid but somewhat unplanned urbanisation. The huge refugee influx from East Bengal/Pakistan to West Bengal in the aftermath of the Partition significantly contributed to these interrelated changes. All this resulted in an increasing pressure on open space and a consequent rise in the commercial value of land from the 1950s. Land, alias open spaces, came to be used more and more for civic, public as well as commercial purposes such as housing, refugee settlements, slums, sanitation and drainage, public building, governmental offices, roads, shops, parks, car parks, temples, etc.

The pressure on land in urban Bengal multiplied with a new wave of refugee influx from Bangladesh to West Bengal in the context of the Bangladesh War of 1971. Forceful acquisition of fallow/waste land and open space for residential and other civic purposes became the order of the day. Official civic bodies like corporations and municipalities came to acquire such land to sustain enhancing pressure of population in concerned localities and settlements. Most importantly, the outskirts and suburbs of Calcutta fell to the full thrust of urbanisation from the 1970s. The result was the gradual but steady contraction of open space, a good quantity of which had hitherto been used as sports/football grounds. In the 1980s–1990s, the process of open space contraction reached a new high with a galloping rise in the commercial value of land in urban areas. The process of conversion of open spaces into urban conglomerations of various sorts was accelerated by the steady growth of a 'promoter raj' in and around Calcutta.[13] These promoters, mostly in liaison with political

---

[11] For an analysis of football's importance as a cultural nationalist force in colonial Bengal, see Chapter 2.

[12] See Chapter 5.

[13] Promoters in West Bengal are those builders and building contractors who acquire land legally or illegally and build multistoried residential buildings and commercial complexes on the same.

parties, openly forced vast open spaces into house building and commercial complexes. Added to this was the civic bodies' drive to beautify Calcutta and other suburban towns by acquiring most of the remaining small pieces of green open space.

The pursuit of the game in urban Bengal suffered a blow owing to a continuous decline in the availability of reasonably good football grounds since the 1970s. The unavailability of playgrounds had the direct impact of depriving different age groups the opportunity to play football from their childhood. Rearing a raw band of future footballers in the unorganised sector was thus nipped in the bud. This social and demographic process of depravity has proved a bane for Bengali football in the long run. To understand the operational aspects and affective dimensions of this complex process, it may be useful here to employ the conceptual model of Y. F. Tuan.[14]

Tuan uses the term *topophilia* to describe the deep affection of people towards particular social spaces, or 'places'.[15] In contradistinction, people may also have feelings of fear or anxiety towards other places: Tuan applies the term *topophobia* to describe such a sentiment.[16] In both cases, a psychological relationship to these spaces emerge as they acquire an embedded meaning for the people that encounter them. As A. Hopcraft remarked in the 1960s: 'Football grounds are not often attractive places in the ornamental sense. Their beauty is the special, environmental kind, appreciable only to people who related the setting to their emotional attachment.'[17]

Tuan's notions seem to have a strong resonance with football ground development in 20th-century Bengal. Every urban locality in colonial Bengal used to have at least one open space, if not more, to play football, breeding a kind of emotional attachment towards that particular space or

---

[14] This employment of Tuan's model has largely drawn from Richard Giulianotti's use of Tuan and John Bale in understanding the relation between football grounds and emotions. For details, see Richard Giulianotti, *Football: A Sociology of the Global Game*, Cambridge: Polity Press, 1999, pp. 69–72. Also see Y. F. Tuan, *Topophilia*, Englewood Cliffs: Prentice Hall, 1974; *Landscapes of Fear*, Oxford: Blackwell, 1979. It was John Bale who first used Tuan to explain the affective dimensions of sports grounds. Bale's work blends the disciplines of social geography and contemporary cultural theory and draws upon worldwide fieldwork. See John Bale, *Landscapes of Modern Sport*, Leicester: Leicester University Press, 1994.

[15] Giulianotti, *Football*, p. 69.

[16] *Ibid.*

[17] A. Hopcraft, *The Football Man*, London: Simon and Schuster, 1988, p. 141.

ground among people around. This unique attachment of the locals to a sporting space is quite akin to topophilia. In the context of the gradual contraction of open space and steady disappearance of such football grounds from the urban landscape in post-colonial Bengal, this topophilic sensation gave way to a topophobic one. As fewer sporting spaces became available for greater number of localities, a sense of distance and detachment began to grow towards certain playgrounds creating topophobic sensations especially among children, adolescents and the youth. The growing distance between *home/locality* and *open space/playground* has largely moulded the nature of spending leisure of the new-generation Bengali middle-class youth. Intending or potential players and spectators could hardly get a chance to nourish their pursuit of the game in such a situation.[18] This had a drastic impact especially in the suburbs that used to provide a rich supply of good footballers to the big and small clubs of Calcutta. The dearth in the number of quality Bengali footballers as well as declining spectators' interest in Calcutta football in the late 1980s and the 1990s may be partly attributed to this development. Arguably, the topophilic or topophobic sensation that I have pointed out is reflective of a crisis in the Bengali's emotional attachment towards football, once considered to be Bengal's most popular mass spectator sport. A study of transition from topophilia to topophobia towards particular sporting spaces, thus, might be a useful model to understand the marked decline in the standard and popularity of football in post-1970s Bengal.[19]

Thus just as the physical geography of a sport has had a dependent relationship with local environment and microclimate, the social and economic viability of a sport has shown a long-term dependence on regional environmental stability. Colonial Bengal afforded greater availability and easier reclamation of open space and hence a flourishing quantity of football grounds. This, in no insignificant way, contributed to football's intensive social popularisation throughout Bengal. Post-colonial West Bengal, however, witnessed gradual entrenchment of open space mostly as a result of refugee influx, population pressure and rapid but somewhat

---

[18] Schools with and without playgrounds might also have affected this transition from topophilia to topophobia from the 1970s onwards because the lack of opportunity to learn and practice the game at the school level could deprive the most important age groups to nurture any attraction towards football.

[19] Similarly, there is further scope to employ this model usefully to study the spatial and social importance of sports stadiums as also enclosed grounds in 20th-century Bengal.

unplanned urbanisation. This led to a crisis in the maintenance and development of football grounds, uniquely articulating power relations at different levels — social, political and economic. The decline in football's standard and popularity in the last three decades of the 20th century can be partly attributed to this environmental imbalance. I have employed the conceptual model of Y. F. Tuan to stress this affective dimension of open space and its impact on Bengali social psyche. Arguably, therefore, the intricate relations of open space, sports grounds and football-play mirrored the emotional attachments and the dynamics of social control in the urban life of post-colonial Bengal.

The Stadium Imbroglio

Despite football's universal popularity all over Bengal, the absence of a proper stadium for the game in Calcutta constituted one major problem for the clubs, fans and the IFA since the 1920s. It has been argued that the need for a stadium was more acutely felt when in 1926 Mohun Bagan defeated North Staffords in the city Football League.[20] While this match generated considerable excitement, the absence of a proper stadium led to thousands of spectators 'failing to gain admission to the temporary structure erected for the match'.[21] In view of overcrowding in many League matches and limited scope of admission, the urge for a stadium became more pronounced. In such a context, prominent Bengali sports patrons including the Maharaja of Santosh, Sir Manmatha Nath Roy Chowdhury, began to advocate the cause of the sports stadium in Kolkata:

> Coming nearer home and speaking for Bengal, I may say, without any fear of contradiction, that a Sports Stadium in Calcutta is the need of the moment. Sport in Bengal will receive serious check if we fail to provide at the psychological moment a central home of sports. Besides, in a city like Calcutta where the huge sporting crowds always cause anxiety to the Police and the people alike, the problem of providing accommodation for spectators can no longer be ignored. Sport is rapidly developing in Bengal — more quickly than many would imagine — and the creation of an ideal center for sport is imperative. We must have a sports stadium which could accommodate in its auditorium no less than 60,000 people.[22]

---

[20] Majumdar, *Twenty-Two Yards to Freedom*, p. 172.
[21] *Ibid.*
[22] Manmatha Nath Ray Chowdhury, 'The Cry for a Stadium', *Calcutta Sports Stadium: An Illustrated Supplement to the I.F.A. Official Shield Programme 1933*, Kolkata: IFA, 1933, p. 5.

He also clearly expressed his desire to have the stadium built in Calcutta:

> I want the stadium in Calcutta because I cannot any longer suffer my heart to see the misery of Indian spectators at big football matches. At times, our football crowds struggle hard, from midday right up to the scheduled time of a game, to make their way to the venue of play. There are occasions when they have to dolefully wait for long hours in their uncomfortable seats, huddled together on ill-constructed public stands, which afford shamefully meagre and scanty accommodation.[23]

However, the real difficulty was the provision of ground on the maidan for the purpose of erecting the stadium. Ray Chowdhury thought that this was 'not insurmountable' and that the 'Civil and Military authorities can easily solve it'.[24] He urged these authorities 'to allocate a plot of land on the Maidan where a Stadium could be established by private capitalists or a Joint Stock Company, under the control of the Calcutta Football Association who have naturally taken the lead in the matter'.[25] He also underlined the financial viability of the stadium scheme as 'a stadium will be paying as a business proposition and may be made a source of revenue to the Government'.[26] To discuss the question in all its bearing, a representative meeting of leading British and Indian sportsmen of Calcutta was held at his residence. The meeting recommended three sites for the proposed stadium: north-west corner of the Eden Gardens facing Strand Road and Auckland Road, Ellenborough Course, and the two grass plots to the north-east corner of the Calcutta Race Course. Of the three sites, the Raja of Santosh preferred the north-east corner of the Eden Gardens as it 'presents less difficulty, inasmuch as it is under the direct control of the Public Works Department of the Government of Bengal'.[27] Moreover, he emphasised: 'In all probability the Military authorities will find it least objectionable from their point of view, as big buildings have already sprang up closely, opposite to that site, I mean the other side of the Auckland Road.'[28] Finally, he urged all to make this venture a reality:

---

[23] *Star of India*, 8 December 1933.
[24] Ray Chowdhury, 'The Cry for a Stadium', p. 5.
[25] *Ibid.*
[26] *Ibid.*
[27] *Ibid.*, pp. 5–6.
[28] *Ibid.*

In any case, a serious cry has been raised for a Stadium which cannot be stilled and I think it is not a cry in the wilderness. I fervently appeal to all Britishers and Indians alike to help the solution of the Stadium problem. Government and the people must combine to wipe out the shame which sits on the fair brow of the City of Palaces for not possessing a Sports Stadium.[29]

The Raja's enthusiastic initiative was much appreciated in the press, and *The Englishman* wrote to that effect:

Thanks largely to the Raja's initiative, the project that has been much talked about and which has the enthusiastic support of followers of every branch of sport, has at last some prospect of being carried through. The main difficulty is the site, which everyone is agreed must be on the *Maidan*, but there is considerable ground for hope that when definite plans have been prepared the authorities concerned may be more sympathetic than they have been in the past. There will, we are assured, be no difficulty about securing the necessary capital for the construction of the Stadium if a suitable site on the Maidan is granted, and there is little doubt that it would be a paying proposition.[30]

The next few years witnessed continued efforts on the part of all concerned with Calcutta football to pursue the military authority as well as the government to implement the stadium scheme. But all went in vain as the military authority refused to release the land without showing any truly tangible reasons.[31] With the death of Santosh in 1937, the scheme also received a setback. Also, the outbreak of the Second World War shelved the cry for a stadium till at least 1943 when it was again raised in an article published in the IFA Shield Souvenir of 1943.

To be candid, Bengal has taken up football as her national game and it can be seen on every important occasion of an important match that if there is a crowd of 15,000 men inside the enclosed galleries round the ground, double the same are forced to remain outside the enclosed ground for want of accommodation.... (S)uch is our lot — in the second city of the British Empire. The Corporation, the Government or the business magnets of the province — can they not come forward to solve this vital

---

[29] *Ibid.*

[30] 'An Editorial Note from *The Englishman*', in *Calcutta Sports Stadium*, p. 3.

[31] For a detailed discussion of the course of events leading to this failure, see Majumdar, *Twenty-Two Yards to Freedom*, pp. 175–82.

and important problem which is being discussed year after year for the last 15 or 20 years?

Thanks to the late Maharaja of Santosh who did yeomen service in this connection, the site was selected near the former Band Stand at the Eden Gardens, the design and sketches were made ready, but to his dismay the late Maharaja had to keep off his scheme for adverse conditions which did not allow him to proceed further to reach his ambition fulfilled.

This crying need however did not cry (die) out and with the passing of years became more acute.[32]

In the same year, the IFA took up the initiative to send 'a circular to all sister organisations of this province for eliciting their opinion as to whether they can join the I.F.A. in their scheme of building a stadium in Calcutta, so that if the scheme materialises all active games may be played inside the stadium'.[33] The IFA's plea met with favourable response from all the associations, who 'have agreed to cooperate with the I.F.A. in the fulfillment of their object in building a stadium immediately in Calcutta'.[34] IFA's plan was to start the construction of the stadium as soon as the War came to an end.

In 1945, the year the War ended, an article appeared in the IFA Shield Souvenir narrating the painful experiences of a 'Weather-Beaten Spectator' at the Calcutta maidan:

> We spectators, who stand in mile-long queues day in and day out under the scorching sun or torrential rains as the weather god decides, before getting into the ground to watch a football match, often to find the galleries overpacked with sweating or wet humanity and return home in crowded buses or trams, sometimes disappointed at the failure of our favourite teams, hear that the news of a stadium is in the air ... smelling the news of a stadium in the air again we cannot but help putting forward a spectator's say in the matter, which may be an eye-opener (?) to those responsible for bringing down the talk of a stadium from the thin air to the more perceptible firmament.[35]

The article also urged the government to ameliorate this long-standing anomaly in Calcutta's sports-field:

---

[32] 'The Need of a Stadium', *IFA Shield Souvenir 1943*, Calcutta: IFA, 1943, p. 17.
[33] *Ibid.*
[34] *Ibid.*
[35] 'Give Us a Stadium', *IFA Shield Souvenir 1945*, Calcutta: IFA, 1945, p. 5.

> We spectators feel that the question of having a stadium, opened once again, must be seen through this time. We appeal to the Governor of Bengal, who comes from a country of stadiums, the Corporation of Calcutta and the IFA to co-operate with one another in the building of a stadium in Calcutta. We do not want a Wembley or a Hindmarsh Oval but let us have a moderate one, which will see the end of an age of long suffering of spectators, not to mention of clubs and Associations.[36]

The article was also accompanied by a cartoon made to satirise the pathos of the spectators, who used to wait outside the temporary erections failing to get inside.[37] Finally, J. C. Guha, a top East Bengal Club official, lamented:

> It is a shocking scandal but Calcutta sleeps. She is a confirmed Rip Van Winkle. In India Brabourne Stadium takes the cake. But Calcutta is never awake. Much water has flown down the Ganges since the idea was first mooted in Calcutta.... Many financiers and contractors wanted to finance the scheme. Ultimately a memorial was sent to H.E. the Governor on the 26th of October 1945. With the departure of Mr. R.G. Cassey, then Governor of the province, again a lull has come to pervade.[38]

It is said that in 1946 Mohamed Ali of Bogra, then finance minister of undivided Bengal, took a leading part for the stadium at the Eden Gardens Band Stand.[39] However, the political temperature of Bengal became too hot by 1946 to allow the stadium scheme a desired smooth run. It further receded following the Calcutta riots of 1946 and the socio-political turmoil preceding the Partition of India in 1947.

The attainment of freedom raised new hope for the building of a stadium. The rays of hope even reached Bombay which could by that time take pride in two stadiums for two different games — Brabourne for cricket and Cooperage for football. As J. C. Maitra, sports reporter for the *Bombay Chronicle*, wrote:

---

[36] *Ibid.*

[37] *Ibid.*, p. 6. The captions in the cartoon read: 'Believe it or Not: The second city of the Empire does not possess a stadium', 'Calcutta Public generally witness their games from outside the field enclosure' and 'A brisk business in soap boxes and periscopes develops in Calcutta during the sporting season because the spectators outside buy these to catch a glimpse of the action'.

[38] J. C. Guha, 'A Burning Question of City's Sports — A Stadium', *IFA Shield Souvenir 1945*.

[39] 'What About the Stadium', *IFA Shield Souvenir 1963*, Calcutta: IFA, 1963.

Now that Bengal has a popular Ministry in power, the long-expected stadium should not take long to materialise. I understand the present Chief Minister, Dr B. C. Roy, was the Chairman of the Standing Committee before he became the head of the Bengal Ministry. He should see his scheme through soon.[40]

The confusion and hope surrounding the stadium scheme was reiterated throughout the early 1950s in a series of reports and articles published in *Sport and Pastime*, one of the foremost popular Indian sports magazines of the time. As one article in 1950 rightly pointed out: 'It is difficult to find out the correct position in regard to the football in Calcutta. It is amazing that although the IFA is keen to have one and the Government of West Bengal is sympathetic towards it and a site at the Eden Gardens has been provisionally fixed, still nobody knows how the whole matter stands.'[41] There were also reports about the government's proposal to move with the idea of a compromise composite stadium at the cricket ground at Eden Gardens, which attracted vehement criticisms from the media. As Pearson Surita, a renowned sports writer of the time, commented:

> The question of a football stadium has also been examined and this has been inspired by a recent governmental suggestion to have a composite stadium on the present cricket ground at Eden Gardens, a proposal that anyone who knows anything about sport in Calcutta has immediately decried. A joint stadium for football, hockey, athletics and certain minor sports, such as exist in every great city of the world, yes, but hardly on the sacred turf where Hobbs and Sutcliffe have trod.[42]

The government, however, seemed to take a serious interest in the matter when, in 1955, it proposed the 'Calcutta Sports Bill' in the autumn session of the State Legislative Assembly.[43] The Bill, apart from placing its proposed administrative measures to put sport in Calcutta on a firm footing, included 'the immediate construction of a football stadium in Calcutta and the control of this stadium and other playgrounds by a body

---

[40] *Bombay Chronicle*, 27 June 1948.
[41] 'The Need is for a Soccer Stadium', *Sport and Pastime*, vol. 4, no. 27, 8 July 1950, p. 4. Similar sentiments were expressed in 'Sport in the Dock', *Sport and Pastime*, vol. 4, no. 30, 29 July 1950, p. 2.
[42] 'Calcutta Letter', *Sport and Pastime*, vol. 6, no. 35, 30 August 1952, p. v.
[43] *Calcutta Gazette*, 6 August 1955.

to be set up by the legislation'.[44] Although the IFA did not recommend the Bill for its objection to certain administrative proposals to control sports in the city, it appreciated the government's urge to build the stadium and promised to cooperate on that count.[45] It was also reported that the construction of the much-needed stadium would commence after the 1955 football season.[46] But the proposed site, as decided by the government, was the ground of the Calcutta Football Club (CFC) which was 'asked to give their views on the suggestion to move to some other plot'.[47] This again led to a debate over the issue of the acquisition of the CFC ground. The CFC claimed, quite justifiably, that 'they have used their premises for the past 70 years even before the IFA came into existence and have spent nearly 20 lakhs of rupees in maintaining the ground and other amenities. While the Club have no intention of going against the wishes of the Government, they will do all in their power to convince the Government of their stand.'[48]

The stadium imbroglio thus continued unabated, and we again come across typical lamentations in the articles published in the IFA Shield official souvenirs of this period, this time with even more pithy and insightful remarks:

> And once again, with that eternal problem of getting admission into a football match, we spectators are moving about with a long expectant look as to who can solve the problem of a stadium. Are we to understand that the question of a stadium will remain a myth for the people of this city after it has been talked out for years in meetings and no tangible movement to this effect?
>
> While every aspect of life has been revolutionized since independence, foreign imperialism made room for a democratic republic, native rulers vanished, Lord Cornwallis's land settlement branded 'permanent settlement' has gone, even the Hindu social system emanating from the Vedic ages was dashed into pieces by the Hindu Code Bill, only one thing remained intact towering like the Pyramid amidst all upheavals, the sufferings of Calcutta Football Public.[49]

---

[44] 'Associations Criticise Sports Bill', *Sport and Pastime*, vol. 9, no. 36, 27 August 1955, p. iv.

[45] *Ibid.*

[46] 'Stadium Idea Takes Shape', *Sport and Pastime*, vol. 9, no. 29, 16 July 1955, p. iv.

[47] *Ibid.*

[48] *Ibid.*

[49] 'New Hope for a Stadium', *IFA Shield Souvenir 1957*, Calcutta: IFA, 1957, pp. 11–12.

In 1957, the popular demand for a stadium was voiced in both Houses of the State Legislature, resulting in an all-party resolution, which urged the government to expedite the matter.[50] The IFA too passed a resolution for a separate stadium for football in the same year and requested the defence minister for a suitable plot of land on the Calcutta maidan for the purpose.[51] Yet the old question of the site once again plagued the scheme while the rival sports bodies — football and cricket — started analysing 'the merits and demerits of a composite stadium where football and cricket could be played alternatively'.[52] The average Bengali sports-lover's demand was very clear: 'We are not interested in any controversy, merits or demerits, we feel that a football stadium is needed most, *far more important and essential than cricket* and we must have it.'[53]

Taking a serious view of such sentiments, Dr B. C. Roy, the chief minister of West Bengal, himself took initiative to accelerate the process of building the stadium. He requested Shib Chandra Banerjee, business magnate of Bombay, 'to prepare a plan for the stadium'.[54] Unfortunately, Banerjee's sudden death provided Dr Roy's plan a setback. Yet he continued his efforts to go ahead with the scheme and invited Mr Vittolozzi, a famous Italian architect, in 1960 to visit the proposed site for the stadium, namely, the Ellenboroguh Course.[55] Vittolozzi, after several visits, submitted his plan for the stadium.[56] The government, on the other hand, appointed a Board of Trustees for the proposed stadium.[57] Unfortunately, the death of B. C. Roy in July 1962 again dealt a jolt to the stadium plan, and the question of allotting a suitable plot for the stadium resurfaced. As a result, the confusion over the issue continued for some time, and the earlier compromise formula of using Eden Gardens as a composite stadium for football and cricket was accepted in 1967. While this step temporarily resolved the problems for the football spectators in Calcutta, the IFA continued to press the state government for building a separate

---

[50] *Ibid.*, p. 12.

[51] The resolution was passed on 6 July 1957 and the letter to the minister was sent on 26 September 1955. For details, see 'What About the Stadium'.

[52] 'New Hope for a Stadium'.

[53] *Ibid.*; emphasis added.

[54] 'What About the Stadium'.

[55] *Ibid.*

[56] *Ibid.*

[57] The trustees included Maharajadhiraj of Burdwan, Maharaja of Mayurbhanj, Sri Biren Mukherjee, Sri G. D. Birla and Dr B. C. Roy.

stadium for football. The newly elected government in 1977 finally decided to build the stadium at Salt Lake, adjacent to Calcutta. It ultimately came into being in the early 1980s with the construction of the Yuba Bharati Krirangan at Salt Lake.

Evolution of Spectator Culture: Fandom, Hooliganism and Violence

With Mohun Bagan's historic Shield victory of 1911 against heavy odds, Bengali sporting nationalism was at its 'moment of arrival', as the win marked Indian football's coming of age.[58] The scattered forms of nationalist spectator culture sometime leading to hooliganism or erupting into violence found typical expression during Mohun Bagan's progress in the 1911 Shield finals.[59] However, Mohun Bagan's consistently remarkable performances against strong European sides since 1906 began to raise more and more winning expectations among native fans, which affected the crowd behaviour on the maidan. Habul Sarkar, a Mohun Bagan regular those days as well as a prominent member of the 1911 Shield-winning team, later recalled an exemplary incident:

> There was an incident in the preliminary round of the Trades Cup probably in 1907 while playing against Dalhousie 'B'. When our opponents were losing by 3 to 2, they lost temper, began to play very rough and even used fists and kicks upon us indiscriminately. This enraged the spectators who rushed into the field and began to assault the offending players and even the members of that Club, and the game had to be abandoned. The spectators were so rowdy that the police had to intervene and as a result of this the Dalhousie 'B' was scratched.[60]

Mohun Bagan's match days in the 1911 Shield provide concrete evidence of the beginning of a typical Bengali spectator culture at the football

---

[58] For details on this, see Chapter 2.

[59] However, stray evidences of players' offences and spectator disturbances were noted even much before 1911. For example, in 1895 the IFA suspended two players of National Association — H. C. Mukherjee and N. K. Das — and one of Seebpore College, N. N. Mukherjee, for one month 'from playing football either for or against any club affiliated to this association'. The cause of this suspension was a disturbance at a match for which a prosecution was instituted in Alipore Police Court. For details, see *The Statesman*, 11 July 1895.

[60] Sarkar, 'My Reminiscences', p. 65.

field. In its report on Mohun Bagan's drawn semifinal match against the Middlesex Regiment, *The Englishman* noted:

> All existing arrangements to keep the crowds under control were swept away and from as far as possible, right up to the touchlines, spectators swarmed and actually fought for places. Once it looked as if a vast riot was in progress at the S.W. corner.... The multitudes in front being pushed by those behind into the football field, rose in a mass to contest their ground. A free fight ensued in which sticks and umbrellas were freely used, and only arrival of the military picket helped to restore order.[61]

A pen picture of the spectators' behaviour at the maidan on 29 July 1911, that is, the day of the final, was vividly depicted two years later by the correspondent of a renowned Bengali periodical.[62] Spectator culture in colonial Bengal of course did not simply imply the on-field behavioural patterns of the Bengali crowd. The European as well as Anglo-Indian spectators, who used to include a sizeable number of ladies as well, voicing their support for their coveted teams, contributed not least to the concretisation of such a typical spectator culture. While European spectatorship on the maidan was often couched in racial overtones implicating anti-Indian attitude, it at times reflected the ethos of sportsmanship as well. The following conversation between a European gentleman and a lady watching the proceedings of the final match bears ample testimony to the latter observation:

> Gentleman: This is quite the finest game of the tournament. It is indeed highclass football.
> Lady: The Bengalee boys are wonderfully plucky and clever. They are playing a rather clean hard game.
> Gentleman: They are really fine exponents of football. They have learned the science and remarkably quick on the ball. They deserve to win.
> Lady: But I hope they won't.
> Gentleman: Ah, that's patriotic, but not sportsmanlike.
> Lady: I don't care. I hope the Argyles (East Yorks) will win.
>
> (After the Argyles alias East Yorks scored the first goal)
> Lady: I am delighted the soldiers have won. They are now sure to get the Shield!

---

[61] *The Englishman*, 25 July 1911.
[62] Gupta, 'Football Final'. The author seemed to have been present at the final match of the Shield in 1911, and later on decided to write a literary narrative on it incorporating his eye-witness experience of the match.

Gentleman: I don't know. It is true, they are leading by a goal but the Bengali lads are a tough lot and bad to beat. I wouldn't bet any thing on the result, as it seems to be quite open yet.
Lady: You want the Bengalis to win. Is that right?
Gentleman: I still think they deserve to win! It'll be hard times, if they don't.

(After the United Bengal alias Mohun Bagan won the match 2-1)
Lady: So the unexpected sometimes happens.
Gentleman: On the contrary it is the expected that has happened. I all along expected the Bengalis to win.
Lady: Is it all over?
Gentleman: Time's up and I think it is all over, including the shouting. Though we may hear some more when the shield is given away.[63]

The tremendous excitement that prevailed and the rejoicing that followed the victory were unprecedented in Bengali social life. Ganen Mallick, sports journalist of the *Amrita Bazar Patrika*, wrote:

> The scene that followed was beyond description. Hats, handkerchiefs, umbrellas and sticks were waved and the tremendous cheering shook haven and earth. It was as if the whole population had gone mad and to compare it with anything would be to minimize the effect.[64]

The description of *Reuter News Agency* or *Amrita Bazar Patrika*, already referred to in Chapter 2, reinforces the same stirrings of fandom in the wake of the Mohun Bagan victory. However, such expressions of fandom did not lead to any recurrent spectator hooliganism or violence till at least the 1920s.[65] Most cases of rowdy crowd behaviour during this period emanated from the decisions of the referees or linesmen, considered to be partial towards European teams by Bengali spectators. For example, in the 1921 first round IFA Shield match between Mohun Bagan and CFC, the green stands of the gallery were set on fire 'after the referee Major Patridge had

---

[63] *Ibid.*

[64] *Amrita Bazar Patrika*, 31 July 1911.

[65] This was so probably because the native spectators could not risk recurrent assault on the Europeans during Mohun Bagan's matches against European teams, given the police protection the minority European spectators enjoyed and also anticipating possible consequences of such assault. More importantly, until the late 1920s, except for Mohun Bagan's few matches against the civil and military European teams, absence of any club rivalry between/among Bengali clubs was one important reason for the non-occurrence of serious spectator clashes.

abandoned the game quite early in the first half as the ground marks had frequently been encroached upon by the indisciplined spectators'.[66]

It was an age neither of great stadia nor of radio or televised sport. Hence 'being in the maidan' was the soul of spectatorship. The nationalist element of the football culture was most obvious in maidan-spectatorship. Spontaneous effusion of nationalist feeling found prolific expression in specific forms of behaviours — pitch-side language, jokes and doggerels, erratic vocal outbursts, peculiar physical gestures, skying umbrellas, tearing shirts, throwing sandals and stones into the ground, torching papers and clothes — and spectator-violence. The most commonplace forms of nationalist spectator culture at Calcutta maidan in the 1920s and 1930s are brilliantly delineated in Achintya Kumar Sengupta's autobiographical *Kallol Yug*. Excerpts from Sengupta's writing deserve reproduction here:

> No age-bar prevailed in those youthful days. Mohun Bagan's match proved a great leveler for Bengalis; young and old, father and son-in-law.... An enthusiastic pat on a man's back in the gallery, the gentleman turning back proved to be a respectable professor. This did not matter! All sailed in the same boat, equal partners in joy and sorrow.... If Mohun Bagan scored a goal by dint of spectators' incarnated good work, that very professor would be delighted, shouting and making eccentric gestures and about to hug his student in joy. All were water of the same river.

> In fact, none could have imagined how one sitting on an eight-anna iron chair and pretending to be a 'bhadralok' might witness a football match. It was not cricket where one had to await a 'glance' or 'drive' once in five or more overs. Every moment in football was filled with anxious excitement. The ball at a close shave of the opponent's goal might suddenly be kicked towards one's own heart, i.e. at his team's goalmouth in a twinkle of an eyelid. One could not really lean on his seat even for a moment. 'Come on, centre, centre it', 'pass him, pass him the ball', 'buck up, buck up', 'make a through' — plenty of such advices and instructions to the players were the norms of real/good spectating. And even that is not all. Rebuking a player was no less important: 'Hey! Why are you playing without any ability'; 'Don't fuss, namby-pamby guy!'; 'Are you drunk and still playing the match?'; 'Come on, fall abreast upon the goal'; 'Injured legs, don't worry, if amputated, would be framed in gold in the museum'. Then, if one missed an open sitter, more desperate and orderly comment could be heard: 'Get out; it's not your place! Just get out of the ground and take refuge in the shadow of your wife's sari.' And if the referee gave any unwanted decision

---

[66] The incident was referred to in *Amrita Bazar Patrika*, 29 June 1956.

one could easily hear the heat of the beat: 'Beat, beat the referee black and blue and thrash him unto his mouth!'

Our shirts used to be frayed and sandals torn thanks to the heat of the game. Not a single drop of rain, yet the ground was found full of knee-deep mud on the eve of the match. Why? The explanation came from a more learned spectator: 'Sweat of the brow made the maidan so slushy'. No umbrella, no waterproof, managing the spectacles became an arduous job. No speculating about how many spectacles fell off the noses by typical elbow pushes!... Many used to crowd outside the gallery penniless, bare head in the sun and barefoot to see their coveted barefooted footballers.

Each of us had to subscribe to every act, convention and tradition of joyous excitement even to the extent of skying forced umbrellas from side sitters.... At noon, under the scorching sun-rays, the only respite was to chew ground-nut if pieces of ice or cucumber or shaddock were not available. Then, the fun lay, of course if you would have liked, in transferring the dry jackets of those ground-nuts into someone's pocket casually.

You must stand up when Mohun-bagan would score a goal. The outburst was often said to have been heard from Bally to Ballygunj. You can't expect to watch such a feat without standing on your feet.

Despite all these efforts, Mohun-Bagan could not win on all occasions. It used to get beaten by weaker teams like Aryan, Kumartuli or Howrah Union when it really mattered. The boat thus drowned just before reaching the shore. It's pathetic to remember those fateful days. Powerless to move on, the situation became so desperate that the only face-saver was to board a second class tram compartment at the expense of luxurious evening travel on a hootless Walford double-decker. A supporter's dejection, which had led him to commit suicide at Mohun-Bagan's defeat, becomes understandable in this light.

To skip the daily heckle of entering the ground through a terrible rush, acquiring a Mohun-Bagan membership won't be a bad idea. However, members are often the most ignorant of the lot. Once during a very important match, we found a few important members smoking outside the gallery during the match with a small gathering encircling them. It was quite unbelievable in view of the mind-blowing match and roaring crowd inside the ground. Someone from the crowd asked in surprise: 'Hey! Why don't you enter the ground?' One of the gentlemen replied: 'We never enter to see the match, rather always stay off. We are the *non-seeing members* of this club.' 'What do you mean?', another exclaimed! 'It means, since we have proved ominous for our team and since our presence in the gallery only results in the defeat of Mohun Bagan, we never see the matches; rather scratch grass with our teeth and listen to the outbursts.'

Such selflessness certainly deserves to be written in golden letters. Staying home won't work during the match. Even when they are eligible to witness the match, they will sit outside to ensure Mohun Bagan's victory. One more instance about a lame gentleman to which I myself was an eyewitness deserves mention here. Enquired as to how his legs were cut off — whether due to a car run-over or not, he said with a grave smile: 'No sir, it's football run-over.' 'What?', I just exclaimed! 'Please, no more words', he stopped me and continued, 'work has been fully extracted from me. It's my plea not only to you but to all our countrymen. All of you instructed to leave the legs on the football ground. I have done accordingly. Don't you feel the obligation to frame my legs in gold in the museum?[67]

With the rise of Mohammedan Sporting Club and East Bengal Club into prominence, club rivalry in Bengal football transcended the earlier binary of Mohun Bagan vs. European teams and came to assume a critical character of inter-club rivalries between strong Bengali sides which included, apart from the three big clubs, other worthy Bengali clubs like Aryan, Kalighat, Sporting Union, or B.N.R.[68] Importantly enough, there was a marked difference in the nature of crowd behaviour in the matches between Indian and European clubs on the one hand and between two Indian clubs on the other. As already noted in Chapter 5, the rivalry between Mohun Bagan and East Bengal had started breeding crowd disorder and hooliganism from the early 1930s. But this trend of maidan hooliganism or crowd violence was not a feature which was confined simply to the arch rivalry of these two clubs, nor could it simply be explained in terms of Ghoti-Bangal conflict later on. Rather, the evidences relating to fan culture and spectator behaviour since the 1930s suggest that football in Bengal had its own behaviourial dynamics, which included elements of tradition, obsession, superstition, coercion, and spontaneity. The usual causes of crowd disorder were either dissatisfaction over perceived 'wrong'

---

[67] Sengupta, *Kallol Yug*, pp. 66–72.

[68] As *Amrita Bazar Patrika* wrote: 'Mohammedan Sporting are slowly but surely replacing Mohun Bagan from the high pedestal they have occupied so long as the crowd's idols. Long before 5-30 all the seats had been sold, and there were 50 yard long queues at every entrance. Thousands were squatting on the turf and thousands had to be turned away for want of accommodation. The most venturesome ones climbed to the branches of the big trees and watched the match from positions of vantage.... The enthusiasm and cheering of the crowd in the green stands and of those outside the enclosure were quite reminiscent of the early days of the premier Indian team (Mohun Bagan).' 5 June 1934.

decisions of the referees and linesmen or effusions of joy or frustration over the result of matches. At the same time, it is also to be noted that while hooliganism and violence on the maidan in the 1930s and 1940s were influenced by the heightening tension in the socio-political life of Bengal during that period, post-colonial Bengal witnessed a much greater and recurrent trend of spectator clashes, which also reflected the contemporary political agitation, social tension, cultural contestation, and economic grievance.[69] There were, of course, ostensible differences between the two socio-political situations of colonial and post-colonial periods.

While the direct causes of spectator hooliganism remained more or less the same over the decades, forms of its expression varied from funny to grotesque, ranging from vocal outbursts, throwing sandals, bricks and stones into the ground or assaulting the referees or linesmen to using soda water bottles, blades and knives in the ground, vandalising club tents or damaging public properties, especially transport and roadside shops on their return from the ground.[70] The role of the police often became a critical factor in controlling such unruly and spontaneous crowd reactions. The IFA, despite its efforts to control and curb spectator violence, could not put a stop to this trend as the government never did have an articulated sports policy, not to speak of any effective crowd control measures till 1980. Moreover, in taking recourse to stern measures in connection with the incidents of crowd violence or on-field offences, the IFA was often plagued by various

---

[69] The rising communal tension in Bengali society in the 1930s–1940s had an obvious impact on fan culture and spectator behaviour. The nature of such impact on the football field has been adequately dealt with in Chapter 3. For example, the social tension and cultural contestation between the host and immigrants as a result of huge refugee influx in the decade following the Partition of 1947, economic restlessness generated by problems of unemployment, or political disorder in the wake of the Naxalite Movement in the early 1970s — all this affected the nature of fan behaviour on the football ground.

[70] A comparative study of football hooliganism in other countries over the same period would reveal the intensity and uniqueness of spectator hooliganism in Bengal football. For such a comparative study, see John Williams, Eric Dunning and Patrick Murphy (eds), *Hooligans Abroad*, London: Routledge, 1984; Eric Dunning, Patrick Murphy and John Williams (eds), *The Roots of Football Hooliganism*, London: Routledge, 1988; R. Giulianotti, N. Bonney and M. Hepworth (eds), *Football, Violence and Social Identity*, London: Routledge, 1994; R. Ingham (ed.), *Football Hooliganism: The Wider Context*, London: Inter Action Imprint, 1978; Paul Darby, Martin Johnes and Gavin Mellor (eds), *Soccer and Disaster: International Perspectives*, London: Routledge, 2005.

pressures within and without, mostly exerted by influential lobbies or even politicians supporting particular clubs. More importantly, such problems of crowd disorder were not confined to Calcutta's First Division League or IFA Shield matches, but gradually extended to engulf football matches — both organised and unorganised — all over Bengal. As a survey of match reports published in contemporary local newspapers reveals, from the late 1930s this became a typical feature of Bengali football. In 1936, 'there was a disturbance after the Lady Hardinge Shield match between the Rangers and East Bengal on police ground yesterday. Referee was assaulted by Indian spectators immediately after the game; the timely arrival of police saved him from serious injury'.[71] In the same year, 'on a complaint made by Rash Bagan to the effect that their members were assaulted by Chetla Union after their League match, Chetla was severely warned and told that a repetition of the offence will entail cancellation of club's affiliation'.[72]

Spectator violence began to assume an alarming proportion from the mid-1940s in coincidence with the rise in political and socio-communal tension in Bengal. This became apparent in course of the League of 1946. In July when Bhowanipur defeated Mohammedan Sporting Club by 1–0, Calcutta maidan witnessed the most 'rowdy scenes' while the assault on the former's club tent was 'deplorable'.[73] As *The Statesman* reported:

> The referee was roughly handled and molested until Mr H. Stanhope — the President of the IFA rushed into the scene with the assistance of Police sergeants and wrapped him up, risking his own person and escorted him to safety amidst a battery of attacks.
>
> Incidents of further assaults are reported to have been made here and there, and the innocent victims of assault included some sports journalists, who had been on duty. But since football grounds are no longer the haunts for amusement, peaceful citizens should take good care to protect themselves against such rowdism in football matches.[74]

The secretary of the Bhowanipur Club, in a letter to the IFA, 'demanded justice and fair play from the Controlling Body considering the heavy damage that the club has sustained thereby in more ways than one' and

---

[71] *The Statesman*, 1 August 1936, p. 11.
[72] *The Statesman*, 11 July 1936, p. 12.
[73] *Amrita Bazar Patrika*, 3 July 1946, p. 6.
[74] *Ibid.* This was probably the first instance when journalists were also assaulted on the Calcutta football maidan as part of spectator violence.

warned that 'if the I.F.A. do not adopt any drastic measure to put a stop to maidan hooliganism and also fail to give adequate protection to the players and members etc., Bhowanipur Club will be compelled under the painful necessity to withdraw their names from the football engagements under the I.F.A.'.[75]

A few days later, when rampant hooliganism followed the East Bengal-Mohun Bagan League encounter, the press raised its strong voice against it and urged the authorities to take drastic measures to stop this trend:

> What the guardians and the controllers of football in Calcutta will be doing now? Whether they will adopt any preventive measure to put a stop to such frequent occurrences or they will be bent upon winding up the show altogether to extinguish the fire of mob violence in football matches, which besides spreading its own evil like the genius of an epidemic disease, is also bringing the fair name of sport and the sporting spirit into disrepute.[76]

The IFA, in its next Governing Body meeting, gave much thought to the issue of maidan hooliganism, and, on the suggestion of J. C. Guha, East Bengal Club's representative, resolved to form a joint enquiry committee comprising the two big clubs to 'found out the root cause', with a view to punish 'the offenders irrespective of their high rank and position in the Clubs'.[77]

The situation continued to worsen even after Independence. In course of the 1948 League, a series of fan violence incidents compelled the D.C. Headquarters, Lalbazar to post plain clothes police inside the ground during the matches, resulting in the arrest of a number of spectators.[78] Next year the situation reached a climax when Calcutta football field witnessed most disgraceful scenes after Aryan defeated East Bengal 2–1 in a return League match at the CFC ground.[79] The match had to be abandoned six minutes from time as pandemonium was let loose on the ground with the referee being assaulted by the disgruntled East Bengal supporters.[80] The *Amrita Bazar Patrika* expressed serious concern over the incident:

> Calcutta's football had many unseemly and regrettable incidents in the past, but the way the mind and temper of a certain section of the spectators

---

[75] *Amrita Bazar Patrika*, 10 July 1946, p. 6.
[76] *Amrita Bazar Patrika*, 8 July 1946, p. 6.
[77] *Amrita Bazar Patrika*, 13 July 1946, p. 6.
[78] *Amrita Bazar Patrika*, 10 July 1948, p. 6.
[79] *Amrita Bazar Patrika*, 8 July 1949, p. 6.
[80] *Ibid.*

has been moving lately, it looked that if football has to be played in the city and played clean, it may be just possible on the point of a pistol and nothing short of it.

What a poor advertisement to the sporting spirit of the premier city in the country! Why play a game if you only play for a win, why watch a football match if you cannot take a defeat, why play for a team if your supporters bring disgrace and discredit to you? Time has now come and it came a long time ago when there must be a show down. The I.F.A. must either govern or get out of it. It is a disgrace to admit that we will only play football if police protection is available.[81]

The IFA stopped all the League matches immediately and called an emergency meeting of its Governing Body to discuss the continuing hooliganism on the maidan.[82] The consensus of opinion at the meeting was that 'football must be resumed at once and the I.F.A. must take drastic and ruthless action against the offending clubs and players irrespective of position and status of any particular club'.[83] The meeting resolved that 'steps to be taken by the I.F.A. on the basis that each club affiliated to the I.F.A. should cooperate in running peaceful football, particularly Mohun Bagan, East Bengal and Mohammedan Sporting'.[84] It also appointed a sub-committee to 'devise ways and means as to how football can be played in smooth and peaceful atmosphere'.[85]

The next decade witnessed serious concerns in both government and police circles over the rising incidence of spectator clashes and assaults on match officials. It has already been shown in Chapter 5 how the chief minister of West Bengal himself had to intervene to settle matters.[86] The major reason for such recurrent occurrence of fan violence was, according to press reports, problems of accommodation:

Football has definitely been a problem sport in the city. It is not fair to criticise anybody since the problem before everybody is the want of accommodation and as and when the accommodation problem will be solved, half the battle will be won and the remaining half will be educating the

---

[81] *Ibid.*
[82] *Amrita Bazar Patrika*, 15 July 1949, p. 6.
[83] *Amrita Bazar Patrika*, 16 July 1949, p. 6.
[84] *Ibid.*
[85] *Ibid.*
[86] See Chapter 5.

public that if a popular team loses, it is not because the referee could not discharge his duty well but the players played badly.[87]

Berry Sarbadhikary, the most illustrious sports journalist of the time, also argued that 'a giant football stadium is, of course, the panacea of most of the football evils and disorders in the city'.[88] He, however, held along with the IFA 'other parties responsible as well in the peculiar set up of Calcutta football — police, leading clubs with their big following members and supporters, and the stand contractors on the maidan'.[89] He also noted: 'with the absurdly low accommodation in the present day football enclosures on the maidan on the face of terrible enthusiasm for the game, the Police are indispensable for the maintenance of law and order and for stopping rowdism which is an unhappy feature of Calcutta football today.'[90] The situation became so uncontrollable that the Calcutta Police requested the IFA to 'stop all league matches until a satisfactory solution was reached', while the chief minister, expressing serious concern over the matter, called a meeting with the representatives of all First Division clubs at his office.[91] The columnist of *Amrita Bazar Patrika* lamented:

> Calcutta football had many problems in the past. There had been occasions when football was temporarily stopped even for a long period but it is difficult to remember whether football was at all dragged to Governmental level in the past. Whither Calcutta football?[92]

The intervention of the chief minister somewhat allayed the impasse over the problem of accommodation and control of gates at the clubs' home grounds, leading to the resumption of the League.[93] Yet the first match on resumption, played between Mohun Bagan and Mohammedan Sporting, had to be abandoned 'as Mohammedan Sporting players stage a walk out on plea of a scare'.[94] Berry Sarbadhikary thus commented:

> And so resumption of first division league football was far from peaceful and heartening.... On the Saturday following Mahomedans 'scared' by the

---

[87] *Amrita Bazar Patrika*, 17 June 1951, p. 6.
[88] *Amrita Bazar Patrika*, 18 June 1951, p. 6.
[89] *Ibid.*
[90] *Ibid.*
[91] *Amrita Bazar Patrika*, 21 June 1951, p. 6.
[92] *Ibid.*
[93] *Amrita Bazar Patrika*, 25 June 1951, p. 6.
[94] *Amrita Bazar Patrika*, 1 July 1951, p. 6.

throwing of a worn-out pair of shoes or two and a few stone chips which, according to them, injured some of their players, left the playing arena with a few seconds to go for half time, and ultimately, the game was abandoned. All round indiscipline therefore stalks the *maidan* and to quote a flogged-to-death expression Calcutta football is once again in the melting pot.[95]

Apart from the problem of accommodation, Sarbadhikary also held the IFA and the big clubs responsible for the continuous troubles at the maidan:

> All our football ills and disorders revolve round the shortage of accommodation for reasons which need not be repeated time and again. The big clubs because of their large following appear to be more important than the I.F.A. and are perhaps in a position to 'dictate' to the I.F.A., if they so wish. The rowdy section of the spectators can get away after indulging in obnoxious practices as there are no proper arrangements to check them, the commendable police vigilance notwithstanding. The referees blunder at times not because they do not know better but owing to the crowd menace which is very real, judging by the assault stories which decorate (!) our sports pages almost every other day.[96]

While the usual targets of the rowdy fans were mostly the match officials, players of small clubs too sometimes had to suffer the same fate. In such cases of fan-wrath, the police, especially the mounted police, played a crucial role in providing safety to them. Instances could be found in galore during these decades from the 1940s when the mounted police saved the match officials and players from physical assault by the furious big club fans, dispersed the hooligans and escorted the attacked to safety. The violent spectators, in their turn, apart from hurling slang words, used to throw umbrellas, shoes, brick bats, stones, sticks, bamboo poles, and soda bottles at their human targets.[97] At times, the clubs too complained to the IFA against poor supervision, requesting even to import referees from abroad. While acknowledging the clubs' right to express grievances to the apex governing body of football, the IFA, however, tried to remain firm to such proposals. In 1956 the League faced a serious crisis as the four leading clubs comprising East Bengal, Mohammedan Sporting club, Aryan, and

---

[95] *Amrita Bazar Patrika*, 2 July 1951, p. 6.

[96] *Ibid*.

[97] For some very striking incidents of this kind in the early 1950s, see *The Statesman*, 2 July 1952, 31 July 1952, 8 August 1952; *Amrita Bazar Patrika*, 6 July 1953, 3–4 July 1954, 25 July 1954, 10, 13 and 15 July 1955.

Rajasthan issued 'some sort of an ultimatum that if concrete steps were not taken by the I.F.A. inside a week from June 21 to set right to the satisfaction of all concerned the indifferent and inefficient refereeing, the signatory-clubs reserve the right or not to field their teams in the future league match'.[98] The IFA bosses also felt at par regarding the general deterioration in the standard of supervision, but took exception to the 'threat' inherent in the ultimatum. Pankaj Gupta, the president of the Calcutta Referees Association, on the other hand, argued that while refereeing in Calcutta definitely needed improvement, 'the present trouble was due to various reasons'.[99] In his opinion, 'partisanship on the part of crowd and club officials, extreme club rivalry and racial and communal feelings of the spectators often created troubles'.[100] Meanwhile, Mohammedan Sporting Club even approached Dr B. C. Roy, the chief minister, alleging that 'their chances for the senior football league championship had received a mortal blow by indifferent and faulty supervision of their matches'.[101] The club also requested the chief minister to pay his attention towards 'improvement of match supervision' and to 'include "indifferent supervision" as a special item in the agenda of Government sponsored Sports Committees'.[102] The spectators' dissatisfaction and unrest over match supervision reached a peak during the League match between East Bengal and Aryan when 'disgraceful scenes of mob-violence in a football league match hitherto unheard and unseen, came before the public view' on 28 June 1956.[103] 'The episode was built around the hooliganism of the green stand spectators, who gave vent to their spleen. They not only created a pandemonium by rushing to the field of play but also made the continuance of play impossible after the nineteenth minute of the second half.'[104] The major issue of dissatisfaction for the spectators emanated from the referee's decision to award the Aryan a penalty, which resulted in the Aryan leading the match 1–0 against a one-man-short East Bengal in the middle of the second half. One newspaper reported the mob violence that ensued as follows:

---

[98] *Amrita Bazar Patrika*, 23 June 1956, p. 8.
[99] *Amrita Bazar Patrika*, 24 June, 1956, p. 8.
[100] *Ibid.*
[101] *Amrita Bazar Patrika*, 27 June 1956, p. 6. By 'indifferent' supervision, the club meant the referees' partisanship towards some of their opponents, including particularly Mohun Bagan.
[102] *Ibid.*
[103] *Amrita Bazar Patrika*, 29 June 1956, p. 8.
[104] *Ibid.*

The referee was man-handled by the mischief mongers on his way back to the C.F.C. tent. But for the timely intervention of Sri J. C. Guha — the Hony. General Secretary of the East Bengal Club, who not only gave him protection risking his own person but also escorted him to safety, the fate of the referee — Bijoli Mukherjee — might have been still worse....

To describe the incident as a tempest in a tea-pot would never be a travesty of truth. Stones, brick-bats, shoes and even the heavy iron-framed chairs were used as the missiles by the green-stand spectators, who in spite of the intervention by the police force made two attempts to set fire to the green stands at the north-east and the south-east ends. Fortunately, however, the situation was brought under control by a tear-gas squad of the Police and the fire was extinguished.[105]

As regards the complaint of the four clubs against poor supervision, the IFA served notices upon the clubs to show cause 'why disciplinary action should not be taken against each of them for writing jointly a letter to the I.F.A. against refereeing'.[106] As this show cause notice came into public via newspapers, the four clubs took strong exception to IFA's course of action, condemning it as 'entirely unconstitutional and improper' and 'opposed to all equity and fairness'.[107] The IFA, in reply, asked the clubs once again to substantiate their allegations with proper evidence.[108] However, it found the explanations offered by those clubs to be 'unsatisfactory' and sternly warned the clubs 'not to indulge in such correspondence to the parent body in future'.[109] Quite naturally, the four clubs remained dissatisfied with such a decision, pending any actual promise or measure to be taken by the parent body with regard to their central grievance — poor and indifferent match supervision.[110] Therefore, more complaints were to come from the clubs in the coming years.[111] Interestingly enough, there were even instances of the members and fans of the big clubs boycotting their favourite club's matches at their own grounds.[112] The situation became so

---

[105] *Ibid.*

[106] *Amrita Bazar Patrika*, 30 June 1956, p. 8.

[107] *Amrita Bazar Patrika*, 3 July 1956, p. 8.

[108] *Amrita Bazar Patrika*, 14 July 1956, p. 8.

[109] *Amrita Bazar Patrika*, 18 July 1956, p. 8.

[110] *Amrita Bazar Patrika*, 19 July 1956, p. 8.

[111] In 1960, Mohammedan Sporting again lodged a petition against poor refereeing and demanded postponement of all their League matches until satisfactory settlement of their grievances. *Amrita Bazar Patrika*, 13 June 1960, p. 8.

[112] For details on such actions by the fans of the three big clubs, see *Amrita Bazar Patrika*, 14 June 1960, p. 8 (Mohammedan Sporting); 28 June 1960, p. 8 (Mohun Bagan); 7 July 1960, p. 8 (East Bengal).

deserving of concern that the IFA had to bring a referee from another state to supervise Mohammedan Sporting's next charity match. The Calcutta Referees Association (CRA), however, strongly objected to this action and its Assistant Secretary Rashbehari Chakraborty resigned in protest.[113]

While the confusion over poor match supervision and the conflict between the IFA and certain clubs continued to prosper, fan hooliganism and maidan violence showed no signs of abatement either. In 1959, after a League encounter between East Bengal and the Sporting Union, one player of the latter club was attacked on his way back to the club tent by a rabid fan and had to be removed to the hospital with a serious injury.[114] In 1960, the commissioner of Police, Calcutta, advised the authorities of the Mohammedan Sporting Club 'to see that their members and supporters behave in a peaceful and orderly manner during the football matches'.[115] In the same year, after Mohun Bagan defeated East Bengal in a crucial match, the CRA was attacked by a large number of demonstrators and partially damaged.[116] The fanatical behaviour of the spectators became so disconcerting that even the chief minister of West Bengal regretted that 'of late there had been tendency among a certain section of club fanatics to indulge in free fights after the conclusion of matches'.[117] He also lamented that 'sports has come to such a stage that even the very spirit of sports was missing'.[118] In fact, the occurrence of fan violence became the order of the day at the maidan in the 1960s.[119] In 1962, the CRA decided not to provide any referees for the supervision of Calcutta League matches following frequent manhandling of referees until and unless 'they were provided adequate security'.[120] In effect, the Governing Body of the IFA met the

---

[113] The referee was imported from Bombay. *Amrita Bazar Patrika*, 27 June 1960, p. 8.

[114] *Amrita Bazar Patrika*, 27 June 1959, p. 8.

[115] *Amrita Bazar Patrika*, 15 June 1960, p. 8.

[116] *Amrita Bazar Patrika*, 3 July 1960, p. 8.

[117] *Amrita Bazar Patrika*, 16 May 1960, p. 8.

[118] *Ibid.*

[119] For serious instances of fan violence, see *Amrita Bazar Patrika*, 22 July 1960, p. 8; 26 May 1962, p. 8; 9–10 June 1962, p. 8; 5 July 1962, p. 8; 23 July 1963, p. 10; 4 July 1964, p. 8; 5 June 1965, p. 1; 15 May 1966, p. 8; 7 June 1966, p. 8; 12 June 1966, p. 1; 18 June 1966, p. 8; 29 June 1968, p. 8; 31 May 1969, p. 8; 29 June 1969, p. 1.

[120] The decision was precipitated by the alleged manhandling of the referee of the Howrah Union vs Wari match on 14 June 1962 by a section of the players and their associates. It was reported that 'while the referee was on his way to the C.R.A. tent he was hit on his head and received bleeding injury'. For details, see *Amrita Bazar Patrika*, 15 June 1962, p. 8.

representatives of all the League clubs at a joint conference and adopted the following resolutions to stop the disturbances in local football:

1. The growing disturbances in local football must be stopped.
2. If during a match it seems that there might be rowdyism, the captains of the rival teams would make an appeal to the spectators and if such appeals do not improve the situation the match would be abandoned.
3. If any allegation is made against a referee, the representatives of the CRA and the IFA will meet together and discuss the matter and, if necessary, action will be taken against the referee.

> It was also agreed that the IFA will issue a statement appealing the spectators to refrain from creating disturbances.[121]

It is important to note in this context that the police, especially the mounted police, used to play a critical role in the process of crowd control during the football matches in these decades. As invasion of ground, stone-throwing and other intimidatory tactics often forced abandonment of games, police had to intervene to keep things under control. They often had to take recourse to lathi-charge and even using tear gas to checkmate the violent spectators. It fell under their regular duty to protect the match officials as well as the players and officials of smaller clubs. At times, however, the police were guilty of committing excesses in the name of suppressing hooliganism. For instance, after the abandonment of a League match between East Bengal and Rajasthan in 1965, the police was accused of 'indiscriminate lathi charge on the members (of the East Bengal Club), injuring many of them, including ladies and players in their uniform' and of 'entering the tent, injuring members and breaking almost all the furniture and memorable photographs'.[122] As one columnist in the *Amrita Bazar Patrika* argued:

> Appropriating the blame now on either the Police or the Public is of little use. Both were guilty of excess, the former certainly more. Determining the quantum of force to be used and observing the sanctity of the club tent are delicate issues involving emotional outbursts and passion. Violent physical injuries on innocent ones, especially on ladies and players in uniform, and mopping up operations within the tent are distressing and condemnable.
>
> There is also the Police point of view: as guardians of law and order they had to act against not football spectators but a riotous mob who had been

---

[121] *Amrita Bazar Patrika*, 17 June 1962, p. 8.
[122] *Amrita Bazar Patrika*, 5 June 1965, pp. 1 and 8.

using the club enclosure, including the tent, as hideouts for their guerilla operations.[123]

As has already been mentioned in Chapter 5, soccer fanaticism over the Mohun Bagan-East Bengal rivalry reached new heights in the 1970s due to demographic, political and social tension. In fact, this fanaticism remained a regular feature of Calcutta football in general throughout the decade.[124] The resultant trend of hooliganism and violence seemed to cross all manageable limits in 1980. The tragedy of 16 August 1980, when 16 football fans died in a stampede at the Eden Gardens during a Mohun Bagan-East Bengal League encounter, was therefore not an incident that happened all of a sudden.[125] Rather the writing on the wall became clear during the Federation Cup of 1980 when supporters of the three big clubs clashed on every occasion their favourite teams met with each other in that tournament. When Mohun Bagan defeated Mohammedan Sporting in the semifinal in the morning fixture on 7 May, 'large areas of central Calcutta witnessed scenes of violence for nearly two hours' as 'groups of rival soccer fans returning from the match … clashed with bombs, soda water bottles and brickbats'.[126] A number of people suffered injuries, while some had to be hospitalised. In fact, law and order in the city was absolutely in tatters following the match. As one newspaper reported:

> Lathi-wielding policemen chased the warring groups, who began to throw stones at shops which hurriedly put down their shutters. Most shops, however, remained closed anticipating such clashes.
>
> The police fired five rounds of teargas shells at the crossing of Dharmatala Street and Chandni Chowk to disperse a mob. Two private cars and a zeep were damaged due to stone throwing.…
>
> The incidents created panic in the affected areas and traffic was disrupted. Office-going people were greatly inconvenienced being caught in the *melee*. A woman was stated to have fainted on Lenin Sarani when she saw some men brandishing daggers.[127]

---

[123] *Amrita Bazar Patrika*, 8 June 1965, p. 8.

[124] For instances of maidan violence in this decade, see *The Statesman*, 16, 28, 30 July, 14 September 1970, p. 10; 10 and 19 August 1971, p. 10; *Amrita Bazar Patrika*, 23 July 1972, p. 8; 3 and 29 July 1976, p. 8; 14 and 20 July 1977, p. 6; 30 July 1977, p. 8; 1 July 1979, p. 10; 4 July 1979, p. 6; 5 July 1979, p. 8.

[125] The background and aftermath of this tragic incident has already been discussed in detail in Chapter 5.

[126] *Amrita Bazar Patrika*, 8 May 1980, p. 1.

[127] *Amrita Bazar Patrika*, pp. 1 and 8; emphasis added.

The final between East Bengal and Mohun Bagan, which ended in a draw, also led to similar incidents of crowd violence.

> Incident-packed and tension-charged, Thursday's final in the end turned into a brawl that was restricted not only to the playing arena itself but spread all over the galleries of the vast stadium....
>
> The repercussions of the unfortunate incidents on the ground were evidenced on the different stands. While almost every stands reported unhappy incidents of free-for-all, the Ranji Stadium and the stands behind the Akashbani Bhavan flared up with serious violence. There were exchanges of brickbats and other missiles; bamboo poles were wantonly swung and there were also free fights atop the stands.
>
> Police, voluntary organisations working inside the ground and several other different club officials were seen carrying injured persons, profusely bleeding, for treatment either in the mini hospital at the Eden Gardens or in other corners of the ground.[128]

The chief minister of West Bengal, Jyoti Basu, vehemently condemned the incident describing it 'unthinkable' and 'regrettable'. He also warned that 'if such incidents would recur, soccer matches might be stopped'.[129] Basu urged the IFA and the teams to restrain the players from making provocative gestures or else punish the guilty players.[130] The police too became extremely worried over the violent incidents on the maidan during the Federation Cup. Mr B. K. Saha, DC Headquarters, stated that 'despite best efforts by the police, chaos in football fields was increasingly becoming a feature of sports'.[131] However, he also made it absolutely clear that 'in the interest of security of other citizens, it was not desirable to engage more policemen in controlling soccer fans'.[132] According to him, 'during the football season other duties of the police like prevention and detection of crime were seriously affected', as 'even during minor matches, policemen were required for protecting the referee, players and officials'.[133]

Similarly, the incident of 16 August 1980 was preceded by a spate of spectator clashes during the League matches. On 18 July 'wanton

---

[128] *Amrita Bazar Patrika*, 9 May 1980, p. 8.
[129] *Amrita Bazar Patrika*, 10 May 1980, p. 1.
[130] *Amrita Bazar Patrika*, 19 July 1980, p. 8.
[131] *Amrita Bazar Patrika*, 16 May 1980, p. 8.
[132] *Ibid.*
[133] *Ibid.*

stone throwing by the crowd that saw a Wari player suffer a deep gash on the back of his head led to the abandonment of Wari's meeting with Mohammedan Sporting in the Group A of the Senior Football League'.[134] On 23 July, after Aryan defeated Sporting Union 1–0, the Sporting Union players 'threw mud and spot at referee Dipak Bhattacharjee's face and kicked to express their displeasure'.[135] The following day 'police had to chase away spectators from the stands and fire teargas shells as a gallant Eastern railway forced East Bengal to part with a point'.[136] On 5 August, 'the R.F.C. players were to be given protecting corging by the police on the Mohun Bagan ground after their Senior League drawn match against Mohun Bagan'.[137] Next day, a decision by the referee during the East Bengal-George Telegraph match 'sparked off almost a free-for-all involving several players on both sides' and 'peace was restored at the initiative of officials of both clubs and the police personnel'.[138] Then, on 7 August, just a week before the tragedy, after the conclusion of the match between Mohammedan Sporting and Kalighat, 'overzealous policemen to compensate for their inactivity during real violence beat lonely supporters black and blue'.[139]

The fateful incident on 16 August 1980, therefore, did not come like a bolt from the blue, although it crossed all limits of anticipation. Many felt that prompt police action could have reduced the magnitude of the tragedy and that medical facilities arranged for on the ground were grossly inadequate for the 80,000 strong gathering. It was also argued: 'As things stand on the Maidan these days, there seems no other alternative than to scrap football programme altogether or stage the matches without spectators.'[140] The chief minister, deploring the recurrent outbreak of mob violence at the maidan, stated that 'such vandalism should not be allowed to continue any more' and ordered a 'fuller enquiry of the incident'.[141] Former sports minister and Aryan Club president Prafulla Kanti Ghosh demanded the chief minister's resignation while the West Bengal Pradesh Congress Committee demanded a judicial enquiry into

---

[134] *Amrita Bazar Patrika*, 19 July 1980, p. 8.
[135] *Amrita Bazar Patrika*, 24 July 1980, p. 8.
[136] *Amrita Bazar Patrika*, 25 July 1980, p. 8.
[137] *Amrita Bazar Patrika*, 6 August 1980, p. 10.
[138] *Amrita Bazar Patrika*, 7 August 1980, p. 8.
[139] *Amrita Bazar Patrika*, 8 August 1980, p. 8.
[140] *Amrita Bazar Patrika*, 17 August 1980, p. 1.
[141] *Amrita Bazar Patrika*, 18 August 1980, p. 1.

the 'violent and tragic' incident.[142] The repercussions on the public were also very serious:

> In public the demand was for 'stop the killer game'. In many parts of the city, flags of the Big Three — Mohun Bagan, East Bengal and Mohammedan Sporting — were found trampled by the same enthusiasts, who till the day before were supporters. Black flags were hoisted in many places to mourn the death of the young men in Saturday's incident.[143]

The state government, realising the gravity of the matter, decided to cancel the remaining football matches of the season and subsequently ordered a judicial enquiry to probe all aspects leading to the unfortunate incident.[144] The chief minister, however, tried to divert the responsibility for such a tragedy more on the rowdy section of the spectators from the police or the administration:

> The Chief Minister said that it would not be proper to blame the police or the administration for the tragedy. It needed a concerted action by all sections of the people to tackle a problem of this magnitude. He said there were about 80000 spectators including two-to-four thousand anti-socials. The anti-socials, although they were small in number, could create havoc.[145]

However, such arguments cannot shun the failed role of the government and the IFA in checkmating the continuous rise in spectator hooliganism and violence over the decades. The controlling authorities of sports in the state could not evade their responsibility with regard to various major factors precipitating the tragedy of 16 August — the inaction of police, black-marketing of tickets, insufficient safety procedures, the violence of the players, problems of accommodation, and effective measures of crowd control during matches. As one columnist in *The Statesman* rightly argued:

> The entire gate proceedings of the football matches besides a few exhibition matches go to the treasury of the State Government. Surely the Government has a vital role apart from the law and order problem.... The time has come for the organizers of the games to ensure the safety of the paying spectators. Even one life lost is too great a price to be paid to remind people that all is

---

[142] Ibid., 20 August 1980, p. 8.
[143] *Ibid.*
[144] *Amrita Bazar Patrika*, 19 August 1980, p. 1; 20 August 1980, p. 1.
[145] *Ibid.*

not well in the football grounds in Calcutta. Surely the lives of the fans are the most important consideration. The problem is too real to be allowed to solve itself and those who run and profit from football should find the solution.[146]

In fact, the solution to the grave problem of crowd violence came in the 1980s mostly from the changing priorities of sports culture in Bengal — the adverse impact of the 1980 tragedy on the society, peoples' increasing preference to watch international football on television, the success of Indian cricket on the international circuit leading the young generation to prefer cricket to soccer, the shifting of the exhibition football matches to the Salt Lake Stadium, helping the police in much better crowd control. Of course, more serious and scientific measures of crowd control and awareness of the spectators played an important role in decreasing the quantum of spectator violence on the maidan.

Changing Facets of Bengali Football Culture

This chapter has tried to identify the variegated and changing facets of football culture in Bengal during the period under review. In this attempt, it has first considered the importance of geographical landscape and social environment in the growth and promotion of the game in colonial and post-colonial Bengal. It has tried to argue how the availability and problems of open space affected the development of sports grounds and social appeal of the game. The internal geography of soccer, that is, the absence of a stadium and the problems of accommodation, on the other hand, always remained a critical factor in the development of football as a mass spectator sport in Bengal. In fact, this was one of the major reasons for crowd disorder and spectator violence, which became a uniquely regular feature of Bengali football culture, at times merging with social or political conflicts of the period. To account for this recurrent hooliganism and violence is truly complex — the match officials, the players, the club authorities and officials, the police, the spectators including the staunchest fans, the IFA and the state government — all having their share of responsibility in the process. It must be admitted, however, that the continuation of this trend for more than five decades certainly pointed to the appalling failure of the

---

[146] *The Statesman*, 18 August 1980, p. 10.

controlling authorities of the game in Bengal to implement any effective long-term measures to stop, or even minimise it. Hooliganism and violence, despite demerits, were always reflective of the Bengali's passion and love for the game, which shaped the cultural peculiarities around football in Bengal. Thus, from environmental and spatial contexts of sports-ground development and stadium building to trends of hooliganism and violence in spectator behaviour and culture, football culture in Bengal could claim to have both embedded socio-political meanings as well as some signs of distinctly autonomous features of its own.

7

Football, Literature and Performing Arts: Perceptions and Sensibilities Towards the Game

The mass following that club football evokes in Bengal is staggering. This universal popular currency of the game, as the earlier chapters of this work have already shown, was due to a variety of factors over the years: football's heightened connection with nationalism, communalism, and in effect, with politics; increasing popularity of club football along sub-regional, community and cultural lines along with growing intense club rivalry; and extensive coverage of football in the media. The growth in population, literacy and urbanisation had also facilitated the growing popularity of football in Bengal since Independence. The variegated patterns of football culture in Bengal have found eloquent expression not only in the on-field and off-field behaviour of spectators, players and officials, but also in the print media, literature as well as in other performing arts like film, theatre and music. With slow but steady mediatisation of sport from the 1950s, a new culture of soccer journalism began to evolve in the Bengali football milieu. The state of sports journalism reached a flourishing standard by 1980. On the other hand, sports journalists and writers generated a new genre of writing sports histories and novels over the same time. More importantly, through the radio commentary of football matches, football culture in Bengal acquired a new dimension reaching out to the remotest of villages. Football also found ready expression in the performing arts like films, theatre and songs. Quite a few popular films were made taking football and its associated culture as viable themes. This chapter will make an attempt to chart, analyse and project these changing representations of football culture in Bengal, examining in effect the immediate tensions and emotions on the maidan as well as the finer perceptions and sensibilities that have grown off-field towards the game in the wider context of political evolution, social transition and economic transformation in Bengal/West Bengal.

Past and Present Glories: Heritage of a Vernacular Football Literature

Books on Indian sport are now abundant in quantity in the last two decades thanks especially to cricket's pre-eminence in Indian life. These books, which include quite a few autobiographies and biographies, mostly encapsulate the moments of glory and failure, key figures and icons and historical narrative of a game's development in India, not to speak of their importance as a huge repository of data and records. Reflective and interpretative accounts of sports history, however, are few and far between. More importantly, the genre of writing the official history of the clubs or institutions has been a rarity in Indian sports writing. Bengal, however, proves to be an exception in this regard. Here, Mohun Bagan and East Bengal, the prime Bengali as well as Indian clubs can boast of a sizeable historical literature around their feats. Though produced wholly by a galaxy of Bengali sports writers and journalists on their own, these sporting histories written mostly in simple and lucid Bengali language provide informative accounts of the history of the clubs at length. But before considering these club histories, it is important to review the first and probably the most comprehensive vernacular history of Bengal football written by RB, alias Rakhal Bhattacharyya.

RB and *Kolkatar Football*

RB's *Kolkatar Football* was first published in 1955 by the East Calcutta Book House, Calcutta. Later, a revised edition of the book became available in 1978 through its republication by Boipatra, another Calcutta publisher. The most recent edition is compiled by Sibram Kumar, a noted sports writer of Bengal and ardent disciple of RB, who, in a bid to accord a fitting tribute to his *guru* (master), has integrated *Kolkatar Football* with RB's other important essays on soccer under one cover.[1] Though the editor had little to add to his master's narrative on the history of football's growth and development in Calcutta, he tries his best to supplement the earlier work with new information wherever possible incorporating recent events of importance. He has also added a few chapters of his own with the objective of filling the gaps in the story of football's transition into a postcolonial sport in Calcutta. The work is also replete with updated statistics, fascinating newspaper cuttings and rare photographs and sketches.

---

[1] RB Rachita Kolkatar Football, Kolkata: Prabhabati Prakashani, 2002.

While the original work of RB, along with his other essays as well as Sibram Kumar's own contributions to the work, does not fall in the domain of mainstream academic writing on sports history, this popular narrative remains significant to the formulation of hypothesis at a more conceptual level. Despite its popular approach, the work is a storehouse of authentic information, primary material and potential interpretations for a sports historian who desires to work on the social and cultural history of football in India. There are arguments galore running through the whole work, which point to the prolific historical sense of the author.

Kolkatar Football begins with a nostalgic approach, drawing attention to Calcutta's traditional football culture in the late 19th and early 20th centuries. In explaining the socio-historical background of football's introduction in Calcutta, RB argues that sports like football and cricket were intended by the British as means to an imperial end, to Anglicise the Indians for purposes of colonial rule. British interest in promoting football, according to him, was actuated by the aim of diverting the Bengali youth from the course of the nationalist movement. But the British could never dream that the Anglicised Bengali, inspired by the European ideals of nationalism and liberty, would subvert the language of the Raj (through sport, which is, football) to propagate anti-Raj sentiments. The themes of 'imperialism', 'nationalism', 'subversion', and 'resistance', which are at the heart of some major arguments regarding British motivations and involvement in colonial Indian sport and the nature of response these elicited from the Indians offered by recent scholars, were all hinted by RB as early as 1955. One is also struck by the fact that at the very beginning of his book, he makes his readers aware of football's universal status as a mass spectator sport in Bengal from Calcutta to the open village green.

After briefly outlining the contributions of the pioneers like Nagendra Prasad Sarvadhikari, the so-called 'Father of Indian Football' and his Sovabazar Club to the growth of the game in the 1880s, RB devotes his attention to give a fairly informative account of the European clubs that dominated the football scene until the early 1930s. It is followed by a neat delineation of the history of four major Bengali clubs of Calcutta—Mohun Bagan, Aryan, Mohammadan Sporting, and East Bengal. The epic IFA Shield victory of Mohun Bagan in 1911 is presented in all its detail. Sibram Kumar, however, has done an excellent job by adding a section entitled 'Amar Ekadas' ('The Immortal Eleven') to it. It provides short biographies of the 11 Mohun Bagan players who won the Shield. The club's growing stature as the premier club of India and the achievements that made it the 'national club' of India, have also been treated eloquently by both the writers. It is interesting to note that RB contextualises the Aryan Club as one of the foremost Bengali outfits in the colonial and early post-colonial Calcutta and considers its founder Dukhiram Majumdar to be the real motivator of footballing interest in and around Calcutta in the late 19th and early 20th centuries.

The rise of Mohammadan Sporting Club as a leading Muslim football club in Calcutta football added a new dimension to the history of soccer in India. RB attributes the club's unique success in the 1930s mainly to its adoption of the Azizian technique of playing barefoot on dry surfaces and wearing light studded boots on the slushy ones. He also notes the importance of Muslim representation and mobilisation in the growing popularity of the club throughout India. In his rather shorter discussion of the rise of East Bengal Club to glory since the 1940s, the author recapitulates the contributions of the founders and the outstanding players. RB also does not fail to offer a brief but useful survey of the history of the smaller clubs of Calcutta like Kumartuli, Town, Sporting Union, Howrah Union, Kalighat, Rajasthan, BNR, Griers, Kidderpore, Bali Pratibha, and the Eastern Railway, most of which had their salad days at different points of time.

RB's *Kolkatar Football* thus charts the trajectory of the game's evolution from a British cultural import from the middle of the 19th century to its becoming an inseparable part of Bengali popular culture and a site for contestation of colonial power by the first half of the 20th century. While the author neatly sums up the origin, growth and development of Calcutta football in its entire vicissitudes until the end of 1940s, the editor updates the entire story with his painstaking research up to the year 2000. However, as we carefully get into RB's narrative, we find that he takes up the more complex aspects of football's socio-historical development in Bengal — imperialism, racialism, nationalism, communalism, maidan culture, violence, and other social aspects of the game. The racist and imperialist dimensions of football's control and maintenance through the Indian Football Association, nationalist implications of Mohun Bagan's Shield victory and communal overtones of Mohammedan Sporting Club's football prowess receive admirable attention in the work.

However, RB seems to have ignored the complex story behind the birth of the East Bengal Club and its promotion to the First Division as well as the importance of the sub-regional and social tension of Ghoti-Bangal manifest in Mohun Bagan-East Bengal football encounters. Neither is he concerned with the nature of football finance in those days. This is striking because RB was aware of the inability of the Indian sports administrators to cope with the changing nature and priorities of the global game. He urged them to substitute traditional attitudes with new ideas to raise the status and standard of Indian football. He concludes by questioning whether 'the change of environment and requirements in independent India has prompted any new awareness amongst the organisers of Indian football?'[2]

In Sibram Kumar edited *RB Rachita Kolkatar Football*, the second section is a collection of 11 essays written by RB in the later part of his career, in the 1960s and 1970s. These had earlier appeared in Bengali periodicals like *Compas*, *Gallery* and *Masik Basumati*. Most of these essays reflect a romanticised nostalgia for Calcutta's glorious footballing past and a wishful longing for a better future as it began to experience a marked decline in standard from the late 1960s. Glorifying the pioneering role the Calcuttans played in the growth and popularisation of the game in India, he goes on to pay tributes to some outstanding footballers and organisers of Calcutta/India. The list includes Revd. Sudhir Chatterjee, a member of the victorious Mohun Bagan team of 1911; Suren Thakur, a class player of the post-1911 period; Gostha Paul, the famous 'Chinese Wall' of Mohun Bagan defence; Samad, the so-called magician of Indian football; Chhoney Majumdar, one of the most 'complete' footballers of the early 20th century; Pankaj Gupta, one of the greatest administrators of Bengali football in the first half of the 20th century; and the *Pandavas* (great five) of Calcutta football — Venkatesh, Apparao, Dhanaraj, Ahmed, and Saleh, who lay behind East Bengal's glorious successes from 1949 to 1951. The last essay in this section, dealing with the decline of Calcutta football, offers interesting insights on the causes of such deterioration. RB strongly condemned the outdated infrastructure of Calcutta football and expresses concerns about the future of Indian football.

In the final section of the book, Sibram Kumar, the editor, tries to put his own imprint on the work by presenting four essays. The first two deal with the performances of foreign teams in Calcutta and of Bengali teams on foreign soil while the third and the fourth respectively take a brief look at the introduction of new tournaments in Calcutta since Independence and some inglorious events in Calcutta football. The book winds up with a final section on the statistics of Calcutta football, which include minute data on the IFA Shield finals, Trades Cup, Elliot Shield and Coochbehar Cup champions, the first two teams and the highest scorers in the First Division Football League, the results of Indo-Europeans matches, and

---

[2] Kumar (ed.), *RB Rachita Kolkatar Football*, p. 280; translation mine.

the representation of Calcutta footballers in Bengal's state team for the Santosh Trophy. Although the work apparently does not intend to offer any interpretative historical argument or analytical framework, it somewhat unwittingly helps us understand football's relation to broader socio-economic processes that shaped colonial and post-colonial urban history in India.

Sporting Literature on 1911

As mentioned in Chapter 2, a rich genre of Bengali sporting literature has cropped up around Mohun Bagan's historic Shield victory in post-colonial West Bengal. Among these works, three exclusively deal with 1911. The first and the most authoritative, Paresh Nandy's *Mohun Bagan 1911* narrates Mohun Bagan's entire venture to win the Shield in every detail.[3] Based primarily on day-to-day newspaper reports, Nandy vividly describes the excitement of the match days, build-up to the final, details of the final match, repercussions of Mohun Bagan's victory, social composition of the playing eleven as well as press reports before and after every match. Rupak Saha's *Ekadashe Suryoday* (Sun-Rise in 1911) is a fascinating narration of the victorious run in 1911 in the garb of a novella.[4] One of the greatest Bengali soccer journalists of all time, Saha sketches the characters of the 1911 victory on the basis of souvenirs, Nandy's book and oral history. If Nandy's work has the flavour of a historical narrative, Saha's work brings out a perfect literary sketch of that historic event. Last but not the least, a most recent publication on 1911 is Sibram Kumar's edited *Sonar Freme Mohun Bagan 1911* (Mohun Bagan 1911 in Golden Frame).[5] This work is a collection of contemporary and later writings on the event and excerpts from contemporary newspaper reports. The editor, by his painstaking effort, has been able to collate some rare pieces of writing and recollection on this famous Indian sporting victory. The newspaper reports are translated in Bengali for the lay reader. This volume will definitely work as a reservoir of sources for the future historian on 1911.

Club Histories

The immortal event of 1911 aside, the Mohun Bagan Club itself could boast of a number of rich sporting histories of the club till date. Since the

---

[3] Calcutta: Karuna Prakashani, 1976.
[4] Calcutta: Karuna Prakashani, 1991.
[5] Calcutta: Prabhabati Prakashani, 2007.

publication of Bhadubhai's *Mohun Baganer Itikatha*, at least four histories of the club were written in the last century.[6] These include Karuna Shankar Bhattacharjee's *Bideshe Mohun Bagan* (Mohun Bagan in Foreign Land), Shantipriya Bandopadhyay's *Cluber Naam Mohun Bagan* (The Name of the Club is Mohun Bagan), Jayanta Dutta's *Victorious Mohun Bagan* and Sibram Kumar edited *Mohun Bagan Omnibus*.[7] Most of these works give a detailed account of the evolution of the club from a modest beginning to its becoming a nationalist institution after 1911, its achievements and moments of glory, and its arch rivalry with Calcutta Football Club and Mohammedan Sporting Club in the colonial age and with East Bengal after Independence.

A most significant recent addition to this trend of club histories is *Chirakaaler Mohun Bagan* (Mohun Bagan Forever).[8] This book, from its cover page to index, is the result of a well thought out plan on the part of its editors to furnish a reflective account of the history of Mohun Bagan Club not only through the writings of sports journalists, literators or sports persons themselves but also through the eyes of people from different walks of life. This popular perception of the club as presented in the work adds a new dimension to the writing of club-histories in India. Hence, one can read in it an engaging story of the social context of the club's foundation, history of the founder families and gradual development of the club through various ups and downs. The publication of *Chirakaaler Mohun Bagan* also defies and goes beyond the historical construction of the club's origin as depicted in earlier treatises on the club. The club's Golden Jubilee Souvenir (1939) as well as the Platinum Jubilee Souvenir (1964) maintained that the club was founded through the initiatives of a few north Calcutta families like the Boses, Sens and Mitras. But how this process actually took place or who really engineered the club's first establishment and what were the ideologies and principles that guided the organisers of the club in its early years would have remained in obscurity but for the publication of this book. For instance, we have now come to learn that Mohun Bagan had to leave its original ground situated at Kirti Mitra's

---

[6] Catalogued in the National Library, Kolkata, this book has never been found on requisition. According to elder sports writers like Moti Nandy, this was the first history of the club known.

[7] Bhattacharjee's work was published in Calcutta: Prabartak Publishers, 1964; Bandopadhyay in Calcutta: New Bengal Press, 1979; Dutta in Calcutta; Sahitya Prakash, 1979; Kumar in Calcutta: Prabhabati Prakashani, 1983.

[8] Chirakaaler Mohun Bagan Prokashona Committee, *Chirakaaler Mohun Bagan*.

Mohun Bagan Villa since the land fell in the covetous eyes of contractors who bought the whole estate and sold the land in plots. It also highlights the objectives and high ideals which motivated the founders of the club.

That Mohun Bagan began to reflect nationalist ethos from the turn of the 20th century becomes clear from the efforts of its then enterprising secretary Major Sailen Bose. Bose, who once played football with the European soldiers, believed in the rejuvenation of physical prowess of the Bengali in order to repudiate the British slur of physical effeminacy labelled against him. The 'immortal eleven' formation of the club that won the IFA Shield in 1911 as the first Indian team was the outcome of his long-term planning. The victory of 1911 has been dealt with quite elaborately. The section on the family of Manmatha Mukherjee, a member of that team, by Partha Rudra, adds a new dimension to its depiction. How Mohun Bagan's win inspired Bengali nationalist sentiments becomes evident when one reads the fascinating poem composed by Karunanidhan Bandopadhyay published in the *Manasi*, September 1911.[9]

The chapter on 'Bibhinna Patro-patrika theke sangrihita Mani-Manikya' ('Jewels from Different Periodicals') is a collection of rare writings on Mohun Bagan through the ages, for which the editors deserve credit. We get a decent reflection of contemporary Bengali society from these pieces which also point to Mohun Bagan's role as a mobiliser of Bengali tradition, thought, desire, and aspirations. The section entitled 'Mohun Bagan sammandhe Bibhinna Rachana' ('Various Writings on Mohun Bagan') also attracts the readers very much as it represents a sincere desire on the part of the editors to place the club in a wider historical perspective. The reprint of Dennis Compton's essay on Mohun Bagan bears testimony to this.

Mohun Bagan's contribution in Indian sport is not confined to football alone, a point that often begs notice. But the present work pays long-deserved attention to other sports like hockey, cricket or tennis in which Mohun Bagan once used to maintain a distinctively glorious record. The essays by Raju Mukherjee, P. B. Dutta or Premangshu Chattopadhyay on these otherwise neglected aspects of the club also provide a fair glimpse of the early development of those sports in colonial Bengal.

The reflective glow of the book is, however, marred by a few silly lapses on the part of the editors, which could have easily been avoided. To give a few instances, Amal Sen's essay on the Bhaduri brothers, the heroes of

---

[9] Already cited in Chapter 2.

the 1911 victory, seems to be a plagiary of Partha Sarathi's one on the same personae. Moreover, the section on 'Samajer Bibhinna Manusher chokhe Mohun Bagan' ('Mohun Bagan in the Eyes of Different Peoples of Society') nearly made this invaluable work a souvenir type. The trend of Western encyclopedic writing on European clubs like Manchester United never entertains such light approaches. Despite these minor hitches, the book has certainly got the quality to become a collector's pride. More importantly, its value for future sports historians is immense.

The history of the East Bengal Club, too, has been encapsulated in various club histories. Since the publication of Ramesh Chandra Goswami's *East Bengal Cluber Itihas* (History of the East Bengal Club) as early as 1963,[10] four more histories of the club have been written. The earlier histories, with the sole exception of Paresh Nandy's *East Bengal Club: Ponchas Bochhorer Sangram o Safalya, 1920–70* (East Bengal Club: Fifty Years' Struggle and Success, 1920–70),[11] which was also the club's acknowledged official history published on the occasion of its golden jubilee in 1970, presented a more or less story telling approach while narrating the activities and achievements of the club over the years. These histories are: Santipriya Bandopadhyay's *Cluber Naam East Bengal* (The Name of the Club is East Bengal) and Jayanta Dutta's *Glorious East Bengal*.[12] Nandy initiated the process of analysing the day-to-day history of the club, making excellent use of daily newspaper reports. The club has had a rich history of its own with success and failure revealing the internal coherence as well as turbulence intricately linked with, and in turn articulating the changing trends of club culture and politics. Rupak Saha recently made a sincere attempt in his work *Itihase East Bengal* (East Bengal in History) to chart and analyse this sensational inner culture of the club through a phase-wise narrative of the club's history in its first 80 years.[13]

As noted in Chapter 5, East Bengal Club was formed in 1920 by a group of respectable East Bengali gentlemen as a part of their reaction against the ill treatment and discrimination meted out to them by their West Bengali counterparts in wider social life including sports. The author rightly places the origin and early development of the club in the context of the Ghoti-Bangal (West Bengali-East Bengali) conflict that came to be reflected in the

---

[10] Calcutta: Book Garden, 1963.

[11] Calcutta: Bichitra, 1973.

[12] Bandopadhyay, published in Calcutta: New Bengal Press, 1979; Dutta in Calcutta: Sahitya Prakash, 1975.

[13] Kolkata: Deep, 2000.

arch rivalry between Mohun Bagan and East Bengal in Bengali football since the 1940s. Saha shows how the history of the club in its first decade of existence points to a complex equation between social power relations and mechanisms of sports administration in contemporary Bengal. Suresh Chaudhuri and Taritbhushan Roy (joint secretaries of the club), both being socially influential in Calcutta and having good relations with British officialdom, utilised their power and position to earn the club's affiliation with the IFA (Indian Football Association). East Bengal was soon allowed to play in the Second Division League and given a ground on the maidan. East Bengal earned a much-deserved promotion to the First Division in 1925 amidst debate and controversy within the rank and file of the IFA. Interestingly enough, he also notes, while the European representatives of the IFA strongly supported East Bengal's cause, the two Indian members representing Mohun Bagan and Aryan strenuously opposed it.

While East Bengal's rise to football prowess in terms of major title wins came in the 1940s, it had already become close runner-up in the Calcutta League thrice in the 1930s and performed well in the IFA Shield too. In fact, it displaced Mohun Bagan to become the arch-rival to Mohammedan Sporting, who dominated that decade in Indian football. In 1939, however, the club withdrew from the League along with Mohammedan Sporting and Kalighat to protest against IFA's partial attitude towards Mohun Bagan and formed the 'Bengal Football Association' to run a new tournament called Brabourne Cup. The conflict came to an end next year through negotiations. The success of East Bengal in the 1940s and early 1950s was due in large measure to the recruitment of a series of quality footballers from other states and even from outside India. The list included Murgesh, Lakshminarayan, Somana, Pagsley, Venkatesh, Apparao, Dhanraj, Ahmed Khan, and Saleh. The last five jointly known as VADAS became famous as the 'Five Pandavas' of Indian football. The selection of Jyotish Guha as the assistant secretary of the club in 1942 was also an important step towards the initiation of new culture in the club. From 1949 to 1953 the club won nearly all the prestigious trophies more than once thanks to the scintillating performance of its five forwards. Saha provides astonishing figures to prove this point: East Bengal scored a total of 387 goals in all the tournaments it played in these five years. The five forwards had scored 260 of these goals. In the late 1950s East Bengal, under Jyotish Guha's leadership, got involved in a serious conflict with the parent body, IFA. Moreover, the recurrent violence and hooliganism on the maidan compelled the chief minister of West Bengal to intervene in football matters. He suggested a change of the club's name as it bore an unhealthy regional overtone. Guha, however, forcefully rejected the proposal. The club also underwent a lamentable phase of inner power conflict since the early 1960s seriously affecting its performance on the football field. Guha had to ultimately pay for his highhandedness in running the club when Dr Nripen Das replaced him as the secretary at the turn of the 1960s. Das's ascendancy to power added a new dimension to the politics and culture of Calcutta club football — induction of musclemen in club elections, administration and player recruitment, Jiban Charaborty and Paltu Das being the two earliest instances of the trend. Das's accession to power boded well for East Bengal and the 1970s proved to be the golden age in the history of the club. It won the League a record six times in a row from 1970 to 1975 and the Shield five times in a row from 1972 to 1976 — a performance still unmatched in the history of Calcutta football. The club also won a prestigious 'Triple', which is, the Shield, Rovers and Durand in 1972. More importantly, it defeated its arch-rival Mohun Bagan 5–0 in the 1975 Shield final that still remains a matter of highest pride for every East Bengal fan and the most ignominious defeat for the Mohun Bagan Club. The heat of the East Bengal-Mohun Bagan rivalry reached a tragic point in 1980 when, during a rather unimportant League match between the two teams at the Eden Gardens in Calcutta, clashes between supporter groups led to widespread violence in the stadium resulting in a stampede that cost 16 diehard fans their lives.

The last two decades of the 20th century in the club have been regarded as what Saha describes as 'the age of Paltu Das'. A stout and confident yet unassuming personality, Paltu Das came to power in 1984 beating Nisith Ghosh in the election and remained the undisputed guide of the club till the turn of the century. In the 1980s Das organised cultural functions as well as football tournaments to stave off the deep economic crisis the club fell in. But such temporary measures could not solve the club's financial crisis in the long run. In 1989 the club again had to experience a bitter inner group conflict over power. Moreover, with the emergence of Tutu Bose and Anjan Mitra, the two enterprising and rich businessmen of Calcutta, at the helm of Mohun Bagan Club, the club was revitalised in the 1990s and posed a formidable challenge to East Bengal's power. Paltu Das, however, was again able to overcome his opposition groups and came to power in the 1991 elections. Under him, the club strongly combatted Mohun Bagan's challenge. But in the face of increasingly stiff competition from the clubs of other states at national tournaments he realised the importance of professionalisation of the club. In the peculiar amateur set-up of Calcutta football, East Bengal found it difficult to find a viable sponsor to create a sustainable professional infrastructure for the club. Initially the club got two minor sponsors — Emami and Khadim. Finally, in late 1997, the club signed a contract with the United Breweries Group, a Bangalore-based liquor company and the football team came to assume the dimension of a company as 'Kingfisher East Bengal'. The impact was obvious: the club tent was modernised, a gymnasium was instituted and the administration was run with an entirely professional outlook.

The book winds up with some interesting and valuable statistics about the club's success in domestic and Asian circuit. The author, however, abstains from furnishing any workable bibliography or index at the end of the book, which would have been amply useful for both the uninitiated club fans as well as interested scholars. Moreover, it is perplexing to find an utter neglect of the club's achievements in other sports like cricket, hockey, tennis, or athletics in Saha's work. Finally, in the construction of a binary equation between Mohun Bagan and East Bengal, the author at times seems to be sympathetic and biased towards the club whose history he is narrating. Despite all this, Saha, working and refining upon an eclectic approach, has been able to utilise a wide variety of primary sources including club souvenirs, reminiscences and otherwise historical literature. Moreover, his close association with the rank and file of the club in the last three decades of the 20th century gave him access to hitherto untapped club documents and records. Most importantly, he has made brilliant use of his personal interaction with, and both formal as well as informal interviews of, the officials, players and common fans of the club in driving home the point that a journalist can write authentic and academically merited club histories no less ably than a historian.

Journalistic and Popular Writings on Bengali Soccer

Apart from these club histories, a number of journalistic and popular historical writings in the vernacular appeared since the 1960s. These writings basically comprise three types of publications: histories of the rivalry among three Calcutta giants, autobiographical writings and biographies of great footballers, and other soccer histories and compilations. The first type of writings is concerned with brief histories of the three big Calcutta clubs — Mohun Bagan, East Bengal and Mohammedan Sporting — and their achievements providing many interesting data and photographs. Ashok Bhattacharya's *Footbaler Tin Pradhan* (Three Major Teams of Football), Chiranjib's *Footbaler Tin Raja* (Three Kings of Football) and Shukharanja Ghosh's *Bharatiya Footballe Tin Protidvandi* (Three Rivals in Indian Football) are the best examples of this trend of writing.[14] Second, Bengali footballers have not really excelled in the genre of producing autobiographies. That is why we have had very few such writings at our disposal till date. These include Chuni Goswami's *Khelte Khelte* (While Playing), Surojit Sengupta's *Back Centre* and Amal Datta's *Jotodin Banchi* (As Long As Alive).[15] However, there are also a few compilations of reminiscences by players and sports commentators-cum-writers, which also fall in the category of auto-biographical writings. These include Ajay Basu's *Maath Theke Bolchhi* (Speaking from the Ground) and Amal Dutta's *Ghera Maath Chhorano Gallery* (Enclosed Ground, Spread Gallery).[16] These writings, apart from their historical value as memoirs, sometimes give us interesting insights into the complex nature of power relations within the rank and file of the football administration and club culture. Among biographical writings, mention may be made of Sourindra Kumar Ghosh's *Kridasamrat Nagendra Prasad Sarvadhikari* (Nagendra Prasad Sarvadhikari, the King of Sports), Rupak Saha's *Chinese Wall*, Jayanta Dutta's *Footbller Mahanayak Gostho Paul* (Gostho Paul, the Super Hero of Football), Ajay Basu's *Maidaner Nayak* (The Heroes of Maidan) and *Footbale Dikpal* (Pioneers in Football), Rupak Saha's *Pancha Pandav* (Five *Pandavas*), Manas Chakraborty's *Amal Dutta*, and *Shatabadir Sera Sailen Manna* (Sailen Manna, the Best of the Century).[17] Finally, there are some useful general works on Bengali sports including football, which throw light on various neglected aspects of the game — power play in the

---

[14] Bhattacharya, published in Calcutta: Gyantirtha, 1972; Chiranjib in Calcutta: Biswabani Prakashani, 1975; Ghosh in Calcutta: Manju Prakashani, 1986.

[15] Goswami, published in Calcutta: Ananda, 1982; Sengupta in Calcutta: Sunny Publishers, 1985; Datta in Kolkata: Aajkal, 2010.

[16] Basu, published in Calcutta: Rooprekha, 1968; Datta in Calcutta: Bisvabani Prakashani, 1982.

[17] Ghosh, published in Calcutta: N. P. Sarvadhikari Memorial Committee, 1963. This is the only vernacular biography of Nagendra Prasad Sarvadhikari.

Saha, published in Calcutta: Hemlata Prakashani, 1979; biography of Gostho Paul, the legendary Mohun Bagan footballer; Dutta in Calcutta: Anima Prakashani, 1986, another biography of Goshto Paul; Basu's both books in

Calcutta: Mandal Book House, 1980. Basu's first book gives a vivid description of the footballing prowess of some of the leading Bengal footballers.

Like the previous work, Basu's *Footbale Dikpal* is also a collection of essays on the charisma of some great Bengal footballers.

Saha's *Pancha Pandav* was published in Calcutta: Karuna Prakasahni, 1991. This work narrates the achievements of the legendary East Bengal forward line of the 1940s and 1950s, comprising Venkatesh, Apparao, Dhanraj, Ajmed, and Saleh.

control and management of the game in Calcutta, politics off the field, journalistic insights into the nature of evolution of the game in Bengal, evolution of the style and technical aspects of the game in general or local histories of the game.[18]

Football and Bengali Fiction

Apart from this rich and variegated repository of vernacular soccer literature, the sport began to get ample reflection in Bengali literature in the 1970s. Moti Nandy was the first among Bengali literateurs, who took up sports in general and soccer in particular as viable theme for his novels and short stories. His two best novels on soccer, namely *Striker* and *Stopper*, earned him fame still unparallelled in Indian sports literature.[19] While *Striker* tells the story of a young footballer's struggle to make a mark in Calcutta's big clubs, the latter informs the fight of a senior footballer to pursue the game against many odds. In other words, *Striker* is about a young striker's future; while *Stopper* hangs on an aging defender's past.[20]

Chakraborty's *Amal Dutta* was published in Kolkata: Sristi, 1999. The author compiles a collection of interesting essays on Amal Dutta, the most controversial but most learned football coach of India.

Chakraborty's *Shatabadir Sera* was published in Kolkata: Deep, 2002. This is the only biography of Sailen Manna, another Mohun Bagan legend and Olympian, who was declared the Indian footballer of the century.

[18] Most important works in this category include Santipriya Bandopadhyay's *Khelar Raja Football* (Football, the King of Sports), Calcutta: Jnanthirthho, 1983 and *Football*, Calcutta: Dey's, 1985; Amal Dutta's *Football Khelte Hole* (For Playing Football), Calcutta, 1971; Jayanta Dutta's *Footbaler Ain Kanun* (The Laws of Football), Calcutta: 1977; Prasun Bandopadhyay's *Football Ghorana: Biplab o Bibartan* (Football Style: Revolution and Evolution), Calcutta: Pratibhas, 1989; Chiranjib's *Bharatiya Football* (Indian Football), Calcutta: Gyantirtha, 1967 and *Khelar Maather Antarale* (Beyond the Sports Field), Calcutta: Nabapatra, 1973; Kali Ray's *Howrah Jelar Football Khelar Itikatha* (History of Football in Howrah District), Calcutta: Bharati Book Stall, 1985; Asoke Dasgupta's. *Khelar Shat* (Sixties of Sport), Kolkata: Deep, 2000; and Shanto Mitra's *Sanghat o Sangharsha: Rajniti ebong Football* (Conflict and Collision: Politics and Football), Kolkata: Saroj Publications, 2005.

[19] *Striker* was published in Calcutta: Ananda, 1973. And *Stopper* in *ibid.*, 1974.

[20] The novellas have recently been translated by Arunava Sinha and published as *Striker, Stopper, Two Novellas*, Gurgaon: Hatchette India, 2010. In deconstructing the stories of Nandy, I have utilised a few interesting reviews of the work available on the following websites: www.roswitha.blogspot.com/2010/05/nandy-striker-stopper.html, www.anuradhagoyal.blogspot.com/.../striker-stopper-by-moti-nandy.html, www.business-standard.com/india/news/it%5Cs-my-life/398713.

Striker is about the young footballer Prasun Bhattacharya, talented and ambitious, poor and deprived. It is not surprising that Nandy chooses to begin Prasun's story with a dream:

> I had a dream last night.... A middle-aged foreigner got out, his complexion as dark as night ... said something to the crowd in Portuguese.... 'I've come from Brazil. I'm sure you've heard of Santos Football club. I'm the manager there. And if Prasun agrees to join us, we want him.'... 'Pele plays for them.'... 'Since Pele plans to retire soon, we want to prepare Prasun immediately so that he can replace him later.'... Wake up, Prasun. It's five o'clock!²¹

Pele, Santos, Brazil — Bengali imagination in post-colonial India was colonised by a solo Latin American flavour. Set in such a romantic and psychologically dreamy ambience, the story lands immediately into the harsh reality of a young man's fight to earn his living by asserting his ability as a footballer. The young Prasun receives no support from his father, a footballer of considerable merit who once played for Juger Jatri, one of the better-known clubs in Calcutta. A school dropout, he begins his career with a second-rung team. The teenaged striker Prasun refuses to buckle down to his little club Sovabazar's demands, and so finds himself working at a petrol pump on a night shift at one point, while he trains on his own in the hope of making it to a bigger club. He is the striker in the novella, and by the time we arrive at the last page, Prasun has overcome all odds — poverty, discrimination, match-fixing, corruption, even his own demons — to achieve success. Anyone who has played any sport knows that there is only one possible result that will please, for sport is structured in the tightest of binaries — either you win or you lose, there is no in-between. So Nandy ends his novella in the afterglow of a goal: 'I raised my eyes and saw the most amazing of sights — the Rangoon United goalkeeper retrieving my black and white world from his goal... Spotting me in the glow of the fireworks, a crowd rushed towards me, chanting, "Prasun, Prasun!"'²²

The striker's great counterpoint is the stopper, in name, in function, in metaphor, and here in Nandy's novella, in age. If Prasun's story is about the caterpillar turning into a butterfly, the ageing Kamal-da's story is a Yeatsian love affair between the game and the footballer, and about a man who is always playing his last game — 'Like a rampaging god, Kamal

---

²¹ Nandy, *Striker*, p. 1.
²² *Ibid.*, pp. 62–63.

danced and swayed all over the room with the ball at his feet, lost in his own world, dodging past his imaginary opponents one by one.'[23] Kamal's story is, like Prasun's, about the beautiful game, but it is also about age and grace, about the limits of the body and the seam-tearing expansiveness of dreams; and, finally, also a fine portrait of a dying tradition, of the grateful disciple and his guru. Nandy makes Kamal-da a solitary figure — his wife is dead, he having been away kicking a football while she lay dying, his son feels no emotion for him, his colleagues despise him, his rivals hate him; one can almost justify his emotional numbness and yet the gratitude he feels for Poltu-da, the guru who dies watching his student play mock football for him, is the stuff of a deep love story. However, at the end of the day, Kamal Guha, who has descended from the heights of success with Juger Jatri to a part-timer's role in Sovabazar, must find a way to keep the club and himself afloat.

What is common to Prasun and Kamal-da's stories is this: 'The only place I would be able to earn money was on the football field. If I couldn't become a great footballer, the only thing I'd be good for was to enlarge the ranks of the unemployed.'[24] For the story of football and poverty is a bit like the story of poetry and penury. The story of football is the story of slums, of school dropouts, of hunger and illiteracy, and much of its charm comes from there — perhaps that is why Nandy names his protagonist 'Kamal', the lotus which proverbially blooms amidst filth. 'Footballers need a lot of protein — if you cannot get meat, milk and eggs, you'll be in deep trouble. I was afraid. What if my body gave way? But where could I find the money for meat?'[25]

Thus the two novellas by Nandy are set in the cultural milieu of Bengali football in the 1960s–70s. Between the two stories the author takes us through the rise and fall of a football star. In the first story the protagonist is a poor, young second-generation footballer who has to fight it out through the maze of various club owners to prove his game till the time his game is so well recognised that the clubs do not have a choice in picking him up. In the second story a footballer is dealing with his sunset days in the game, where he thinks he can still give the younger generation competition, while balancing his job that he got because of football. He keeps looking at his balance sheet of life which has footballs in every row. He wants to leave his legacy in football by grooming a young player just the way his coach

---

[23] Nandy, *Stopper*, p. 40.
[24] Nandy, *Striker*, p. 22.
[25] *Ibid.*, p. 39.

groomed him. Taken together, the fictions depict a kaleidoscopic scenario full of characters whose life revolves around football: 'The failed footballer Ratan, the impoverished but idealistic coach Paltuda, the politicking officials Bipinda and Dakuda, the disgraced ex-player Anilbabu (Prasun's father), the fanatical supporters of *Yuger Yatri*, the soft romantic moments between Prasun and Neeleema, and the lively conversations amongst the spectators in the gallery, all add up to a memorable portrait of the constrained but optimistic Bengali middle-class life associated intimately with Kolkata soccer.'[26]

Besides the personal struggle of the two players, the stories provide a look at the management of sports in Bengal alias India, how the clubs are like personal properties of a select few. The match fixing and buying the players to play in a certain way almost seems like a rule than an exception. The pathetic conditions in which the players have to live and the only things still driving them to the field is their passion for the game. Even the basic requirements like ample nutritious food is not available to most players and a whole lot of them are driven away from the game in lure of a small job here and there. It amazes one that rival clubs would sign up some players only to make them sit at the bench and loose their magic touch on the field. Stories take one through the dirty world of sports which the audience has no clue of and which the players have to go through before they can present themselves to the public. The beauty of Nandy's writing is that the two stories integrate the challenges of soccer in Bengal: of how truly wearying and alienating the obsession can be, and how manipulative and traitorous the practice of it is. Nandy's heroes actually do fight crime, in the form of Calcutta's abject football bureaucracy. It is a corrupt world. The little clubs will fight to keep their best players from leaving, scrap and trade favours among themselves to stay up. The big ones will intimidate and bully the smaller ones for reasons of their own. Perhaps inescapably, the journeys of both young man and old mirror each other. If Prasun, with all his ambition and integrity, must learn to be selfish — so selfish that he must eat even when his family cannot — then Guha's quest is that of a man who already knows that all things come to pass, and must sacrifice to achieve them anyway.

At another level, the novellas take us through journeys which have lows which are extremely lonely and can break a person if he is not mentally strong or does not have a strong support system. This is where the role of

---

[26] Somshankar Ray, '"The Kindred Points of Heaven and Home": Kolkata Football in Bangla Fiction and Critique', *90 Minutes*, vol. 1, no. 1, January 2009, 73–74.

a coach becomes very important. On the other hand are the highs which can get to a player's head, and become the very reason of his downfall. Players have to keep oscillating between these two extremes for most of their playing lives. It requires as much mental strength to deal with all the opposing forces to stay in the game, as honing the talent and maintaining the passion for the game. What is heartening is the fact that in the end it is always the game that wins, because once a player attains a certain status with the crowd, no one else matters.

Nandy's other soccer novels, *Ferari* (The Lost) and *Dalbadaler Aage* (Before the Change of Club), depict respectively the passion, ecstasy and pathos of spectatorship articulating its impact on family and social relations, and the cultural politics of club transfer in Bengali football, highlighting the complex power relations, club rivalry and musclemanship in the process.[27] Besides Nandy, Santipriya Bandopadhyay's *Goal* and *Offside* and Nimai Bhattacharjee's *Footballar*, although published in the 1990s, realistically dealt with Bengali soccer culture of the 1960s–70s.[28] Short stories on soccer also began to appear in periodicals and sports magazines from the 1980s. A few collections of short stories on various sports in Bengal were compiled later, which included the ones on soccer.[29] Thus a rich variety of soccer fiction abounded in Bengali language in the 1970s and 1980s although the momentum was probably lost from the 1990s reflecting a more general decline in soccer literature in India.

Radio and Football in Post-colonial West Bengal

One of the integral parts of Bengali football culture in the pre-television era was the live commentary of matches on radio. In fact, it was radio that took the game to the remotest corners of Bengal after Independence.[30] On

---

[27] Ferari was published in Calcutta: Ananda, 1990. And *Dalbadaler Aage* in *ibid.*, 1992

[28] Both Bandopadhyay's works were published in 1990 by Dey's Publishing, Calcutta, while Bhattacharjee's work was published in Calcutta: Dey's, 1993.

[29] See, for example, Siddhartha Ghosh (ed.), *Khela aar Khela*, Calcutta: Ananda, 1994; Asoke Sen (ed.), *Kishor Golpo Khela*, Calcutta: Dey's Publishing, 1998; Santipriya Bandopadhyay, *Srra Khelar Golpo*, Kolkata: Bijayan Prakashani, 2001.

[30] The most interesting autobiographical narrative of radio commentary in Bengali football can be found in Ajay Basu, *Maath Theke Bolchhi* (Speaking from the Gallery), Calcutta: Rooprekha, 1982.

the other hand, the popularity of All India Radio aired from Akashbani Kolkata depended greatly on the transmission of commentary and news on sports, particularly football.[31] While the first sports news was relayed in English in 1930, the first ever running commentary of football in Bengali was broadcast in 1934 when B. K. Bhadra and Rai Chand Boral made an experimental relay of a soccer League match between the Calcutta Football Club and Mohan Bagan Club.[32] However, this initial attempt to broadcast running soccer commentary did not have a smooth run and was stopped soon. Many pointed fingers to the poor quality of running commentary in Bengali. This was in striking contrast to the huge popularity of cricket commentary in the same decades. The India-Australia and India-West Indies cricket matches during 1947–48 provided one important occasion for live relay from Calcutta station.[33] However, as sports writer Chiranjib has pointed out,

> Transistors were not in vogue when commentaries became popular. The size of the radios was quite big but only few households possessed one. But interestingly, irrespective of the size, big or medium, almost all the saloons had radios and to increase their customer base the proprietors of the saloons used to place a speaker near the entrance.[34]

Towering sports-commentators like Ajoy Basu and Kamal Bhattacharya, who covered the India-Australia cricket matches in 1959 from the Eden Gardens, very soon made Bengali cricket commentary hugely popular around the same time. The duo, along with Pushpen Sarkar, Beri Sarbadhikari and Pearson Surita lent their inimitable voices while relaying cricket and football events in English and Bengali on a regular basis from the 1950s.[35] It was with the Mohan Bagan vs Rajasthan League match on

---

[31] For more layers on this aspect, see Nabanita Mitra, 'All India Radio: Politics and Culture', in Kausik Bandyopadhyay (ed.), *Asia Annual 2008: Understanding Popular Culture*, New Delhi: Manohar, 2010, p. 87.

[32] For details on this first radio commentary of Bengali soccer, see Sushanta Kumar Bhowmik, 'Calcutta Football, Akashbani and Bengali Nostalgia', *90 Minutes*, vol. 1, no. 3, July–September 2009.

[33] Mitra, 'All India Radio'.

[34] Chiranjib, 'Kolkatar Btear: 50 Bochhor', Radio Broadcast, Part-29, Kolkata A, 10 March 2002 at 8 a.m., cited in Bhowmik, 'Calcutta Football, Akashbani and Bengali Nostalgia', p. 90.

[35] Mitra, 'All India Radio', p. 87. Also see Susanta Kumar Bhowmik, 'Swadhinata-uttar pashchim bange betar jagater itibritta' (History of the Radio

15 July 1957 that Ajay Basu and Pushpen Sarkar made a remarkably steady beginning of radio commentary of football in Bengali at a time when the Bengali public were not yet ready to believe that 'running commentary of matches can be made in Bengali'.[36] As Ajay Basu recounted:

> One such sad memory dates back to an evening of the 1950s, it was this time when running commentary of matches had just started. I was coming down the stairs leaving the commentary box when I suddenly heard a comment, 'here comes the commentator! What did he say? In which colour saree did you drape the goal, ball and free kick? Can there be a running commentary of a football match in Bengali? With complete disgust in his voice the gentleman shouted, 'what do all have to bear with?' I could well understand that all these were meant for me.[37]

However, Bengali commentary became widely popular within a few years. As Basu, referring to the earlier incident, wrote: 'I wish to meet that gentleman now. The age old belief of him and every other individual has been proved wrong. Is he going to react the same way hearing Bengali running commentary of matches? Is he still going to make faces?'[38]

The popularity of radio commentary in Bengal centred on the match days of the three big clubs of Calcutta football — Mohun Bagan, East Bengal and Mohammedan Sporting. People all over Bengal from the city to the remotest of villages would gather in front of the radio during the matches of their favourite clubs. It has been argued that 'the popular frenzy surrounding the Mohan Bagan-East Bengal matches (embodying the proverbial *Ghoti-Bangal* rivalry) proved to be so contagious that it drew both **NRI** Bengalis as well as Bengali women towards listening to commentaries, talks, interviews and discussions on soccer, with rapt attention!'[39]

World in Post-Independence West Bengal), in Rahul Roy (ed.), *Paschim Banga: Phire Dekha*, Chinsurah: Pratiti, 2003. Ajay Basu reflected on the brilliance of each of his co-commentators on several occasions in his writings. See, for example, Ajay Basu, 'Garer Mather Gariyan', *Desh*, Binodan sankhya, 1988, pp. 68–77.

[36] *Ananda Bazar* Patrika, 16 July 1957. Also see Ratan Chandra Das, *No 1 Garstin Place Theke* (From 1, Garstin Place), Kolkata: Akashbani Bhavan, 2001, referred to in Bhowmik, 'Calcutta Football. Akashbani and Bengali Nostalgia', p. 91.

Basu, *Maath Theke Bolchhi*, p. 6. Also see Bhowmik, 'Calcutta Football. Akashbani and Bengali Nostalgia', p. 91.

[37] Ajay Basu, *Phire Phire Chai* (Looking Back Again and Again), Calcutta, 2005, p. 54, cited in Bhowmik, 'Calcutta Football. Akashbani and Bengali Nostalgia', p. 91.

[38] *Ibid.*

[39] Mitra, 'All India Radio', p. 87.

In fact, the Bengali sports commentators took football to the kitchen of nearly every Bengali household.[40] The commentary became so popular that 'even in the matches in the localities one could hear running commentaries imitating Ajay Basu, Pushpen Sarkar or Kamal Bhattacharya, the three musketeers of Bengali sports commentary'.[41]

Among Bengal's best-known commentators, the most enduring contribution came from Ajay Basu, the most versatile 'homegrown superhero' of the vernacular commentary.[42] A player of some decent merit, Basu utilised his sporting knowledge to the best of his advantage when he took up commentary on radio. His voice and choice of words created an unmatched legacy of soccer/sports commentary in Bengal. His trendsetting career as a commentator showed that radio commentary could become a viable career option in an age when sports writing/commentary in the vernacular was hardly given its due recognition in Bengal. As Boria Majumdar has rightly commented:

> Guided by the *bhadralok* ethic of respectability, Basu was instrumental in instituting a new genre of Bengali sports commentary. 'Namaskar, Eden Udyan theke Ajay Basu bolchhi' — had been internalised by the Bengali bhadrolok of the 60s and 70s. It was romantic, yet rational, nostalgic yet ethical, critical yet consistent. His commentary, which shaped sporting sensibilities in the state, was no less part of the Bengali heritage than Briendrakrishna Bhadra's chants of the *Mahalaya*. Basu was a cult — his followers imbibed sport as their religion ... he combined the skills of a novelist with that of an orator. The product – a unique brand of commentary that was peculiarly his own. His commentary was poetry and drama, pitching sport as no less than an art form.... In an age when television had not reached the country, when the radio was the only means that could make sporting hearts beat pit-a-pat, Basu was the best. He was the pied piper of Bengal and his listeners the mice that followed his melody.[43]

A few months before his death, the Indian Football Association conferred a written felicitation on him and it was read out to him while he was in a critical condition in hospital: 'We used to hear *Mahishashurmardini* being

---

[40] 'Betare Dharabhasya ekhono Nikhunt Noy' (Commentary on radio is not yet flawless), *Khelar Asar*, 12 May 1978, p. 5.

[41] Bhowmik, 'Calcutta Football. Akashbani and Bengali Nostalgia', p. 91.

[42] Boria Majumdar, 'Voice of Eden Gardens', *Sahara Time*, 29 November 2003, p. 15.

[43] *Ibid*.

recited by Birendrakrishna Bhadra only once every year, but we used to hear this voice (Ajay Basu's) the entire football season. He could create a magic with his words. Even the listener sitting thousands of miles away could visualise the happenings in the field. Your baritone voice is equally well known to the Bengalese like Manna and Hemanta.'[44] In fact, with the death of Ajay Basu, the golden era of Bengali running commentary came to an end.[45]

As Ajay Basu argued, radio commentators were part and parcel of Bengali football.[46] In fact, while a number of programmes on sports and games were introduced on All India Radio (Kolkata), in course of time, it was the running commentary that remained the most popular attraction for the sports lovers of Bengal till the 1970s.[47] Thus radio played a key role in the social popularisation of football as also the spread of football fandom in post-colonial West Bengal. However, with the onset of live or recorded television coverage of matches on Doordarshan from the early 1980s, radio commentary gradually began to lose its social currency although radio retained its position of importance in the rural or suburban Bengali football milieu till the beginning of live coverage of national and regional tournaments by satellite television from the late 1990s.

Football in Performing Arts: The Other Voices of Bengal's Mass Spectator Sport

The Bengali passion for football, documented and commented upon by many observers, has not only been the subject of popular fiction, but has, to a lesser extent, been featured in Bengali popular performing arts. While there are several Bengali films that have bits of soccer, it is noteworthy that there are only a handful of films that have plots centring on the game, or that at least feature the game as the key element.[48] It is strange to understand as to why the Bengali filmmakers until the 1970s were not eager to appropriate the Bengalis' passion for football through their films with

---

[44] Cited in Bhowmik, 'Calcutta Football. Akashbani and Bengali Nostalgia', p. 92.

[45] *Ananda Bazar Patrika*, 14 February 2004, p. 9.

[46] Ajay Basu, 'Dharabhasyer Birambana', *Khelar* 19–25 July 1991, p. 62.

[47] These programmes included *Khelar Jagat* (1973 — later renamed as *Krirangan*) and sports news in the evening.

[48] Gooptu, 'Celluloid Soccer', p. 689.

great effect.[49] Yet football films, albeit produced few and far between, have always been popular in Bengal. *Saptapadi*, a film starring Uttam Kumar, the greatest hero of Bengali cinema, gave a glimpse of the anti-colonial struggle on the football field, intensified by the fact that the opponents were representative of the imperial British rulers.[50] Uttam Kumar helps beat them in a football match at the very beginning of the film.

Striker, starring footballer Shyam Thapa and Subhas Bhowmik, was the filmic adaptation of Moti Nandy's novel about a player (the role played by Samit Bhanja) who aspires to feature in the Calcutta League. *Dhanyi Meye* (Sporty Girl!) and *Mohun Baganer Meye* (The Daughter of Mohun Bagan) are about team rivalries getting in the way of love.[51] It was *Dhanyi Meye*, which stole the cake in terms of popularity. Viewers cannot forget the effortless appeal of Uttam Kumar, president of a playing club who eats, drinks and dreams goals that would fetch him the 'Harbhanga Cup'. It is a dream that finds him 'kicking' his wife in sleep, forbidding marriage for his striker brother, and taking on his feisty girlfriend Jaya Bhaduri. The second, featuring Utpal Dutt, Mahua Roy Chowdhury, Dipankar De, and Chinmoy Roy, transferred the rivalry between the supporters of the leading football teams, to the two families in a Bengali marriage. Utpal Dutt, a diehard Mohun Bagan supporter, refuses to let his son marry an East Bengal fan. But that is precisely what happens, although his daughter-in-law pretends to support his team, with hilarious consequences.

Saheb, starring Utpal Dutt, Tapas Paul and Mahua Roy Chowdhury, on the other hand, depicted the career of a young promising goalkeeper, cut short by the compulsion of a lower-middle-class family.[52] Saheb, the youngest son in a joint family, is a talented footballer all set to play the Junior League. But misfortune strikes in the form of economic crisis: retired father cannot marry off his daughter, Saheb's sister; Saheb sacrifices his career and comes to the rescue by selling his kidney. Later on other films

---

[49] For a brief discussion on these football films in Bengal, see Oindrila Mukherjee, 'Movers, Movies and Mores', *The Statesman* (Midweek), 15 August 2001, p.2; Ratnottama Sengupta, 'Scoring on Screen', *Sunday Times of India*, 9 July 2006, p.2. The only academic piece that deals with football's representation in Bengali films in a socio-historical perspective is Sharmishtha Gooptu's 'Celluloid Soccer', pp. 689–98.

[50] Directed by Ajay Kar, it was released in 1961.

[51] *Dhanyi Meye* was directed by Aravinda Mukhopadhyay and released in 1971. *Mohun Baganer Meye* was directed by Manu Sen, the film was released in 1976.

[52] Directed by Bijoy Basu and released in 1981.

like *East Bengaler Chhele* (The Son of East Bengal) and *Ashray* (Refuge) (2000) also took football as a prism to reflect upon the cultural politics of Bengali football as well as complexities of everyday culture and social relations in contemporary Bengal.[53]

The marginality of Bengali's football passion was all the more discernible in the realm of theatre. It was not until 1977 that a play with football as the central plot could be produced in Bengal. In that year a very perceptive and widely popular play, *Football*, made on the passion and obsession surrounding Bengali football, was produced by *Nandikar*. This play, adapted from British playwright Peter Derson's *Zigger Zagger* and directed by Rudra Prasad Sengupta, was first performed on 10 March 1977. It tells the story of fan culture around a particular club, namely, East Bengal, and the intricate power play and emotions associated with the club culture.[54]

Among the songs composed on Bengali football, Manna Dey's 'Sab Khelar Sera Bangalir Tumi Football' (King of all sports, you are Bengalis' favourite, football), a song that features in the film *Dhanyi Meye*, has retained the most enduring appeal. Written by Pulak Bandopadhyay and composed by Nachiketa Ghosh, this song captures the universal currency and mass appeal football used to enjoy in Bengal till the 1980s. In fact, the few songs dwelling on the game in *Dhanyi Meye* and *Mohun Baganer Meye* became very popular during the 1970s. Manna De sang another very sensitive and popular song 'Khela Football Khela' (Sport, football, the sport) in response to the tragedy of 16 August 1980 that claimed the lives of 16 football fans at the Eden Gardens.

The marginal depiction of soccer in Bengali cinema, stage and music remains an interesting yet unresolved question in the history of modern Bengali popular culture. Given the centrality of the game in Bengali everyday life during most of the 20th century, there should have been a more potent representation of soccer in the performing arts of the time. As noted by Sharmishtha Gooptu in the case of cinema, there are just a handful of Bengali films that deal with soccer to any reasonable extent, and here too the sport itself is compromised in favour of other priorities, with the sport element simply fizzling out at various points during the

---

[53] The film, *East Bengal Chhele* intended to be produced in the mid-1990s with Chiranjit as the hero, could not ultimately see the light of the day.

[54] For an interesting discussion on the background, production and theme of the play, see Samrat Mukhopadhyay, 'Football: Mancha Jokhon Maidan', *90 Minutes*, vol. 1, no. 3, July–September 2009, pp. 95–101.

latter halves of the films.[55] It was only in the 1970s that soccer began to attract attention from the logic of commercialism in film, theatre or music industries of Bengal. But here again the initial enthusiasm could not produce a lasting legacy and the representation of the game in such performing arts became nearly illusive from the late 1980s.

Representing the Game

The vernacular soccer literature of post-colonial Bengal, which comprises histories of the game and the clubs, autobiographies and biographies of players, journalistic writings as well as novels and other literary pieces, throws light on hitherto-neglected cultural peculiarities of the game in Bengal. The impact of soccer on public life could also be discernable in the way it was represented in performing arts like cinema, theatre and music. Thus the wider cultural repercussions of the game as reflected in literature, be it journalistic, literary or historical, popular media like the radio and creative arts including films, theatre and songs, albeit occasionally, implicated football as an integral part of the Bengali's everyday life and projected the game as a socially viable cultural force in colonial and post-colonial Bengal.

---

[55] Gooptu, 'Celluloid Soccer'.

Epilogue

The present work is pursued with the premise that the social history of South Asian sport can be meaningfully understood only by looking beyond the sports field. This study, using sport as a lens, has tried to consider some relevant themes of social history, and brought forth some important issues of political and cultural history of 20th-century Bengal. It has attempted to construct a social history of football in Bengal from 1911 to 1980, mainly pointing to the relevance of football as a popular cultural force and its centrality in the everyday life of Bengal. It charts the trajectory of the game's evolution from its introduction and adoption as an unimportant pastime to its adaptation and popularisation as a mass spectator sport in colonial and post-colonial Bengal, bringing into light the nationalist, communal, regional, local, and cultural manifestations of the game. The study also highlights football's transformed role as an instrument of reaction, resistance and subversion. It has endeavoured to indicate that the football field of Bengal proves to be a mirror image of what society experiences in its cultural and political field, through a series of historical projections of *identity, difference* and *culture*.

Scoring Off the Field intends to bring to light the importance of soccer in colonial and post-colonial Bengal as an essentially cultural experience, political tool, social instrument, and commercial force. In this sense, it contributes to the growing body of literature on the history of sport in South Asia. More importantly, viewing sport as an integral part of popular culture, the work also intends to make a contribution to the wider historical literature on popular culture in modern India. Second, it also shows how Bengali society and culture shaped the history of the game while the game in turn influenced the various processes at work in Bengali society, politics and culture. As the work is based on an eclectic interdisciplinary approach, it neither really follows the Sports Studies paradigm nor the Cultural Studies paradigm, fashionable of late. Rather, the study is conceived within the broader contours of Social History, of course drawing necessary methodological support at times from other paradigms and disciplines. In this context, the work addresses the question of viability of placing the history of sport in what Ramachandra Guha calls 'a ghetto of its own'.[1] While a history of sport can become a viable area of study in its own right, I would argue that it is best pursued within the wider perspective and methodology of historical discipline. In other words, as Guha rightly asserts: 'the attempt should rather be to use ignored or previously marginal spheres, such as sport . . . to illuminate the historical centre itself'.[2]

Finally, the work comes quite close to the study of contemporary history in terms of methodological exercise. That is why it has also tried to identify questions that still need to be asked, raise issues that urge serious debates and offer insights that can stimulate future research. These questions and issues relate to the ways football experienced a downswing in terms of standard and popularity since the 1980s, sports journalism and literature has experienced changes with cricket replacing soccer as more important subject, transformation in the nature of regional and club rivalries have unfolded in the last two decades, and the clash between amateurism and professionalism proved a bane for the commercial uplift of the game in India.

In Bengal alias India, soccer has long been a site, albeit ignored by historians, which articulates the complexities and diversities of the everyday life of the nation. In view of the complexities of Bengali/Indian soccer, it is easy to comprehend that a single work cannot do justice to all aspects of football culture. *Scoring Off the Field* therefore has attempted to reveal at least part, if not the whole, of the process of how significant soccer had become for Bengal — politically, socially, culturally, and emotionally. While football's growth as a mass spectator sport has been analysed in this work against the backdrop of imperialism, nationalism and communalism in colonial Bengal and regionalism in post-colonial India, the importance of landmark events like Mohun Bagan's IFA Shield victory in 1911 or the role of the Bengali clubs like Sovabazar, Aryan, National Association, Mohun Bagan, Kumartuli, or Mohammedan Sporting in that process can be undertaken for further research. The gradual decline of the Mohammedan Sporting Club since Independence with occasional flurries and the wider question of community-representation in cultural fields such as sport can also form an interesting area of historical enquiry.

James Walvin once suggested, 'more emphasis needs to be placed on local studies without losing sight of the broader context'.[3] The macrocosm

---

[1] Guha, *A Corner of a Foreign Field*, p. xiv. This has actually happened with the histories of women and environment.

[2] *Ibid.*

[3] Walvin, 'Sport, Social History and the Historian', p. 10.

of Bengali football, into which the work has tried to weave the microcosms of local histories, is expected to generate future forays into more specialised regional and local studies. Such forays could also be able to address more specifically Walvin's notion that 'general structures do indeed have a place, but they will inevitably be subjected to the qualifications of specific and local peculiarities'.[4] While the local roots of football in Bengal have been analysed in this work, the local growth of the game in the 20th century remains a legitimate area of future study.

Finally, while *Scoring Off the Field* highlights various facets of football culture in Bengal, the politics, sub-cultures and groups that grew around the game and the maidan — for example, *dalbadal* or transfer from clubs, club administration and election, conventions and superstitions of the game, role and fate of the referees, story of the club and ground maintenance staff — remain to be taken up as viable themes of future research, particularly with due emphasis on oral and anecdotal history. Last but not the least, the book studies the cultural history of *men*'s football in Bengal, implying that *women*'s football still awaits its historian for its historical narrative and analysis.

---

[4] *Ibid.*

Appendix I

Excerpts from Nagendra Prasad Sarvadhikari's only Biography in English

part of those who call themselves sportsman. I can not allow myself to be a party to it.'

Thereupon Nagendra Prasad intimated the audience to leave the club then and there. Strenuous attempts were made to make Nagendra Prasad change his mind. Raj Chunder Chunder (afterwards Solicitor) the son of Ganesh Chunder Chunder, the famous Solicitor, did his utmost to prevail on Nagendra Prasad pointing out that the mean mover was sure to be out-voted. It was of no avail.

The very idea of the movers was nauseating to Nagendra Prasad. He could not reconcile himself to belong to a circle the minutest part of which is putrid. Being a stern constitutionalist he was bound to bring the matter up to vote. He knew the result of voting will be disastrous to the movers. All the same, an out and out sportsman as he was he considered it ignoble to be a party to it. So Nagendra Prasad left the club, the club of his own creation. This was followed by resignation of no less than 450 of its members. Thus "Wellington" met with its tragic end. Town Club was founded not long after this.

It did not take long also to Nagendra Prasad to start a new organisation. He thought it best to amalgamate the Boy's Club, The Presidency Club, and the broken up Wellington Club into one body. Luckily, the Sovabazar Rajbati Club which was purely a Tennis Club alos joined hands with Nagendra Prasad and the four clubs merged into one and came to be known as Sovabazar Club. Kumar

Jisnendra Krishna Dev Bahadur of Sovabazar Raj Family along with Nagendra Prasad became the Joint Hony. Secretaries to the Club. The then Maharajah of Cooch Behar held the office of the President.

No doubt, the confectioner's son was one of the first members of the Sovabazar Club, In came also member who were by caste weaver, carpenter, irom-smith, and fisherman. On the other hand members from the cultured class of Hindus, Mohammedans, and Parsis simply poured in. Gates were equally open to Anglo-Indians and Europeans and the club had in its roll not few of them. The ideal of Nagendra Prasad in the matter was very high. Calcutta now possesses the Calcutta Club. Sovabazar Club however had a more practical vision. Its success was therefore at once unprecedented. Sportsmen are a class by themselves. They know no communalism. Look to the old records of the Sovabazar Club and see how it has demonstrated it sixteen annas to the rupee.

Sovabazar Club is popularly known as the premier Indian Club. Whoever has happened any day to be at the club tent near about dusk must not have failed to notice a congregation including amongst others a galaxy of European high officials both civil and military. Moreover members of Dalhousie and Naval Volunteers massed not in small number. Every body took each other a brother of the same faith Sportsman. This was what Sovabazar did and one can well surmise the usefulness of it in nation-building work.

The Regimental Band (Buffs) of its own accord has played on the Sovabazar ground on some match days. What "The Englishman" described as "Babus vs Syces Fight" proved in a court of law, thanks to Mr. Harrision the then Commissioner of Police as a downright agression on the part of a notable European Firm on the ground of what they knew as an Indian club only. The Viceroy's body-guard coming from Alipur to the Government House used to cross the club grounds. Sovabazar took exception

Taking this 'Chakra' as a nucleus Nagendra Prasad was about to expand it at the beginning of the present war for doing A.R.P. and allied works, but Providence willed otherwise. Mr. C.E.S. Faireweather, the Commissioner of Police Calcutta readily gave his permission to the expansion of the Chakra and the Viceroy of India Lord Linlithgow wrote to Nagendra Prasad through His Excellency's Secretary of His Excellency's high appreciation of the task undertaken by Nagendra Prasad voluntarily. The dreams of the Father of Indian Football, the founder of the I.F.A. and the foremost pioneer of all Branches of Sports were about to be fulfilled in his life-time but inscrutable destiny took away this indomittable but silent servant of the country to an unknown sphere where perhaps a worker of his ilk was needed.

As a true Sportsman the spirit of strict discipline and ready submission to the accredited authority has religiously been attempted by Nagendra Prasad all through to be instilled into the hearts of those who chose to come within the fold of a sporting club. Under his lead the attempt was a brilliant success. This being so it was possible for him to turn out a number of players who would have been real assets to any club in any country. To name only a few the names of Mona Chowdhury, Benoy Prasad, Upen Mukerji (Bara Babu) Bama Charan, S. Banerji (Khiri) and the cricketeers who have already been named come to the forefront. Later Kali Mukerji (Canal Club) Sarat Sarbadhikary and Susil Prasad (from Hare Sporting) Dwijen Bose (from Mohun Bagan) Durgadas Bhaduri (from C. E. College) Duhkiram (from Aryans) and a number of others joined the illustrious band to keep the banner proudly flowing. Kali Mitter (deputed by Nagendra Prasad to be the first Indian member of the I.F.A. Council) of the Canal Club came with Kali Mukerji to join the Sovabazar Club and served the club all his life loyally. With these Sovabazar Club proved its mettle pitted against even the best of European teams both civil and military. Its brilliant feat by vanquishing East Surrey in the trades Cup (then Senior Competition) is an historical event. True devotion of Nagendra Prasad made matters thought impossible, possible. And thus at the fourth memorial meeting held at the Commercial Museum Hall the President Mr. N. K. Basu Advocate remarked "for more than two generations I have known Nagendra Prasad as a great nation builder, a strong desciplinarian, a devout Indian who preached the Gospel of unity by bringing and tethering in the field the Hindus, the Moslem and Christians and tied them with the bond of Universal brotherhood. In his youth he was acquainted with Sir Surendra Nath Banerji, Shelly Bonerji etc. but he never paid heed to politics. His conviction was that politics will bring disunity more than unity".

Mr. E. M. Wheeler the wellknown educationists and sportsman happening to be connected with the Hughly College on or about 1890 took the lead in introducing out-door games in the district of Hughly. He started with Tennis. Football and Cricket followed soon in collaboration with Nagendra Prasad. By 1890 such clubs as Hare Sporting, Koomurtooli, National Association, Mohunbagan, Diana, Aryans, Chinsurah Town, Chinsurah Sporting and Howrah Sporting were supplementing the execution of the task undertaken by Nagendra Prasad. Chandernagore Sporting, Pickwick Club (Uttarpara) and a number of school and college clubs came into existence also in quick succession. Patna and Dacca were not slow in following the lead given by Calcutta in this direction. Arsenal boys (Indian) of the Fort William got up a splendid team. On Nagendra Prasad's advice the Muhammedan members of the Sovabazar Club took the lead in founding the Muhammedan Sporting Club with the express idea of course to supplement the work of the Sovabazar Club.

Bengal then was practically in Football Fever and other provinces were eagerly waiting their turn. In the meantime the I. F. A. was founded Nagendra Prasad taking the leading roll in it. With the growth of numerous clubs the urgency for forming a governing association was keenly felt by him. To keep discipline and morale of the clubs intact it was essential that a central governing body must come into existence. As a matter of fact the idea first originated in the Sovabazar tent. The matter was discussed informally there. Leading members of the Dalhousie (formerly Trades Club) Naval Volunteers (now Rangers Club) etc. had a heart to heart talk with Nagendra Prasad and the proposal of having a governing Association had the blessings of all. Nagendra Prasad in his usual wont as a wonderful organiser moved briskly and begged the then Maharajah of Cooch Behar who graciously presented the Cooch Behar Cup. The Trades Cup was there but it was turned into a Second Fiddle. The Shield was formed, liberal contributions coming from all quarters. It has in time proved a real Shield to Bengal against vile onslaughters. The then lieutenant governor of Bengal came forward also to present the Elliot Shield. Cadet enthusiasts missed not also to present the Cadet Cup. Charged with running these important competitions the popularity of the I. F. A. became India wide. The name and fame of Bengal as the home of Football in India reached England and the continent. Nagendra Prasad the 10 year old boy going to Manton's for a Football and Nagendra Prasad, the Founder of the I. F. A., in his undergraduate days needs no colouring indeed. The potrait is vivid.

When Nagendra Prasad saw Hare Sporting, National Association and Mohun Bagan were dependable to carry on his work and the work of the Sovabazar Club, when he saw that Sarada Ranjan was moving whole heartedly in the interest of Indian Cricket he felt at ease. So long

Nagendra Prasad was their guardian angel. There was no necessity for him to be always hovering over them any longer. So step by step he let them chalk out their own path till he saw the line clear, when he made everything over to them.

After graduating from the Presidency College, Nagendra Prasad went for Solicitorship Examination which he ultimately passed and became a Solicitor of the High Court in due course. Though a solicitor he never solicited any work from any body. Work came to him however of its own accord and some brother solicitors off ond on thrust on him work full of legal intricacies. The Sportsman-solicitor's angle of vision was not of a stereotyped character. His sporting spirit even here was uppermost and this helped him to make the matter easy and highly satisfactory to both the parties in dispute. The professional litigant however was always afraid of him and used to keep him at a distance.

'Out and out a sportsman Nagendra Prasad was no less a zealot in the domain of literature, English and Bengali" said a contemporary of a local daily. As a student of Shakespeare and Girish Chandra the name of

Source: P. L. Dutt, *Memoir of "Father of Indian Football" Nagendra Prosad Sarvadhikari*, Calcutta: N. P. Sarvadhikari Memorial Committee, 1944.

Appendix II

Editorial of *Amrita Bazaar Patrika* after Mohun Bagan's IFA Shield Victory in 1911

Amrita Bazar Patrika

CALCUTTA, JULY 31, 1911 MONDAY.

THE IMMORTAL ELEVEN

MAY GOD BLESS THE Immortal Eleven of Mohun Bagan for raising their nation in the estimation of the Western people by their brilliant feat on Saturday last.

The victory is no doubt ours and that in the line of physical culture wherein the Bengalees at any rate were so long held to be lamentably deficient.

Let us use these incidents to cultivate confidence in ourselves, to feed the legitimate ambition and aspiration of fulfilling ourselves; but let also love and gratitude for those who are taking us by the hand and teaching us to win spurs in fresh fields and pastures new, fill our hearts.

THE MEMORABLE CROWD

AT LAST THE LONGED FOR Final in the Shield tournament — the Mohun Bagan — East York match came off on Saturday last on the Calcutta ground. The spectators who packed every inch of the Maidan simply defied calculation. They might have been eighty thousand or they might have been more. Spectators came from far and near and I know that a gentleman actually came from Patna to witness the game. A special train was run between Howrah and Burdwan. The splendid exhibition of football by the Mohun Bagan team will not be forgotten for many years to come.

THESE WERE THE EXPRESSIONS OF THE OLDEST NATIONALIST DAILY CONGRATULATING THE PREMIER INDIAN SPORTS CLUB ON ITS HISTORIC VICTORY IN I.F.A. SHIELD FINAL ON JULY 29, 1911

Both the Institutions have stood the test of time and to-day one greets the other for its achievements and aspirations

POSTERITY PAYS HOMAGE TO THE PIONEERS

PUBLISHED IN THE LANGUAGE OF THOSE IMMORTAL ELEVEN AND READ BY ANOTHER HALF A MILLION THE PROGRESSIVE CALCUTTA DAILY SHARES COMMON GOOD FEELINGS WITH ALL LOVERS OF SPORTS

JUGANTAR

Appendix III

History of the IFA Shield

History of the I. F. A. Shield

INSTITUTED in 1893, the present Indian Football Association Shield Tournament promises, in its forty-third year, to be as successful as any of its illustrious predecessors. Though not as old as the Trades Cup or the Durand Cup (the Shield, being open to civilian and military, European and Indian teams, has grown to be the most coveted trophy in the country. To the credit of successive boards of management is it that there has been a steady rise in interest and in attractiveness which has, year after year, secured the rivalry of the greatest exponents from the various provinces.

The game of Association Football in Calcutta dates back to the early seventies, but it was not till 1888 that the idea of organising a tournament of a knock-out nature was conceived. Ten years prior to that, the Dalhousie Athletic Club had come into existence under the name of the Trades Club. Indians were quick to follow suit, Mr. N. Sarbadhikari being instrumental in forming the Sovabazar Club, and the Calcutta Football Club originally confining their energies to the handling code, the Naval Volunteer Club and European colleges and schools fell into line.

With the formation of an Association, which was honoured in due course with

Calcutta Football Club, Shield Winners, in 1911.

Calcutta Football Club, Shield Winners in 1922, 1923 and 1924. Photograph of 1923.

2nd Bn. Sherwood Foresters, Shield Winners in 1925, 1927 and 1928.

the recognition of the English Football Association, who granted affiliation as a Hall Mark of sound administration, the Trades Cup, presented by the Trades Association, came into being. Thus was the foundation laid of open competitive football in this country, and there has been no looking back.

In its first year, the Trades Cup attracted thirteen entrants, and the first name to appear on it is that of the Dalhousie Athletic Club. They beat the Buffs in the final, but in the following year the position was reversed. In an entry of nine teams. Entrants rose to thirteen again in 1891, when the 2nd King's Liverpool Regiment were the winners, and to seventeen in 1892, the 1st East Lancashire Regiment being the last team to have their name on the Cup in open competition.

It was not till 1893 that the Calcutta Football Club entered the tournament, and then they withdrew after getting through the first two rounds owing to several of their players being requisitioned for the Rugby team to meet their great rivals, the Buffs. The same was the case again in 1895 when, after drawing a tie, they beat the Rifle Brigade and then played three goalless draws before giving the ultimate winners of the Calcutta group a

walk-over — their
Nagpur engagement on
this occasion was
with Bombay.

At the end of the
1892 season, the time
was thought to be
ripe for the establish-
ment of a more pre-
tentious tournament
which would attract
the strongest combin-
ations from other
parts of the country.
The chief movers
were Mr A R Brown,
the honorary secre-
tary, and Mr B K
Lindsay, both of
whom figured with
distinction in the
Dalhousie Athletic
Club team,
Mr. Watson of the
Calcutta Football
Club and Mr Sar-
bedhikary. From
these meetings rose
the I. F. A. Shield,
and the Trades Cup
was relegated to the
status of a junior
tournament. Volun-
tary contributions
procured for the pur-
chase of a Shield of
the value of over
Rs. 1,600 and for
medals. To reduce
the expenses further-
more, four of the
limited entrants
were asked to play-
off at Lucknow.

Members of the
Lucknow group in
that first year were
the Royal Irish Regi-
ment and of the
Calcutta group the
5th Western Divi-
sion Royal Artillery.
The latter beat
Howrah Union, who
had defeated the
Dalhousie Athletic
Club, in the final,
the Royal Irish won
by the only goal of
the match. The
Dalhousie Athletic
Club ground was the
only one in use in those days, and the attendance was estimated at 7,000, which shows the
extent to which the game had caught the public

2nd Bn. 5th West Riding Shield Winners in 1924.

2nd Bn. Seaforth Highlanders, Shield Winners in 1912.

2nd Bn. Highland Light Infantry, Shield Winners in 1921.

and 1904. They were Runners Up to the Calcutta
Football Club in 1922 and to the 2nd Sherwood
Foresters in 1928. The former of these matches

fancy even at that
time.

The Royal Irish
were winners again
in the next year, and
Irish successes were
registered by the
Irish Rifles in 1901,
1912 and 1913. Six-
teen years later the
2nd Royal Ulster
Rifles augmented
these beating the
Rangoon Gordons in
the final. The
Runners-Up Cup was
instituted in 1913,
and the first holders
were the 91st High-
landers. In that
year there were
twenty-two entrants
and the only occa-
sion on which the
number has dropped
below twenty since
then was in 1924,
when there were
nineteen.

Morila the best re-
cord amongst civilian
clubs is the one held
by the Calcutta Foot-
ball Club, but for the
past eight years mili-
tary teams have do-
minated. The
premier club held
the Shield during
the following years,
1899, 1900, 1902, 1904,
1906 and 1915, before
equalling the feat of
the Gordons of win-
ning for three succes-
sive years from 1922
to 1924. In 1914 they
were Runners-Up
to the King's Own,
in 1916 to the 2nd
North Staffords, in
1919 to the 1st
Dorsetshires (E.W.B.)
and in 1927 to the
2nd Sherwood
Foresters.

Following their
success in the Trades
Cup, the Dalhousie
Athletic Club won
the Shield in 1897

History of the I. F. A. Shield

will be remembered as keenly by followers of the game as the 1923 final, in which the Calcutta Football Club beat Mohun Bagan. The leading Indian Club earned the only success scored by a barefooted team when they prevailed in 1911, beating the East Yorks in the final. In 1920, they reached the semi-final only to lose to another Indian side in Kumartuli, who lost to the Black Watch in the final. Like the Rangoon branch of the same service, the Calcutta Customs have reached the final once. That was in 1915, when they eventually lost to the Calcutta Football Club.

Of military teams, the Gordons, from 1906 to 1910, were first to win the Shield for three successive years. As remarked above, the Calcutta Football Club emulated that performance, and in 1928 the 2nd Sherwood Foresters completed a similar series of triumphs. The Highland Light Infantry have two successes to their credit, but there was

2nd Bn. Essex Regiment, Shield Winners in 1932

1st Bn. Duke of Cornwall's Light Infantry, Shield Winners in 1933

1st Bn. East Yorkshire, Shield Winners in 1935

a gap of twenty-four years between them. The wonderful goal-scoring ability of their centre forward, Graves, will always be associated with their 1931 achievement.

With the magnificent trophies now under the control of the Indian Football Association, the necessity for financial assistance in the supplying of these does not arise, but voluntary contributions are required nevertheless. Donations by clubs and those concerned with the business side of the game continue to be made, and these are largely responsible for increasing the interest in the tournament. Few military units can boast of a sports fund sufficiently substantial to allow of their patronising the various centres who look to them to brighten up their engagements. The generosity of those who have the welfare of the game at heart makes it possible for Calcutta to stage a meeting of the leading teams of all denominations which is unequalled even in Simla.

The Editor of this publication tenders his thanks to all who have so courteously responded to his request for information, particularly the officials of the various Clubs.

Source: *IFA Shield Illustrated Souvenir,* Calcutta: IFA, 1933.

Appendix IV

Salim: The Indian Juggler in Scotland in 1936

Source: *The Scottish Daily Express*, 23 August 1936.

Appendix V

Cry for a Stadium

An Editorial Note from The Englishman

WE publish an article from the Raja of Santosh, President of the Bengal Legislative Council, and one of the keenest sportsmen in Bengal, strongly supporting the movement for the erection of a Sports Stadium in Calcutta. Thanks largely to the Raja's initiative, the project that has been much talked about and which has the enthusiastic support of followers of every branch of sport, has at last some prospect of being carried through. The main difficulty is the site, which every one is agreed must be on the Maidan, but there is considerable ground for hope that when definite plans have been prepared the authorities concerned may be more sympathetic than they have been in the past. There will, we are assured, be no difficulty about securing the necessary capital for the construction of the Stadium if a suitable site on the Maidan is granted, and there is little doubt that it would be a paying proposition.

The Cry for a Stadium

[*Specially written for "The Englishman" by The Hon'ble Raja Sir Manmatha Nath Ray Chowdhury, Kt., of Santosh, President, I.F.A.*]

IT may be true that in no period of her history could India actually boast of an Olympia, but it is undeniable that she has at all times been prominent in her keen enthusiasm for manly games and sports.

I felt a surge of emotion within me when, from a terrace of the Agra Fort, I saw the enclosed arena down below, where brave athletes and sportsmen of India performed glorious deeds of courage and heroism under the eyes of the great Moguls. There, on that historic spot, during a great sports meeting, Aurangzeb, then a mere youngster, gave undoubted proof of his valour and chivalry by rushing to the rescue of an intrepid competitor, who was engaged in a deadly contest with a huge tusker. The Prince separated them with great courage and pluck and killed the infuriated brute. "Though not the eldest, thou art the fittest of my sons to fill the throne after me," exclaimed his Royal father, Emperor Shahjahan—a prophecy which came to pass.

Our history is replete with such instances which bear eloquent testimony to India's sporting spirit. So, if India had no Olympia, she had her "Olympic Games." Like Greece, India also fixed her gaze as much upon the glory of the body of man as upon the glory of his intellect and spirit. She attached great importance to the harmonious culture of body and mind. Her religion enjoined that both should alike be disciplined.

"Then there came a change, as all human things change." With the inroad of modernism, a certain type of games, sports of yore, were found to be on their last legs. The days of "Olympia," or of the death-defying Roman gladiators, or of Indian sportsmen of old-time virility and valour completely disappeared in the mists of the past. The tide which came to sweep away worn-out landmarks from the world of sport not only seized India, but more or less all the civilized countries of Asia and Europe.

But it is not to be forgotten that after the world-wide emasculation of manly games and sports, there was an abnormal set-back in sport in India. This was far below the world depression. Of all her provinces, Bengal suffered most. Her sporting spirit was almost crushed out of existence. There were no doubt spasmodic efforts here and there to recoup but the atmosphere was so adversely changed that her efforts to recover the lost ground were slackened to an alarming extent. Thanks to England and English culture, India in general

MR. PRESIDENT STILL GOING STRONG!

ELEVATION TO STRAND ROAD

and Bengal in particular were gradually able to imbibe the sporting spirit of the British.

The recovery was slow because the difficulties of the situation were great and many. Of late, India has again come into her own and although she is yet behind many of her competitors in the world race for athletic supremacy. Military authorities can easily solve it. Sooner or later they have got to face it and sooner they tackle it the better. There can be no compromise with it and they must make up their mind to treat it radically as it has a tendency to grow larger. Each year brings new complications and larger crowds to intensify it.

her progress is remarkable. Bright hopes are now cherished of her future and her achievements have already proved beyond the shadow of a doubt that of all the gifts which India has received from England, her manly games and sports constitute one of the very best. But example and self-help can no longer carry her forward. She is now more than ever in need of material help to augment her resources, if she is to claim her rightful place in sport and if her physical culture is to continue in an unimpaired state, till her teeming population becomes strong and healthy, judged by the world standard.

Coming nearer home and speaking for Bengal, I may say, without any fear of contradiction, that a Sports Stadium in Calcutta is the need of the moment. Sport in Bengal will receive serious check if we fail to provide at the psychological moment a central home of sports. Besides, in a city like Calcutta where the huge sporting crowds always cause anxiety to the Police and the people alike, the problem of providing accommodation for spectators can no longer be ignored. Sport is rapidly developing in Bengal—more quickly than many would imagine—and the creation of an ideal centre for sport is imperative. We must have a sports stadium which could accommodate in its auditorium no less that 60,000 people.

The real difficulty is the provision of ground on the Maidan for the purpose; but, to my mind, it is not insurmountable. The Civil and of the Public Works Department of the Government of Bengal. In all probability, the Military authorities will find it least objectionable from their point of view, as big buildings have already sprung up closely opposite to that site, I mean on the other side of the Auckland Road. This plot of ground has outlived its usefulness as a part of a public park. If the Stadium is constructed there it will not affect the Eden Gardens, as the lawn and the surrounding bowers will be left intact and it will not interfere with the boundaries of the old cricket ground. Although the site is a part of the Maidan, it is already detached from the vast expanse of the Maidan, which is rightly called the "lungs of Calcutta." On the other hand, the frontages to roads on all sides will simplify the control of the traffic and the playing field. Besides, it has one more advantage in having a long and lovely lake along its side which, if it is brought within the limits of the Stadium, may be improved upon to give us a fine water course for aquatic sports, so that the whole project may be as much for the benefit

There is no doubt that a very large amount of capital shall have to be sunk for the construction and maintenance of a Stadium worthy of Calcutta but no money will be required from the public exchequer. All that the Civil and Military authorities will have to do is to allocate a plot of land on the Maidan where a Stadium could be established by private capitalists or a Joint Stock Company, under the control of the Calcutta Football Association who have naturally taken the lead in the matter.

It is my considered opinion that a Stadium will be paying as a business proposition and may be made a source of revenue to the Government. A representative conference of leading British and Indian sportsmen of Calcutta was held at my house to discuss the question in all its bearing. The Stadium Scheme was unanimously accepted by that great body, on my motion, and the following sites were recommended to the authorities concerned :—

(1) North-West corner of the Eden Gardens facing the Strand Road and Auckland Road.

(2) Ellenborough Course.

(3) The two grass plots to the North-East corner of the Calcutta Race Course including the short public road (Hospital Road) in and between them having on its sides the Kidderpore Road and Casuarina Avenue.

Of the three sites, the one in the North-West corner of the Eden Gardens presents less difficulty, inasmuch as it is under the direct control of our "Wet Bobs" as it is for our "Dry Bobs."

In any case, a serious cry has been raised for a Stadium which cannot be stilled and I think it is not a cry in the wilderness. I fervently appeal to all Britishers and Indians alike to help the solution of the Stadium problem. Government and the people must combine to wipe out the shame which sits on the fair brow of the City of Palaces for not possessing a Sports Stadium. There can be no doubt that the magnificent panorama of the superb edifice of an Amphitheatre, like the one contemplated, standing side by side with one of Calcutta's historic and most charming landmarks, the Burmese Pagoda, within the picturesque environment of the Eden Gardens, apart from its intrinsic value as a training ground for athletic efficiency, honour and fame, is bound to thrill our people through and through and prove to be an enduring monument to Government's solicitude for the welfare of the people committed to its care.

Source: *Calcutta Sports Stadium: An Illustrated Supplement to the IFA Official Shield Programme 1933*, Calcutta: IFA, 1933.

Appendix VI

Footballers in Commercial Advertisements in the 1930s

Noor Mohamed, the sturdy centre half back of the Mohammedan Sporting Club, writes: "Of all the drinks, I consider a hot cup of tea most refreshing and stimulating. After a hard match in rain and mud a hot cup of tea is a great boon."

TEA for Endurance

Read our new Sports Brochure entitled: "*Now for a Cup of Tea*" and see why the leading sportsmen of India recommend tea for endurance and stamina during and after games. Please cut out this coupon and send it, together with your name, address and occupation to the Commissioner for India, Indian Tea Market Expansion Board, P. O. Box No. 2172, Calcutta who will send you free of charge a copy of the Brochure.

INSERTED BY THE INDIAN TEA MARKET EXPANSION BOARD

Source: *Calcutta Football League Official Programme 1940*, Calcutta: IFA, 1940.

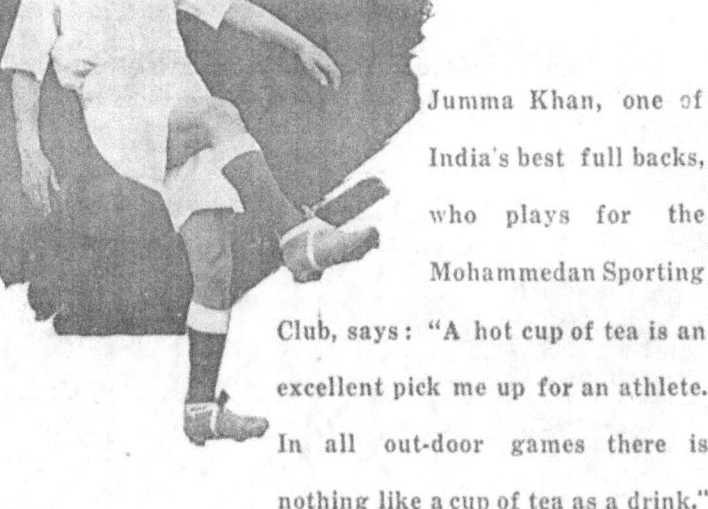

Jumma Khan, one of India's best full backs, who plays for the Mohammedan Sporting Club, says: "A hot cup of tea is an excellent pick me up for an athlete. In all out-door games there is nothing like a cup of tea as a drink."

TEA *for Endurance*

Read our Sports Brochure entitled, "Now for a Cup of Tea" and see why the world's most renowned sportsmen recommend tea as the best refresher and safest stimulant. Please cut out this coupon and send it, together with your name, address and occupation to the Commissioner for India, Indian Tea Market Expansion Board, P. O. Box No. 2172, Calcutta, who will send you free of charge a copy of the Brochure.

INSERTED BY THE INDIAN TEA MARKET EXPANSION BOARD

Source: *Calcutta Football League Official Programme 1938*, Calcutta: IFA, 1938.

Appendix VII

Correspondence between the Football Association, England and the Indian Football Association, Calcutta

THE FOOTBALL ASSOCIATION.

PATRON:
HIS MAJESTY THE KING.
PRESIDENT:
SIR CHARLES CLEGG, J.P.

SECRETARY:
S. F. ROUS

TELEGRAPHIC ADDRESS:
"FOOTBALL ASSOCIATION
PADD. LONDON."

22, LANCASTER GATE,
LONDON, W. 2.

18th September, 1936.

SD/M. Enc:

The Hon'ble Maharaja Sir Chowdhury, Kt., M.L.C., M.R.A.S., F.R.S.A.,
Santosh House,   F.R.C.I., of Santosh.
1, Raja Santosh Road,
Alipore, Calcutta.

Dear Sir,

We thank you for sending us a copy of the circular letter which has been issued to the Indian Provinces and Presidencies.

We have received by the same post a letter dated 3rd September from the "All-India Football Association" whose General Secretary is Rai Bahadur J.P. Sinha, Gorakhpur, U.P., and a further letter dated 5th September. In the second letter they refer to the last paragraph on page 2 of your printed letter in which you say that the President of the Army Sports Control Board approves the suggestion that a Conference of the Representatives of the Provinces and Presidencies be arranged. In this connection the "A.I.F.A." say they have referred to the Army Sports Control Board and their views on the subject are as follows :-

(i) The object of the proposed conference is to settle, if possible, the difference between the two Associations and not to discuss the I.F.A. scheme which has been found unacceptable.

(ii) It is presumed that the invitation to and agenda for such a conference should emanate from the A.I.F.A. and that, if possible, it should be held at Delhi at a time when the Presidents or senior representatives of both Associations can be present.

We should like to have your observations upon the above.

Enclosed please find a copy of our reply to the "A.I.F.A."

Yours faithfully,

S. Roy
Secretary.

Source: *Private Papers of the Maharaja of Santosh (MSPP)*. © Late Raja B.N. Roy Chowdhury of Santosh

Appendix VIII

Correspondence between the Army Sports Control Board and the Indian Football Association, Calcutta

Personal.

No.

Army Headquarters, India,

GENERAL STAFF BRANCH,

Simla, the 29th May 1937.

Dear Maharaja Sahib,

Thank you for your letter of the 25th May.

I am sorry to say that it is quite impossible to accede to your request that the meeting, to be held next month at Simla and/which we hope to bring into being the All India Football Federation, should be postponed until July. As you know, the original date has already been put back one month to suit the I.F.A. with considerable inconvenience to the other parties concerned, and any further postponement would I know, cause great offence to them and upset all their arrangements. Further, I am hoping to go to England about the middle of July for a short period of leave.

I regret that the present date of our meeting is not very convenient for the I.F.A., but I am sure that you will agree that any postponement is out of the question for the reasons stated. I hope very much that you will find it possible to send a suitable representative to the meeting.

2. Your question regarding the number of representatives which the I.F.A. should send to the meeting is a little complicated.

The meeting is being held to inaugurate the proposed All India Football Federation and is governed by no rules. All we could do was to ask all the parties concerned to send a representative each. The first thing to do will be to bring into being the Federation; when that has been done, the next step will be to consider and approve the draft rules. Until these rules have been approved, there can be no authority for the I.F.A. to have more than one representative. I suggest therefore that the only possible solution is for the I.F.A. to send one representative to the meeting; for the initial proceedings he will have only one vote; after the draft rules have been approved he will have two votes for all subsequent business. I hope you will agree that this is a suitable arrangement.

3. I agree that there is much to be said for accepting Calcutta as the Headquarters of the A.I.F.F for the first few years. Obviously, however, the decision cannot rest with me as the question will have to be decided by the forthcoming meeting.

4. I regret very much that you consider that the I.F.A. has not been well treated. Since I became connected with this affair I have tried to be quite impartial and incidentally to ensure that sufficient weight was given to the prestige and traditions of the I.F.A. The alternative suggestion that the I.F.A. should to all intents and purposes absorb the A.I.F.A. was never of course a practical proposition.

5.	I must confess that I find the last few lines of your letter rather perturbing as they imply that even at this late stage in the proceedings you may find it impossible to accept the A.I.F.F. or to co-operate loyally with such a body. Accordingly, I think it is only right that I should make my position in this matter quite clear.

I am a busy man, and during recent months this football controversy has made demands on my time which I can ill afford. I certainly cannot continue on these lines indefinitely, though I am prepared to do all in my power within reason to help to find a satisfactory solution. I have, however, decided that, if the meeting in Simla next month is unsuccessful and does not result in the formation of the A.I.F.F. to be loyally supported by all concerned, I shall be forced to refrain from any further participation in this football controversy. In such a contingency I should be forced to forward to the F.A. in England a report on the happenings of the last few months and on the reasons for the break-down of negotiations, and thereafter events in India would have to follow their normal course. I venture to think that the history of the formation of the All India Cricket and Hockey Bodies shows that such a situation is unlikely to prove in the best interests of Bengal, and I certainly hope that it will not arise.

I have written to you very frankly to avoid any possible misunderstanding, as I feel that this is what you would wish me to do. I shall be glad if you will kindly treat this letter as private and personal.

Yours Sincerely,

Ross Majindie

The Hon'ble Maharaja of Santosh,
President, I.F.A.,
Santosh House,
21 Raja Santosh Road,
Alipore,
Calcutta.

Source: *MSPP*. © Late Raja B.N. Roy Chowdhury of Santosh

Appendix IX

Spectator Violence at Calcutta Maidan

MOB-VIOLENCE IN SENIOR SOCCER
East Bengal-Aryans Match Abandoned: Referee Attacked
Green Stand Crowd Invade Play Ground

Disgraceful scenes of mob-violence in a football league match hitherto unheard and unseen, came before the public view on Thursday afternoon when East Bengal met the Aryans in their senior league encounter on the C.F.C. ground. The episode was built around the hooliganism of the green stand spectators, who gave vent to their spleen. They not only created a pandemonium by rushing to the field of play but also made the continuance of play impossible after the nineteenth minute of the second half. The referee was the target once again.

The referee was man-handled by the mischief-mongers on his way back to the C.F.C. tent. But for the timely intervention of Sri J. C. Guha, the Hony. General Secretary of the East Bengal Club, who not only gave him protection risking his own person, but also escorted him to safety, the fate of the referee (Bijoy) Mukherjee might have been still worse. The match was thus abandoned six minutes from time.

To describe the incident as a tempest in a tea-pot would never be a travesty of truth. Stones, brickbats, shoes and even the heavy confirmed chairs were used as the missiles by the green-stand spectators, who, inspite of the intervention by the police force, made two attempts to set fire to the green stands at the north-east and the south-east ends. Fortunately however, the situation was brought under control by a teargas squad of the Police and the fire was extinguished.

To an old-stager Thursday's incidents were but the repetition of history. It may be recalled that in the I.F.A. Shield first round match between Calcutta F.C. and Mohun Bagan in 1921, the green stands were in flames after the referee—Major Pickridge, had abandoned the game (quite early in the first-half of the ground was frequently lit been embattled upon by the indisciplined spectators.

evidently become a bit excited and their vociferous protests could be heard from the distance. Sri Jyotish Guha, the Hony. Secretary, East Bengal Club, at this stage made gallant efforts to pacify the crowd on the white stands.

The unruly crowd from the eastern galleries made their way towards the white stands and apparently looked out for the referee. Some of the officials of both the contending clubs, however, extricated the referee from the crowd and escorted him to safety. The referee, it is gathered, received some blows from the crowd before he was brought out of the ground.

Alongwith the referee being escorted to safety East Bengal players left the field but the Aryans player were still there. Hurling of missiles from the eastern galleries was gradually intensified till a teargas squad made their appearance on the ground. Several policemen were also sent to the other side of the ground. This had some effect on the crowd at they began to thin away but at this stage attempts were made on two occasions to set fire to the galleries on the eastern side. The policemen being very alert the attempts were foiled on both occasions. The Calcutta Club ground was practically cleared of the unruly crowd by the dusk.

THE GAME

Now about the match. The Aryans put up a brilliant display and had more of the play until it was abandoned. Their forwards moved about in a more purposive fashion than their opposite numbers. Chyguay also clever their way but their shooting was not upto the mark.

Reddy, who partnered P. Kumar at back of the East Bengal team was injured quite early in the match and although he came out once on the first half he had to leave the ground soon for good and thus East Bengal had to play with ten players for the better part of the match.

Teams :—

Aryans: S. Sett, M. Pal and Joseph D. Chatterjee. A. Barkadhikary and Kipoo T. Roy, S. Dasgupta, Mewalai, P. Mitra and R. Bose.

East Bengal: Dr. S. Dasgupta and Dr. P. Kumar, Hassan, Sk/ Reddy and Rampival Balasubrahmaniam Ahmed, T. Rao, Kitoo and Moosa.

Referee: Bijoy Mukherjee

OTHER FOOTBALL RESULTS

Third Division: K F A Inst. (2); Young Bengal (1); Calcutta Police (3); Police (1); Aikya Sammilani (1),

ARYANS LEADING

Aryans (1): East Bengal (0)

It was nothing short of a mob violence that led to the abandonment of the senior football league match between East Bengal and the Aryans six minutes from the final whistle on the C.F.C. ground on Thursday when the match was abandoned the Aryans were one-goal up. Mewalal, their leader of attack converting a penalty kick in the 18th minute of the second half.

The scene that was enacted was disgraceful enough to tarnish the fair name of sports. A frenzied crowd in the cheaper stands apparently to express their dissatisfaction against the supervision, resorted to the pelting of stones, shoes, iron-framed wooden chairs and other missiles до the ground when play was still in progress and even after play was stopped.

The match drew an enormous placed for the spot-kick a few East Bengal players were seen talking with the referee. The man-in-charge of whistle was, however, adamant and the penalty kick was taken. Mewalal who was entrusted with the spot-kick, made no mistake.

Immediately after play had resumed after the goal the activities of the spectators on the eastern galleries were intensified. At this stage a police constable was found running across the field even though play was in progress. The linesman from that side also came down running almost to the heels of the police constable. Meanwhile, a free-kick was awarded to East Bengal. But before the free-kick was taken a section of crowd from the green galleries scaled the American fencing and invaded the field.

Although there were not as violent as the spectators on green galleries the spectators in the white stands...

[unreadable column — league results]

BASKETBALL KNOCKOUT

The postponement final of the junior knockout basketball championship between Boys' Training Association vs Dragons Club will be played to-day (Friday) commencing on the Association ground, maidan at 5 p.m.

Source: *Amrita Bazar Patrika*, 29 June 1956.

Appendix X

Referee in Bengal Football

Can you imagine a Football Match without a Referee

Can you imagine a game of soccer sans the man with the whistle? Referee what a word. It, in effect, means the ENFORCER OF THE LAW! Unlike the Enforcer of the film, the referee is not allowed to carry or to use a pistol. He could do with a machinegun sometimes. However he is permitted to carry a whisle which he uses with as deadly effect.

It is all work and no play for the referee. He commands greater attention than any cricket umpire is ever likely to achieve but no kudos for him ever. He is not the star centre-forward, is the true cynosure of eyes. The public is ever watching the referee. A million hopes depend on him.

There is nothing sluggish about the soccer referee. His is no sleeping-on—the feet job. He cannot dream, speculate or wonder about the mysteries of the universe or his thoughts to stray over to some American movie girls seen in films or picture books.

If the game has been advertised to start at 4-30 p. m. the referee slips furtively past the gateman at 4.15. He is early. He waits for the teams to turn up. When they do, he enters the arena, escorted by his two aiders and abaiters known as the linesmen.

The lot of the linesmen is as unenviable as the Referee's. They have more fun, through dodging flying saucers and shoes from the stands. They become such expert dodgers that when some of them win a sweepstake and become capitalists, the Income tax officers have a tough time trying to catch up with them. During the game to wave or not to wave his flag is the linesman's question. Either action puts him in immediate dislavour with one section of the crowd. His moments are filled with peril. One of these days a linesman, I am sure, will be awarded the Param Vir Chakra. The rival captains shake hands first with the referee, then with his accomplices and finally with each other. Note the order of precedence. They smile with pity at the referee and learn from him of the odds. The referee borrows a coin from a press photographer and tosses it. He later pockets it absent-mindedly. He has other and bigger things on his mind.

Now is the referee seen in his true colours. He is a pervert, a sadist, a crook; or else why does he pull up that winger for off-side? The infringement, as supporters of the offending side tell you, only exists in his imagination. Transgressing players, blown up by him, cast indignant looks at him. Varying sections of the crowd cheated of the exultation of victory, often call for his immediate liquidation by lynching. It is indeed a humane lot that turns up to see a soccer. A section, with their favourites one goal down, questions the referee's ancestry. The fellow next to you, to all appearances as decent, cultured among the spectators knows no bounds. They pour scorn on him. He should not have allowed that clean goal; They shout obscenities at him and threaten with the cruelest fate.

The linesman signals: one minute to go! And the referee thanks the Lord and blows a long whistle which is almost a wail. The game has been won and lost. Tired, wet, panting, the players make their way through the lane made up of guarding lines of the special police, to the tent for cool

and civilised as you are, reels off a string of epithets which would put a fisherman to shame.

The referee is too absorbed in keeping law and order among twenty-two players to pay any attention to the vociferous gallery. Long sufferances of the inevitable multitude has thickened his skin into tough hide and deafened him to abuse. He is a martyr made. At half time his shirt is wetter than Cherrapunji and any of the player's. The ordeal is resumed and the referee bravely carries on, playing, in the opinion of the partisan crowds, now for one side and now for the other. How nice would it be for him were the game to end in a drawn! Cruel chance gives the game to the less deserving team. The disappointment of the majority

drinks. The referee joins them and tells some one,"Yes it was not a bad game at all".

No applause for him, nobody thanks him, neither winners, losers nor spectators. Nobody ever admires his courage. He does not care. For he knows that his has been the sovereign for that brief hour of glory and that not a single pair of eyes among the thousands had ever been off him. He slips unobtrusively out, even as he came in.

Source: *IFA Shield Programme 1962*, Calcutta: IFA, 1962.

Appendix XI

The Need of a Stadium

The Need of a Stadium

Calcutta in particular and Bengal in general is a sports-loving province and time and again it has been proved that in any competitive match, in whatever branch of sports, a good crowd is always inevitable. To be candid Bengal has taken up football as her national game and it can be seen on every important occasion of an important match that if there is a crowd of 15,000 men inside the enclosed galleries round the ground, double the same are forced to remain outside the enclosed ground for want of accommodation and another 5,000 remain satisfied listening either to the Radio or sitting in their homes enquiring and disturbing all the time the telephone operator for the result of the match. It is also painful to look at the crowd in cheap stands in a Ranji Trophy cricket match witnessing the game from 11 a.m. to 5 p.m. under a scorching sun for 2 and three days. And such is our lot —in the second city of the British Empire. The Corporation, the Government or the business magnets of the province—can they not come forward to solve this vital and important problem which is being discussed year in after year for the last 15 or 20 years?

Thanks to the late Maharaja of Santosh who did yeomen service in this connection. The site was selected near the former Band Stand at the Eden Gardens, the design and sketches were made ready, but to his dismay the late Maharaja had to keep off his scheme for adverse conditions which did not allow him to proceed further to reach his ambition fulfilled.

This crying need however did not cry out and with the passing of years became more and more acute. The I. F. A. however judging from all angle this year has themselves taken up the initiative and has sent in a circular to all sister organisations of this province for eliciting their opinion as to whether they can join the I. F. A. in their scheme of building a stadium in Calcutta, so that if the scheme materialises, all active games may be played inside the stadium. We understand that all the Associations have agreed to co-operate with the I. F. A. in the fulfilment of their object in building a stadium immediately in Calcutta.

It is of course not possible to start with the object even if the I. F. A. is permitted to build the stadium by the Government until the war is over. But at the same time it is essential that all formalities in this connection should be overcome at once so that the work of the stadium is possible to start immediately after the cessation of hostilities. In this connection it should be mentioned that although this project is laudable and is crying need of the hour, it involves a heavy financial responsibility and obligation. But even this problem can be easily solved provided the Government approves the scheme immediately and extends its helping hand to the Indian Football Association by allowing the Association to set apart one important League Fixture and another important Shield Fixture every year for the Stadium Fund. This will solve the problem and the I. F. A. which is no doubt the biggest sports organisation in the East with a record of 50 years of unique service for the cause of the game will be able to fulfil an essential and longfelt need of the city.

A huge crowd witnessing an important match on the C. F. C. Ground from outside the enclosed Galleries.

Source: *IFA Shield Souvenir 1943*, Calcutta: IFA, 1943, p. 17.

Appendix XII

Bulletin about the Stadium

Bulletin about the Stadium

For god's shake hold your Umbrella for few years more and you will get your stadium. Do you know that the site is sighted—Ellenborough course, the idea is mooted—the Italian Architect and at last our government has taken the initiative. But ofcourse with a great "But" and that is the availability of materials. Any how later or sooner—sooner or later we may hope, our time immemorial need may be fulfilled.

Here again we have both ways sympathy for some important personages who are at the helm of affairs of some particular big Clubs and also for the secretary of the I. F. A. While the secretary will be relieved from constant embarrasment that there is no ticket and even to hide himself a day before an important match where only V. I. P. have access and also the officials of the Clubs they will have peace on one hand but their importance will be diminished to

a great extent. There are sports observers working behind the scene who sometimes say probably this was the main reason that hindered the construction of a stadium in Calcutta for long many years.

Source: *IFA Shield Programme 1962*, Calcutta: IFA, 1962.

Bibliography

Official Records

Home Police Proceedings, Government of Bengal (1936–37) (West Bengal State Archives, Kolkata).

Private Papers

Maharaja of Santosh Private Papers (Nehru Memorial Museum and Library, New Delhi).

Publications of Government, Semi-Official and Public Bodies

Calcutta Municipal Gazette, Calcutta (selected years).
Hundred Years of the University of Calcutta, A history of the university issued in commemoration of the centenary celebrations, Calcutta: University of Calcutta, 1957.
Medical College, Bengal. 1835–1984, Commemorative volume on the occasion of golden jubilee memoriam and terjubilee year of Medical College, Calcutta: Medical College Ex-Students Association, 1984.
National Physical Efficiency Drive: 1965–66, New Delhi: Ministry of Education, Government of India, 1965.
Presidency College Centenary Volume, 1955, Calcutta: Superintendent, Government of West Bengal Press, 1956.
Sports in India, Delhi: The Publication Division, Ministry of Information & Broadcasting, Government of India, 1959.
The Centenary of Medical College, Bengal, 1835–1934: A Souvenir, Calcutta: Medical College, 1935.

Publications of Private Institutions and Clubs

93rd IFA Shield Tournament Souvenir, Calcutta: IFA, 1985.
Balurghat Town Club Centenary Souvenir, Balurghat: Balurghat Town Club, 2001.
Beximco Pharma Abul Hashem Table Tennis Championship 2004 Souvenir, Dhaka: Wari Club, 2004.
Calcutta Football League Official Programme / Souvenir (selected years).
DCM Football Tournament Journal, Delhi, 1986.

Dhaka Mohammedan Sporting Club er Sankhipta Itihas (A Brief History of the Dhaka Mohammedan Sporting Club), Dhaka: Mohammedan Sporting Club, 2004.
East Bengal Club Golden Jubilee Souvenir, Calcutta: East Bengal Club, 1967.
I.F.A. Shield Illustrated Souvenir, Calcutta: IFA, 1936.
I.F.A. Shield Souvenir, Calcutta: IFA, 1935–1980: selected years.
Indian Football Association Golden Jubilee Souvenir, ed. Pankaj Gupta, Calcutta, 1943.
Mohammedan Sporting Club Souvenir, Calcutta: Mohammedan Sporting Club, 1939.
Mohammedan Sporting Club. Calcutta League Champions. 1934–1935, A Souvenir, Calcutta: Mohammedan Sporting Club, 1935.
Mohun Bagan A. C. Meets Cosmos. A Souvenir, Calcutta: Mohun Bagan A.C., 1977.
Mohun Bagan Athletic Club Golden Jubilee Souvenir, Calcutta: Mohun Bagan A.C., 1939.
Mohun Bagan Athletic Club Platinum Jubilee Souvenir, Calcutta: Mohun Bagan A.C., 1964.
Platinum Jubilee: Calcutta Customs Club, 1892–1967, Calcutta: Customs Club, 1967.
The Grass is Green in Goa: 40 Years Yield a Lot of Goals, ed. Francis Xavier Janim Rebeirro, Panjim: Goa Football Association, 2000.
The Scottish Church College Ter Jubilee Volume. 1979, Calcutta: The Scottish Church College, 1979.
Victoria Sporting Club Platinum Jubilee Souvenir, Dhaka: Victoria Sporting Club, 1991.
VIIth Jawaharlal Nehru Invitation International Gold Cup Football Tournament Souvenir, Siliguri: AIFF & IFA, 1988.
Wari Club: Shatabarsho Smarani, 1898–1998, Wari Club: Centenary Memoriam, 1898–1998, Dhaka: Wari Club, 2000.
WIFA Golden Jubilee Souvenir, Bombay: Western India Football Association, 1961.
XIX National Football Championship for the Santosh Trophy Souvenir, Bangalore: Mysore State Football Association, 1962.
XXXIV National Football Championship for Santosh Trophy, Official Souvenir, Kolkata: IFA, 1977.
XXXVII National Football Championship for Santosh Trophy, Official Souvenir, Coimbatore: AIFF, 1980.

Printed Reports

Annual Report, 1932–33, Mohammedan Sporting Club.
Annual Reports and the Statement of Accounts of the I.F.A., Calcutta: IFA Office. 1894–1980 (available years).
Report of the Indian National Congress (1896).
Report on the Native Newspapers of Bengal (1911).
University of Calcutta Reports on Mofussil Colleges (1908).

Memoirs, Autobiographies and Reminiscences

Basu, Ajay, *Maath Theke Balchhi* (Speaking from the Ground), Calcutta: Rooprekha, 1968.
Basu, Rajnarayan, *Se kal aar e kal* (That Age and This Age), Calcutta: Bangiya Sahitya Parisat, 1874.

Bose, Subhas Chandra, *An Indian Pilgrim: An Unfinished Autobiography and Collected Letters, 1897–1921*, ed. Netaji Research Bureau, London: Asia Publishing House, 1965.

Campbell, Sir George, *Memoirs of My Indian Career*, ed. Sir C. E. Bernard, vol. 2, London: Macmillan, 1893.

Chaudhuri, Nirad C, *Autobiography of an Unknown Indian*, London: Macmillan, 1951.

———, *Thy Hand, Great Anarch! India: 1921–1952*, London: Chatto & Windus, 1987.

Cox, Sir Edmund L., *My Thirty Years in India*, London: Mills & Boon, 1909.

Debi, Sarala, *Jibaner Jharapata* (Broken Leaves of Life), Calcutta, Rupa, 1964.

Dutta, Amal, *Ghera Maath Chhadano Gallery* (Enclosed Ground, Spread Gallery), Calcutta: Bisvabani Prakashani, 1982.

———, *Jotodin Banchi* (As Long As Alive), Kolkata: Aajkal, 2010.

Goswami, Chuni, *Khelte Khelte* (While Playing), Calcutta: Ananda, 1982.

Mitra, Krisnakumar, *Atmacharit* (Memoirs), Calcutta, 1937.

Pal, Bipin Chandra, *Memories of My Life and Times*, 2 vols, Calcutta, 1932–51, vol. 1 Modern Book Agency, vol. 2, Yugoyatri Prakashak.

Pennell, T. L., *Among the Wild Tribes of the Afghan Frontier*, London: Seeley Service, 1909.

Ray, Prafulla Chandra, *Life and Experiences of a Bengali Chemist*, vol. 1, Calcutta: Chuckerverty, Chatterjee & Co., Ltd., 1932.

Sengupta, Achintya Kumar, *Kallol Yug*, Calcutta: M.C. Sircar & Sons, 1950.

Sengupta, Surajit, *Back Centre*, Calcutta: Sunny Publishers, 1986.

Shamsuddin, Abul Kalam, *Atit Diner Smriti* (Memories of Olden Days), Dacca, 1968.

Tyndale-Biscoe, C. E., *Tyndale-Biscoe of Kashmir: An Autobiography*, London: Seeley Service, 1951.

———, *Character-Building in Kashmir*, London: Church Missionary Society, 1920.

———, *A Valiant Man of Kashmir*, London: Church Missionary Society, 1930.

Tyndale-Biscoe, Eric Dallas, *Memoirs of Eric Dallas Tyndale-Biscoe* (in transcript form: personal collection).

Contemporary Literary Works, Tracts and Pamphlets

Bagal, Yoges Chandra, *Hindu Melar Itibritta* (History of Hindu Mela), Calcutta: Maitryaee, 1945.

Bahurupi (pseud.), *Mohun Baganer Meye o Tarpor* (The Daughter of Mohun Bagan and afterwards), Calcutta: Bahurupi, 1978.

Basu, Abanindrakrisna, *Bangalir Sarcus* (Bengali's Circus), Calcutta, 1936.

Chattopadhyay, Bankim Chandra, *Bankim Rachanabali* (Collected Works of Bankim Chandra), 3 vols, Calcutta: Sahitya Samsad, 1953–69.

Ghose, Birendranath, *Bangalir Bahubal* (Physical Valour of the Bengalis), Calcutta, 1932.

Gupta, Bipinbihari, *Puratan Prasanga* (Old Contexts), Calcutta, 1913.

Mallik, Umes, *Yader gaye jor ache* (Those Who Have Physical Strength), Calcutta, 1946.

Nandy, Moti, *Striker*, Calcutta: Ananda, 1973.
———, *Stopper*, Calcutta: Ananda, 1974.
———, *Ferari* (The Lost), Calcutta: Ananda, 1990.
———, *Dalbadaler Aage* (Before the Change of Club), Calcutta: Ananda, 1992.

Other Contemporary Published Sources

Bose, Pramatha Nath, *Swaraj — Cultural and Political*, New Delhi: Usha Publications, 1929.
Dutt, P. L., *Memoir of 'Father of Indian Football' Nagendra Prosad Sarvadhikari*, Calcutta: N. P. Sarvadhikari Memorial Committee, 1944.
Gilbert, M., *Servant of India: A Study of Imperial Rule from 1905 to 1910 as Told through the Correspondence and Diaries of Sir James Dunlop Smith*, London: Longman, 1966.
Ispahani, M. A. H., *Quid-e-Azam Jinnah, As I Knew Him*, Karachi: Forward Publications, 1965.
Macaulay, T. B., *Critical and Historical Essays*, vol. 3, London: J. M. Dent & Sons Ltd., 1961.
Raleigh, Sir Thomas, *Lord Curzon in India: Being a Selection from his Speeches as Viceroy and Governor General, 1898–1905*, London: Macmillan, 1906.
Sarbadhikary, Berry (ed.), *Indian Footballer Annual: A Digest of Football Affairs in India and the World*, Calcutta: S. G. Publications, 1956.
Sherring, H., *The Mayo College, Ajmere, 'The Eton of India': A Record of Twenty Years 1875–1895*, 2 vols, Calcutta: Thacker and Spink, 1897.
Steevens, G. W., *In India*, London: Thomas Nelson & Sons, 1899.
Strachey, John, *India: Its Administration and Progress*, London: Macmillan and Company, 1911 (first published 1888).
Trust and Fear Not, Ought Natives to be Welcomed as Volunteers? Calcutta: Thacker, Spink & Co., 1885.
Tyndale-Biscoe, C. E., *Grinding Grit into Kashmir*, London, Seeley Service, 1922.
———, *Kashmir in Light and Shade*, London: Seeley Service, 1922.
Tyndale-Biscoe, E. D., *Fifty Years against the Stream*, Mysore: Wesleyan Missionary Press, 1930.

Newspapers and Periodicals

Bengali Language

Ananda Bazar Patrika
Balok
Bharatvarsha
Desh
Manasi o Marmabani
Masik Basumoti
Nayak
Prabartak
Prabasi

English Language

Amrita Bazar Patrika
Bombay Chronicle
Hindustan Standard
The Indian Daily News
Star of India
The Englishman
The Statesman
The Telegraph

Magazines

Bengali Language

Khelar Katha
Khelar Mathe
Olympic
Krirangan
Khelar Asar
Khela
Kick-Off

English Language

The Scottish Church College Magazine
Sport and Pastime
Sportstar

Oral Evidences

Interviews and Discussions

Sailen Manna (footballer)
Arun Ghosh (footballer-turned-coach)
Shanto Mitra (footballer)
Ranjit Gupta (ex-IFA honorary secretary)
Sultan Ahmed (president, Mohammedan Sporting Club)
Surojit Sengupta (footballer-turned-sports editor)
Rupak Saha (sports journalist)
Binay Bhushan Chaudhury (historian)
Gautam Bhadra (historian)
Surendra Gopal (historian)

Audio Cassette (music)

Manna Der Sera Gaaner Sankolon (Collection of Manna De's Best Songs), Calcutta: Gathani Records, 1994.

Shotoborsher Mohun Bagan (Mohun Bagan in its Centenary), Produced by Tutu Basu and directed by Sankar Banerjee, Calcutta: UD Industries, 1999.

Visual Sources
Photographs from Mona Chowdhury, and Sabyasachi Mallick
Cartoons
Theatre: *Football*
Films: *Saptapadi, Mohunbaganer Meye, Saheb, Dhanyi Meye, Aasray*

Books

In English
Ahmad, Sufia, *Muslim Community in Bengal. 1884–1912*, Dacca: Asiatic Press, 1974.
Alter, J., *The Wrestler's Body: Identity and Ideology in North India*, Berkeley, CA: University of California Press, 1992.
Anderson, Benedict, *Imagined Communities: Reflections on the Origin and Spread of Nationalism*, rev. edn, New York: Verso, 1991.
Armstrong, G. and R. Giulianotti (eds), *Fear and Loathing in World Football*, Oxford: Berg, 2001.
Ashton, S. R., *British Policy towards the Indian States, 1905–39*, London: Curzon Press, 1982.
Bale, John, *Sports Geography*, London: Spon, 1989.
———, *Sport, Space, Society*, London: Routledge, 1992.
———, *Landscapes of Modern Sport*, Leicester: Leicester University Press, 1994.
Bandyopadhyay, Kausik, *Playing for Freedom: A Historic Sports Victory*, New Delhi: Standard Publisher, 2008.
Basu, Jaydeep, *Stories from Indian Football*, New Delhi: UBS Publishers' Distributors Pvt. Ltd, 2003.
Begg, W. D., *Cricket and Cricketers in India*, Ajmer: published by author, 1934.
Bose, Mihir, *A History of Indian Cricket*, London: Andre Deutsch Ltd., 1990.
Broomfield, J. H., *Elite Conflict in a Plural Society: Twentieth Century Bengal*, Los Angeles: University of California Press, 1968.
Brown, Judith M., *Gandhi and Civil Disobedience: The Mahatma in Indian Politics*, Cambridge: Cambridge University Press, 1977.
Cardoso, Fernando Henqique and Enzo Faletto, *Dependency and Development in Latin America*, trans. Marjory Mattingly Urquidi, 1971, Berkeley: University of California Press, 1979.
Cashman, Richard, *Patrons, Players and the Crowd*, Calcutta: Orient Longman, 1979.
Carr, E. H., *What is History?* London: Pelican, 1961.
Chakrabarty, Prafulla K., *The Marginal Men, The Refugees and the Left Political Syndrome in West Bengal*, Calcutta: Lumiere Books, 1990.
Chatterjee, Partha, *Nationalist Thought and the Colonial World: A Derivative Discourse?* London: Zed Books, 1986.

Chatterjee, Partha, *The Nation and Its Fragments: Colonial and Postcolonial Histories*, Calcutta: Oxford University Press, 1995.
Chatterji, Joya, *Bengal Divided: Hindu Communalism and Partition, 1932–1947*, Cambridge: Cambridge University Press, 1995.
Cockcroft, James D., Andre Gunder Frank and Dale L. Johnson (eds), *Dependence and Underdevelopment*, Garden City: Double-day-Anchor Books, 1972.
Cornell, S. and D. Hartman, *Ethnicity and Race: Making Identities in a Changing World*, London: Pine Forge Press, 1998.
Darby, Paul, Martin Johnes and Gavin Mellor (eds), *Soccer and Disaster: International Perspectives*, London: Routledge, 2005.
Das, Suranjan, *Communal Riots in Bengal: 1905–1947*, New Delhi: Oxford University Press, 1991.
Datta, Pradip Kumar, *Carving Blocs: Communal Ideology in Early Twentieth Century Bengal*, New Delhi: Oxford University Press, 1999.
De Mellow, Melville (ed.), *Indigenous Games and Martial Arts of India*, vol. 1, New Delhi: Sports Authority of India, 1987.
———, *Reaching for Excellence: The Glory and Decay of Sport in India*, New Delhi: Kalyani Publishers, 1979.
Desai, A. R., *Social Background of Indian Nationalism*, Bombay: Popolar Prakashan, 1948.
Dimeo, Paul, and James Mills (eds), *Soccer in South Asia: Empire, Nation, Diaspora*, London: Frank Cass, 2001.
Dunning, Eric, Patrick Murphy and John Williams (eds), *The Roots of Football Hooliganism*, London: Routledge, 1988.
Finn, Gerry P. T. and Richard Giulianotti (eds), *Football Culture: Local Contests, Global Visions*, London & Portland, OR: Frank Cass, 2000.
Fishwick, Nicholas, *English Football and Society: 1910–1950*, Manchester: Manchester University Press, 1989.
Forbes, Geraldine, *Women in Modern India*, paperback edition, Cambridge: Cambridge University Press, 1998.
Giulianotti, Richard, *Football: A Sociology of the Global Game*, Cambridge: Polity Press, 1999.
Giulianotti, R., N. Bonney and M. Hepworth (eds), *Football, Violence and Social Identity*, London: Routledge, 1994.
Ghosh, Niranjan, *Role of Women in the Freedom Movement in Bengal, 1919–47: Midnapore*, Kolkata: Firma KLM, 1988.
Gordon, M. M., *Assimilations in American Life: The Role of Race, Religion and National Origins*, New York: Oxford University Press, 1964.
Gordon, Leonard, *Bengal: The Nationalist Movement, 1876–1940*, New York: Columbia University Press, 1974.
Gramsci, Antonio, *Selection from the Prison Notebooks*, trans. and ed. by Quinton Hoare and Geoffrey Nowell Smith, New York: International Publishers, 1971.
Guha, Ramachandra, *A Corner of a Foreign Field: The Indian History of a British Sport*, Delhi: Picador, 2002.

Gunder Frank, Andre, *Capitalism and Underdevelopment in Latin America*, New York: Monthly Review Press, 1967.
Guttmann, Allen, *Games and Empires: Modern Sports and Cultural Imperialism*, New York: Columbia University Press, 1994.
Hignell, Andrew, *Rain Stops Play: Cricketing Climates*, London: Frank Cass, 2003.
Hobsbawm Eric and Terence Ranger (eds), *The Invention of Tradition*, Cambridge: Cambridge University Press, 1983.
Holt, Richard, *Sport and the British: A Modern History*, Oxford: Oxford University Press, 1989.
Hopcraft, A., *The Football Man*, London: Simon and Schuster, 1988.
Hutchins, Francis, *Illusion of Permanence: British Imperialism in India*, Princeton: Princeton University Press, 1967.
Hyam, Robert, *Britain's Imperial Century, 1851–1914*, London: Macmillan, 1976.
Ingham, R. (ed.), *Football Hooliganism: The Wider Context*, London: Inter Action Imprint, 1978.
Jeffrey, Robin (ed.), *People, Princes and Paramount Power: Society and Politics in the Indian Princely States*, Delhi: Oxford University Press, 1978.
Mandle, R. Jay and Joan D. Mandle, *Grass Roots Commitment: Basketball and Society in Trinidad and Tobago*, Parkersburg, Iowa: Caribbean Books, 1988.
Majumdar, Boria and J. A. Mangan, (eds), *Sport in South Asian Society: Past and Present*. London: Routledge, 2005.
Majumdar, Boria and Kausik Bandyopadhyay, *Goalless: The Story of a Unique Footballing Nation*, New Delhi: Penguin/Viking, 2006.
Majumdar, Boria, *Once Upon a Furore: Lost Pages of Indian Cricket*, New Delhi: Yoda Press, 2004.
———, *Twenty-Two Years to Freedom: A Social History of Indian Cricket*, New Delhi: Penguin/Viking, 2004.
Mangan, J. A., *Athleticism in Victorian and Edwardian Public School: The Emergence and Consolidation of an Educational Ideology*, Cambridge: Cambridge University Press, 1981 and London: Frank Cass, 2000 (with a new introduction).
——— (ed.), *The Cultural Bond: Sport, Empire, Society*, London: Frank Cass, 1992.
———, *The Games Ethic and Imperialism: Aspects of the Diffusion of an Ideal*, London: Frank Cass, 1998.
Mangan J. A. and Andrew Ritchie (eds), *Ethnicity, Sport, Identity: Struggle for Status*, London: Frank Cass, 2003.
Mcpherson, Kenneth, *The Muslim Microcosm: Calcutta, 1918–1935*, Wiesbaden: Franz Steinar Verlag, 1974.
Metcalf, Thomas R., *The Aftermath of Revolt: India 1857–1870*, Princeton: Princeton University Press, 1964.
Mitra, Soumen, *In Search of an Identity: History of Football in Colonial Calcutta*, Kolkata: Dasgupta & Co., 2006.
Momen, Humaira, *Muslim Politics in Bengal: A Study of Krishak Praja Party and the Elections of 1937*, Dacca: Sunny House, 1972.

Morrow, Ann, *The Maharajas of India*, London: Grafton Books, 1986.
Mukherjee, Kumar, *The Story of Football*, New Delhi: Publications Division, Ministry of Information and Broadcasting, Government of India, 2002.
Mukherjee, S. N., *Calcutta: Myths and History*, Calcutta: Subarnarekha, 1977.
———, *Citizen Historian: Explorations in Historiography*, Delhi: Manohar, 1996.
Nandy, Ashis, *The Intimate Enemy: Loss and Recovery of Self under Colonialism*, Oxford: Oxford University Press, 1983.
———, *The Tao of Cricket: On Games of Destiny and the Destiny of Games*, London: Viking, 1989.
Phadnis, Urmila, *Ethnicity and Nation-Building in South Asia*, New Delhi: Sage Publications, 1990.
Rahman, Hossainur, *Hindu-Muslim Relations in Bengal, 1905–1947: Study in Cultural Confrontation*, Bombay: Nachiketa Publications, 1974.
Rao, C. V. H., *Civil Disobedience Movement in India: Or, The Indian Struggle for Freedom*, Chandigarh: Lion Press, 1946.
Ray, Rajat Kanta, *Social Conflict and Political Unrest in Bengal: 1875–1927*, Delhi: Oxford University Press, 1984.
Rodrigues, Mario, *Batting for the Empire: A Political Biography of Ranjitsinhji*, New Delhi: Penguin, 2003.
Said, Edward W., *Culture and Imperialism*, New York: Knopf, 1993.
Sarkar, Sumit, *Swadeshi Movement in Bengal, 1903–1908*, New Delhi: People's Publishing House, 1973.
———, *Modern India: 1885–1947*, Madras: Macmillan India Ltd, 1983.
———, *Writing Social History*, New Delhi: Oxford University Press, 1997.
Sen, Shila, *Muslim Politics in Bengal: 1937–1947*, New Delhi: Impex India, 1976.
Sharma, Radha Krishna, *Nationalism, Social Reform and Indian Women: A Study of the Interaction between Our National Movement and the Movement of Social Reform among Indian Women, 1921–1937*, Delhi: Janaki Prakashan, 1981.
Siddiqui, M. K. A., *Muslims of Calcutta: A Study in Aspects of their Social Organization*, Calcutta: Anthropological Survey of India, 1974.
Sinha, Mrinalini, *Colonial Masculinity: The 'Manly Englishman' and the 'Effeminate Bengali' in the Late Nineteenth Century*, Manchester: Manchester University Press, 1995.
Sinha, Pradip, *Calcutta in Urban History*, Calcutta: Firma KLM, 1978.
Stein, Burton, *A History of India*, Oxford: Blackwell, 1998.
Taneja, Anup, *Gandhi, Women, and the National Movement, 1920–47*, New Delhi: Har Anand, 2005.
Thapar-Bjorkert, Suruchi, *Women in the Indian National Movement: Unseen Faces and Unheard Voices, 1930–42*, paperback edition, New Delhi: Sage, 2006.
Thompson, Edward, *The Making of the Indian Princes*, London: Curzon Press, 1978.
Tomlinson, John, *Cultural Imperialism*, Baltimore: Johns Hopkins University Press, 1991.
Vassili, Phil, *The First Black Footballer*, London, Frank Cass, 1998.
Williams, John, Eric Dunning and Patrick Murphy (eds), *Hooligans Abroad*, London: Routledge, 1984.

In Bengali

Bandopadhyay, Prasun, *Football Ghorana: Biplab o Bibartan* (Football Tradition: Revolution and Evolution), Calcutta: Pratibhas, 1989.

Bandopadhyay, Shantipriya, *Cluber Naam East Bengal* (The Name of the Club is East Bengal), Calcutta: New Bengal Press, 1979.

———, *Cluber Naam Mohun Bagan* (The Name of the Club is Mohun Bagan), Calcutta: New Bengal Press, 1979.

———, *Football*, Calcutta: Dey's, 1985.

———, *Khelar Raja Football* (Football, the King of Sports), Calcutta: Jnanthirthho, 1983.

———, *Sera Khelar Golpo* (Best Sports Stories), Kolkata: Bijayan Prakashani, 2001.

Banerjee, Upendra Krishna, *Karnel Suresh Bishvas* (Cornel Suresh Biswas), Calcutta: 1900.

Basu, Ajay, *Footbale Dikpal* (Pioneers in Football), Calcutta: Mandal Book House, 1980.

———, *Maidaner Nayak* (Heroes of Maidan), Calcutta: Mandal Book House, 1980.

Bhattacharya, Ashok, *Footbaler Tin Pradhan* (Three Major Teams of Football), Calcutta: Gyantirtha, 1972.

Bhattacharyya, Karuna Shankar, *Bideshe Mohun Bagan* (Mohun Bagan in Foreign land), Calcutta: Prabartak Publishers, 1964.

Bhattacharjee, Nimai, *Footballar*, Calcutta: Dey's, 1993.

Chakraborty, Kamakhya Prasad, *Sekaler Jalpaiguri Sahar ebong Samajik Jibaner Kichhu Kotha* (The Town of Jalpaiguri of That Age and Some Aspects of Social Life), Jalpaiguri: Chakraborty Paribar, 2004.

Chakraborty, Manas (ed.), *Amal Dutta*, Kolkata: Deep, 2002.

———, *Mohun Bagan East Bengal Reshareshi* (Mohun Bagan-East Bengal Conflict), Kolkata: Deep Prokashon, 2008.

———, *Shotabdir Sera Sailen Manna* (Sailen Manna, the Best of the Century), Kolkata: Sristi, 1999.

Chirakaaler Mohun Bagan Prokashona Committee, *Chirakaaler Mohun Bagan* (Mohun Bagan For Ever), Kolkata: Amal Kumar Sen, 2003.

Chiranjib (Chitta Biswas), *Bharatiya Football* (Indian Football), Calcutta: Gyantirtha, 1967.

———, *Footbaler Tin Raja* (Three Kings of Football), Calcutta: Biswabani Prakashani, 1975.

———, *Khelar Maather Antarale* (Beyond the Sports-field), Calcutta: Nabapatra, 1973.

Dasgupta, Asoke, *Khelar Shat* (Sixties of Sport), Calcutta: Deep, 2000.

Dutta, Jayanta, *Footbller Mahanayak Gostho Paul* (Gostho Paul: The Great Hero of Football), Calcutta: Anima Prakashani, 1986.

———, *Victorious Mohunbagan*, Calcutta: Sahitya Prakash, 1979.

———, *Glorious East Bengal*, Calcutta: Sahitya Prakash, 1975.

Ghosh, Birendranath, *Bangalir Bahubal* (Physical Valour of the Bengalis), Calcutta, 1932.

Ghosh, Shukharanjan, *Bharatiya Footballe Tin Protidvandi* (Three Main Competitors of Calcutta Football), Calcutta: Manju Prakashani, 1986.
Ghosh, Siddhartha (ed.), *Khela aar Khela* (Sport and Sport), Calcutta: Ananda, 1994.
Ghosh, Sourindra Kumar, *Kridasamrat Nagendra Prasad Sarvadhikari* (Nagendra Prasad Sarvadhikari: The King of Sports), Calcutta: N. P. Sarvadhikari.Memorial Committee, 1963.
Kumar, Sibram (ed.), *Mohunbagan Omnibus*, Calcutta: Prabhabati Prakashani, 1983.
—— (ed.), *RB Rachita Kolkatar Football* (Calcutta's Football written by RB), Kolkata: Prabhabati Prakashani, 2002.
—— (ed.), *Sonar Freme Mohun Bagan 1911* (Mohun Bagan 1911 in Golden Frame), Kolkata: Prabhabati Prakashani, 2007.
Mitra, Shanta, *Sanghat o Sangharsha: Rajniti ebong Football* (Conflict and Battle: Politics and Football), Kolkata: Saroj Publications, 2005.
Mukherjee, Hirendranath, *Nirbachita Probondho* (Selected Essays), vol. 1, Kolkata: Mitra & Ghosh, 1998.
Nandy, Paresh, *East Bengal Club, 1920–1970: 50 Bochhorer Sangram o Safalya* (East Bengal Club, 1920–1970: Fifty Years' Struggle and Achievements), Calcutta: Bichitra, 1973.
——, *Mohun Bagan 1911*, Calcutta: Karuna Prakashani, 1976.
Pandit Mashai (Ramesh Chandra Goswami), *East Bengal Cluber Itihas* (History of the East Bengal Club), Calcutta: Book Garden, 1963.
Ray, Kali, *Howrah Jelar Football Khelar Itikatha* (History of Football in Howrah District), Calcutta: Bharati Book Stall, 1985.
RB (Rakhal Bhattacharya), *Kolkatar Football* (Calcutta's Football), Calcutta: East Light Book House, 1955.
Ritan, Lutfar Rahman, *Football*. Dacca: Bangla Academy, 1985.
Saha, Rupak, *Chinese Wall*, Calcutta: Hemlata Prakashani, 1979.
——, *Ekadashe Suryodoy* (Sun-Rise in 1911), Calcutta: Karuna Prakashani, 1990.
——, *Itihase East Bengal* (East Bengal in History), Calcutta: Deep, 2000.
——, *Pancha Pandav* (Five Pandavas), Calcutta: Karuna Prakasahni, 1991.
Sen, Asoke (ed.), *Kishor Golpo Khela* (Sports Stories for Adolescents), Calcutta: Dey's Publishing, 1998.
Sen, Sachin, *Kheladhular Bichitra Kahini* (Peculiar Stories of Games and Sports), Calcutta: R. M. Gupta/Geetanjali Book Centre, 1983.

Articles

In English

Alter, J, '*Kabaddi*, a National Sport of India: The Internationalism of Nationalism and the Foreignness of Indianness", in N. Dyck (ed.), *Games, Sports and Cultures*, Oxford: Berg, 2000.
Appadurai, Arjun, 'Playing with Modernity: The Decolonization of Indian Cricket', in C. A. Breckenridge (ed.), *Consuming Modernity: Public Culture in a South Asian World*, Minneapolis, MN: University of Minnesota Press, 1995.

Arbena, Joseph L., 'Sport and Revolution: The Continuing Cuban Experience', *Studies in Latin American Popular Culture*, vol. 9 (1990): 319–28.

———, 'The Diffusion of Modern European Sport in Latin America: A Case Study of Cultural Imperialism', *South Eastern Latin Americanist*, vol. 33, no. 4, March 1990.

Bandyopadhyay, Kausik, 'Race, Nation and Sport: Footballing Nationalism in Colonial Calcutta', *Soccer and Society*, vol. 4, no. 1, 2003, pp. 1–19.

———, '1911 in Retrospect: A Revisionist Perspective on a Famous Indian Sporting Victory', in J. A. Mangan and Boria Majumdar (eds), *Sport in South Asian Society: Past and Present, The International Journal of the History of Sport*, vol. 21, nos 3–4, 2004, pp. 363–83.

Bhowmik, Sushanta Kumar, 'Calcutta Football, Akashbani and Bengali Nostalgia', *90 Minutes*, vol. 1, no. 3, July–September 2009.

Cabral, Amilcar, 'National Liberation and Culture', *Transition*, no. 45, 1974, 12–17.

Cashman, Richard, 'Cricket and Colonialism: Colonial Hegemony and Indigenous Subversion', in J. A. Mangan (ed.), *Pleasure, Profit, Proselytism: British Culture and Sport at Home and Abroad, 1700–1914*, London: Frank Cass, 1988.

Chowdhury-Sengupta, I., 'The Effeminate and the Masculine: Nationalism and the Concept of Race in Colonial Bengal', in Peter Robb (ed.), *The Concept of Race in South Asia*, Oxford: Oxford University Press, 1995.

Dimeo, Paul. '"Team Loyalty Splits the City into Two": Football, Ethnicity and Rivalry in Calcutta', in G. Armstrong and R. Giulianotti (eds), *Fear and Loathing in World Football*, Oxford: Berg, 2001.

———, 'Colonial Bodies, Colonial Sport: "Martial" Punjabis, "Effeminate" Bengalis and the Development of Indian Football', *The International Journal of the History of Sport*, vol. 19, no. 1, March 2002, pp. 72–90.

———, 'Football and Politics in Bengal: Colonialism, Nationalism, Communalism', in Paul Dimeo and James Mills (eds), *Soccer in South Asia: Empire, Nation, Diaspora*, London: Frank Cass, 2001.

———, '"With Political Pakistan in the Offing …": Football and Communal Politics in South Asia, 1887–1947', *Journal of Contemporary History*, vol. 38, no. 3, July 2003, pp. 377–94.

Francis, E. K., 'The Nature of Ethnic Groups', *American Journal of Sociology*, vol. 52, no. 5, March 1947, pp. 393–400.

Galtung, Johan, 'The Sport System as a Metaphor for the World System', in Fernand Landry, Marc Landry and Magdeleine Yerles (eds), *Sport: The Third Millennium*, Sainte-Foye: Presses de l'Universite Laval, 1991.

Gooptu, Sharmishtha, 'Celluloid Soccer: the Peculiarities of Soccer in Bengali Cinema', *The International Journal of the History of Sport*, vol. 22, no. 4, July 2005, pp. 689–98.

Gruneau, Richard, 'The Critique of Sport in Modernity', in Eric G. Dunning, Joseph A. Maguire and Robert E. Pearton (eds), *The Sports Process*, Champaign: Human Kinetics, 1993.

Guha, Ramachandra, 'Cricket and Politics in Colonial India', *Past and Present*, vol. 161, no. 1, November 1998, pp. 155–90.

Habib, Irfan, 'Civil Disobedience, 1930–31'. *Social Scientist*, vol. 25, nos 9–10, September–October 1997, pp. 43–66.

Kapadia, Novy, 'The Story of Indian Football, 1889–2000', in Paul Dimeo and James Mills (eds), *Soccer in South Asia: Empire, Nation, Diaspora*, London: Frank Cass, 2002.

Klein, Alan, 'Baseball as Underdevelopment: The Political Economy of Sport in the Dominican Republic', *Sociology of Sport Journal*, vol. 6, no. 2, June 1989, pp. 95–112.

Kudaisya, Gyanesh, 'Divided Landscapes, Fragmented Identities: East Bengal Refugees and their Rehabilitation in India, 1947–79', in D. A. Low and Howard Brasted (eds), *Freedom, Trauma and Continuities: Northern India and Independence*, New Delhi: Sage, 1998.

Leitao, Noel da Lima, 'Goan football has little cause to look back', in *The Grass is Green in Goa: 40 Years Yield a Lot of Goals*, Panjim: Goa Football Association, 2000.

Maguire, Joseph, 'Globalization, Sport and National Identities: "The Empire Strikes Back"', *Loisir et Societe*, vol. 16, no. 2, Autumn 1993.

Majumdar, Boria. 'Imperial Tool "For" Nationalist Resistance: The "Games Ethic" in Indian History', *The International Journal of the History of Sport*, vol. 21, nos 3/4, 2004, pp. 377–98.

———, 'On a Political Pitch', *Biblio — A Review of Books*, vol. 8, nos 7–8, 2003, pp. 21–22.

———, 'Politics of Leisure in Colonial India — *Lagaan*: Invocaion of Lost History', *Culture, Sport, Society*, vol. 5, no. 2, 2002, pp. 29–44.

———, 'The Politics of Soccer in Colonial India, 1930–37: The Years of Turmoil', *Soccer and Society*, vol. 3, no. 1, 2002, pp. 22–36.

———, 'The Vernacular in Sports History', *Economic and Political Weekly*, vol. 37, no. 29, 20 July 2002, pp. 3069–75.

Mangan, J. A. 'Eton in India: The Careful creation of Oriental Englishmen', in J. A. Mangan, *The Games Ethic and Imperialism: Aspects of the Diffusion of an Ideal*, London: Frank Cass, 1998.

———, 'Introduction', in J. A. Mangan (ed.), *Pleasure, Profit, Proselytism: British Culture and Sport at Home and Abroad: 1700–1914*, London: Frank Cass, 1988.

———, 'Soccer as Moral Training: Missionary Intentions and Imperial Legacies', in Paul Dimeo and James Mills (eds), *Soccer in South Asia: Empire, Nation, Diaspora*, London: Frank Cass, 2001.

Mason, Tony, 'Football on the Maidan: Cultural Imperialism in Calcutta', in J. A. Mangan (ed.), *The Cultural Bond: Sport, Empire, Society*, London: Frank Cass, 1992.

Mitra, Nabanita, 'All India Radio: Politics and Culture', in Kausik Bandyopadhyay (ed.), *Asia Annual 2008: Understanding Popular Culture*, New Delhi: Manohar, 2010.

Mitra, Soumen, 'Babu at Play: Sporting Nationalism in Bengal, 1880–1911', in Nisith Ray and Ranjit Roy (eds), *Bengal: Yesterday and Today*, Calcutta: Papyrus, 1991.

Mookerjee, Surapriya, 'Early Decades of Calcutta Football', in *An Economic Times Special Feature: Calcutta 300*, Calcutta: Bennett and Coleman and Co Ltd, 1990.

Nandy, Moti, 'Calcutta Soccer', in Sukanta Chaudhuri (ed.), *Calcutta: The Living City, 2: The Present and Future*, Calcutta: Oxford University Press, 1990.

———, trans. Shampa Banerjee, 'Football and Nationalism', in Geeti Sen (ed.), *The Calcutta Psyche*, New Delhi: India International Centre, 1990.

Perkin, Harold, 'Teaching the Nations How to Play: Sport and Society in the British Empire and Commonwealth', *The International Journal of the History of Sport*, vol. 6, no. 2, Sept. 1989, pp. 145–55.

Plamenatz, John, 'Two Types of Nationalism', in Eugene Kamenka (ed.), *Nationalism: The Nature and Evolution of an Idea*, London: Edward Arnold, 1976.

Ray, Somshankar, '"The Kindred Points of Heaven and Home": Kolkata Football in Bangla Fiction and Critique', *90 Minutes*, vol. 1, no. 1, January 2009, pp. 73–74.

Rosselli, John, 'The Self-Image of Effeteness: Physical Education and Nationalism in Nineteenth-Century Bengal', *Past and Present*, vol. 86, no. 1, 1980, pp. 121–48.

Sarkar, Sumit, 'The Logic of Gandhian Nationalism: Civil Disobedience and the Gandhi-Irwin Pact, 1930-31', *Indian Historical Review*, vol. 3, pp. 114–48, July 1976.

Sarkar, Tanika, 'Communal Riots in Bengal', in Mushirul Haasan (ed.), *Communal and Pan-Islamic Trends in Colonial India*, New Delhi: Manohar, 1985.

Sen, Asit Kumar, 'Glimpses of College History', in *Scottish Church College Ter Jubilee Commemoration Volume*, Calcutta: Scottish Church College, 1980.

Stoddart, Brian, 'Sport, Cultural Imperialism, and Colonial Response in the British Empire', *Comparative Studies in Society and History*, vol. 30, no. 4, 1988, pp. 649–73.

Walvin, James, 'Sport, Social History and the Historian', *The British Journal of Sports History*, vol. 1, no.1, 1984, pp. 5–13.

Zagoria, Donald S., 'The Social Bases of Indian Communism', in Richard Lowenthal (ed.), *Issues in the Future of Asia: Communist and Non-Communist Alternatives*, London: Pall Mall, 1969, pp. 97–124.

In Bengali

Badruddin, S. M., 'Nadia-r Kheladhulo — Atit o Bartaman' (Games and Sports in Nadia), *Paschimbanga*, Special Number on Nadia District, 1997.

Bhowmik, Susanta Kumar, 'Swadhinata-uttar pashchim bange betar jagater itibritta' (History of the Radio World in Post-Independence West Bengal), in Rahul Roy (ed.), *Paschim Banga: Phire Dekha*, Chinsurah: Pratiti, 2003.

Biswas, Niraj, 'Khelay Cooch Behar' (Coochbehar in Sports), *Madhuparni*, Special Number on Cooch Behar, 1989.

Mahalanbis, Jiten, 'Khelar Maathe' (On the Sports-field), in C. C. Sanyal et al. (eds), *Jalpaiguri District Centenary Volume: 1869–1968*, Jalpaiguri, 1970.

Majumdar, Swapan, 'Kheladhulay Paschim Dinajpur' (West Dinajpur in Games and Sports), *Madhuparni*, West Dinajpur District Number, 1992–93.

Moulik, Tathagata, 'Hoogly Jelar Oitihyapurna Kheladhulo' (Traditional Sports of Hoogly District), *Paschimbanga*, Special Number on Hoogly, 1998.

Musa, Mansur, 'Ghoti-Bangal er Birodh Nispatti' (Resolving the Ghoti-Bangal Conflict), in Nitish Biswas and Mukulesh Biswas (eds), *Banga Sanskritir Sanhatir Oitihya* (Tradition of Cohesion in Bengali Culture), Kolkata: Oikotan Gobeshona Samsad, 1995, pp. 235–42.

Prasad, Bhabani, 'Harano Din: Kheladhular Itibritta', (Lost Days: Chronicles of Games and Sports), *Uttaradhikar Balurghat, Dadhichi*, Special Issue, 2000–2001.

Saha, Rupak, 'Bangalir Football' (Bengalis' Football), *Desh*, 28 August 1993, pp. 21–23.

Sengupta, Tanaji, 'Nirapade Bhinna Clube' (Safely in other clubs), *Desh* (Binodon sankhya), 1988, pp. 184–89.

Unpublished Theses

Majumdar, Boria, 'Cricket in Colonial India, 1780–1947', D. Phil dissertation, Oxford University, 2004.

Mitra, Soumen, 'Nationalism, Communalism and Sub-regionalism: A Study of Football in Bengal, 1880–1950', M. Phil Dissertation, Centre for Historical Studies, Jawaharlal Nehru University, 1988.

Shil, Amrita Kumar, 'Cultural Diffusion and Popular Adoption of Modern Sports in Northern Bengal: A Case Study of the Districts of Darjeeling, Cooch Behar and Jalpaiguri in the Colonial Period', M. Phil Dissertation, Department of History, University of North Bengal, 2004–2005.

Websites

www.kolkatafootball.com
www.indianfootball.com
www.mohunbaganac.com
www.eastbengalfootballclub.com
www.the-aiff.com

About the Author

Kausik Bandyopadhyay teaches history at West Bengal State University, Barasat, India. He is Associate Editor, *Soccer and Society*, Routledge. He has previously taught at Kidderpore College, Kolkata and at the Department of History, University of North Bengal.

He was also Fellow, International Olympic Museum, Lausanne. A former Fellow of the Maulana Abul Kalam Azad Institute of Asian Studies, Kolkata, he is the author of *Playing for Freedom: A Historic Sports Victory* (2008) and *Playing Off the Field: Explorations in the History of Sport* (2007); co-author of *Goalless: The Story of a Unique Footballing Nation* (2006); editor of *Why Minorities Play or Don't Play Soccer: A Global Exploration* (2010) and *Modernities in Asian Perspective* (2010); issue editor of *Asia Annual 2008: Understanding Popular Culture* (2010); and co-editor of *Fringe Nations in World Soccer* (2008) and *Sikkim's Tryst with Nathu La: What Awaits India's East and Northeast?* (2009). He has also published several articles in national and international journals.

Index

Adi Arya Saraswat Samaj 88
'age of consent' controversy (1891) 29
Akashbani Kolkata 254
akhras 28, 140
Ali, Maulana Mohammed 82, 112
All India Council of Sports 147
All India Federal Council 153, 154, 156, 157
All India Football Association (AIFA) 18, 144, 145, 156, 158; formation of 148–52
All Indian Football Federation (AIFF) 145, 147, 148, 154, 165, 166; formation of 161–64
All India Radio 254, 257
Amal Dutta (Chakraborty) 248, 249
Amrita Bazar Patrika 69, 73, 89, 90, 95, 96, 171, 194, 216, 222, 229; editorial after Mohun Bagan's IFA Shield victory in 1911 270–71
Ananta Sporting Club 52
Anderson, Benedict 103; theory of 'imagined communities' 63
Anglo-Indian press 69, 76–78
Anglo-Saxon sports 28
anti-colonial nationalism 13, 79, 107
anti-Partition movement (1905–8) 40, 57, 64
Army Sports Control Board (ASCB) of India 18, 143, 145, 147, 158; correspondence with Indian Football Association 283–85; role of 152–57
Aryan Club 40, 46, 48, 94, 98, 136, 164, 178–80, 190, 219, 222, 226, 232, 238, 239

Ashray (film) 15, 259

Back Centre (Sengupta) 248
Bagbazar Club 83
Balurghat High School 52
Bandopadhyay, Santipriya: *Cluber Naam Mohun Bagan* 242, *Cluber Naam East Bengal* 244; *Goal* 253; *Offside* 253
Bangladesh War (1971) 203
Basu, Ajay 248, 255–57
Basumati 76, 80
Bengal: anti-Partition movement 40, 57, 64; development of vernacular sports journalism in 86; football and communalism in 137–42; football and nationalist politics in 96–101; footballing nationalism 101–7; partition of 64, 67, 172; pent-up nationalism 102; renaissance 19; self-image of effeteness 26–30; transition from physical culture to football culture 26–30
Bengal Congress Provincial Committee 97
Bengalee, The 89
Bengal Football Association 136, 183, 245
Bengal football culture 6, 123; adoption and social adaptation 42–48; changing facets of 234–35; communalisation of 13; European discrimination against 92–95; and evolution of spectator culture 214–34; first matches and earliest clubs 30–32; and Hindu–Muslim

Index

relations 122; and live commentary of matches on radio in post-colonial West Bengal 253–57; local factors influencing growth of 48–53; racialism and nationalism 91–96; and social struggle of national liberation 101–7; and stadium imbroglio 206–14; Swadeshi Movement and 64–68; transition from nationalist force to communal identity 17
Bengali fiction, and Indian football 249–53; *see also* vernacular football literature, heritage of
Bengali soccer: clubs in colonial India 63, 83; journalistic and popular writings on 247–49; *see also* Bengal football culture
Bharatbarsha (Bengali periodical) 138, 139
Bharatiya Footballe Tin Protidvandi (Ghosh) 247
Bhattacharjee, Karuna Shankar 242
Bhattacharjee, Nimai 253
Bhattacharya, Ashok 247
Bhattacharyya, Subrata 192
Bideshe Mohun Bagan (Bhattacharjee) 242
Bihar Olympic Association 147
'Bodyline' series 4
Bombay Chronicle 210
Bombay Football Association 146
Boys' Club 34
Brabourne Cup 136, 183, 245
Brabourne League 136
British Football Association 145, 152, 166
British Journal of Sports History (1984) 1, 2
British missionaries, role in popularisation of soccer in India 22–25
British Raj 20, 24, 54, 78
British rule after 1857, 'orientalisation' of 20

Cabral, Amilcar 57, 106
Cadet Cup 92
Calcutta football 6, 205, 239; first matches and earliest clubs 30–32; Muslim representation in 108–12
Calcutta Football Club (1872) 31, 38, 49, 65, 66, 93, 110, 207, 212, 254
Calcutta Football League 11, 17, 90, 92, 98, 114, 116–18, 123–24, 133, 142, 177, 179, 182, 187, 228, 245, 258
Calcutta Monthly 109–11
Calcutta Referees Association (CRA) 101, 226, 228
Calcutta riots (1946) 140, 210
Campbell, Sir George 28–29
Carr, E. H. 6–7
Cashman, Richard 104–5
Celtic Football Club 122–24
Chakrabarty, Prafulla 189
Chakraborty, Manas 248
Chatterjee, Nirmal Kumar 140
Chatterjee, Partha 103
Chatterji, Joya 126
Chiefs Colleges 20, 23
Chinese Wall (Saha) 248
Chinsurah Sporting 48, 83
Chinsurah Town Club 98
Chirakaaler Mohun Bagan 242
Civil Disobedience movement (1929–31) 96, 98, 101, 148
club conflict in Calcutta football 13, 18, 83, 113
Cluber Naam East Bengal (Bandopadhyay) 244
Cluber Naam Mohun Bagan (Bandopadhyay) 242
colonial Indian sports 8, 238
commentary of matches on radio, in post-colonial West Bengal 253–57
Communal Award (1932) 126, 138
communal riots 141
Compas 240
Comrade, The 82, 111–12

Coochbehar Cup 41, 45, 47, 51, 65, 92, 110, 175, 182, 240
Crescent Club 41, 109
cricket in colonial India 6
cultural hegemony: concept of 60; Gramscian notion of 61
cultural imperialism 10, 16, 17, 59–62, 69, 77, 104, 106
cultural indigenisation, of soccer 53–56
cultural nationalism 17, 57, 83, 104, 106, 108, 202
Curzon, Lord 20

Dalbadaler Aage (Nandy) 253
Dalhousie Athletic Club 31, 49
Dalhousie Club of Calcutta 31, 38
Das, Paltu 246
Datta, Amal 195, 248
Delhi Football Association 159
Derson, Peter 259
Dhaka Mohammedan Sporting Club 121
Dhanyi Meye (film) 15, 258, 259
Diamond Jubilee Reading Room 110
Dimeo, Paul 12, 143–44, 165, 168, 173, 181, 195, 196
Doordarshan 257
Durand Cup 12, 92, 187
Dutta, Jayanta 242, 244, 248

East Bengal Club 11, 91, 118, 239; origin and growth of 174–81; rivalry with Mohun Bagan club 13, 168–74, 182, 196–98, 246; sporting histories depicted in literature 244–47; *see also* Ghoti-Bangal rivalry
East Bengal Cluber Itihas (Goswami) 244
East Bengal Club: Ponchas Bochhorer Sangram o Safalya, 1920–70 (Nandy) 244
East Bengaler Chhele (film) 259
East India Company 30
East Punjab Football Association 147

East Surrey Regiment 38
East York Regiments 16, 17, 41, 48, 71
Eden Gardens, Calcutta 16, 213, 230, 254
Ekadashe Suryoday (Saha) 241
Ellenboroguh Course 213
Elliot Shield 67, 68, 92, 240
Empire, The 77
Englishman, The 31, 69, 78, 79, 208, 215
ethnic group, definition and components of 169
European Cup 122

Federation Cup 193, 195, 230, 231
Federation Internationale de Football Association (FIFA) 165, 199
Ferari (Nandy) 253
First Division Football League 39, 50, 94, 113, 116, 177–78, 240
'Five Pandavas' of Indian football 186, 245
Footbale Dikpal (Basu) 248
Footbaler Tin Pradhan (Bhattacharya) 247
Footbaler Tin Raja (Chiranjib) 247
football: and Bengali fiction 249–53; boot *vs.* barefoot 53–56; communalisation of 13, 96, 108; and communalism in Bengal 137–42; cultural indigenisation of 53; in culture of 20th-century India 2; games ethic 19–25; historiography of, in India 7–15; local factors for growth of football in Bengal 48–53; Mohammedan Sporting Club and representation of Muslim community 41, 108–12; and national consciousness 64–68; in performing arts 257–60; popularisation of 22–23; regional politics 143, 164–66; role of British missionaries 22–24; role of Nagendra Prasad Sarvadhikari in popularising 32–42; socio-historical development

Index ✦ 311

in Bengal 10; socio-political issues 19–25
Football (play) 259
Footballar (Bhattacharjee) 253
Football Association (FA) of England 18, 143, 149, 158–61; correspondence with Indian Football Association 281–82
football culture, in Bengal 15–18
Football Culture: Local Contests, Global Visions (Finn and Giulianotti) 167
footballers, in commercial advertisements 279–80
Football Federation Conference 155
football grounds, development of 199–206, 276
footballing communalism 13, 96, 108, 137–42
football rivalry in West Bengal, influence of partition of India and refugee influx on 184–90
football tournament in India 37–38
Footbller Mahanayak Gostho Paul (Dutta) 248
Frank, Andre Gunder, theories of 'development of dependency' 60
Friends Club 35, 37

Gallery (Bengali periodical) 240
gambling 71, 90
games ethic, concept of 19–25
Ganguly, Manmatha 45, 54
Ghera Maath Chhorano Gallery (Dutta) 248
Ghosh, Kumar 248
Ghosh, Shukharanjan 247
Ghoti-Bangal rivalry 13, 167, 203, 219, 255; club rivalry 191–93; on football field 181–84; social aspects of 168–74; tragedy of 16 August 1980 193–95, 230
Ghuznavi, Abdul Halim 119
Gladstone Cup 48, 65
Glorious East Bengal (Dutta) 244
Goal (Bandopadhyay) 253

Goalless: The Story of a Unique Footballing Nation 13
Gooptu, Sharmishtha 15, 259
Goswami, Chuni 248
Goswami, Ramesh Chandra 244
Government of India Act (1935) 126
Gramscian theory of cultural hegemony 61
Guha, J. C. 210
Guha, Ramachandra 3, 80, 262
Gupta, Pankaj 226

Hamidia Club 41, 109
Hare School 32–34, 35
Harwood League 88, 146
Hercules Cup 176
Hindu Code Bill 212
Hindu Mahasabha 138, 140
Hindu Mela 28–29
Hobsbawm, Eric 1
Howrah Sporting Club 48
Hurtebize, Claude 58
Hyderabad Football Association 146

Ilbert Bill (1883–84) 29
Indian Football Association (IFA) 13, 17, 38–39, 92, 98, 108, 118, 143, 161, 209, 239, 245, 256; *vs.* AIFA 152–57; conflict with Mohammedan Sporting Club 125–37; correspondence with Army Sports Control Board 283–85; correspondence with Football Association, England 281–82
Indian Football Association (IFA) Shield 16, 17, 39, 69, 92, 125, 176; history of 272–74
Indian Football League of Bombay 152
Indian National Congress 148, 164
Indian Railways Athletic Association 147
Itihase East Bengal (Saha) 244

Jalpaiguri Town Club 51

Jorabagan Club 175
Jotodin Banchi (Datta) 248
Jubilee Club 41, 109

kabaddi 8
Kallol Yug (Sengupta) 94, 217
Karnataka Football Association. *See* Mysore Football Association
Khelte Khelte (Goswami) 248
Kingfisher East Bengal 247
Kolkatar Football (RB) 237–41
Kridasamrat Nagendra Prasad Sarvadhikari (Ghosh) 248
Kumar, Sibram 241, 242
Kumudini Cup 50

lady picketers: and nationalist politics in colonial Bengal 96–101; political boycott of 96
Lakshibilas Cup 65, 66
London War Office 163, 166

Maath Theke Bolchhi (Basu) 248
Macaulay Minute (1835) 20
Macaulay, Thomas 26
Madras Football Association 146
Maidaner Nayak (Basu) 248
Maitra, J. C. 152
Majumdar, Boria 3, 105, 153, 163, 166
Majumdar, Dukhiram. *See* Majumdar, Oomesh Chandra
Majumdar, Oomesh Chandra 45–46
Mallick, Ganen 73, 216
Mangan, J. A. 11, 12, 21–23, 104, 105, 199
Masik Basumati (Bengali periodical) 240
Mason, Tony 8, 10, 21, 69, 76, 81, 86, 93, 104
Mills, James 143, 145, 165
Minto Fete Tournament 65, 66
Mitra, Dinabandhu 170
mob-violence. *See* spectator culture, evolution of
modern sports, cultural imperialism and colonial response to 58–64
Mohammedan Sporting Club 13, 90, 186, 190, 228; conflict with IFA 125–37; decline since independence of India 262; early history of 108–12; impact of communalism 137–42; impact of successive league victories 117–22; representation of Muslim community in game of football 108–12; revival and success of 112–17; Salim, Mohammed 122–25
Mohun Bagan 1911 (Nandy) 241
Mohun Bagan Challenge Shield 89
Mohun Bagan Club 37, 41, 57, 64, 254; club conflict 13; Coochbehar Cup 65; Gladstone Cup 65; Golden Jubilee Souvenir (1939) 242; ideals and moral codes 47; IFA Shield victory (1911) 10–12, 14, 17, 41, 48, 62, 80, 83, 85, 90, 262; Lakshibilas Cup 65, 66; moment of arrival (1911) 73–81; moment of departure (1911) 68–73; Platinum Jubilee Souvenir (1964) 242; rivalry with East Bengal club 13, 196–98, 246; *see also* Ghoti-Bangal rivalry; social, cultural and commercial implications 81–91; sporting histories depicted in literature 241–47; tension with European outfit 66–67; Trades Cup 65, 66; victory over European East York Regiments 16, 17; win over Calcutta Football Club (CFC) 65
Mohun Baganer Itikatha (Bhadubhai) 242
Mohun Baganer Meye (film) 15, 258, 259
Mohun Bagan Omnibus (Kumar) 242
Mukherjee, Hiren 93
Mukherjee, S. N. 6
Muslim League 113, 122, 139–41

Muslim Sporting Club 82, 119, 121, 139
Mussalman, The 73, 82, 111
Mysore Football Association 146

Naidu, Sarojini 100
Nandikar (play) 259
Nandy, Ashis 106
Nandy, Moti 10, 32, 141, 258; *Dalbadaler Aage* 253; *Ferari* 253; *Stopper* 249; *Striker* 249–50
Nandy, Paresh 241, 244
Nari Satyagraha Samiti 97–100
National Association 12, 39, 40, 41, 45, 54, 64, 65, 262
nationalism, types of 103
nationalist movement 96–101, 148
Nationality Promotion Society 27
Native Volunteer Movement (1884–85) 29
Nawab Begum Football Cup 109
Naxalite movement 191
New Muslim Majlis 113
Nooruddin, Khwaja 113
North-West Indian Football Association 147, 160

Pancha Pandav (Saha) 248
para clubs 51
Paul, Gostho 174–75
pent-up nationalism 102
performing arts, football in 257–60
Phadnis, Urmila 169
physical culture movement, in Bengal 27–30
physical education 28–29, 51
picketing movement 96–101
Plamenatz, John 103, 104
Playing for Freedom: A Historic Sports Victory 14
Presidency College 7, 31, 34, 35, 67, 68, 85, 98

provincial football associations, in colonial India 146–47
public school games 21, 24, 25
public school system 20
Public Service Commission (1886–87) 29
Punjab Football Association 147

Quit India movement (1942) 141

racial discrimination 92–95
Rafique, M. 120
Railways Athletic Association 147
Railways Sports Control Board 147
Rajasthan Football Association 147
Rajputana Football Association. *See* Rajasthan Football Association
Rashid, S. A. 110, 115
referee, in Bengal football 70, 93–94, 101, 188, 228–29, 288–89
regional politics of soccer, in colonial India: Bengal *vs.* other states 148–52; formation of All India Football Federation (AIFF) 161–64; historical aspects of 143–45; IFA *vs.* AIFA 152–57; IFA, AIFA and British support for resolving 157–60; and impact of regionalism in Indian soccer 164–66; provincial football associations 146–47
religious communalism 13
Reuters News Agency 76, 216
Ripon A.C. 48
Robinson, Sir Hercules 21
Rous, Stanley 157
Rovers Cup 92, 146, 187
Roy, B. C. 213
Roychaudhuri, Manmathanath 177–78
rugby football 31

Sadhabar Ekadashi (Mitra) 170
Saha, Rupak 171, 241, 244, 248

Saheb (film) 15, 258
Salim, Mohammed 122–25, 275
Salt Lake Stadium 234
Santosh, Maharaja of 132–34, 144, 145, 150, 155, 159–64, 206
Santosh Trophy 147, 241
Saptapadi (film) 258
Sarbadhikary, Berry 186, 224, 225
Sarkar, Tanika 140
Sarvadhikari, Nagendra Prasad: excerpts from biography in English 264–69; as Father of Indian Football 30, 32, 238; role in popularising game of football 32–42
Scottish Church College Magazine 67
Scottish Daily Express 123, 124
Second Division League 94, 116, 176–77, 245
Sen, Dwaipayan 14
Sengupta, Achintya Kumar 94, 112
Sengupta, Surojit 191, 248
Services Sport Control Board 147
Shatabadir Sera Sailen Manna (Chakraborty) 248
soccer. *See* football
Soccer in South Asia: Empire, Nation, Diaspora (2001) 10
social differentiation 18, 167
Sonar Freme Mohun Bagan 1911 (Kumar) 241
Sovabazar Club 11, 36–39, 44, 54, 238
spectator culture, evolution of 214–34
spectator violence, at Calcutta Maidan 14, 128, 184, 187, 214–34, 286–87; tragedy of 16 August 1980 193–95
Sport and Pastime 211
sporting nationalism 41, 73, 100, 142, 181, 214
Sporting Union 228
sports, Indian: academic writings on 7–15; caste-based discrimination 36; communalisation of 108; cultural imperialism and colonial response to 58–64; influence of politics, culture and economy on 4; relevance in history 2; in social history 3–7; study of 2
sports journalism 85, 86, 236, 262
stadium: bulletin about 291; demand for 276–78; imbroglio 206–14; need of 290
Star of India 117, 128, 130
Statesman, The 69, 77, 88, 97, 99, 100, 117, 121, 138, 179, 233
Steevens, G. W. 26
Stoddart, Brian 91, 107
Stopper (Nandy) 249
Striker (film) 258
Striker (Nandy) 249–50
Swadeshi movement (1905–8) 55, 64–68, 81, 99

Tamil Nadu Football Association. *See* Madras Football Association
Times of India Illustrated Weekly, The 70–71
T-20 Indian Premier League 4
Tomlinson, John 59
Town Club 40, 48, 51, 52, 98
Trades Cup 37–38, 41, 45, 64–66, 240
tragedy of 16 August 1980 193–95, 230, 231
Tuan, Y. F., model for understanding relation between football grounds and emotion 204
Tyndale-Biscoe, Cecil Earle 22–23

United Breweries Group 197, 247

Vangiya Sahitya Parishat 72
vernacular football literature, heritage of: club histories 241–47; journalistic and popular writings on Bengali soccer 247–49; RB and *Kolkatar Football* 237–41; sporting literature on 1911 241

vernacular sports journalism in Bengal, development of 86
Victorian English public schools 23
Victoria Sporting Club 49
Victorious Mohun Bagan (Dutta) 242
Vivekananda, Swami 27, 42

Walvin, James 1, 3, 5, 7, 262–63
Wari Club 49
Wellington Club 35–37
West Bengal Pradesh Congress Committee 232

Western India Football Association (WIFA) 146, 150, 152, 160
Wheeler, E. M. 48
wrestling 8, 27, 29

Yuba Bharati Krirangan 214
Yuva Sampradaya 140

Zagoria, Donald S. 189
Zigger Zagger (Derson) 259

For Product Safety Concerns and Information please contact our EU
representative GPSR@taylorandfrancis.com
Taylor & Francis Verlag GmbH, Kaufingerstraße 24, 80331 München, Germany

www.ingramcontent.com/pod-product-compliance
Lightning Source LLC
Chambersburg PA
CBHW071759300426
44116CB00009B/1146